Japanese Idioms

By

Nobuo Akiyama
Professorial Lecturer in Japane
The Paul H. Nitze
School of Advanced International
The Johns Hopkins University, Washi   C.
and
Carol Akiyama
Language Training Consultant
Washington, D.C.

BARRON'S

Contents

日本人読者への序文

イディオムとは何か

　イディオムを、ことわざや、単なる複合語と混同している著書がなきにしもあらず。しかし定義としては、二つ以上の単語を組み合わせ、全体として別の意味を表すものと見なすべきだろう。英語の イディオム も、日本語の慣用句も、その点では共通といえる。但しことわざとの違いは、人生の知恵や教訓のような特別の意味合いが無いことだ。本書はこの観点に基づき、日本語の慣用句を扱っている。

　イディオム、即ち 慣用句 は、その国の文化、国民の発想法を如実に反映し、日常生活と密接な関係を持っている。その場その場にふさわしい考え、感情、ユーモアなどを込め、言いたいことに味を添える。このような背景や機能があるだけに、慣用句はその言葉が母国語の人々が好んで使う表現。だが同時に、文字通り解釈しても分からないのが難点だ。外国語を学ぶ人にとっては、やっかいなことになる。

日本人としての使い方

　日本人も、英語で苦労する点では、その例に漏れない。本書は、日本語を学ぶ欧米人を意図してはいる。しかし日本人を除外するどころか、この本を積極的に利用できるようにも構成してある。日常会話の日本語を、つまり、言いたいことを同じようなニュアンスの英語で伝えたい。そんな考えがある人ならば、本書を大いに活用できることは疑いない。

　英語を学ぶ日本人が、言葉に詰まってしまうことがしばしばある。その理由には、言いたい日本語の慣用句が英語で出てこなかったり、それをどう言えばいいか頭を捻りすぎてしまうことだ。

　日本語の慣用句の入ったセンテンスを英語で話そうとする。その時、文字通りに訳してしまうと、意味をなさなくなるのは当然のこと。だがその危険を知ってはいても、ではどうすればいいのか。そのような場合に本書を使い、英語らしい表

現をすることが可能になる。つまり、日本人は、この本を日本語イディオムの和英辞典として手引きに出来る。

ここには、ことわざもある程度含まれてはいるが、主として二千を越す純粋な日本語の慣用句が選ばれている。慣用句の基礎概念になる見出し語をアルファベット順に載せ、見出し語の下に、関連した慣用句が、これもアルファベット順に載せてある。

紙面の制限上、選択を強いられたが、本書の掲載分で、普段使う日本語を英語で話し書くためには、これでまず十分といえる。慣用句を含めた日本語のニュアンスを自然な英語で伝えられるようになれば、コミュニケーションの度合いも一段と深まるだろう。

体裁と使い方

本書は、次のようにアレンジされている。

先ず見出し語が、ローマ字と日本語と英語の順に載せてある。その後は、見出し語に関連するイディオムの例が、日本語、ローマ字、英語の順で書かれている。

[lit. ...]は、ほぼ純粋な直訳を用い、語源に基づき、日本人の考え方の発展を外国人に知って貰うのが目的。日本人でも語学に興味のある人は、日本語を再考する上でも、注意を払うといいだろう。理屈はともかく、日本語の考えを英語で伝えられればそれでいい。そう思う人は、これを無視して何の差し障りもない。

用例のセンテンスに関しては、ローマ字は明らかに日本語を学ぶ外国人を助けるために含まれている。これが目障りならば、これを全く無視して構わない。但し漢字の読みを確かめるためには、辞書を引くより、最初にここにあるローマ字を読んでみる方が効率的かも知れない。

最後に

　日本語の慣用句は、先ずそれに相当する英語のイディオムがあればそれを、無ければ、それに近い口語的表現を用いるようにしている。これによって、現代アメリカ英語を理解する上の一助となることはまず間違いない。日米両国の言語と意思流通の架け橋として、幾分でも貢献できれば幸いである。

Preface

For the language learner, idioms are a dimension beyond grammar, pronunciation, and vocabulary. They add color, spice, and humor. They provide insights into the culture. If you know the idioms, you can understand expressions that cannot be translated by just their constituent parts. A speaker of English who hears the phrase "a fly on the wall" knows that it means "an eavesdropper," or that "to get someone's goat" means "to annoy someone." If you are learning Japanese, or if you have already achieved some proficiency and want to enrich your knowledge, you will find it invaluable to develop similar awarenesses in your new language. This book will help you achieve your goal.

You can look up idioms as you hear or read them. Or you can browse through the more than 2,000 entries at your leisure to see how the idioms reveal Japanese views on life, love, respect, duty, honor, shame, work, relationships, nature, deities, and much more.

Idioms are entered by key Japanese words, usually nouns, listed alphabetically in Romaji. Thus if you hear the Japanese word for "bean paste" in an expression you don't know, you look it up under the key word "*miso.*" Under this heading appear the most common idioms containing the word. Each entry contains the idiom in both Romaji and Japanese characters, the English meaning, the literal translation, and finally, a Japanese sentence to illustrate the usage with the English translation. Look up "*miso o tsukeru*" this way, and you'll find it means "to make a mess of something," literally, "to spread bean paste on something." Or if you hear an unfamiliar expression containing the Japanese for "cat," look it up under the key word "*neko,*" then the expression, "*neko no hitai,*" which means "a very small area,". literally, "a cat's forehead." This is the only size piece of land the average person in Japan can afford!

Because each entry is based on the Japanese idiom and the Japanese illustrative sentence, there are certain implications for the English. For the literal translations, the language conveys the Japanese words as closely as possible. For the English meanings and the illustrative sentences, every attempt is made to use language that is as natural as possible under the circumstances. But since the two languages and cultures are so different, some translations may leave you shaking your head. For example, the idiom that means "a bride's changing clothes during the wedding reception," and the illustrative sentence "How often did the bride change her clothes during the wedding reception?" may strike the English speaker as odd. But to the Japanese, it's quite normal.

As you use the book, you'll enjoy seeing how the literal meanings of the idioms relate to the actual usage. And you'll continue enriching your knowledge of the unique ways in which the Japanese express things in their daily lives.

PRONUNCIATION GUIDE

This book assumes that you are already somewhat familiar with the basic pronunciation rules of Japanese, but for those who need a little help, here are some guidelines.

Writing Conventions

For each Japanese phrase or vocabulary item used in this book, both the Japanese writing and the Hepburn spelling are given. The latter is the most common system of Romanization of Japanese words; it's called *romaji*.

Vowels

Japanese vowels are more like those of Spanish than English.

The following vowels are short and pure, with no glide—that is, they are not diphthongs.

JAPANESE VOWEL	SOUND IN ENGLISH	EXAMPLE	
a	as in f**a**ther	*akai*	ah-kah-ee
e	as in m**e**n	*ebi*	eh-bee
i	as in s**ee**	*imi*	ee-mee
o	as in b**oa**t	*otoko*	oh-toh-koh
u	as in f**oo**d	*uma*	oo-mah

The following vowels are like the ones above, but lengthened.

JAPANESE VOWEL	SOUND IN ENGLISH	EXAMPLE	
ā	as in f**a**ther, but lengthened	*batā*	bah-tah̄
ei	as in m**e**n, but lengthened	*eigo*	ēh-goh
ii	as in s**ee**, but lengthened	*iiharu*	ēē-hah-roo
ō	as in b**oa**t, but lengthened	*ōsama*	oh-sah-mah
ū	as in f**oo**d, but lengthened	*yūbin*	yōō-been

And keep in mind:

1. Long vowels are important: pronouncing a long vowel incorrectly can result in a different word or even an unintelligible one. For instance, *obasan* (oh-bah-sahn) means aunt; *obāsan* (oh-bah̄-sahn) means grandmother. *Ojisan* (oh-jee-sahn) means uncle; *ojiisan* (oh-jēē-sahn) means grandfather. *Seki* (seh-kee) means seat; *seiki* (seh̄-kee) means century.

2. Sometimes the **i** and the **u** are not pronounced. This usually occurs between voiceless consonants (p, t, k, ch, f, h, s, sh), or at the end of a word following a voiceless consonant. An example you may already know is *sukiyaki* (skee-yah-kee). This word for a popular Japanese dish begins not with soo, but with skee. You omit the **u** entirely. In *tabemashita* (tah-beh-mahsh-tah), which means "I ate," the last **i** is omitted.

Consonants

With a few exceptions, Japanese consonants are similar to those of English. Note the differences:

f The English **f** is pronounced by a passage of air between the upper teeth and the lower lip. To make the Japanese **f**, blow air lightly between your lips as if you were just beginning a whistle.

g As in **g**o. You may also hear it pronounced as the **ng** sound in ri**ng**, although not at the beginning of a word.

r This is different from the English **r**. The Japanese **r** is made by lightly touching the tip of the tongue to the bony ridge behind the upper teeth, almost in the English **d** position. It's more like the Spanish **r**, but it's not flapped or trilled.

s It's always hissed, as in **s**o; it's never pronounced as in hi**s** or plea**s**ure.

Please note:

1. If you have trouble making these consonants the Japanese way, your English pronunciation will be intelligible and will not be considered incorrect.

2. Some Japanese consonants are doubled. In English, this is just a feature of spelling and often doesn't affect pronunciation. In Japanese, the doubling is important and may change the meaning of a word. For example, *kite*

kudasai (kee-teh koo-dah-sah-ee) means "please put it on (clothing)." *Kitte kudasai* (keet-teh koo-dah-sah-ee) means "please cut it." In a word with a doubled consonant, don't say the consonant twice—just hold the sound longer.

Loan Words

If you know English, you may already know more Japanese than you think. There are thousands of English loan words in everday use in Japan. Most of these common words have been borrowed with no change in meaning. But there is a change in pronunciation. This can be tricky. On the one hand, you're secure with the familiar words; on the other, if you pronounce them as you're used to doing, you won't be understood, and you won't understand the words when Japanese use them. For example, **baseball** won't work; *bēsubōru* (beh-soo-boh-roo) will! If you order a **beer**, you might not get one; say bīru (bee-roo) and you will. (Note the long vowel: biru with a short vowel means **building**.)

Here are a few more examples of familiar words with somewhat different pronunciations in Japanese:

gasoline	*gasorin*	gah-soh-reen
pocket	*poketto*	poh-keht-toh
pink	*pinku*	peen-koo
ballpoint pen	*bōru pen*	boh-roo pehn
supermarket	*sūpā*	soo-pah
yacht	*yotto*	yoht-toh
handkerchief	*hankachi*	hahn-kah-chee

Japanese Idioms

A

---

abura   油   *oil*

abura ga kireru   油が切れる   *to be exhausted*
[lit. Oil runs out.]

油が切れそうなので、バカンスが必要です。Abura ga kiresō nanode, bakansu ga hitsuyō desu.   *I need a vacation because I'm just about exhausted.*

abura o shiboru   油をしぼる   *to take someone to task*
[lit. to squeeze oil]

顧客に連絡するのを忘れて、課長に油をしぼられました。Kokyaku ni renraku suru no o wasurete, kachō ni abura o shiboraremashita.   *Because I forgot to get in touch with the client, I was taken to task by the section chief.*

abura o sosogu   油を注ぐ   *to fuel, to inflame*
[lit. to pour oil]

その新聞の記事は、彼の怒りに油を注ぎました。Sono shinbun no kiji wa, kare no ikari ni abura o sosogimashita.   *That newspaper article fueled his anger.*

abura o uru   油を売る   *to goof off, to loaf*
[lit. to sell oil]

あの人は仕事をするより、油を売るのが得意です。Ano hito wa shigoto o suru yori, abura o uru no ga tokui desu.   *He's better at goofing off than working.*

---

abura   脂   *fat*

abura ga noru   脂がのる   *to be in one's prime*
[lit. to increase in fat content]

あの歌手は、最近脂がのってきました。Ano kashu wa, saikin abura ga notte kimashita.   *That singer has recently come into her prime.*

---

ago   顎   *chin, jaw*

ago de tsukau   顎で使う   *to order someone around*
[lit. to use someone with one's chin]
彼は人を顎で使うので、彼が好きな人はあまりいません。
Kare wa hito o ago de tsukau node, kare ga suki na hito wa
amari imasen.   *Because he orders everyone around, not many
people like him.*

ago ga hazureru   顎が外れる   *to die laughing*
[lit. One's jaw gets dislocated.]
彼女の話があまり面白いので、顎が外れるほど笑いました。
Kanojo no hanashi ga amari omoshiroi node, ago ga hazureru
hodo waraimashita.   *Her story was so funny that I almost died
laughing.*

ago ga hiagaru   顎が干上がる   *to suffer from loss of income*
[lit. One's jaw dries up.]
遊んでばかりいると、そのうち顎が干上がってしまいますよ。
Asonde bakari iru to, sono uchi ago ga hiagatte shimaimasu yo.
*If you keep playing around, you won't be able to pay your
bills.*

ago o dasu   顎を出す   *to get exhausted*
[lit. to stick one's chin out]
久しぶりに運動したので、すぐに顎を出してしまいました。
Hisashiburi ni undō shita node, sugu ni ago o dashite
shimaimashita.   *Because I exercised for the first time in ages, I
got exhausted fast.*

ago o naderu   顎をなでる   *to pride oneself on something*
[lit. to stroke one's own chin]
彼はテニスの試合に勝って、顎をなでていました。Kare wa
tenisu no shiai ni katte, ago o nadete imashita.   *He prided
himself on winning the tennis match.*

---

ai   愛   *love*

ai no kesshō   愛の結晶   *child(ren)*
[lit. the crystallization of love]

あの夫婦に、先月愛の結晶が生まれました。Ano fūfu ni, sengetsu ai no kesshō ga umaremashita. *That couple had a baby last month.*

ai no su 愛の巣 *the home of a newlywed couple*
[lit. a love nest]
新婚の太郎と花子は、京都に愛の巣を構えました。Shinkon no Tarō to Hanako wa, Kyōto ni ai no su o kamaemashita. *The newlyweds Taro and Hanako set up their new home in Kyoto.*

---

aji 味 *taste*

aji mo sokke mo nai 味も素気もない *curt*
[lit. no taste, no warmth]
親切に聞いてあげたのに、その女性は味も素気もない返事をしました。Shinsetsu ni kiite ageta noni, sono josei wa aji mo sokke mo nai henji o shimashita. *I offered to help her, but she gave me a curt reply.*

aji na koto o yaru 味なことをやる *to act smart*
[lit. to do something of taste]
パーティーでギターを弾くなんて、彼もなかなか味なことをやるね。Pātī de gitā o hiku nante, kare mo nakanaka aji na koto o yaru ne. *How smart of him to play the guitar during the party!*

aji o shimeru 味を占める *to get a taste of something*
[lit. to occupy taste]
一度の成功に味を占めて、彼は相変わらず同じ事をしています。Ichido no seikō ni aji o shimete, kare wa aikawarazu onaji koto o shite imasu. *After tasting success once, he's still doing the same old thing.*

aji o shiru 味を知る *to experience something*
[lit. to get to know the taste]
一度贅沢の味を知ると、元に戻るのは容易ではありません。Ichido zeitaku no aji o shiru to, moto ni modoru no wa yōi dewa arimasen. *When you experience luxury once, it's not easy to go back to your old lifestyle.*

aka   赤   *red*

aka no tanin   赤の他人   *total stranger*
[lit. a red stranger]

赤の他人に、そんな話をしてはいけません。Aka no tanin ni, sonna hanashi o shitewa ikemasen.   *Don't tell such a story to a total stranger.*

akahaji   赤恥   *utter shame, total disgrace*
[lit. red shame]

この間は会議に出ることを忘れて、赤恥をかきました。
Kono aida wa kaigi ni deru koto o wasurete, akahaji o kakimashita.   *The other day, I totally disgraced myself by forgetting to attend the meeting.*

akashingō ga tsuku   赤信号が付く   *to become precarious*
[lit. A red light comes on.]

社長が病気になって、会社の運営に赤信号が付きました。
Shachō ga byōki ni natte, kaisha no un-ei ni akashingō ga tsukimashita.   *With the president's illness, the management of the company has become precarious.*

---

aka   垢   *grime*

akanuke shinai   垢抜けしない   *unpolished, crude*
[lit. grime not coming off]

あの人は都会に来て十年たつのに、まだ垢抜けしていません。
Ano hito wa tokai ni kite jū nen tatsu noni, mada akanuke shite imasen.   *Although it's been 10 years since he came to the city, he's still not urbane.*

akanuke shita   垢抜けした   *polished, refined*
[lit. grime off]

彼女は、いつも垢抜けした服装をしています。Kanojo wa, itsumo akanuke shita fukusō o shite imasu.   *She always wears sophisticated clothes.*

---

akashi   証し   *proof*

mi no akashi o tateru   身の証しを立てる   *to prove one's innocence*

4

[lit. to make proof stand up]

汚職をマスコミに非難された政治家は、身の証を立てるために弁護士を雇いました。Oshoku o masukomi ni hinan sareta seijika wa, mi no akashi o tateru tame ni bengoshi o yatoimashita. *When the media accused him of corruption, the politician hired a lawyer to prove his innocence.*

---

aki   秋   *autumn*

aki no sora   秋の空   *to be fickle (love)*

[lit. autumn sky]

彼は、彼女の秋の空のような心に悩みました。Kare wa, kanojo no aki no sora no yō na kokoro ni nayamimashita. *He was hurt by her fickleness.*

akikaze ga tatsu   秋風が立つ   *to cool mutually (love)*

[lit. Autumn breeze begins to blow.]

半年もたたない内に、二人の間に秋風が立ち始めました。Hantoshi mo tatanai uchi ni, futari no aida ni akikaze ga tachihajimemashita. *Their love began to cool in less than a half year.*

---

ama   天   *heaven*

amakudari   天下り   *senior government official landing a high position in the private sector*

[lit. to descend from heaven]

彼は政府を定年退職した後、天下りで銀行の社長になりました。Kare wa seifu o teinen taishoku shita ato, amakudari de ginkō no shachō ni narimashita. *He landed a position as a bank president after retiring from the government.*

amanojaku   天の邪鬼   *perverse person*

[lit. a devil in heaven]

彼は天の邪鬼だから、人の助言に従いません。Kare wa amanojaku dakara, hito no jogen ni shitagaimasen. *He is perverse and doesn't follow other people's advice.*

---

amai   甘い   *sweet*

amai kotoba ni noru   甘い言葉に乗る   *to believe*

sweet talk

[lit. to ride on sweet words]

彼女は彼の甘い言葉に乗って、結婚してしまいました。

Kanojo wa kare no amai kotoba ni notte, kekkon shite
shimaimashita.   *.Unfortunately, she married him believing his
sweet talk.*

amai shiru o suu   甘い汁を吸う   *to benefit oneself by
exploiting others*

[lit. to suck sweet juice]

あの人は周りの人から甘い汁を吸って、金持ちになりました。

Ano hito wa mawari no hito kara amai shiru o sutte, kanemochi ni
narimashita.   *He became rich by exploiting people around him.*

amaku kangaeru   甘く考える   *to take things too easy*

[lit. to consider things sweetly]

物理の試験は甘く考えていたために、成績はあまり良くあ
りませんでした。 Butsuri no shiken wa amaku kangaete ita
tame ni, seiseki wa amari yoku arimasen deshita.   *Since I
didn't take the physics exam seriously, my grade wasn't that
good.*

amaku miru   甘く見る   *to take someone lightly*

[lit. to view a person sweetly]

相手を甘く見たため、交渉はうまくいきませんでした。

Aite o amaku mita tame, kōshō wa umaku ikimasen deshita.
*The negotiations failed because I took my counterpart too
lightly.*

amatō   甘党   *to have a sweet tooth*

[lit. a partisan of something sweet]

彼は甘党で、特にチョコレートに目がありません。Kare wa
amatō de, toku ni chokorēto ni me ga arimasen.
He has a sweet tooth, especially for chocolate.

---

ame   雨   *rain*

ame ga furō ga yari ga furō ga   雨が降ろうが槍が降ろうが
no matter what

[lit. even if it rains or spears shower down]

雨が降ろうが槍が降ろうが、計画は実行します。Ame ga
furō ga yari ga furō ga, keikaku wa jikkō shimasu. *No matter
what happens, I'll carry out the plan.*

ame onna/ame otoko   雨女／雨男   *woman/man who
brings rain wherever she/he goes*

[lit. a rain woman/ a rain man]

彼女は雨女なので、誘うと危ないです。Kanojo wa ame onna
nanode, sasou to abunai desu. *It's risky to invite her, because
she brings rain wherever she goes.*

ame tsuyu o shinogu seikatsu   雨露をしのぐ生活 *poverty*

[lit. living by sheltering oneself from the rain and dew]

あの作家は成功する前、雨露をしのぐ生活を経験しました。
Ano sakka wa seikō suru mae, ame tsuyu o shinogu seikatsu o
keiken shimashita.   *That novelist experienced poverty before
he became successful.*

---

ami   網   *net*

ami no me o kuguru   網の目をくぐる   *to evade the law*

[lit. to pass through the mesh of a net]

彼は、網の目をくぐって象牙を輸入しました。Kare wa, ami
no me o kugutte zōge o yunyū shimashita.   *He evaded the law
and imported ivory.*

ami o haru   網を張る   *to set up a dragnet*

[lit. to stretch a net]

警察は誘拐の容疑者を捕らえようと、全国に網を張りました。
Keisatsu wa yūkai no yōgisha o toraeyō to, zenkoku ni ami o
harimashita.   *The police set up a nationwide dragnet for the
kidnapping suspect.*

---

ana   穴   *hole*

ana ga attara hairitai   穴があったら入りたい   *to be
ashamed, to be humiliated*

[lit. to want to crawl into a hole if there is one]

みんなの前で大失敗して、穴があったら入りたい気持ちで

7

した。Minna no mae de daishippai shite, ana ga attara hairitai
kimochi deshita.   *When I made a mistake in front of everybody,
I was so ashamed.*

ana no aku hodo mitsumeru   穴のあくほど見つめる   *to
stare at someone or something*

[lit. to look at something to the extent that a hole will open up]
その絵のあまりの見事さに、穴のあくほど見つめずにはい
　られませんでした。Sono e no amari no migotosa ni, ana no
aku hodo mitsumezu niwa iraremasen deshita.   *The painting
was so fantastic that I couldn't stop staring at it.*

ana o akeru   穴をあける   *to cause a deficit*

[lit. to dig a hole]
今月は買い物をしすぎて、家計に穴をあけてしまいました。
Kongetsu wa kaimono o shisugite, kakei ni ana o akete
　shimaimashita.   *I made a hole in the family budget this
month because I shopped too much.*

anaba   穴場   *great secret spot*

[lit. a place with a hole]
あそこに釣りに行くなら、穴場を教えてあげましょう。
　Asoko ni tsuri ni iku nara, anaba o oshiete agemashō.   *If you
go fishing there, I'll tell you a great secret spot.*

anaume o suru   穴埋めをする   *to make up a loss*

[lit. to fill in a hole]
政府は財政赤字の穴埋めをするために、増税しなければな
　りませんでした。Seifu wa zaisei akaji no anaume o suru
tame ni, zōzei shinakereba narimasen deshita.   *To make up the
financial deficit, the government had to raise taxes.*

---

anbai   塩梅   *condition*
ii anbai ni   いい塩梅に   *fortunately*

[lit. with good salt and plums]
雨が降ってきたら、いい塩梅にタクシーが来ました。Ame
ga futte kitara, ii anbai ni takushī ga kimashita.   *Fortunately, a
taxi came by when it started to rain.*

anraku 安楽   *comfort*
  anraku shi 安楽死   *euthanasia*
  [lit. death for comfort]
  その患者は苦しみに耐えかねて、安楽死を求めました。
    Sono kanja wa kurushimi ni taekanete, anraku shi o
    motomemashita. *The patient couldn't bear the pain and
    asked for euthanasia.*

---

anshō 暗礁   *submerged reef*
  anshō ni noriageru 暗礁に乗り上げる   *to hit a snag*
  [lit. to run aground on a submerged reef]
  その計画が暗礁に乗り上げることは、最初から分かってい
  ました。Sono keikaku ga anshō ni noriageru koto wa, saisho
  kara wakatte imashita. *I knew all along that the plan would
  hit a snag.*

---

ao 青   *blue, green*
  aoiki toiki 青息吐息   *to be suffering*
  [lit. sighing with blue breath]
  不景気のため、どの店も青息吐息です。Fukeiki no tame,
  dono mise mo aoiki toiki desu. *All the stores are suffering
  because of the recession.*

  aojashin 青写真   *blueprint*
  [lit. a blue photograph]
  今度のプロジェクトのための青写真を作りました。Kondo
  no purojekuto no tame no aojashin o tsukurimashita. *I made a
  blueprint for the upcoming project.*

  aokusai 青臭い   *inexperienced*
  [lit. green-smelling]
  あんな青臭い人に、この企画は任せられません。Anna
  aokusai hito ni, kono kikaku wa makaseraremasen. *We can't
  trust someone so inexperienced with this project.*

  aonisai 青二才   *greenhorn*
  [lit. a green two-year-old]
  あの男は青二才のくせに、ずいぶん生意気なことをいいます。

Ano otoko wa aonisai no kuse ni, zuibun namaiki na koto o iimasu.   *Although he's just a greenhorn, he says such arrogant things.*

aosuji o tateru   青筋を立てる   *to become enraged*
[lit. to show blue veins]

そんなつまらないことに青筋を立てるなよ。Sonna tsumaranai koto ni, aosuji o tateruna yo.   *Don't become enraged over something so trivial.*

aotagai   青田買い   *to contract to employ college students prematurely*
[lit. to buy green rice-fields]

青田買いは禁じられていますが、それはなかなか無くなりません。Aotagai wa kinjirarete imasu ga, sore wa nakanaka nakunarimasen.   *Although the premature hiring of college students is forbidden, it doesn't go away easily.*

---

arau   洗う   *to wash*

arainaosu   洗い直す   *to reexamine*
[lit. to wash again]

その計画は洗い直すべきです。Sono keikaku wa arainaosu beki desu.   *We should reexamine the project.*

araitateru   洗い立てる   *to expose*
[lit. to wash incessantly]

新聞は、その政治家の過去を洗い立てました。Shinbun wa, sono seijika no kako o araitatemashita.   *The newspaper exposed the politician's past.*

araizarai   洗いざらい   *everything*
[lit. to wash and carry off]

殺人の容疑者は、犯した罪を洗いざらい白状しました。Satsujin no yōgisha wa, okashita tsumi o araizarai hakujō shimashita.   *The murder suspect confessed to every crime he committed.*

---

ari   蟻   *ant*
ari no haideru sukima mo nai   蟻の這い出る隙間もない

to guard closely

[lit. no gap for even ants to crawl from]

警察は、首相官邸を蟻の這い出る隙間もないほど警戒しました。Keisatsu wa, shushō kantei o ari no haideru sukima mo nai hodo keikai shimashita. *The police closely guarded the prime minister's official residence.*

---

asa 朝 *morning*
  asameshi mae 朝飯前 *easy, a piece of cake*
  [lit. before breakfast]
  そんな仕事は朝飯前です。Sonna shigoto wa asameshi mae desu. *That's a cinch.*

---

ase 汗 *sweat*
  ase no kesshō 汗の結晶 *result of one's hard work*
  [lit. a crystal of sweat]
  この小説は、あの作家の汗の結晶です。Kono shōsetsu wa, ano sakka no ase no kesshō desu. *This is the result of that writer's hard work.*

  asemizu tarasu 汗水垂らす *to toil*
  [lit. to drip sweat]
  彼は大家族を養うため、汗水垂らして働いています。Kare wa dai kazoku o yashinau tame, asemizu tarashite hataraite imasu. *He has been toiling to support his big family.*

  te ni ase o nigiru 手に汗を握る *breathtaking*
  [lit. to hold sweat in one's palm]
  その試合は、手に汗を握る大接戦でした。Sono shiai wa, te ni ase o nigiru daisessen deshita. *The game was breathtakingly close.*

---

ashi 足 *leg, foot*
  ageashi o toru 揚げ足を取る *to carp, to nitpick*
  [lit. to grab someone's raised leg]
  彼には、いつも人の揚げ足を取る悪い癖があります。Kare niwa, itsumo hito no ageashi o toru warui kuse ga arimasu. *He has a bad habit of always nitpicking.*

ashi ga bō ni naru   足が棒になる   *One's legs become stiff.*
[lit. The legs become sticks.]
彼女は、足が棒になるまで歩き続けました。Kanojo wa, ashi ga bō ni naru made arukitsuzukemashita. *She kept walking till her legs got very stiff.*

ashi ga chi ni tsukanai   足が地に着かない   *to be restless and excited*
[lit. One's legs don't touch the ground.]
結婚式が近付いて、彼女は足が地に着きません。Kekkon shiki ga chikazuite, kanojo wa ashi ga chi ni tsukimasen. *With her wedding approaching, she's restless and excited.*

ashi ga deru   足が出る   *to exceed one's budget or income*
[lit. Legs stick out.]
新年会では、予算よりかなり足が出てしまいました。Shinnen kai dewa, yosan yori kanari ashi ga dete shimaimashita. *We spent considerably more than our budget for the New Year's party.*

ashi ga muku   足が向く   *to head somewhere spontaneously*
[lit. One's legs turn toward somewhere.]
夏の暑い日には、仕事の後よくビヤホールに足が向いてしまいます。Natsu no atsui hi niwa, shigoto no ato yoku biyahōru ni ashi ga muite shimaimasu. *On hot summer days, I often find myself heading toward a beer hall after work.*

ashi ga niburu   足が鈍る   *to be less eager to go*
[lit. One's legs become dull.]
フランスに行きたいけれど、言葉のことを考えると足が鈍ります。Furansu ni ikitai keredo, kotoba no koto o kangaeru to ashi ga niburimasu. *I want to go to France, but when I think about the language, I become less eager.*

ashi ga omoi   足が重い   *to be reluctant to go*
[lit. One's legs are heavy.]
試験は出来なかったのが分かっているので、結果を見に行くのは足が重いです。Shiken wa dekinakatta no ga wakatte

iru node, kekka o mini iku no wa ashi ga omoi desu. *Since I know I didn't do well, I'm reluctant to go see the results of the exam.*

ashi ga tōnoku 足が遠のく *to come and go less frequently than before, to come and go at longer intervals*
[lit. One's legs become distant.]

最近、銀座のバーから足が遠のいています。Saikin, Ginza no bā kara ashi ga tōnoite imasu. *These days, I've been going to bars in Ginza less frequently.*

ashi ga tsuku 足が付く *identity to be learned*
[lit. One's legs are connected.]

現場に残した指紋から、犯人の足が付きました。Genba ni nokoshita shimon kara, hannin no ashi ga tsukimashita. *The criminal's identity was learned from his fingerprints at the scene of the crime.*

ashi o arau 足を洗う *to wash one's hands of something*
[lit. to wash one's feet]

彼女は芸能界から足を洗って、結婚しました。Kanojo wa geinō kai kara ashi o aratte, kekkon shimashita. *She washed her hands of show business and got married.*

ashi o fumiireru 足を踏み入れる *to get involved in something*
[lit. to put one's legs in something]

彼が政治に足を踏み入れてから、二十年たちます。Kare ga seiji ni ashi o fumiirete kara, nijū nen tachimasu. *It's been 20 years since he got involved in politics.*

ashi o hakobu 足を運ぶ *to go to visit*
[lit. to carry one's legs]

野球のチームに入りたくて、監督の家に何度も足を運びました。Yakyū no chīmu ni hairitakute, kantoku no ie ni nando mo ashi o hakobimashita. *Since I wanted to join the baseball team, I often went to visit the manager's home.*

ashi o hipparu 足を引っ張る *to drag someone down*
[lit. to drag someone's legs]

同僚は彼女の成功を妬んで、足を引っ張ろうとしました。

Dōryō wa kanojo no seikō o netande, ashi o hipparō to shimashita. *Her colleagues were jealous of her success and tried to drag her down.*

ashi o ireru   足を入れる   *to set foot in*
[lit. to put one's feet in]

夫は、飲屋街には決して足を入れません。Otto wa, nomiya gai niwa kesshite ashi o iremasen. *My husband never sets foot in a bar district.*

ashi o nobasu   足を延ばす   *to extend a trip*
[lit. to stretch a leg]

アメリカへ行ったとき、メキシコまで足を延ばしました。

Amerika e itta toki, Mekishiko made ashi o nobashimashita. *When I went to the United States, I extended the trip to include Mexico.*

ashi o sukuu   足をすくう   *to trip someone up*
[lit. to scoop up someone's legs]

彼女を信用して、足をすくわれた人が沢山います。Kanojo o shin-yō shite, ashi o sukuwareta hito ga takusan imasu. *There are many people who were tripped up by her while they trusted her.*

ashi o torareru   足を取られる   *to lose one's footing*
[lit. to get one's feet taken away]

階段で足を取られて、下まで転げ落ちてしまいました。

Kaidan de ashi o torarete, shita made korogeochite shimaimashita. *I lost my footing and tumbled to the bottom of the stairs.*

ashi o ubawareru   足を奪われる   *to be deprived of transportation*
[lit. to get one's legs stolen]

地下鉄のストで足を奪われて、会社に行けませんでした。

Chikatetsu no suto de ashi o ubawarete, kaisha ni ikemasen deshita. *I couldn't go to work because the subway was on strike.*

ashiba o katameru　　足場を固める　　*to secure a foothold*
[lit. to set up scaffolding]

彼は、その町で立候補するための足場を固めています。
　Kare wa, sono machi de rikkōho suru tame no ashiba o
　katamete imasu.　*He's securing a foothold to run for election
　in that town.*

ashibumi suru　　足踏みする　　*to be at a standstill*
[lit. to step on a spot]

いくら勉強しても、成績は足踏みを続けています。Ikura
　benkyō shitemo, seiseki wa ashibumi o tsuzukete imasu.　*No
　matter how much I study, my grades stay the same.*

ashidai　　足代　　*transportation costs*
[lit. leg price]

そこへ行く足代は、会社が払ってくれました。Soko e iku
　ashidai wa, kaisha ga haratte kuremashita.　*The company paid
　my transportation costs to get there.*

ashidome　　足止め　　*restrictions on travel*
[lit. to stop one's legs]

政府は、災害地域への足止めを解きました。Seifu wa, saigai
　chiiki e no ashidome o tokimashita.　*The government lifted the
　restrictions on travel to the disaster area.*

ashigatame　　足固め　　*preparations for the future*
[lit. to fix one's legs]

もうそろそろ、結婚のために足固めをして置いた方がいい
　ですよ。Mō sorosoro, kekkon no tame ni ashigatame o shite
　oita hō ga ii desu yo.　*It's about time that you start preparing
　yourself for marriage.*

ashige ni suru　　足蹴にする　　*to treat someone horribly*
[lit. to kick someone]

彼は人を足蹴にしても、自分の利益を得ようとします。
　Kare wa hito o ashige ni shite mo, jibun no rieki o eyō to
　shimasu.　*He tries to profit even if he has to treat other people
　horribly.*

ashikase ni naru　　足枷になる　　*to become a hindrance*

[lit. to become shackles]

足枷になりませんから、作業班に入れて下さい。Ashikase
ni narimasen kara, sagyō han ni irete kudasai.   *I won't be a
hindrance, so please let me join the task force.*

ashimoto e tsukekomu   足下へつけ込む   *to take unfair
advantage of someone's weakness*

[lit. to enter close to someone's feet]

あの人は、友達の足下につけ込んで借金しました。Ano hito
wa, tomodachi no ashimoto ni tsukekonde shakkin shimashita.
*He borrowed money from his friend by taking advantage of her
weakness.*

ashimoto ni hi ga tsuku   足下に火が付く   *Danger is
imminent.*

[lit. Fire ignites at one's foot.]

信頼不足で、現政権の足下に火が付いています。Shinrai
busoku de, gen seiken no ashimoto ni hi ga tsuite imasu.   *The
current administration is in imminent danger because of lack
of confidence.*

ashimoto nimo oyobanai   足下にも及ばない   *to be no
match for someone*

[lit. to be unable to reach someone's feet]

柔道では、あの人の足下にも及びません。Jūdō dewa, ano
hito no ashimoto nimo oyobimasen.   *Where judo is
concerned, I'm no match for him.*

ashimoto nimo yoritsukenai   足下にも寄りつけない
to be unable to touch someone

[lit. to be unable to come close even to someone's feet]

雄弁さでは、誰も彼の足下にも寄りつけません。Yūbensa
dewa, daremo kare no ashimoto nimo yoritsukemasen.   *With
respect to eloquence, nobody can touch him.*

ashimoto o miru   足下を見る   *to take unfair advantage
of someone's weakness*

[lit. to look at someone's feet]

値段の交渉をするときには、足下を見られないように気を

付けなさい。Nedan no kōshō o suru toki niwa, ashimoto o mirarenai yō ni ki o tsukenasai. *When you try to negotiate a price, be careful not to be taken advantage of.*

ashinami ga midareru   足並みが乱れる   *to fall apart*
[lit. The pace gets disturbed.]
政府と民間の景気回復協力の足並みが乱れ始めました。
   Seifu to minkan no keiki kaifuku kyōryoku no ashinami ga midarehajimemashita. *The collaboration between the government and the private sector on economic recovery has started to fall apart.*

ashinami ga sorou   足並みが揃う   *to fall into line*
[lit. The pace is in harmony.]
やっとの事で、参加者全員の足並みが揃いました。Yatto no koto de, sankasha zen-in no ashinami ga soroimashita. *Finally, all the participants have fallen into line.*

ashite matoi   足手まとい   *to be a drag*
[lit. to cling to one's legs and hands]
あの人は、何をするにもいつも足手まといになります。
   Ano hito wa, nani o suru ni mo itsumo ashite matoi ni narimasu. *No matter what we do, he's always a drag.*

ni no ashi o fumu   二の足を踏む   *to hesitate*
[lit. to step on the same spot with the second foot]
彼女は結婚について二の足を踏んでいます。Kanojo wa kekkon ni tsuite ni no ashi o funde imasu. *She's hesitating about getting married.*

ukiashidatsu   浮き足立つ   *to begin to waver*
[lit. Legs start floating.]
指導者が辞めて、抗議中の学生は浮き足立ってしまいました。
   Shidōsha ga yamete, kōgi chū no gakusei wa ukiashidatte shimaimashita. *When their leader quit, the protesting students began to waver.*

---

atama   頭   *head*
   atama ga agaranai   頭が上がらない   *to feel deep*

indebtedness or respect

[lit. One's head does not go up.]

あの人にはいつも助けてもらっているので、頭が上がりません。Ano hito niwa itsumo tasukete moratte iru node, atama ga agarimasen. *Because I have been getting help from him constantly, I feel deeply indebted.*

atama ga itai　頭が痛い　　*It's a pain.*

[lit. One's head hurts.]

借金のことを考えると、頭が痛いです。Shakkin no koto o kangaeru to, atama ga itai desu. *It's a pain to think about my debts.*

atama ga furui　頭が古い　　*to be old-fashioned*

[lit. One's head is old.]

彼女のお父さんは、頭が古いです。Kanojo no otōsan wa, atama ga furui desu. *Her father is an old fogy.*

atama ga hikui　頭が低い　　*to be humble*

[lit. One's head is low.]

彼女は、有名になっても頭が低いです。Kanojo wa, yūmei ni nattemo atama ga hikui desu. *Even though she has become famous, she's still humble.*

atama ga ippai　頭が一杯　　*to be preoccupied*

[lit. One's head is full.]

試験のことで頭が一杯で、あまりご飯が食べられません。Shiken no koto de atama ga ippai de, amari gohan ga taberaremasen. *Since I'm preoccupied with the exam, I can't eat much.*

atama ga katai　頭が固い　　*to be inflexible*

[lit. One's head is hard.]

彼は頭が固くて、違う意見を聞き入れません。Kare wa atama ga katakute, chigau iken o kikiiremasen. *Because he's inflexible, he doesn't listen to opinions different from his.*

atama ga sagaru　頭が下がる　　*to take off one's hat to someone or something*

[lit. One's head goes lower.]

彼女の努力には、頭が下がります。Kanojo no doryoku niwa,
   atama ga sagarimasu.   *I take off my hat to her efforts.*

atama ni ireru   頭に入れる   *to learn something by heart*
[lit. to put something in one's head]
日本に行く前に、大切な語句を頭に入れておきました。
   Nihon ni iku mae ni, taisetsu na goku o atama ni irete
   okimashita.   *Before going to Japan, I learned some useful
   phrases by heart.*

atama ni kuru   頭に来る   *to get mad*
[lit. go to one's head]
家族の前で馬鹿にされて、頭に来ました。Kazoku no mae de
   baka ni sarete, atama ni kimashita.   *I got mad at being
   slighted in front of my family.*

atama no kaiten ga hayai   頭の回転が速い   *sharp*
[lit. The spin of one's head is fast.]
彼女は、頭の回転がとても速いです。Kanojo wa, atama no
   kaiten ga totemo hayai desu.   *She's a very sharp person.*

atama no kaiten ga osoi   頭の回転が遅い   *slow*
[lit. The spin of one's head is slow.]
あの学生は、やや頭の回転が遅いです。Ano gakusei wa,
   yaya atama no kaiten ga osoi desu.   *That student is somewhat
   slow.*

atama o haneru   頭をはねる   *to pocket a percentage of
   money*
[lit. to cut off a head]
あの仕事の仲介者は、日雇い賃金の三割も頭をはねています。
   Ano shigoto no chūkaisha wa, hiyatoi chingin no san wari mo
   atama o hanete imasu.   *That middleman is pocketing as much
   as 30 percent of the day laborers' wages.*

atama o hineru   頭をひねる   *to rack one's brains*
[lit. to incline one's head]
新事業計画の発案に、頭をひねりました。Shin jigyō keikaku
   no hatsuan ni, atama o hinerimashita.   *I racked my brains to
   come up with a new business plan.*

atama o hiyasu　　頭を冷やす　　　*to calm down*
[lit. to cool one's head]
喧嘩をやめて、頭を冷やしなさい。Kenka o yamete, atama o
　hiyashinasai.　　*Stop fighting and take it easy.*

atama o itameru　　頭を痛める　　　*to be concerned about
someone or something*
[lit. to make one's head hurt]
彼は、引退後の暮らしについて頭を痛めています。Kare wa,
　intai go no kurashi ni tsuite atama o itamete imasu.　*He's
　concerned about his life after he retires.*

atama o kakaeru　　頭を抱える　　　*at one's wit's end*
[lit. to hold one's head]
彼は、難問に頭を抱えています。Kare wa, nanmon ni atama o
　kakaete imasu.　*He's at his wit's end facing a very difficult
　problem.*

atama o marumeru　　頭を丸める　　　*to become a Buddhist
monk*
[lit. to shave one's head]
彼は、最近頭を丸める決心をしました。Kare wa, saikin
　atama o marumeru kesshin o shimashita.　*Recently, he
　decided to become a Buddhist monk.*

atama o motageru　　頭をもたげる　　　*to come to the fore,
to emerge*
[lit. to hold up one's head]
彼女は、最近一流の歌手として頭をもたげてきました。
　Kanojo wa, saikin ichiryū no kashu to shite atama o motagete
　kimashita.　*Recently, she has emerged as a top-class singer.*

atama o nayamasu　　頭を悩ます　　　*to rack one's brains*
[lit. to bother one's head]
彼女は、子供の教育のことで頭を悩ましています。Kanojo
　wa, kodomo no kyōiku no koto de atama o nayamashite imasu.
　She's racking her brains over her children's education.

atama o osaeru　　頭を抑える　　　*to keep someone under
control*

20

[lit. to hold someone's head down]

映画監督はスターの頭を抑えるのに苦労しました。Eiga kantoku wa sutā no atama o osaeru noni kurō shimashita. *The movie director had a difficult time keeping the star under control.*

atama o sageru   頭を下げる   *to knuckle under*

[lit. to lower one's head]

チームワークのために、先輩に頭を下げなければなりませんでした。Chīmuwāku no tame ni, senpai ni atama o sagenakereba narimasen deshita. *For the sake of teamwork, we had to knuckle under to the senior members.*

atama o shiboru   頭を絞る   *to rack one's brains*

[lit. to squeeze one's head]

いくら頭を絞っても、良い考えが浮かびませんでした。Ikura atama o shibottemo, ii kangae ga ukabimasen deshita. *No matter how much I racked my brains, I couldn't come up with a good idea.*

atamakabu   頭株   *key figure*

[lit. a head stump]

暴動の頭株が逮捕されました。Bōdō no atamakabu ga taiho saremashita. *The key figure in the riot was arrested.*

atamakazu   頭数   *head count*

[lit. the number of heads]

頭数が揃わなくて、野球が出来ませんでした。Atamakazu ga sorowanakute, yakyū ga dekimasen deshita. *We couldn't play baseball because we didn't have enough people.*

atamakin   頭金   *down payment*

[lit. head money]

家を買う頭金のために、貯金しています。Ie o kau atamakin no tame ni, chokin shite imasu. *I'm saving money for a down payment to buy a house.*

atamauchi   頭打ち   *lagging*

[lit. hitting one's head]

あの俳優の人気は、最近頭打ちです。Ano haiyū no ninki wa,

saikin atamauchi desu.   *Recently, the popularity of that actor
has been lagging.*

atamawari   頭割り   *Dutch treat, to pay an equal share*
[lit. to divide a bill by the head count]
宴会の費用は、頭割りで払いましょう。Enkai no hiyō wa,
atamawari de haraimashō.   *Let's go Dutch for the party
expenses.*

---

ato   後   *back, rear, consequences, after, later*
ato no matsuri   後の祭り   *too late*
[lit. the day after a festival]
今一生懸命勉強を始めても、後の祭りですよ。Ima
isshōkenmei benkyō o hajimetemo, ato no matsuri desu yo.
Even if you start studying hard now, it's too late.

ato o hiku   後を引く   *It's hard to quit something after
starting.*
[lit. to drag the consequences]
一度甘い物を食べ出すと、後を引くので困ります。Ichido
amai mono o tabedasu to, ato o hiku node komarimasu.   *Once
I start eating sweets, I'm in trouble because it's hard to stop.*

atoaji ga warui   後味が悪い   *to leave a bad taste in
one's mouth*
[lit. The aftertaste is bad.]
友達と口論した後は、後味が悪かったです。Tomodachi to
kōron shita ato wa, atoaji ga warukatta desu.   *The quarrel
with my friend left me with a bad taste in my mouth.*

atobō o katsugu   後棒を担ぐ   *to be a party to
something*
[lit. to shoulder the back end of a stick]
あの人は、社長失脚の陰謀の後棒を担ぎました。Ano hito
wa, shachō shikkyaku no inbō no atobō o katsugimashita.   *He
was a party to the conspiracy for the president's downfall.*

atogama ni suwaru   後がまに座る   *to step into
another's shoes*

[lit. to sit as a replacement pot]

社長が死んだ後、奥さんが後がまに座りました。Shachō ga shinda ato, okusan ga atogama ni suwarimashita. *After the president of the company died, his wife stepped into his shoes.*

atogusare   後腐れ   *trouble later*

[lit. future rot]

後腐れを避けるために、問題があれば今解決しておきなさい。 Atogusare o sakeru tame ni, mondai ga areba ima kaiketsu shite okinasai. *If there's a problem, you should solve it now to avoid trouble later.*

atooshi   後押し   *to back someone*

[lit. to push someone's back]

この間の選挙では、大勢の人が彼を後押ししました。Kono aida no senkyo dewa, ōzei no hito ga kare o atooshi shimashita. *A lot of people backed him in the recent election.*

atosaki kamawazu   後先構わず   *without thinking*

[lit. not caring if it's front or rear]

彼は、後先構わず家を飛び出しました。Kare wa, atosaki kamawazu ie o tobidashimashita. *Without thinking, he rushed out of his house.*

---

ato   跡   *mark, trace*

ato o ou   跡を追う   *to die following the death of someone close*

[lit. to chase a trace]

彼は奥さんの死の一年後に跡を追いました。Kare wa okusan no shi no ichi nen go ni ato o oimashita. *He died one year after his wife's death.*

ato o tatanai   跡を絶たない   *no end to something*

[lit. not to cut off traces]

就職希望者が、跡を絶ちませんでした。Shūshoku kibōsha ga, ato o tachimasen deshita. *The job applicants kept coming.*

ato o tatsu   跡を絶つ   *to disappear without a trace*

[lit. to cut off traces]

あの人が後を絶ってから、三年になります。Ano hito ga ato o tatte kara, san nen ni narimasu.   *It's been three years since he disappeared without a trace.*

ato o tsukeru　　跡をつける　　　*to tail, to shadow*
[lit. to follow a mark]
刑事は、一日中容疑者の跡をつけました。keiji wa, ichi nichi jū yōgisha no ato o tsukemashita.   *The police detective tailed the suspect all day long.*

atome o tsugu　　　跡目を継ぐ　　　*to succeed the head of a group*
[lit. to sew the mesh of a trace]
彼は、茶道の流派の家元としてお父さんの跡目を継ぎました。Kare wa, sadō no ryūha no iemoto to shite otōsan no atome o tsugimashita.   *He succeeded his father as headmaster of the tea ceremony school.*

atotori　　跡取り　　　*heir, heiress*
[lit. picking up a trace]
彼の跡取りは、ビジネスの感覚が欠けています。Kare no atotori wa, bijinesu no kankaku ga kakete imasu.   *His heir is lacking in business sense.*

---

awa　　泡　　*bubble, foam, froth*
awa o fukaseru　　泡を吹かせる　　　*to defeat someone to the point of humiliation*
[lit. to let someone blow bubbles]
彼女は討論で相手に勝って泡を吹かせました。Kanojo wa tōron de aite ni katte awa o fukasemashita.   *While winning the debate, she humiliated her opponent.*

awa o kuu　　泡を食う　　　*to be taken aback*
[lit. to eat foam]
試験の難しさに泡を食いました。Shiken no muzukashisa ni awa o kuimashita.   *I was taken aback by the difficulty of the exam.*

mizu no awa to naru　　水の泡となる　　　*to come to nothing*

[lit. to become a water bubble]

私の調停の努力は水の泡となりました。Watakushi no chōtei no doryoku wa mizu no awa to narimashita. *My efforts at mediation came to nothing.*

B

ba   馬   *horse*

bakyaku o arawasu   馬脚を現す   *to show one's true colors*

[lit. to reveal the legs of a horse]

彼は慎ましい振りをしていましたが、じきに馬脚を現しました。Kare wa tsutsumashii furi o shite imashita ga, jiki ni bakyaku o arawashimashita. *He was pretending to be modest, but he soon showed his true colors.*

bariki ga aru   馬力がある   *to have stamina*

[lit. to have horsepower]

あのマラソンの選手は、非常に馬力があります。Ano marason no senshu wa, hijō ni bariki ga arimasu. *That marathon runner has great stamina.*

bariki o kakeru   馬力をかける   *to work one's fingers to the bone*

[lit. to apply horsepower]

渡辺さんは、卒業試験のために馬力をかけて勉強しています。Watanabe san wa, sotsùgyō shiken no tame ni bariki o kakete benkyō shite imasu. *Miss Watanabe is working her fingers to the bone to pass the graduation exam.*

ba   場   *place, spot*

bachigai   場違い   *inappropriate*

[lit. The place is wrong.]

ここでそんなことをするのは、場違いです。Koko de sonna *koto o suru no wa, bachigai desu. It's inappropriate to do such things.*

bakazu o fumu   場数を踏む   *to be experienced*
[lit. to step on a number of spots]
この仕事には、場数を踏んだ人が必要です。Kono shigoto niwa, bakazu o funda hito ga hitsuyō desu. *We need an old hand for this job.*

baokure suru   場遅れする   *to get nervous*
[lit. to come late to a place]
歌を歌おうとしましたが、大勢の人がいるので場遅れして しまいました。Uta o utaō to shimashita ga, ōzei no hito ga iru node baokure shite shimaimashita. *I tried to sing a song, but I got nervous because there were so many people.*

---

baka   馬鹿   *fool, idiot, absurdity*

baka na mane o suru   馬鹿なまねをする   *to act silly*
[lit. to pretend to be a fool]
人前で馬鹿なまねをするんじゃありません。Hitomae de baka na mane o surunja arimasen. *Don't act silly in front of the other people.*

baka ni naranai   馬鹿にならない   *substantial, nothing to sneeze at*
[lit. to not become absurdity]
彼女の地域社会への貢献は馬鹿になりません。Kanojo no chiiki shakai e no kōken wa baka ni narimasen. *Her contribution to local society is substantial.*

baka ni suru   馬鹿にする   *to slight, to insult, to make fun of*
[lit. to make a fool of someone]
学生たちは、あの先生を馬鹿にしています。Gakusei tachi wa, ano sensei o baka ni shite imasu. *The students are making fun of that teacher.*

baka o miru   馬鹿を見る   *to make a fool of oneself*
[lit. to see a fool]
安物を買って馬鹿を見ました。Yasumono o katte baka o mimashita. *I made a fool of myself buying that junk.*

bakaatari   馬鹿当たり   *smash hit*
[lit. a crazy hit]
あのショーは、馬鹿当たりしています。Ano shō wa,
  bakaatari shite imasu. *That show is a smash hit.*

bakabakashii   馬鹿馬鹿しい   *absurd, ridiculous*
[lit. fool-like]
あの人は、馬鹿馬鹿しい将来の夢を持っています。Ano
  hito wa, bakabakashii shōrai no yume o motte imasu. *He has
  an absurd dream for his future.*

bakabanashi   馬鹿話   *foolish talk*
[lit. a fool's talk]
仕事中に、馬鹿話はやめて下さい。Shigoto chū ni,
  bakabanashi wa yamete kudasai. *Please stop the foolish
  conversation during work.*

bakajikara   馬鹿力   *great physical strength*
[lit. a fool's power]
彼は引っ越しの時、馬鹿力を発揮しました。Kare wa
  hikkoshi no toki, bakajikara o hakki shimashita. *He showed
  great physical strength during the move.*

bakakusai   馬鹿臭い   *foolish, absurd*
[lit. smelling like a fool]
そんなことにお金を使うのは、馬鹿臭いです。Sonna koto ni
  okane o tsukau no wa bakakusai desu. *It's absurd to spend
  money for such a thing.*

bakasawagi   馬鹿騒ぎ   *racket*
[lit. a fool's commotion]
馬鹿騒ぎをやめなさい。Bakasawagi o yamenasai. *Stop
  making such a racket.*

bakashōjiki   馬鹿正直   *excessively honest*
[lit. a fool's honesty]
彼は馬鹿正直なので、気分を損ねる人が大勢います。Kare
  wa bakashōjiki nanode, kibun o sokoneru hito ga ōzei imasu.
  *There are many people who get upset at him because he's too
  honest.*

27

bakateinei 馬鹿丁寧   *excessively polite*
[lit. a fool's politeness]
丁寧なのは大切ですが、あまり馬鹿丁寧にならないように
気をつけなさい。 Teinei nano wa taisetsu desu ga, amari
bakateinei ni naranai yō ni ki o tsukenasai. *It's important to
be polite, but be careful not to be too polite.*

bakawarai 馬鹿笑い   *to laugh like an idiot*
[lit. an idiot's laugh]
みっともないから、馬鹿笑いはやめなさい。 Mittomonai
kara, bakawarai wa yamenasai. *Stop laughing like an idiot;
it's unseemly.*

---

ban 万   *10,000, everything, all things*
banji kyūsu 万事休す   *It's all over. It's finished.*
[lit. Ten thousand things rest.]
旅行の途中で財布をなくして、万事休すになりました。
Ryokō no tochū de saifu o nakushite, banji kyūsu ni narimashita.
I lost my wallet in the middle of the trip, and it was all over.

bannan o haishite 万難を排して   *at all costs*
[lit. by eliminating 10,000 difficulties]
ご招待、有り難うございます。パーティーには、万難を排
して伺います。 Goshōtai, arigatō gozaimasu. Pātī niwa,
bannan o haishite ukagaimasu. *Thank you very much for the
invitation. I'll come to your party at all costs.*

bansaku tsukiru 万策尽きる   *to be at the end of one's
rope*
[lit. Ten thousand schemes end.]
彼女は万策尽きて、留学をあきらめました。 Kanojo wa
bansaku tsukite, ryūgaku o akiramemashita. *She was at the
end of her rope and gave up studying abroad.*

---

batsu ばつ   *circumstances, convenience*
batsu ga warui ばつが悪い
to feel awkward, to be embarrassed
[lit. The circumstances are bad.]

ばつが悪いけれど、友達のお父さんに仕事を頼みに行きました。Batsu ga warui keredo, tomodachi no otōsan ni shigoto o tanomini ikimashita. *Although I felt awkward, I went to see my friend's father to ask for a job.*

batsu o awaseru　　ばつを合わせる　　*to make one's story sound plausible*
[lit. to fit the circumstances]
私の言い訳に、彼がばつを合わせてくれました。Watakushi no iiwake ni, kare ga batsu o awasete kuremashita. *He was kind enough to make my excuse sound plausible.*

---

benkyō　　勉強　　*study*
benkyō ni naru　　勉強になる　　*to gain good experience*
[lit. to become useful for study]
初めて中国へ行って、良い勉強になりました。Hajimete Chūgoku e itte, ii benkyō ni narimashita. *When I first went to visit China, I gained some good experience.*

benkyōka　　勉強家　　*hard worker*
[lit. a study expert]
彼女は勉強家だから、新しいことでもすぐ覚えます。Kanojo wa benkyōka dakara, atarashii koto demo sugu oboemasu. *Since she is a hard worker, she learns even new things quickly.*

nedan o benkyō suru　　値段を勉強する　　*to lower a price*
[lit. to study a price]
これを買っても良いけれど、値段をもう少し勉強してもらえませんか。Kore o kattemo ii keredo, nedan o mō sukoshi benkyō shite moraemasen ka. *I may buy it, but would you lower the price a little?*

---

benri　　便利　　*convenience*
benriya　　便利屋　　*handyman*
[lit. a person of convenience]
彼は便利屋で、何でも直せます。Kare wa benriya de, nandemo naosemasu. *He's such a good handyman that he*

can fix anything for you.

---

benzetsu   弁舌   *speech*

benzetsu no tatsu   弁舌の立つ   *eloquent*

[lit. the tongue standing up for a speech]

あの評論家は、弁舌の立つ人としても知られています。

Ano hyōronka wa, benzetsu no tatsu hito to shite mo shirarete imasu.   *That critic is also known as an eloquent speaker.*

benzetsu o furuu   弁舌を振るう   *to speak eloquently*

[lit. to shake the tongue for a speech]

部長は、会議で弁舌を振るいました。Buchō wa, kaigi de benzetsu o furuimashita.   *The department chief spoke eloquently at the meeting.*

---

binbō   貧乏   *poverty*

binbōkuji o hiku   貧乏くじを引く   *to be the least lucky of all*

[lit. to draw a poor lottery ticket]

貧乏くじを引いてしまい、みんなのためにお使いをしなければなりませんでした。Binbōkuji o hiite shimai, minna no tame ni otsukai o shinakereba narimasen deshita.   *Because I was the least lucky of all, I had to do errands for everybody.*

binbōkusai   貧乏臭い   *shabby*

[lit. smelling like a poor person]

彼は金持ちなのに、いつも貧乏くさい服を着ています。

Kare wa kanemochi nanoni, itsumo binbōkusai fuku o kite imasu.   *Although he's rich, he's always wearing shabby clothes.*

---

bō   棒   *stick, pole*

bō ni furu   棒に振る   *to waste, to ruin*

[lit. to swing something like a stick]

あの人は、麻薬で人生を棒に振りました。Ano hito wa, mayaku de jinsei o bō ni furimashita.   *He ruined his life with drugs.*

bō o furu   棒を振る   *to conduct music*
[lit. to swing a stick]

一度でも、オーケストラで棒を振ってみたいです。Ichido
  demo, ōkesutora de bō o futte mitai desu. *I would love to
  conduct an orchestra even once.*

bōanki   棒暗記   *memorizing without understanding,
  straight memorization*
[lit. stick memorization]

試験では、答えの棒暗記はしないように。Shiken dewa,
  kotae no bōanki wa shinai yō ni. *Don't memorize answers for
  an exam without understanding the meaning.*

bōbiki   棒引き   *to write off, to cancel*
[lit. to draw a stick]

あなたの借金を、棒引きしてあげましょう。Anata no
  shakkin o, bōbiki shite agemashō. *I'll write off your debt.*

bōdachisuru   棒立ちする   *to stand stiffly*
[lit. to stand like a stick]

彼女はあまりの恐さに、棒立ちしてしまいました。Kanojo
  wa amari no kowasa ni, bōdachishite shimaimashita. *Fearful,
  she stood stiffly.*

bōyomisuru   棒読みする   *to read in a monotone*
[lit. to read like a stick]

詩を棒読みしても、感情が伝わりません。Shi o
  bōyomishitemo, kanjō ga tsutawarimasen. *If you read poetry
  in a monotone, you can't convey feelings.*

katabō o katsugu   片棒を担ぐ   *to take part in something*
[lit. to carry one end of a stick]

彼は、社内の陰謀の片棒を担いで出世した男です。Kare wa,
  shanai no inbō no katabō o katsuide shusse shita otoko desu.
  *He is the man who made it by taking part in a company
  conspiracy.*

bōzu   坊主   *Buddhist priest*
　mikkabōzu   三日坊主   *quitter*
　[lit. a Buddhist priest for three days]
　あの人は三日坊主で、何をやっても長続きしません。Ano
　hito wa mikkabōzu de, nani o yattemo nagatsuzuki shimasen.
　Because she's a quitter, she can't last long at anything she does.

---

bu   分   *rate, percentage*
　bu ga aru   分が有る   *to be at an advantage*
　[lit. There is a percentage.]
　明日の試合は、こちら側に分があります。Ashita no shiai
　wa, kochiragawa ni bu ga arimasu.   *We have an advantage in
　the game tomorrow.*

　bu ga warui   分が悪い   *to be at a disadvantage*
　[lit. The percentage is bad.]
　わが社の分が悪い市場で、競争しなければなりません。
　Waga sha no bu ga warui shijō de, kyōsō shinakereba
　narimasen.   *Our company has to compete in a market where
　we're at a disadvantage.*

C

cha   茶   *tea, green tea*
　chaban   茶番   *farce, sham*
　[lit. a facetious Noh drama]
　彼女は泣いて謝っているけれど、また茶番です。Kanojo wa
　naite ayamatte iru keredo, mata chaban desu.   *Although she's
　crying and apologizing, once again it's a farce.*

　chacha o ireru   茶々を入れる   *to interrupt with banter*
　[lit. to make tea after tea]
　彼女は、私が話すといつも茶々を入れます。

Kanojo wa, watakushi ga hanasu to itsumo chacha o iremasu.
She interrupts me with banter whenever I talk.

ocha o nigosu　　お茶を濁す　　　*to pussyfoot*
[lit. to make tea cloudy]
政府は環境問題について、お茶を濁しています。Seifu wa
kankyō mondai ni tsuite, ocha o nigoshite imasu.　　*The
government is pussyfooting on environmental issues.*

ochame　　お茶目　　　*playful, mischievous (a child)*
[lit. an eye of tea]
あの子は、お茶目なことが大好きです。Ano ko wa, ochame
na koto ga daisuki desu.　　*That child loves to play pranks.*

---

chi　　血　　　*blood*

chi de chi o arau arasoi　　血で血を洗う争い　　　*intense
internal strife*
[lit. to wash blood with blood]
今党では次の党首を選ぶために、血で血を洗う争いが起こ
っています。Ima tō dewa tsugi no tōshu o erabu tame ni, chi
de chi o arau arasoi ga okotte imasu. *The party is experiencing
intense internal strife over the choice of their next president.*

chi ga hiku omoi　　血が引く思い　　　*to be horrified, to
make one's flesh crawl*
[lit. One's blood recedes.]
交通事故の現場を見て、血が引く思いをしました。Kōtsū
jiko no genba o mite, chi ga hiku omoi o shimashita.　　*The
scene of the traffic accident made my flesh crawl.*

chi ga kayotta　　血が通った　　　*warm, humane, thoughtful*
[lit. blood flowing]
政府は、血が通った政策を約束しています。Seifu wa, chi ga
kayotta seisaku o yakusokushite imasu.　　*The government
promises people-oriented policies.*

chi ga kayotte iru　　血が通っている　　　*alive*
[lit. One's blood flows.]
血が通っている間は、働き続けるつもりです。Chi ga

kayotte iru aida wa, hataraki tsuzukeru tsumori desu.   *I intend to keep working as long as I'm alive.*

chi ga noboru   血が上る   *to fly off the handle*
[lit. One's blood rushes up.]

彼があまりにも無礼なので、頭に血が上りました。Kare ga amari nimo burei nanode, atama ni chi ga noborimashita.   *His rudeness made me fly off the handle.*

chi ga sawagu   血が騒ぐ   *to get excited*
[lit. One's blood makes noises.]

明日の旅行のことを考えると、血が騒ぎます。Ashita no ryokō no koto o kangaeru to, chi ga sawagimasu.   *I get excited when I think about tomorrow's trip.*

chi ga tsunagaru   血がつながる   *to be a blood relative*
[lit. One's blood is connected.]

叔父は血がつながっているのに、私にとても冷淡です。Oji wa chi ga tsunagatte iru noni, watakushi ni totemo reitan desu.
My uncle is very cold to me although he is a blood relative.

chi ga waku   血が沸く   *stirring, thrilling*
[lit. One's blood boils.]

昨日私たちのチームが勝って、血が沸きました。Kinō watakushitachi no chīmu ga katte, chi ga wakimashita.   *Our team's victory yesterday was thrilling.*

chi mo namida mo nai   血も涙もない   *cold-blooded*
[lit. having no blood and no tears]

社員は、会社の血も涙もない仕打ちに憤慨しています。Shain wa, kaisha no chi mo namida mo nai shiuchi ni fungai shite imasu.   *The employees are enraged at their cold-blooded treatment by the company.*

chi no ame   血の雨   *bloodshed*
[lit. rain of blood]

今の状態が続くと、血の雨を降らせる恐れがあります。Ima no jōtai ga tsuzuku to, chi no ame o furaseru osore ga arimasu.
If the current situation continues, there is great danger of bloodshed.

chi no deru yō na   血の出るような   *extremely hard*
[lit. like bleeding]

彼女は、血の出るような努力をしてお金を貯めました。

  Kanojo wa, chi no deru yō na doryoku o shite okane o
  tamemashita.   *She saved money by working extremely hard.*

chi no ke no ōi   血の気の多い   *hotheaded*
[lit. much indication of blood]

あの人は血の気が多くてすぐ怒るので、気をつけなさい。

  Ano hito wa chi no ke ga ōkute sugu okoru node, ki o
  tsukenasai.   *You should be careful of him becuase he's
  hotheaded and gets angry easily.*

chi no meguri no warui   血の巡りの悪い   *stupid*
[lit. poor blood circulation]

彼は血の巡りが悪いから、よく失敗します。Kare wa chi no
  meguri ga warui kara, yoku shippai shimasu.   *Because he's
  stupid, he makes mistakes often.*

chi no namida   血の涙   *tears of anguish*
[lit. tears of blood]

両親に突然死なれて、彼女は血の涙を流しました。Ryōshin
  ni totsuzen shinarete, kanojo wa chi no namida o
  nagashimashita.   *She shed tears of anguish over the sudden
  deaths of her parents.*

chi o haku omoi   血を吐く思い   *determination*
[lit. a feeling of vomiting blood]

彼は大学に行くために、血を吐く思いで勉強しました。

  Kare wa daigaku ni iku tame ni, chi o haku omoi de benkyō
  shimashita.   *Because of his determination to go to college, he
  studied hard.*

chi o hiku   血を引く   *to inherit a trait or talent*
[lit. to draw blood]

あの子はお母さんの音楽の才能の血を引いています。Ano
  ko wa okāsan no ongaku no sainō no chi o hiite imasu.   *That
  child inherited her mother's talent for music.*

chi o miru   血を見る   *to cause casualties*

[lit. to see blood]

デモ隊が機動隊と衝突して、血を見ることになりました。
Demotai ga kidōtai to shōtotsu shite, chi o miru koto ni narimashita. *When the demonstrators clashed with the mobile police units, there were casualties.*

chi o wakeru　　血を分ける　　*to be blood relatives*
[lit. to share same blood]

兄と私は血を分けた仲でも、考え方がまるで違います。Ani to watakushi wa chi o waketa naka demo, kangaekata ga marude chigaimasu. *Although we're blood relatives, my brother and I have totally different ways of thinking.*

chi to ase no kesshō　　血と汗の結晶　　*fruit of someone's blood, sweat, and tears*
[lit. a crystal of blood and sweat]

彼女の博士号は、血と汗の結晶です。Kanojo no hakasegō wa, chi to ase no kesshō desu. *Her Ph.D. is the fruit of her blood, sweat, and tears.*

chi to nari niku to naru　　血となり肉となる　　*to be a key*
[lit. to become blood and muscles]

若いときの経験が、今の成功の血となり肉となっています。
Wakai toki no keiken ga, ima no seikō no chi to nari niku to natte imasu. *An experience in my youth was the key to my current success.*

chi wa arasoenai　　血は争えない　　*in the blood*
[lit. The blood can't compete.]

あの医者の子供はみんな医者になりました。血は争えないものです。Ano isha no kodomo wa minna isha ni narimashita. Chi wa arasoenai mono desu. *That doctor's children all became doctors. It's indeed in the blood.*

chimanako ni naru　　血眼になる　　*to become frantic*
[lit. to get bloodshot eyes]

落とした財布を、血眼になって探しました。Otoshita saifu o, chimanako ni natte sagashimashita. *I looked frantically for my lost wallet.*

chimatsuri ni ageru　血祭りに上げる　　*to make
someone a scapegoat*
[lit. to hoist someone for a blood festival]
チームのオーナーは、監督を血祭りに上げて首を切りました。
Chīmu no ōnā wa, kantoku o chimatsuri ni agete kubi o
kirimashita.　*The team owner made a scapegoat of the head
coach and fired him.*

chimayou　血迷う　*to lose one's mind*
[lit. One's blood is at a loss.]
その学生は、血迷って先生を殴りつけました。Sono gakusei
wa, chimayotte sensei o naguritsukemashita.　*The student lost
his mind and punched his teacher.*

chimichi o ageru　血道を上げる　　*to be infatuated with
someone*
[lit. to raise blood vessels]
彼は、赤坂の芸者に血道を上げています。Kare wa, Akasaka
no geisha ni chimichi o agete imasu.　*He's infatuated with a
geisha in Akasaka.*

chisuji　血筋　*lineage, ancestry*
[lit. a line of blood]
彼は、貴族の血筋を引いています。Kare wa, kizoku no
chisuji o hiite imasu.　*He's from a family of noble ancestry.*

---

chi　地　*ground, soil*
chi ni mamireru　地にまみれる　*to be defeated*
[lit. to be covered with mud]
あの政治家は、この前の選挙で地にまみれました。Ano
seijika wa, kono mae no senkyo de chi ni mamiremashita.
That politician lost the last election.

chi ni ochiru　地に落ちる　*to decline, to drop*
[lit. to fall to the ground]
あの学者の名声は、急激に地に落ちました。Ano gakusha no
meisei wa, kyūgeki ni chi ni ochimashita.　*The fame of that
scholar rapidly declined.*

chiho o katameru   地歩を固める   *to secure a foothold*
[lit. to occupy the ground for one's own steps]
彼は、将来重役になるための地歩を固めました。Kare wa,
shōrai jūyaku ni naru tame no chiho o katamemashita.   *He
secured a foothold to become a senior executive in the future.*

---

chichi   乳   *milk*
chichikusai   乳臭い   *green, immature*
[lit. smelling of milk]
あの人は大学生なのに、まだ乳臭いです。Ano hito wa
daigakusei nanoni, mada chichikusai desu.   *He's a college
student, but he's still immature.*

---

chie   知恵   *wisdom, intelligence*
chie ga asai   知恵が浅い   *slow, dull-witted*
[lit. One's wisdom is shallow.]
彼は知恵が浅いから、大切な仕事は頼めません。Kare wa
chie ga asai kara, taisetsu na shigoto wa tanomemasen.   *We
can't ask him to do anything important because he's slow.*

chie ga mawaru   知恵が回る   *to be resourceful*
[lit. One's wisdom spins.]
彼女は知恵が回るので、旅行中は頼りになります。Kanojo
wa chie ga mawaru node, ryokō chū wa tayori ni narimasu.
During a trip, you can rely on her because she's resourceful.

chie o kariru   知恵を借りる   *to ask for advice*
[lit. to borrow wisdom]
留学について、先生に知恵を借りました。Ryūgaku ni tsuite,
sensei ni chie o karimashita.   *I asked my teacher's advice
about my studying abroad.*

chie o kasu   知恵を貸す   *to give advice*
[lit. to lend wisdom]
会計士は、投資についていとこに知恵を貸しました。
Kaikeishi wa, tōshi ni tsuite itoko ni chie o kashimashita.   *The
accountant gave advice about investments to my cousin.*

chie o shiboru   知恵を絞る   *to exert one's wits*

[lit. to squeeze wisdom]

新しい事業計画を提出するために、知恵を絞りました。

Atarashii jigyō keikaku o teishutsusuru tame ni, chie o shiborimashita. *I exerted my wits to submit a new business plan.*

chie o tsukeru   知恵を付ける   *to instigate, to incite*
[lit. to fasten wisdom to someone]

彼は同僚にストライキを起こすように知恵を付けました。

Kare wa dōryō ni sutoraiki o okosu yō ni chie o tsukemashita. *He instigated his colleagues to strike.*

---

chikai   誓い   *oath, vow*
　chikai o tateru   誓いを立てる   *to make a vow*
　[lit. to erect a vow]

彼は、毎日運動する誓いを立てました。Kare wa, mainichi undō suru chikai o tatemashita. *He made a vow to exercise every day.*

---

chikara   力   *power, force*
　chikara ni amaru   力に余る   *beyond one's ability*
　[lit. more than one's power]

その要求は、私の力に余りました。Sono yōkyū wa, watakushi no chikara ni amarimashita. *The request was beyond my capability.*

chikara ni naru   力になる   *to help*
[lit. to become power]

彼女が困っているので、力になってあげました。Kanojo ga komatte iru node, chikara ni natte agemashita. *I helped her because she was having trouble.*

chikara no aru   力のある   *convincing*
[lit. There is power.]

彼は力のある話し方で、理由を説明しました。Kare wa chikara no aru hanashikata de, riyū o setsumei shimashita. *He explained the reasons in a convincing speech.*

chikara o furuu   力を振るう   *to be influential*

[lit. to brandish power]

あの教授は、経済理論の分野で力を振るっています。

Ano kyōju wa, keizai riron no bun-ya de chikara o furutte imasu. *That professor is influential in the field of economic theory.*

chikara o ireru   力を入れる   *to take great interest in someone or something*

[lit. to put power in]

あの政党は、環境問題に力を入れています。Ano seitō wa, kankyō mondai ni chikara o irete imasu. *That political party is taking great interest in environmental issues.*

chikara o kariru   力を借りる   *to enlist the help of someone*

[lit. to borrow power]

難問を解決するために、弁護士の力を借りました。Nanmon o kaiketsu suru tame ni, bengoshi no chikara o karimashita. *We enlisted the help of a lawyer to solve some difficult problems.*

chikara o kasu   力を貸す   *to help*

[lit. to lend power]

友達が自分の会社を作るとき、力を貸しました。Tomodachi ga jibun no kaisha o tsukuru toki, chikara o kashimashita. *I helped my friend when she set up her own company.*

chikara o otosu   力を落とす   *to be dejected*

[lit. to drop power]

彼は彼女が婚約を解消して以来、力を落としています。Kare wa kanojo ga kon-yaku o kaishō shite irai, chikara o otoshite imasu. *He's been dejected since she broke off their engagement.*

chikarakobu o ireru   力瘤を入れる   *to help actively, to make efforts*

[lit. to make one's biceps swell]

彼女は、政治改革の草の根運動に力瘤を入れています。Kanojo wa, seiji kaikaku no kusa no ne undō ni chikarakobu o irete imasu. *She's actively helping the grass-roots movement for political reform.*

chikarazoe 　力添え　*help*
[lit. to accompany power]
友達のお父さんの力添えで、いい仕事を見つけることが出来ました。Tomodachi no otōsan no chikarazoe de, ii shigoto o mitsukeru koto ga dekimashita. *I was able to find a good job with the help of my friend's father.*

chikarazukeru 　力付ける　*to encourage, to reassure*
[lit. to attach power]
彼がインタビューを心配していたので、力付けてあげました。
Kare ga intabyū o shinpai shite ita node, chikarazukete agemashita. *Because he was worried about his interview, I reassured him.*

chikarazuku de 　力ずくで　*by sheer force*
[lit. for the sake of force]
彼は、力ずくで今の地位を築きました。Kare wa, chikarazuku de ima no chii o kizukimashita. *He established his current status by sheer force.*

---

chōchin 　提灯　*lantern*
chōchin o motsu 　提灯を持つ　*to flatter*
[lit. to hold a lantern]
彼女は、社長の提灯を持つ機会を見逃しません。Kanojo wa, shachō no chōchin o motsu kikai o minogashimasen. *She never misses a chance to flatter the president.*

---

chōshi 　調子　*tune*
chōshi ga ii 　調子がいい　*fawning, obsequious*
[lit. The tune is good.]
彼は調子がいいから、あまり信用できません。Kare wa chōhi ga ii kara, amari shin-yō dekimasen. *Because he's obsequious, I can't trust him much.*

chōshi ni noru 　調子に乗る　*to be on a roll*
[lit. to ride on a tune]
私たちは仕事がやっと調子に乗って、締め切りに間に合います。

Watakushitachi wa shigoto ga yatto chōshi ni notte, shimekiri ni maniaimasu.   *Now that we're on a roll, we can meet the deadline.*

chōshi ni noru　　調子に乗る　　*to get a swelled head*
[lit. to ride on a tune]
あの人は、誉められるとすぐ調子に乗ります。Ano hito wa, homerareru to sugu chōshi ni norimasu.   *She easily gets a swelled head when she's praised.*

chōshi o awaseru　　調子を合わせる　　*to play along with someone*
[lit. to fit a tune]
彼は、上司が言うことには何でも調子を合わせます。Kare wa, jōshi ga iu koto niwa nandemo chōshi o awasemasu.   *He plays along with whatever his boss says.*

chōshi o nomikomu　　調子を飲み込む　　*to get the hang of something*
[lit. to swallow a tune]
先月コンピュータを買いましたが、やっと調子を飲み込むことが出来ました。Sengetsu konpyūta o kaimashita ga, yatto chōshi o nomikomu koto ga dekimashita.   *I bought a computer last month, and I've finally gotten the hang of it.*

chōshi o otosu　　調子を落とす　　*to slow down, to be in a slump*
[lit. to drop a tune]
あの選手は、初夏以来調子を落としています。Ano senshu wa, shoka irai chōshi o otoshite imasu.   *That player has been in a slump since the beginning of summer.*

chōshi o yawarageru　　調子を和らげる　　*to tone down*
[lit. to soften a tune]
マスコミは政府攻撃の調子を和らげました。Masukomi wa seifu kōgeki no chōshi o yawaragemashita.   *The mass media toned down their attack on the government.*

---

chū　宙　*space, air*
　chū de yomu　宙で読む　*to recite from memory*

[lit. to read in space]

あの女優は、詩を宙で読むことが得意です。Ano joyū wa, shi o chū de yomu koto ga tokui desu.   *That actress is good at reciting poems from memory.*

chū ni mayou   宙に迷う   *to remain unsettled*
[lit. to get lost in space]

交渉は、意見の衝突で宙に迷っています。Kōshō wa, iken no shōtotsu de chū ni mayotte imasu.   *The negotiations remain unsettled because of the clash of opinions.*

chū ni uku   宙に浮く   *to be suspended, to be up in the air*
[lit. to float in the air]

建築計画は、住民の反対で宙に浮いています。 Kenchiku keikaku wa, jūmin no hantai de chū ni uite imasu.   *The construction project is up in the air because of opposition by the residents.*

---

chūmon   注文   *order*
  chūmon no urusai   注文のうるさい   *fussy*
[lit. An order is noisy.]

彼は、礼儀については注文がうるさい人です。Kare wa, reigi ni tsuite wa chūmon ga urusai hito desu.   *He's fussy about etiquette.*

  chūmon o tsukeru   注文を付ける   *to attach conditions*
[lit. to attach an order]

母はもっと勉強する注文を付けて、コンピュータを買ってくれました。Haha wa motto benkyō suru chūmon o tsukete, konpyūta o katte kuremashita.   *My mother bought me a computer on the condition that I study harder.*

D

daiji   大事   *important, valuable*
  daiji ni itaru   大事にいたる   *to get out of control, to*

reach a serious level
[lit. to reach an important thing]

犯罪が大事にいたる前に、予防策を作るべきです。Hanzai ga daiji ni itaru mae ni, yobō saku o tsukuru beki desu. *We should establish prevention measures before crime gets out of control.*

daiji o toru　　大事をとる　　　*to be cautious, to play it safe*
[lit. to pick up an important thing]

風邪だと思いますが、大事をとって明日医者に行きます。
Kaze da to omoimasu ga, daiji o totte ashita isha ni ikimasu. *I think it's a cold, but to play it safe, I'm going to see a doctor tomorrow.*

---

daku　　抱く　　　*to embrace*

dakikomu　　抱き込む　　　*to win someone over*
[lit. to hold someone to one's chest]

彼は、彼女を策略に抱き込みました。Kare wa, kanojo o sakuryaku ni dakikomimashita. *He won her over to his plot.*

---

dakyō　　妥協　　　*compromise*

dakyōan o neru　　妥協案を練る　　　*to work out a compromise*
[lit. to knead a compromise plan]

急いで決着するために、妥協案を練っています。Isoide ketchaku suru tame ni, dakyōan o nette imasu. *To settle quickly, we're working out a compromise.*

---

dame　　駄目　　　*useless, no use*

dame o dasu　　駄目を出す　　　*to reject, to not accept*
[lit. to issue uselessness]

学校は、学生の要求に駄目を出しました。Gakkō wa, gakusei no yōkyū ni dame o dashimashita. *The school rejected the students' demands.*

dame o osu　　駄目を押す　　　*to make sure*
[lit. to press uselessness]

医者は、患者が薬を規則的に飲むように駄目を押しました。

Isha wa, kanja ga kusuri o kisokuteki ni nomu yō ni dame o oshimashita.   *The doctor made sure his patient would take the medicine regularly.*

---

dashi   だし   *stock, broth*
    dashi ni tsukau   だしに使う   *to use someone, to exploit someone*
  [lit. to use someone for stock]
  彼女は、パートナーをだしに使って目的を遂げました。
  Kanojo wa, pātonā o dashi ni tsukatte mokuteki o togemashita.   *She achieved her goal by exploiting her partner.*

---

da   蛇   *snake*
    dasoku   蛇足   *excessive, superfluous*
  [lit. snake legs]
  その説明の、最後の言葉は蛇足です。Sono setsumei no, saigo no kotoba wa dasoku desu.   *The last part of the explanation is superfluous.*

---

debana   出鼻   *extruding nose*
    debana o kujiku   出鼻を挫く   *to squelch someone's initial enthusiasm*
  [lit. to break someone's nose]
  教授は講義の出鼻を挫かれて、後を続けられませんでした。
  Kyōju wa kōgi no debana o kujikarete, ato o tsuzukeraremasen deshita.   *The professor's enthusiasm was squelched at the beginning of his lecture and he couldn't go on.*

---

do   度   *degree, time(s)*
    do o sugosu   度を過ごす   *to go too far, to be overbearing*
  [lit. to exceed a degree]
  監督の度を過ごした態度に、選手は憤っています。Kantoku no do o sugoshita taido ni, senshu wa ikidootte imasu.   *The players resent the manager's overbearing attitude.*

    do o ushinau   度を失う   *to lose one's composure*
  [lit. to lose a degree]

彼女は突然演説を頼まれて、度を失いました。Kanojo wa totsuzen enzetsu o tanomarete, do o ushinaimashita. *She lost her composure at the sudden request for her to give a speech.*

---

dogimo   度肝   *liver*
dogimo o nukareru   度肝を抜かれる   *to be dumbfounded*
[lit. One's liver is extracted.]
娘に婚約を告げられて、度肝を抜かれました。Musume ni kon-yaku o tsugerarete, dogimo o nukaremashita. *I was dumbfounded by my daughter's announcing her engagement.*

---

doko   どこ   *where*
doko fuku kaze   どこ吹く風   *complete indifference*
[lit. Where is the wind blowing?]
彼は何度注意されても、どこ吹く風といった様子です。Kare wa nando chūi saretemo, doko fuku kaze to itta yōsu desu. *No matter how many times he is warned, he seems completely indifferent.*

---

doku   毒   *poison*
dokudokushii   毒々しい   *venomous, spiteful*
[lit. poison-like]
あの人は、毒々しい話し方で反論しました。Ano hito wa, dokudokushii hanashikata de hanron shimashita. *He argued back using spiteful language.*

dokuke ni aterareru   毒気に当てられる   *to be stunned*
[lit. to be exposed to the poisonous air]
私は、図々しく好意を要求する彼女の毒気に当てられてしまいました。Watakushi wa, zūzūshiku kōi o yōkyū suru kanojo no dokuke ni aterarete shimaimashita. *I was stunned by her brazen demands for favors.*

dokuke o nukareru   毒気を抜かれる   *to be deflated (feelings)*
[lit. the poisonous air to be drawn out]
抗議するつもりだったら謝られて、毒気を抜かれてしまい

ました。Kōgi suru tsumori dattara ayamararete, dokuke o
nukarete shimaimashita. *I intended to protest, but when they
apologized, my anger subsided.*

---

doro 泥 *mud*

doro o haku 泥を吐く   *to confess to one's crime*
[lit. to vomit mud]
容疑者は、逮捕されるとすぐに泥を吐きました。Yōgisha
wa, taiho sareru to sugu ni doro o hakimashita. *The suspect
confessed to the crime right after his arrest.*

doro o kaburu 泥をかぶる   *to assume someone else's
responsibility*
[lit. to pour mud upon oneself]
課長は部下の失敗の泥をかぶって、辞職しました。Kachō
wa buka no shippai no doro o kabutte, jishoku shimashita.
*The section chief assumed responsibility for his subordinate's
mistake by resigning.*

dorojiai 泥仕合   *mudslinging*
[lit. a mud bout]
この選挙戦では、候補者が泥仕合を繰り広げています。
Kono senkyo sen dewa, kōhosha ga dorojiai o kurihirogete
imasu. *In this election campaign, the candidates are
engaging in mudslinging.*

dorokusai 泥臭い   *unrefined, sloppy*
[lit. smelling like mud]
彼は、いつも泥臭い服装をしています。Kare wa, itsumo
dorokusai fukusō o shite imasu. *He's always wearing sloppy
clothes.*

doronawashiki 泥縄式   *after the fact*
[lit. a method of making a rope after seeing a thief]
政府の災害予防対策は、泥縄式でした。Seifu no saigai yobō
taisaku wa, doronawashiki deshita. *The government took
disaster-prevention measures after the fact.*

doronuma ni hamaru 泥沼にはまる   *to be bogged down*

[lit. to fall into a muddy marsh]

友達は賭事の泥沼にはまっています。Tomodachi wa kakegoto no doronuma ni hamatte imasu. *My friend is bogged down in gambling.*

kao ni doro o nuru   顔に泥を塗る   *to disgrace someone*
[lit. to apply mud to someone's face]

あの人は、親の顔に泥を塗っても平気です。Ano hito wa, oya no kao ni doro o nuttemo heiki desu. *She doesn't care even if she disgraces her parents.*

---

dokyō   度胸   *courage, pluck*

dokyō ga ii   度胸が良い   *bold*
[lit. One's courage is good.]

彼女は度胸が良いから、質問をためらうことはありません。Kanojo wa dokyō ga ii kara, shitsumon o tamerau koto wa arimasen. *She's bold and never hesitates to ask questions.*

dokyō ga suwaru   度胸が据わる   *to have nerves of steel*
[lit. One's courage is in position.]

彼は、度胸が据わっています。Kare wa, dokyō ga suwatte imasu. *He has nerves of steel.*

dokyō o sueru   度胸を据える   *to pluck up one's courage*
[lit. to set one's courage]

度胸を据えて、社長に昇給を頼みに行きました。Dokyō o suete, shachō ni shōkyū o tanomini ikimashita. *After plucking up my courage, I went to the president to ask for a raise.*

---

dosu   どす   *dagger*

dosu no kiita   どすの利いた   *intimidating*
[lit. A dagger is effective.]

やくざは、ドスの利いた声でキャバレーの客にすごみました。Yakuza wa, dosu no kiita koe de kyabarē no kyaku ni sugomimashita. *The gangster threatened the cabaret patrons in an intimidating voice.*

E

eiki 英気   *spirit*
   eiki o yashinau   英気を養う   *to renew one's spirits*
   [lit. to nourish one's spirit]
   英気を養うために、`を取りました。Eiki o yashinau tame
   ni, kyūka o torimashita. *I took a vacation to renew my spirits.*

---

eimin 永眠   *eternal rest*
   eiminsuru   永眠する   *to pass away*
   [lit. to sleep forever]
   彼は、長い病気の末永眠しました。Kare wa, nagai byōki no
   sue eimin shimashita. *He passed away after a long illness.*

---

eiri 営利   *profit*
   eiri o musaboru   営利を貪る   *to make undue profits*
   [lit. to devour profit]
   彼は営利を貪るので、悪名が高いです。Kare wa eiri o
   musaboru node, akumei ga takai desu. *He is notorious for
   making undue profits.*

---

eiten 栄転   *job transfer on promotion*
   eitensuru   栄転する   *to be transferred on promotion*
   [lit. an honorable switchover]
   彼は、パリの支店長に栄転しました。Kare wa, Pari no
   shitenchō ni eiten shimashita. *He was transferred to head the
   Paris branch office.*

---

ejiki 餌食   *prey*
   ejiki ni naru   餌食になる   *to fall victim to someone or
   something*
   [lit. to become prey]
   彼女は、詐欺の餌食になりました。Kanojo wa, sagi no ejiki
   ni narimashita. *She fell victim to a fraud.*

---

en 縁   *blood relation, connection*

en ga nai   縁が無い   *to have no connection to something*
[lit. no relation]
私は、お金とは縁がありません。Watakushi wa, okane to wa en ga arimasen. *I have no luck with money.*

en mo yukari mo nai hito   縁もゆかりもない人
perfect stranger
[lit. a person to whom one has no relation]
あの人とは、縁もゆかりもありません。Ano hito to wa, en mo yukari mo arimasen. *He's a perfect stranger to me.*

en o kiru   縁を切る   *to break off with someone, to sever a relationship*
[lit. to sever a relationship]
彼女は、ボーイフレンドと縁を切りたがっています。
Kanojo wa, bōifurendo to en o kiritagatte imasu. *She wants to break off with her boyfriend.*

en o musubu   縁を結ぶ   *to tie the knot*
[lit. to conclude a relationship]
大学の級友は長年の交際の後、縁を結びました。Daigaku no kyūyū wa naganen no kōsai no ato, en o musubimashita. *The college classmates tied the knot after dating for many years.*

---

en   縁   *veranda*

en no shita no chikaramochi   縁の下の力持ち   *to work in the background*
[lit. a strong man under a veranda]
彼は政策決定で、縁の下の力持ちの役を果たしています。
Kare wa seisaku kettei de, en no shita no chikaramochi no yaku o hatashite imasu. *He's functioning as the brains behind the scenes for policy formulation.*

---

engi   縁起   *omen, luck*

engi demo nai   縁起でもない   *ominous*
[lit. no luck]
結婚の日に、縁起でもない話はやめて下さい。Kekkon no hi

ni, engi demo nai hanashi wa yamete kudasai.   *Please stop talking about ominous things on the wedding day.*

engi o katsugu   縁起を担ぐ   *to be superstitious*
[lit. to carry an omen]
あの野球の選手は縁起を担いで、試合の日には髭を剃りません。Ano yakyū no senshu wa engi o katsuide, shiai no hi ni wa hige o sorimasen.   *That baseball player is superstitious and doesn't shave on game day.*

---

eri   襟   *collar*
eri o tadasu   襟を正す   *to be awestruck*
[lit. to straighten one's own collar]
その人の過去を知って、襟を正しました。Sono hito no kako o shitte, eri o tadashimashita.   *I was awestruck when I learned of his past.*

---

etsu   悦   *joy*
etsu ni iru   悦に入る   *to gloat*
[lit. to enter into joy]
彼はゴルフで勝って、悦に入っています。Kare wa gorufu de katte, etsu ni itte imasu.   *He's gloating over his win in the golf tournament.*

F

fu   腑   *bowels*
fu ni ochinai   腑に落ちない   *to be hard to swallow*
[lit. not going down to the bowels]
その説明は、腑に落ちません。Sono setsumei wa, fu ni ochimasen.   *That explanation is hard to swallow.*

fu no nuketa yō na   腑の抜けたような   *to be numb*
[lit. like the bowels being removed]
彼は離婚してから、腑の抜けたような顔をしています。

Kare wa rikon shite kara, fu no nuketa yō na kao o shite imasu. *He's been looking numb since his divorce.*

---

fuda   札   *card, ticket*
fudadome   札止め   *sellout*
[lit. stopping the sale of tickets]
相撲は、毎日札止めの人気です。Sumō wa, mainichi fudadome no ninki desu. *The sumo tournament is so popular that every day is a sellout.*

fudatsuki no   札付きの   *notorious*
[lit. card-bearing]
彼女は、札付きのうそつきです。Kanojo wa, fudatsuki no usotsuki desu. *She's a notorious liar.*

---

fude   筆   *writing brush*
fude ga suberu   筆が滑る   *slip of the pen*
[lit. A writing brush glides.]
筆が滑って、報告書に間違いを書いてしまいました。Fude ga subette, hōkokusho ni machigai o kaite shimaimashita. *With a slip of the pen, I made a mistake in the report.*

fude ga tatsu   筆が立つ   *to have a gift for literature*
[lit. A writing brush stands out.]
彼女は筆が立つから、大作家になるでしょう。Kanojo wa fude ga tatsu kara, dai sakka ni naru deshō. *With her gift for literature, she'll become a great novelist.*

fude no ayamari   筆の誤り   *slip of the pen*
[lit. a mistake by a writing brush]
手紙を書くときには、筆の誤りに気をつけなさい。Tegami o kaku toki niwa, fude no ayamari ni ki o tsukenasai. *When you write a letter, be careful not to make any slips of the pen.*

fude o hashiraseru   筆を走らせる   *to write fast*
[lit. to let a writing brush run]
素晴らしいニュースを急いでお知らせしようと、筆を走らせました。Subarashii nyūsu o isoide oshirase shiyō to, fude o

hashirasemashita.   *I wrote quickly to let you know the wonderful news.*

fude o ireru   筆を入れる   *to edit, to correct (writing)*
[lit. to insert a writing brush]
先生は、私の作文にたくさん筆を入れました。Sensei wa, watakushi no sakubun ni takusan fude o iremashita.   *My teacher made a lot of corrections in my composition.*

fude o kuwaeru   筆を加える   *to edit, to refine (writing)*
[lit. to add a writing brush]
報告書を提出する前に、もう一度筆を加えました。Hōkokusho o teishutsu suru mae ni, mō ichido fude o kuwaemashita.   *Before submitting the report, I edited it once more.*

fude o oku   筆を置く   *to stop writing*
[lit. to put down a writing brush]
長い手紙になりましたので、この辺で筆を置きます。Nagai tegami ni narimashita node, kono hen de fude o okimasu. *Since the letter has gotten very long, I'll stop here.*

fude o oru   筆を折る   *to end one's literary career*
[lit. to break a writing brush]
あの作家は、健康が理由で筆を折りました。Ano sakka wa, kenkō ga riyū de fude o orimashita.   *That novelist ended his literary career for reasons of health.*

fude o someru   筆を染める   *to start writing*
[lit. to dye a writing brush]
良い考えが浮かばないので、まだ筆を染めていません。Ii kangae ga ukabanai node, mada fude o somete imasen.   *I can't come up with great ideas, so I haven't started writing yet.*

fude o toru   筆を執る   *to write*
[lit. to pick up a writing brush]
お願いすることがあって、筆を執りました。Onegai suru koto ga atte, fude o torimashita.   *I'm writing to you to ask a favor.*

fudebushō   筆無精   *lazy writer*
[lit. lazy with a writing brush]

彼女は筆無精で、旅先からご主人に手紙を書いたことがありません。Kanojo wa fudebushō de, tabisaki kara goshujin ni tegami o kaita koto ga arimasen. *Because she's a lazy writer, she's never written a letter to her husband when she's been away.*

fudemame   筆まめ   *diligent writer*
[lit. hardworking with a writing brush]
彼女は筆まめで、毎週お母さんに手紙を書きます。Kanojo wa fudemame de, maishū okāsan ni tegami o kakimasu. *She's a diligent writer and writes a letter to her mother every week.*

---

fui   不意   *sudden and unexpected*
fui o kuu   不意を食う   *to be taken by surprise*
[lit. to eat unexpectedness]
突然のお客に不意を食いました。Totsuzen no okyaku ni fui o kuimashita. *I was taken by surprise by a sudden guest.*

fui o tsuku   不意をつく   *to take someone by surprise*
[lit. to charge at unexpectedness]
競争相手の不意をついて、ビジネスに成功しました。Kyōsō aite no fui o tsuite, bijinesu ni seikō shimashita. *We succeeded in business by taking our competitors by surprise.*

fui o utsu   不意を打つ   *to take someone by surprise*
[lit. to hit unexpectedness]
討論会では他の参加者の不意を打って、勝つことが出来ました。Tōronkai dewa hoka no sankasha no fui o utte, katsu koto ga dekimashita. *I won the debate by taking the other participants by surprise.*

fuiuchi o kuu   不意打ちを食う   *to be taken by surprise*
[lit. to eat a surprise attack]
彼女は選挙に勝つべきでしたが、不意打ちを食って負けました。Kanojo wa senkyo ni katsu beki deshita ga, fuiuchi o kutte makemashita. *She should have won the election but lost because she was taken by surprise.*

---

fuku   腹   *abdomen, belly*

54

fukuan 腹案   *rough idea*
[lit. a belly idea]

腹案はありますが、本格的な計画はまだです。Fukuan wa
arimasu ga, honkakuteki na keikaku wa mada desu.   *I have a
rough idea but not a full-scale plan yet.*

fukushin 腹心   *one's confidante*
[lit. a belly and a soul]

彼女は私の腹心で、何でも打ち明けることが出来ます。
Kanojo wa watakushi no fukushin de, nandemo uchiakeru koto
ga dekimasu.   *She is my confidante, and I can tell her
anything.*

fukuzō no nai 腹蔵のない   *frank*
[lit. without storing anything in one's belly]

何でも、腹蔵無くお話下さい。Nandemo, fukuzō naku
ohanashi kudasai.   *Please say whatever is on your mind.*

---

fune 船   *ship*

norikakatta fune 乗りかかった船   *having obligated
oneself*
[lit. a ship one is about to board]

乗りかかった船だから、ずっと手伝ってあげましょう。
Norikakatta fune dakara, zutto tetsudatte agemashō.   *Since
I've obligated myself, I'll help you see it through.*

ōbune ni notta yō 大船に乗ったよう   *to be at ease*
[lit. like boarding a big ship]

仕事は彼が手伝ってくれるので、大船に乗ったような気持
ちです。Shigoto wa kare ga tetsudatte kureru node, ōbune ni
notta yō na kimochi desu.   *I'm at ease because he's going to
help me.*

watari ni fune 渡りに船   *chance, opportunity*
[lit. a ship at a ferry landing]

彼女はその申し出に、渡りに船と飛びつきました。Kanojo
wa sono mōshide ni, watari ni fune to tobitsukimashita.   *She
jumped at the offer as a great opportunity.*

furoshiki　　風呂敷　　　*wrapping cloth*
　ōburoshiki o hirogeru　　大風呂敷を広げる　　　*to brag*
　[lit. to spread a big wrapping cloth]
　彼はいつも大風呂敷を広げるので、彼の話は信用できません。
　　Kare wa itsumo ōburoshiki o hirogeru node, kare no hanashi
　　wa shin-yō dekimasen.　*Since he brags all the time, I can't
　　trust his stories.*

---

fushin　　不審　　　*doubt, suspicion*
　fushin o idaku　　不審を抱く　　　*to have a suspicion, to be
　suspicious*
　[lit. to embrace a suspicion]
　国民は、政府の動きに不審を抱いています。Kokumin wa,
　　seifu no ugoki ni fushin o idaite imasu.　*The people were
　　suspicious of the move by the government.*

　fushin o kau　　不審を買う　　　*to incur suspicion*
　[lit. to buy suspicion]
　あの政治家はインタビューで失言して、不審を買ってしま
　　いました。Ano seijika wa intabyū de shitsugen shite, fushin o
　　katte shimaimashita.　*That politician incurred suspicion by
　　making a slip of the tongue in an interview.*

---

futa　　蓋　　　*lid*
　futa o akeru　　蓋を開ける　　　*to start, to open*
　[lit. to lift a lid]
　野球のシーズンが蓋を開けました。Yakyū no shīzun ga futa o
　　akemashita.　*Baseball season has started.*

---

futatsu　　二つ　　　*two*
　futatsu ni hitotsu　　二つに一つ　　　*one way or another*
　[lit. one out of two]
　行くのかどうか、彼らは二つに一つの返事を迫りました。
　　Iku no ka dō ka, karera wa futatsu ni hitotsu no henji o
　　semarimashita.　*They pressed me to give them an answer one
　　way or another about going.*

futatsuhenji   二つ返事   *enthusiastic consent*
[lit. two answers]
彼女の招待に、二つ返事で承諾しました。Kanojo no shōtai
ni, futatsuhenji de shōdaku shimashita.   *I readily accepted her
invitation.*

---

futoi   太い   *thick*
   futoi koto   太いこと   *shameless thing*
   [lit. a thick thing]
   あの人は太いことを平気でします。Ano hito wa futoi koto o
      heiki de shimasu.   *He does shameless things without any
      concern for the consequences.*

   futoi yatsu   太い奴   *shameless fellow*
   [lit. a thick fellow]
   あれは借りた金を返さない太い奴です。Are wa karita kane o
      kaesanai futoi yatsu desu.   *A shameless fellow, he doesn't pay
      back money he borrows.*

---

futokoro   懐   *pocket, breast*
   futokoro ga atatakai   懐が暖かい   *to have a lot of money*
   [lit. One's pocket is warm.]
   今日は懐が暖かいから、晩御飯をご馳走してあげましょう。
      Kyō wa futokoro ga atatakai kara, bangohan o gochisō shite
      agemashō.   *I have a lot of money today, so I'll take you out
      for dinner.*

   futokoro ga fukai   懐が深い   *to be big-hearted*
   [lit. One's breast is deep.]
   彼は懐が深いので、何でも話しやすいです。Kare wa
      futokoro ga fukai node, nandemo hanashiyasui desu.   *Because
      he's big-hearted, it's easy to talk to him about anything.*

   futokoro ga itamu   懐が痛む   *financially burdensome*
   [lit. One's pocket hurts.]
   先月は思わぬ出費があって、懐が痛みました。Sengetsu
      wa omowanu shuppi ga atte, futokoro ga itamimashita.

Because of an unexpected expense last month, things were
tough financially.

futokoro ga sabishii　懐が寂しい　　*to be short of money*
[lit. One's pocket is lonely.]

懐が寂しいので、映画を見に行けません。Futokoro ga
sabishii node, eiga o mini ikemasen.　*I can't go to a movie*
because I'm short of money.

futokoro ga samui　　懐が寒い　　*to be short of money*
[lit. One's pocket is cold.]

無駄遣いばかりしていると、すぐに懐が寒くなりますよ。
Mudazukai bakari shite iru to, sugu ni futokoro ga samuku
narimasu yo.　*If you keep wasting it, you'll be short of money soon.*

futokoro o itameru　　懐を痛める　　*to suffer financially*
[lit. to hurt one's pocket]

懐を痛めても、子供はぜんぶ大学にやるつもりです。
Futokoro o itametemo, kodomo wa zenbu daigaku ni yaru
tsumori desu.　*Even if I suffer financially, I'll send all my*
children to college.

futokoro o koyasu　　懐を肥やす　　*to feather one's nest*
[lit. to fatten one's pocket]

彼女は周りの人を犠牲にして、自分の懐を肥やしました。
Kanojo wa mawari no hito o gisei ni shite, jibun no futokoro o
koyashimashita.　*She feathered her nest at the expense of*
those around her.

futokorogatana　　懐刀　　*one's right-hand man*
[lit. a dagger in a pocket]

息子は、有力な政治家の懐刀です。Musuko wa, yūryoku na
seijika no futokorogatana desu.　*My son is the right-hand man*
of an influential politician.

futokoroguai　　懐具合　　*one's financial position*
[lit. the state of one's pocket]

やっと、懐具合がよくなってきました。Yatto, futokoroguai
ga yoku natte kimashita.　*Finally, my financial position is*
getting better.

G

---

ga   我   *ego, self*
  ga ga tsuyoi   我が強い   *egoistic*
  [lit. One's ego is strong.]
  彼女は我が強くて、つき合いづらいです。Kanojo wa ga ga
    tsuyokute, tsukiaizurai desu.   *She is egoistic, and it's difficult
    to be around her.*

  ga o haru   我を張る   *to assert oneself*
  [lit. to put up one's ego]
  彼は我を張って、誰の意見にも従いませんでした。Kare wa
    ga o hatte, dare no iken nimo shitagaimasen deshita.   *He
    asserted himself and followed nobody else's opinions.*

  ga o oru   我を折る   *to yield to someone's will*
  [lit. to break one's own ego]
  彼女は我を折って、お母さんの意見に従いました。Kanojo
    wa ga o otte, okāsan no iken ni shitagaimashita.   *She yielded
    to her mother's opinion.*

  ga o seisuru   我を制する   *to control oneself*
  [lit. to limit one's ego]
  理由がないのに非難されて、我を制するのに苦労しました。
    Riyū ga nai noni hinan sarete, ga o sei suru noni kurō
    shimashita.   *Because I was criticized for no reason, I had a
    tough time controlling myself.*

  ga o tōsu   我を通す   *to have one's own way*
  [lit. to put through one's ego]
  彼は、つまらないことまで我を通そうとします。Kare wa,
    tsumaranai koto made ga o tōsō to shimasu.   *He tries to have
    his own way even for insignificant things.*

---

gara   柄   *character, nature*
  gara no ii   柄のいい   *genteel, elegant*
  [lit. One's character is fine.]
  あの柄のいい女性は、友達のお婆さんです。Ano gara no ii

josei wa, tomodachi no obāsan desu. *That elegant woman is my friend's grandmother.*

gara no warui   柄の悪い   *vulgar*
[lit. One's character is bad.]
柄の悪い人とは、つき合わない方がいいですよ。Gara no warui hito to wa, tsukiawanai hō ga ii desu yo. *You'd better not socialize with vulgar people.*

---

gei   芸   *performance*
gei ga komakai   芸が細かい   *to be mindful of details*
[lit. A performance is detailed.]
彼は、何をするにも芸が細かいです。Kare wa, nani o suru nimo gei ga komakai desu. *He's mindful of details in anything he does.*

gei ga nai   芸がない   *to lack creativity*
[lit. There is no performance.]
あの人は芸がないから、いつも同じ事ばかりしています。Ano hito wa gei ga nai kara, itsumo onaji koto bakari shite imasu. *Since he lacks creativity, he does the same things repeatedly.*

---

geijutsu   芸術   *art*
geijutsuhada   芸術肌   *artistic nature*
[lit. artistic skin]
彼女には、芸術肌の所があります。Kanojo niwa, geijutsu hada no tokoro ga arimasu. *She has something of an artistic nature.*

---

genkin   現金   *cash*
genkin na   現金な   *calculating*
[lit. cash-like]
あの人は、現金な人です。Ano hito wa, genkin na hito desu. *He's eager to promote his own interests.*

---

geta   下駄   *wooden clogs*

geta o azukeru   下駄を預ける   *to leave everything up to someone*

[lit. to check one's wooden clogs in]

最終決定は、彼に下駄を預けました。Saishū kettei wa, kare ni geta o azukemashita. *We left the final decision to him.*

geta o hakaseru   下駄を履かせる   *to inflate figures*

[lit. to let someone put wooden clogs on]

まじめな学生の試験の結果には、少し下駄を履かせました。Majime na gakusei no shiken no kekka niwa, sukoshi geta o hakasemashita. *I padded the test scores of the good students a little.*

---

gō   業   *someone's action*

gō o niyasu   業を煮やす   *to become irritated*

[lit. to boil someone's action]

会議ではつまらないことを討議し続けるので、業を煮やしました。Kaigi dewa tsumaranai koto o tōgi shitsuzukeru node, gō o niyashimashita. *In the meeting, I became irritated by the long debate over trivial matters.*

---

goma   胡麻   *sesame*

goma o suru   胡麻を擂る   *to toady, to flatter*

[lit. to grind sesame]

彼は、いつも上役に胡麻を擂っています。Kare wa, itsumo uwayaku ni goma o sutte imasu. *He's constantly flattering his boss.*

gomashio atama   胡麻塩頭   *salt-and-pepper hair*

[lit. sesame-and-salt head]

父はまだ若いのに、もう胡麻塩頭になっています。Chichi wa mada wakai noni, mō gomashio atama ni natte imasu. *Although my father is still young, he already has salt-and-pepper hair.*

gomasuri   胡麻擂り   *apple polisher*

[lit. a sesame grinder]

彼女は会社で、胡麻擂りとして知られています。Kanojo wa,

kaisha de gomasuri toshite shirarete imasu.   *She's known as an apple polisher in the company.*

---

gu   愚   *folly*

gu nimo tsukanai   愚にもつかない   *absurd*
[lit. to not even reach the level of absurdity]
愚にもつかない言い訳はやめなさい。 Gu nimo tsukanai iiwake wa yamenasai.   *Stop making absurd excuses.*

gu no kotchō   愚の骨頂   *the height of folly*
[lit. the high point of a bone regarding absurdity]
そんなことをするのは、愚の骨頂ですよ。 Sonna koto o suru no wa, gu no kotchō desu yo.   *If you do such a thing, it'll be the height of folly.*

---

gun   群   *crowd*

gun o nuku   群を抜く   *to excel*
[lit. to surpass the crowd]
彼女は、英語にかけては群を抜いています。 Kanojo wa, eigo ni kakete wa gun o nuite imasu.   *She excels in English.*

---

gyū   牛   *ox*

gyūho   牛歩   *snail's pace*
[lit. an ox's walk]
審議は、牛歩で進みました。 Shingi wa, gyūho de susumimashita.   *The deliberations progressed at a snail's pace.*

gyūji o toru   牛耳を執る   *to have a firm grip on something*
[lit. to hold an ox's ear]
あの政治家は、党の防衛政策の牛耳を執っています。 Ano seijika wa, tō no bōei seisaku no gyūji o totte imasu.   *That politician has a firm grip on the defense policy of his party.*

gyūjiru   牛耳る   *to control*
[lit. to grab an ox's ear]
極端な意見を持つ人が、クラブを牛耳っています。

Kyokutan na iken o motsu hito ga, kurabu o gyūjitte imasu.
Those with the most extreme opinions are controlling our club.

H

---

ha   歯   *tooth, teeth*

ha ga tatanai   歯が立たない   *to be no match for, not able to handle something*
[lit. to be unable to sink one's teeth into something]
テニスでは、彼に歯が立ちません。Tenisu dewa, kare ni ha ga tachimasen.   *As far as tennis is concerned, I'm no match for him.*

ha ga uku   歯が浮く   *nauseating*
[lit. to loosen one's teeth]
あの人の話を聞くと、いつも歯が浮きます。Ano hito no hanashi o kiku to, itsumo ha ga ukimasu.   *His talk is always nauseating.*

ha ni kinu kisenu   歯に衣着せぬ   *to not mince words*
[lit. to not put clothes on one's teeth]
彼は誰に対しても、歯に衣を着せません。Kare wa dare ni taishite mo, ha ni kinu o kisemasen.   *He doesn't mince words with anybody.*

ha no nuketayō   歯の抜けたよう   *deserted*
[lit. as if some teeth are missing]
地元のチームが負けてばかりいるので、球場は歯が抜けたようです。Jimoto no chīmu ga makete bakari iru node, kyūjō wa ha ga nuketa yō desu.   *Since the local team has been losing, the ball park has a lot of empty seats.*

hagayui   歯痒い   *to feel impatient*
[lit. One's teeth itch.]
彼の仕事があまり遅いので、見ていると歯痒くなります。Kare no shigoto ga amari osoi node, mite iru to hagayuku narimasu.   *Because he works so slowly, watching him makes*

me feel impatient.

hagishiri suru   歯ぎしりする   *to be mortified at something*

[lit. to grind one's teeth]

勝てるはずの試合に負けて、歯ぎしりしてしまいました。
Kateru hazu no shiai ni makete, hagishiri shite shimaimashita.
I was mortified at losing the game we should have won.

hagotae ga aru   歯ごたえがある   *tough*

[lit. There is resistance to one's teeth.]

もっと歯ごたえがある仕事がしてみたいです。 Motto
hagotae ga aru shigoto ga shitemitai desu.   *I'd like to try tougher work.*

hagotae ga nai   歯ごたえがない   *too easy*

[lit. There is no resistance to one's teeth.]

歯ごたえがない仕事は、したくありません。 Hagotae ga nai
shigoto wa, shitaku arimasen.   *I don't want to do work that's too easy.*

---

haba   幅   *width, range*

haba ga kiku   幅が利く   *to be influential*

[lit. One's range is effective.]

あの学者は、保守的な政治家の間で幅が利いています。
Ano gakusha wa, hoshuteki na seijika no aida de haba ga kiite
imasu.   *That scholar is influential among the conservative politicians.*

haba o kikaseru   幅を利かせる   *to carry a lot of weight, to be powerful*

[lit. to make one's range effective]

あのビジネスマンは、そこの地方政治で幅を利かせています。
Ano bijinesuman wa, soko no chihō seiji de haba o kikasete
imasu.   *That businessman carries a lot of weight in local politics there.*

---

haburi   羽振り   *flapping of wings*

haburi ga ii   羽振りがいい   *to be popular, to have*

money or power

[lit. The flapping of wings is great.]

あの歌手は、中年の男性の間で羽振りがいいです。Ano
kashu wa, chūnen no dansei no aida de haburi ga ii desu.
That singer is popular among middle-aged men.

haburi o kikaseru   羽振りを利かせる   *to exercise one's influence*

[lit. to apply the flapping of wings]

この町で、何事にも羽振りを利かせているのがあの人です。
Kono machi de, nanigoto nimo haburi o kikasete iru no ga ano
hito desu.   *He is the man who exercises his influence over
everything in this town.*

---

hada   肌   *skin*

hada de kanjiru   肌で感じる   *to have first-hand experience*

[lit. to feel it with one's own skin]

コンピュータは役に立つ道具であることを肌で感じました。
Konpyūta wa yaku ni tatsu dōgu dearu koto o hada de
kanjimashita.   *I have first-hand experience that the computer
is a useful tool.*

hada ga au   肌が合う   *to get along well*

[lit. The skin matches.]

彼は彼女と肌が合います。Kare wa kanojo to hada ga aimasu.
He gets along well with her.

hada ga awanai   肌が合わない   *to not get along well*

[lit. The skin does not match.]

彼女とは、全然肌が合いません。Kanojo to wa, zenzen hada
ga aimasen.   *I can't get along well with her at all.*

hitohada nugu   一肌脱ぐ   *to help*

[lit. to take off one's skin]

親友が契約を取るために、一肌脱ぎました。Shin-yū ga
keiyaku o toru tame ni, hitohada nugimashita.   *I helped my
best friend to win the contract.*

---

hadaka   裸   *naked body*

hadaka ikkan de   裸一貫で   *starting from scratch*
[lit. thoroughly naked]
彼は巨額の富を、裸一貫から築き上げました。Kare wa
kyogaku no tomi o, hadaka ikkan kara kizukiagemashita. *He
built an enormous fortune starting from scratch.*

hadaka ni naru   裸になる   *to go broke*
[lit. to become naked]
彼は賭事に夢中になって、すっかり裸になってしまいました。
Kare wa kakegoto ni muchū ni natte, sukkari hadaka ni natte
shimaimashita. *He went crazy gambling and went totally
broke.*

---

haji   恥   *shame, humiliation, disgrace, dishonor*

haji no uwanuri   恥の上塗り   *to incur further disgrace*
[lit. to apply a second coat of disgrace over the first one]
自分の失敗なのに人を非難するなんて、恥の上塗りです。
Jibun no shippai nanoni hito o hinan suru nante, haji no
uwanuri desu. *It's a further disgrace to blame others for
your own mistakes.*

haji o kakaseru   恥をかかせる   *to humiliate someone*
[lit. to make someone's shame surface]
傲慢な奴に人前で恥をかかせて、いい気持がしました。
Gōman na yatsu ni hitomae de haji o kakasete, ii kimochi ga
shimashita. *It felt good to humiliate the arrogant scoundrel
in front of everyone.*

haji o kaku   恥をかく   *to disgrace oneself*
[lit. to make one's own shame surface]
社長を掃除夫と間違えて、恥をかきました。Shachō o sōjifu
to machigaete, haji o kakimashita. *I disgraced myself by
mistaking the president for a janitor.*

haji o sarasu   恥をさらす   *to make a spectacle of oneself*
[lit. to expose one's own shame]
彼は友達の結婚披露宴で酔っぱらって、恥をさらしました。
Kare wa tomodachi no kekkon hirōen de yopparatte, haji o

sarashimashita.   *He made a spectacle of himself by getting drunk at his friend's wedding reception.*

haji o shinobu   恥を忍ぶ   *to suppress one's shame*
[lit. to endure one's own shame]
恥を忍んで、友達の親からお金を借りました。Haji o shinonde, tomodachi no oya kara okane o karimashita. *Suppressing my shame, I borrowed money from my friend's parents.*

haji o shiranai   恥を知らない   *shameless*
[lit. to not know shame]
あの人は恥を知らずに、いつも人の悪口ばかり言っています。Ano hito wa haji o shirazuni, itsumo hito no warukuchi bakari itte imasu.   *She's always badmouthing other people shamelessly.*

haji o shiru hito   恥を知る人   *honorable person*
[lit. a person who knows what shame is]
彼女は恥を知る人だから、信頼できます。Kanojo wa haji o shiru hito dakara, shinrai dekimasu.   *We can trust her because she is an honorable person.*

haji o sosogu   恥をそそぐ   *to clear one's name*
[lit. to wash one's own shame]
非難が間違っていることを証明して、恥をそそぎました。Hinan ga machigatte iru koto o shōmei shite, haji o sosogimashita.   *By proving that the charges against me were wrong, I cleared my name.*

hajisarashi   恥さらし   *disgrace*
[lit. exposing one's own shame]
そんなことをすると家族の恥さらしになるからやめなさい。Sonna koto o suru to kazoku no hajisarashi ni naru kara yamenasai.   *Stop doing such things, or you'll disgrace your family.*

hajishirazu   恥知らず   *shameless person*
[lit. someone who is not aware of his or her own shame]
あの人は、自分の家族の面倒を見ない恥知らずです。Ano

hito wa, jibun no kazoku no mendō o minai hajishirazu desu.
He is a shameless person who doesn't take care of his own family.

---

haku   箔   *foil, leaf, tinsel*

haku ga ochiru   箔が落ちる   *to lose some prestige*
[lit. The tinsel falls.]
首相は公約が果たせなくて、箔が落ちてしまいました。
   Shushō wa kōyaku ga hatasenakute, haku ga ochite
   shimaimashita. *The prime minister lost some prestige when
   he couldn't keep his public pledge.*

haku ga tsuku   箔がつく   *to gain prestige*
[lit. The tinsel is put on someone.]
先生は博士号を取って、箔がつきました。Sensei wa
   hakasegō o totte, haku ga tsukimashita. *My teacher gained
   prestige by getting a Ph. D.*

---

hakuhyō   薄氷   *thin ice*

hakuhyō o fumu   薄氷を踏む   *to be on thin ice*
[lit. to step on thin ice]
上司に昇給を頼みに行くのに、薄氷を踏む思いをしました。
   Jōshi ni shōkyū o tanomini iku noni, hakuhyō o fumu omoi o
   shimashita. *I felt as if I were on thin ice when I went to see
   my boss to ask for a raise.*

---

hakusha   拍車   *spur*

hakusha o kakeru   拍車を掛ける   *to give impetus to something*
[lit. to spur]
相次ぐスキャンダルが、政治改革運動に拍車をかけています。
   Aitsugu sukyandaru ga, seiji kaikaku undō ni hakusha o kakete
   imasu. *A series of scandals is giving impetus to a political
   reform movement.*

---

hakushi   白紙   *blank paper*

hakushi ni modosu   白紙に戻す   *to go back to the*

drawing board

[lit. to put something back on a blank paper]

計画は条件が変わったため、白紙に戻すことにしました。
Keikaku wa jōken ga kawatta tame, hakushi ni modosu koto ni shimashita. *Because conditions changed, we decided to go back to the drawing board.*

---

hame 羽目 *paneling*

hame o hazusu 羽目を外す *to make a racket*

[lit. to detach paneling]

パーティーを開くのはいいけれど、羽目を外さないようにしなさい。Pātī o hiraku no wa ii keredo, hame o hazusanai yō ni shinasai. *It's all right to have a party, but don't make a racket.*

---

hamon 波紋 *ripple*

hamon o tōjiru 波紋を投じる *to create a stir*

[lit. to cast a ripple]

大蔵省の声明が、財界に波紋を投じました。Ōkurashō no seimei ga, zaikai ni hamon o tōjimashita. *The statement by the Finance Ministry created a stir in the financial world.*

---

han 判 *seal, stamp*

han de oshita yō ni 判で押したように *like clockwork*

[lit. just like affixing a seal]

彼女は毎朝、判で押したように七時に家を出ます。Kanojo wa maiasa, han de oshita yō ni shichiji ni ie o demasu. *Like clockwork, she leaves her home every morning at seven.*

---

hana 花 *flower*

hana ga saku 花が咲く *to grow, to develop, to thrive*

[lit. A flower blooms.]

彼との友情に花が咲きました。Kare to no yūjō ni hana ga sakimashita. *My friendship with him grew.*

hana mo mi mo aru 花も実もある *warmhearted*

[lit. There are both flowers and fruit.]

69

彼は花も実もある人として尊敬されています。Kare wa hana mo mi mo aru hito toshite sonkei sarete imasu. *He's respected for being warmhearted.*

hana o chirasu   花を散らす   *to die young*
[lit. to let a flower go]
友達は二十二歳で花を散らしました。
　　Tomodachi wa nijūni sai de hana o chirashimashita. *My friend died when she was 22 years old.*

hana o motaseru   花を持たせる   *to give someone the credit for something*
[lit. to let someone have flowers]
事業の成功について、社長は奥さんに花を持たせました。
　　Jigyō no seikō ni tsuite, shachō wa okusan ni hana o motasemashita. *The president gave his wife the credit for his successful business.*

hana o sakaseru   花を咲かせる   *to attain success*
[lit. to let a flower bloom]
彼女は十五歳の時、音楽界ですでに花を咲かせました。
　　Kanojo wa jūgo sai no toki, ongaku kai de sude ni hana o sakasemashita. *When she was 15 years old, she had already attained success in the music world.*

hanamichi o kazaru   花道を飾る   *to make a graceful exit (retirement)*
[lit. to decorate a runway]
あの選手は最後の試合でホームランを打って、花道を飾りました。Ano senshu wa saigo no shiai de hōmuran o utte, hanamichi o kazarimashita. *That player made a graceful exit by hitting a home run in his last game.*

hanashi ni hana ga saku   話に花が咲く   *to have a lively conversation*
[lit. Flowers bloom in a conversation.]
友達との話に花が咲きました。Tomodachi tono hanashi ni hana ga sakimashita. *I had a lively conversation with my friends.*

iwanu ga hana   言わぬが花   *It's better left unsaid.*
[lit. Saying nothing is the flower.]

それを彼女に言いたいかも知れないけれど、言わぬが花で
すよ。 Sore o kanojo ni iitai kamoshirenai keredo, iwanu ga
hana desu yo. *You may want to tell her that, but it's better
left unsaid.*

ryōte ni hana   両手に花   *to be doubly blessed*
[lit. to have a flower in each hand]

彼は素晴らしい奥さんといい仕事を持って、両手に花です。
Kare wa subarashii okusan to ii shigoto o motte, ryōte ni hana
desu. *He's doubly blessed because he has a wonderful wife
and a great job.*

takane no hana   高嶺の花   *beyond one's reach*
[lit. a flower on a high mountain]

彼女は良家の出身で、私にとっては高嶺の花です。Kanojo
wa ryōke no shusshin de, watakushi ni totte wa takane no hana
desu. *Because she's from an upper-class family, she's beyond
my reach.*

---

hana   鼻   *nose*

hana de ashirau   鼻であしらう   *to turn up one's nose
at something*
[lit. to treat someone with one's nose]

夫は妻の願いを鼻であしらいました。Otto wa tsuma no negai
o hana de ashiraimashita. *The husband turned up his nose at
his wife's wishes.*

hana de warau   鼻で笑う   *to snicker*
[lit. to laugh with one's nose]

聴衆は、政治家の言い訳を鼻で笑いました。Chōshū wa,
seijika no iiwake o hana de waraimashita. *The audience
snickered at the politician's excuses.*

hana ga takai   鼻が高い   *to be proud*
[lit. One's nose is high.]

お嬢さんが医者になって、鼻が高いでしょう。Ojōsan ga
isha ni natte, hana ga takai deshō. *You must be proud that*

your daughter has become a doctor!

hana ni kakeru　鼻に掛ける　　*to be vain*
[lit. to hang something on one's nose]
彼は家族が金持ちなのを鼻にかけています。Kare wa kazoku
ga kanemochi nano o hana ni kakete imasu.　*He's vain about
his family's wealth.*

hana ni tsuku　鼻につく　　*to be disgusting, to stink*
[lit. to assail one's nose]
彼女の図々しさは鼻につきます。Kanojo no zūzūshisa wa
hana ni tsukimasu.　*Her pushiness is disgusting.*

hana no sa de　鼻の差で　　*by a nose*
[lit. with the difference of a nose]
この前の選挙では、運良く鼻の差で勝ちました。Kono mae
no senkyo dewa, un yoku hana no sa de kachimashita.　*In the
last election, luckily, I won by a nose.*

hana no saki　鼻の先　　*very close*
[lit. the tip of a nose]
その店は、すぐ鼻の先です。Sono mise wa, sugu hana no saki
desu.　*That shop is very close to here.*

hana no shita ga nagai　鼻の下が長い　　*to be lewd
toward women*
[lit. The space below a nose is long.]
彼は、鼻の下が長いのが大欠点です。Kare wa, hana no shita
ga nagai no ga dai ketten desu.　*His big shortcoming is
lewdness toward women.*

hana o akasu　鼻を明かす　　*to succeed despite others'
low expectations*
[lit. to make someone's nose open]
一流の会社に入って、回りの鼻を明かしました。Ichiryū no
kaisha ni haitte, mawari no hana o akashimashita.　*I surprised
everyone when I was hired by a top company.*

hana o narasu　鼻を鳴らす　　*to sweet-talk someone*
[lit. to speak through the nose]
ガールフレンドは、鼻を鳴らして指輪をねだりました。

Gārufurendo wa, hana o narashite yubiwa o nedarimashita.
My girlfriend tried to sweet-talk me into buying her a ring.

hana o oru   鼻を折る   *to mortify, to take someone down a peg*

[lit. to break someone's nose]

あの高慢な男の鼻を折る機会をうかがっています。Ano kōman na otoko no hana o oru kikai o ukagatte imasu.   *I'm looking for an opportunity to take the guy down a peg or two.*

hana o takakusuru   鼻を高くする   *to brag, to boast*

[lit. to make one's own nose taller]

彼は大した成功ではないのに、鼻を高くしています。Kare wa taishita seikō dewa nai noni, hana o takaku shite imasu. *He's bragging over nothing.*

hana o tsukiawaseru   鼻を突き合わせる   *to be face to face*

[lit. to bring one's nose against someone's]

彼と鼻を突き合わせて相談しました。Kare to hana o tsukiawasete sodan shimashita.   *I consulted with him face to face.*

hanamochi naranai   鼻持ちならない   *appalling*

[lit. to stink even when holding one's nose]

彼女の無神経さは鼻持ちなりません。Kanojo no mushinkeisa wa hanamochi narimasen.   *Her insensitivity is appalling.*

hanatsumami   鼻摘まみ   *a nuisance*

[lit. someone for whom one holds one's nose]

彼は会社で鼻摘まみになっています。Kare wa kaisha de hanatsumami ni natte imasu.   *He is a nuisance in our company.*

---

hana   はな   *nasal mucus*

hana mo hikkakenai   はなも引っかけない   *to ignore someone or something*

[lit. to not even dash nasal mucus on someone]

彼女はお金のない人には、はなも引っかけません。Kanojo

wa okane no nai hito niwa, hana mo hikkakemasen. *She ignores men who aren't rich.*

---

hanabashira   鼻柱   *bridge of a nose*
   hanabashira ga tsuyoi   鼻柱が強い   *obstinate*
[lit. The bridge of a nose is strong.]
彼は新入社員なのに、鼻柱が強いです。Kare wa shinnyū shain nanoni, hanabashira ga tsuyoi desu. *Although he's a new employee, he's obstinate.*

   hanabashira o oru   鼻柱を折る   *to humiliate someone*
[lit. to break the bridge of someone's nose]
討論で高慢な男の鼻柱を折って、すっきりしました。Tōron de kōman na otoko no hanabashira o otte, sukkiri shimashita. *It felt good to humiliate the arrogant guy in the debate.*

---

hanage   鼻毛   *hair of the nostrils*
   hanage o nuku   鼻毛を抜く   *to dupe someone*
[lit. to pull the hair out of someone's nostrils]
彼は人の鼻毛を抜きかねない男だから、気をつけなさい。
   Kare wa hito no hanage o nukikanenai otoko dakara, ki o tsukenasai. *Be careful of him; he can dupe anyone.*

---

hanagusuri   鼻薬   *nose medicine*
   hanagusuri o kikaseru   鼻薬を効かせる   *to grease someone's palm*
[lit. to make nose medicine effective]
彼は政治家に鼻薬を効かせて、建築許可をもらいました。
   Kare wa seijika ni hanagusuri o kikasete, kenchiku kyoka o moraimashita. *He obtained the building permit by greasing a politician's palm.*

---

hanaiki   鼻息   *breathing through the nose*
   hanaiki ga arai   鼻息が荒い   *to be keyed up*
[lit. One's breathing through the nose is heavy.]
友達は明日の試合に勝つのだと、鼻息が荒いです。
   Tomodachi wa ashita no shiai ni katsu no da to, hanaiki ga arai

desu.   *My friend is all keyed up to win the game tomorrow.*

hanaiki o ukagau   鼻息をうかがう   *to curry favor with
someone*

[lit. to look out for someone's breathing through the nose]

彼はいつも上役の鼻息をうかがっています。Kare wa itsumo
uwayaku no hanaiki o ukagatte imasu.   *He's always currying
favor with his boss.*

---

hanashi   話   *talk*

hanashi ga au   話が合う   *to find each other's company
enjoyable*

[lit. The talk fits.]

彼女と私は話がよく合います。Kanojo to watakushi wa
hanashi ga yoku aimasu.   *She and I find each other's company
enjoyable.*

hanashi ga hayai   話が早い   *easy to get to the point*

[lit. The talk is fast.]

あなたも同じ考えなら、話が早いです。Anata mo onaji
kangae nara, hanashi ga hayai desu.   *If your idea is the same
as mine, it'll be easy to get to the point.*

hanashi ga hazumu   話が弾む   *The conversation
becomes lively.*

[lit. The talk bounces.]

久しぶりに友達にあって、話が弾みました。Hisashiburi ni
tomodachi ni atte, hanashi ga hazumimashita.   *I met my friend
after a long time, and the conversation got lively.*

hanashi ga kamiawanai   話がかみ合わない   *to not go
anywhere*

[lit. The talk doesn't engage one.]

いくら交渉しても、話がかみ合いませんでした。Ikura
kōshō shitemo, hanashi ga kamiaimasen deshita.   *No matter
how much we negotiated, it didn't go anywhere.*

hanashi ga ochiru   話が落ちる   *The talk becomes lewd.*

[lit. The talk falls.]

話が落ちてきたので、席を外しました。Hanashi ga ochite
   kita node, seki o hazushimashita.   *Because the talk became
   lewd, I left the table.*

hanashi ga tsuku   話がつく   *to come to an agreement*
[lit. The talk arrives.]
交渉は簡単に話がつきました。Kōshō wa kantan ni hanashi ga
   tsukimashita.   *We easily came to an agreement in the
   negotiations.*

hanashi ga wakaru   話が分かる   *sensible*
[lit. to understand the talk]
彼女は話が分かるから、何でも相談できます。Kanojo wa
   hanashi ga wakaru kara, nandemo sōdan dekimasu.   *Since she
   is sensible, you can consult with her about anything.*

hanashi ni mi ga hairu   話に実が入る   *to be engrossed
   in a story*
[lit. A fruit enters the talk.]
友達との話に実が入って、家に帰るのが遅くなりました。
   Tomodachi to no hanashi ni mi ga haitte, ie ni kaeru no ga
   osoku narimashita.   *Because I was engrossed in conversation
   with my friend, I was late going back home.*

hanashi ni naranai   話にならない   *to be out of the
   question*
[lit. to not become talk]
車を買いたくても、それだけのお金では話になりません。
   Kuruma o kaitakutemo, sore dake no okane dewa hanashi ni
   narimasen.   *You may want to buy a car, but with that little
   money, it's out of the question.*

hanashi ni noru   話に乗る   *to counsel*
[lit. to ride the talk]
仕事のことで話に乗ってもらえますか。Shigoto no koto de
   hanashi ni notte moraemasu ka.   *Would you counsel me about
   a job?*

hanashi no tane   話の種   *topic of conversation*
[lit. the seed of a talk]

それはここでの話の種として、相応しくありません。Sore
wa koko de no hanashi no tane to shite, fusawashiku arimasen.
That isn't suitable as a topic of a conversation here.

hanashi o tsukeru   話をつける   *to settle something*
[lit. to fix the talk]

話をつけるために、妥協しました。Hanashi o tsukeru tame
ni, dakyō shimashita. *To settle the matter, I compromised.*

hanashihanbun   話半分   *to take something with a grain
of salt*
[lit. half of the talk]

彼は彼女の説明を話半分で聞きました。Kare wa kanojo no
setsumei o hanashihanbun de kikimashita. *He listened to her
explanation with a grain of salt.*

hayai hanashi ga   早い話が   *to make a long story short*
[lit. A fast story is . . . .]

早い話が、結果は良かったという事です。Hayai hanashi ga,
kekka wa yokatta to iu koto desu. *To make a long story short,
it turned out to be fine.*

---

hane   羽   *feather, wing*
hane ga haeta yō ni   羽が生えたように   *like hot cakes*
[lit. as if wings spring up]

この本は、羽が生えたように売れています。Kono hon wa,
hane ga haeta yō ni urete imasu. *This book is selling like hot
cakes.*

hane o nobasu   羽を伸ばす   *to kick up one's heels*
[lit. to spread one's wings]

父がいないので、羽を伸ばしています。Chichi ga inai node,
hane o nobashite imasu. *With my father away, I'm kicking up
my heels.*

---

hanjō   半畳   *half a tatami mat*
hanjō o ireru   半畳を入れる   *to interrupt*
[lit. to throw in half a tatami mat]

人が深刻な話をしているとき、半畳を入れてはなりません。

Hito ga shinkoku na hanashi o shite iru toki, hanjō o irete wa narimasen. *Don't interrupt when others are talking about serious matters.*

hanki   反旗   *standard of revolt*
hanki o hirugaesu   反旗を翻す   *to rise in revolt*
[lit. to unfurl the standard of revolt]
学生は厳しい学校の規則に反旗を翻しました。Gakusei wa kibishii gakkō no kisoku ni hanki o hirugaeshimashita. *The students rose in revolt against the rigid school regulations.*

happa   発破   *blasting*
happa o kakeru   発破をかける   *to urge someone on*
[lit. to set dynamite]
先生はもっと勉強するように、生徒に発破をかけました。Sensei wa motto benkyō suru yō ni, seito ni happa o kakemashita. *The teacher urged the pupils on to study harder.*

happō   八方   *all directions*
happōbijin   八方美人   *a sycophant*
[lit. a beauty to all eight directions]
彼は八方美人だから、本音が分かりません。Kare wa happōbijin dakara, honne ga wakarimasen. *Since he is a sycophant, you don't know his true intentions.*

happōfusagari   八方塞がり   *in a fix*
[lit. all directions being closed]
借金がたまって、八方塞がりの状態です。Shakkin ga tamatte, happōfusagari no jōtai desu. *Since I've accumulated so much debt, now I'm in a fix.*

hara   腹   *abdomen, belly, stomach*
hara ga dekiru   腹ができる   *to be resolved*
[lit. One's belly is ready.]
やっと、大学院へ行く腹ができました。Yatto, daigakuin e iku hara ga dekimashita. *Finally, I'm resolved to go to graduate school.*

---

hara ga fukureru   腹が膨れる   *to get frustrated (from keeping quiet)*
[lit. One's belly balloons.]

言いたい意見が言えないで、腹が膨れました。Iitai iken ga ienai de, hara ga fukuremashita. *Because I couldn't say what I wanted to, I got frustrated.*

hara ga futoi   腹が太い   *big-hearted*
[lit. One's belly is thick.]

彼は腹が太いから、人が失敗しても咎めません。Kare wa hara ga futoi kara, hito ga shippai shitemo togamemasen. *Since he's big-hearted, he doesn't blame people even if they make mistakes.*

hara ga ieru   腹がいえる   *anger to subside*
[lit. One's belly gets cured.]

彼女に対して腹がいえるのに、一ヶ月かかりました。
Kanojo ni taishite hara ga ieru no ni, ikkagetsu kakarimashita. *It took an entire month for my anger toward her to subside.*

hara ga kudaru   腹が下る   *to have diarrhea*
[lit. One's stomach comes down.]

キャンプで腹が下ったのは、水のせいでした。Kyanpu de hara ga kudatta nowa, mizu no sei deshita. *The water was the cause of diarrhea on the camping trip.*

hara ga kuroi   腹が黒い   *deceitful*
[lit. One's belly is black.]

あの人は親切そうでも、実は腹がとても黒いです。Ano hito wa shinsetsu sō demo, jitsu wa hara ga totemo kuroi desu. *She looks kind, but she's actually quite deceitful.*

hara ga kusatta   腹が腐った   *despicable*
[lit. One's belly is rotten.]

彼は、金儲けしか興味のない腹が腐った人間です。Kare wa, kane mōke shika kyōmi no nai hara ga kusatta ningen desu. *He is a despicable person who doesn't care about anything but making money.*

hara ga miesuku　　腹が見え透く　　*One's true intentions are obvious.*

[lit. One's belly is transparent.]

どんなにお世辞を言っても、彼の腹は見え透いています。

Donna ni oseji o ittemo, kare no hara wa miesuite imasu.　*No matter how much he flatters me, his true intentions are obvious.*

hara ga niekurikaeru　　腹が煮えくり返る　　*to be furious*

[lit. One's belly boils over.]

汚職の疑いをかけられて、腹が煮えくり返っています。

Oshoku no utagai o kakerarete, hara ga niekurikaette imasu.　*I'm furious that I was suspected of corruption.*

hara ga ōkii　　腹が大きい　　*generous*

[lit. One's belly is big.]

彼は腹が大きい人で、頼み事はいつでも聞いてくれます。

Kare wa hara ga ōkii hito de, tanomigoto wa itsudemo kiite kuremasu.　*He is a generous person, and he always agrees to my requests.*

hara ga osamaru　　腹が収まる　　*to calm down*

[lit. One's stomach is restored.]

彼に憤慨していましたが、謝ったので腹が収まりました。

Kare ni fungai shite imashita ga, ayamatta node hara ga osamarimashita.　*I was very angry with him, but I calmed down when he apologized.*

hara ga suwaru　　腹が据わる　　*to become bolder*

[lit. One's stomach is set.]

一度それをやる決心をしたら、腹が据わりました。Ichido sore o yaru kesshin o shitara, hara ga suwarimashita.　*Once I decided to do it, I became bolder.*

hara ga tatsu　　腹が立つ　　*to be angry*

[lit. One's belly stands up.]

彼の嘘には、本当に腹が立ちます。Kare no uso niwa, hontō ni hara ga tachimasu.　*I'm really angry about his lie.*

hara ni ichimotsu aru　　腹に一物有る　　*to have an*

ulterior motive

[lit. There's something in someone's belly.]

あの男には、腹に一物ありそうです。 Ano otoko niwa, hara ni ichimotsu arisō desu.   *He seems to have an ulterior motive.*

hara ni suekaneru   腹に据えかねる   *hard to take*

[lit. to be unable to set something in one's belly]

息子の怠け癖は、腹に据えかねます。 Musuko no namakeguse wa, hara ni suekanemasu.   *It's hard to take my son's laziness.*

hara no kawa ga yojireru   腹の皮がよじれる   *to nearly die laughing*

[lit. One's stomach skin is distorted.]

彼女の滑稽な話に、腹の皮がよじれました。 Kanojo no kokkei na hanashi ni, hara no kawa ga yojiremashita.   *I nearly died laughing at her hilarious story.*

hara no mushi ga osamaranai   腹の虫が治まらない   *One's anger doesn't subside.*

[lit. Worms in one's belly don't calm down.]

理由もなく非難されて、腹の虫が治まりません。 Riyū mo naku hinan sarete, hara no mushi ga osamarimasen.   *Since I was wrongly accused, my anger won't go away.*

hara o awaseru   腹を合わせる   *to conspire*

[lit. to put one's belly with someone's]

あの二人は腹を合わせて、社長を失脚させました。 Ano futari wa hara o awasete, shachō o shikkyaku sasemashita.   *Those two conspired for the president's downfall.*

hara o eguru   腹をえぐる   *penetrating, piercing*

[lit. to gouge someone's belly]

腹をえぐる質問に、ちょっと答えが詰まりました。 Hara o eguru shitsumon ni, chotto kotae ga tsumarimashita.   *I was momentarily at a loss for an answer to a penetrating question.*

hara o itameta ko   腹を痛めた子   *one's own child*

[lit. a child who pained one's own abdomen]

腹を痛めた子なのに、ちっとも親に似ていません。 Hara o

itameta ko nanoni, chittomo oya ni nite imasen.   *Although she's my own child, she doesn't bear any resemblance to me.*

hara o iyasu   腹をいやす   *to get revenge*
[lit. to cure one's belly]

この前負けたチームに今度は大勝して、腹をいやしました。
Kono mae maketa chīmu ni kondo wa taishō shite, hara o iyashimashita.   *By winning big, we got our revenge against the team that had defeated us before.*

hara o kakaeru   腹を抱える   *to laugh one's head off*
[lit. to embrace one's own belly]

とてもおかしくて、腹を抱えずにはいられませんでした。
Totemo okashikute, hara o kakaezu niwa iraremasen deshita.   *It was so funny that I laughed my head off.*

hara o katameru   腹を固める   *to set one's mind*
[lit. to tighten one's belly]

アメリカに行って、英語を勉強する腹を固めました。
Amerika ni itte, eigo o benkyō suru hara o katamemashita.   *I set my mind to go to the United States and study English.*

hara o kimeru   腹を決める   *to be resolved*
[lit. to decide on something in one's belly]

彼女は離婚する腹を決めました。Kanojo wa rikon suru hara o kimemashita.   *She was resolved to divorce her husband.*

hara o kiru   腹を切る   *to take responsibility and resign*
[lit. to cut one's belly]

会社の業績が低下したら、腹を切るつもりです。Kaisha no gyōseki ga teika shitara, hara o kiru tsumori desu.   *If the company's performance declines, I'll take responsibility and resign.*

hara o koshiraeru   腹をこしらえる   *to eat*
[lit. to build one's stomach]

仕事を始める前に、腹をこしらえましょう。Shigoto o hajimeru mae ni, hara o koshiraemashō.   *Let's eat before starting to work.*

hara o koyasu   腹を肥やす   *to feather one's own nest*

[lit. to make one's belly fat]

彼は慈善事業を運営する振りをしながら、腹を肥やしました。
Kare wa jizenjigyō o uneisuru furi o shinagara, hara o koyashimashita. *He feathered his own nest while pretending to run a charitable organization.*

hara o kukuru   腹をくくる   *to be determined*

[lit. to fasten one's belly]

その仕事は、腹をくくってやらないと出来ませんよ。Sono shigoto wa, hara o kukutte yaranai to dekimasen yo. *You can't complete the work unless you show some determination.*

hara o minuku   腹を見抜く   *to see through someone's scheme*

[lit. to see through someone's belly]

彼の滑らかな言葉にかかわらず、腹を見抜くことが出来ました。Kare no nameraka na kotoba ni kakawarazu, hara o minuku koto ga dekimashita. *In spite of his smooth talk, I could see through his scheme.*

hara o mirareru   腹を見られる   *to have one's thoughts found out*

[lit. one's belly being seen]

宴会で、早く帰りたい腹を見られてしまいました。Enkai de, hayaku kaeritai hara o mirarete shimaimashita. *At the party, it was detected that I wanted to leave early.*

hara o misukasu   腹を見透かす   *to read someone's mind*

[lit. to see through someone's belly]

彼は複雑な人で、腹を見透かすのは容易ではありません。Kare wa fukuzatsu na hito de, hara o misukasu nowa yōi dewa arimasen. *Since he's quite complex, it isn't easy to read his mind.*

hara o saguru   腹を探る   *to feel someone out*

[lit. to search someone's belly]

交渉では、双方とも相手の腹を探ろうとしました。Kōshō dewa, sōhō tomo aite no hara o sagurō to shimashita. *In the negotiations, both sides tried to feel each other out.*

hara o sueru   腹を据える   *to be prepared*
[lit. to set one's belly]

この一年は、一生懸命勉強する腹を据えました。Kono
 ichinen wa, isshōkenmei benkyō suru hara o suemashita.   *I'm
 prepared to study hard for one year.*

hara o tateru   腹を立てる   *to get mad*
[lit. to make one's belly stand up]

彼は彼女がまた約束を破ったので、腹を立てました。Kare
 wa kanojo ga mata yakusoku o yabutta node, hara o
 tatemashita.   *He got mad at her because she broke her
 promise again.*

hara o watte   腹を割って   *frankly*
[lit. by cutting one's belly open]

私たちは、腹を割って話し合いました。Watakushitachi wa,
 hara o watte hanashiaimashita.   *We talked frankly to each
 other.*

hara o yomu   腹を読む   *to read someone's mind*
[lit. to read someone's belly]

あの人の腹を読むのは、容易ではありません。Ano hito no
 hara o yomu no wa, yōi dewa arimasen.   *It's not easy to read
 his mind.*

harachigai no   腹違いの   *half-siblings with different
 mothers*
[lit. by a different belly]

これが、私の腹違いの妹です。Kore ga, watakushi no
 harachigai no imōto desu.   *This is my half-sister.*

haradachimagire ni   腹立ち紛れに   *in a fit of anger*
[lit. in the chaos of a belly standing up]

腹立ち紛れに、言うべきでないことを言ってしまいました。
 Haradachimagire ni, iu beki de nai koto o itte shimaimashita.
 In a fit of anger, I said what I shouldn't have.

haragei   腹芸   *maneuvering skills*
[lit. a belly act]

84

彼は腹芸で、論争を解決しました。Kare wa haragei de, ronsō o kaiketsu shimashita. *He solved the dispute by applying his maneuvering skills.*

haraguroi   腹黒い   *wicked*
[lit. black-bellied]
あの人は腹黒いから気をつけなさい。Ano hito wa haraguroi kara ki o tsukenasai. *Be careful of him; he's wicked.*

haraise   腹いせ   *to vent one's anger*
[lit. to press one's belly]
彼女がデートを断ったので、彼は悪口を言って腹いせをしています。Kanojo ga dēto o kotowatta node, kare wa warukuchi o itte haraise o shite imasu. *Since she turned him down for a date, he's venting his anger by badmouthing her.*

haratsuzumi o utsu   腹鼓を打つ   *to eat to one's heart's content*
[lit. to beat a belly drum]
イタリアに行ったとき、毎日毎日腹鼓を打ちました。Itaria ni itta toki, mainichi mainichi haratsuzumi o uchimashita. *When I visited Italy, I ate to my heart's content every day.*

katahara itai   片腹痛い   *ridiculous*
[lit. The side of one's stomach hurts.]
彼が勤勉を説くなんて片腹痛いです。Kare ga kinben o toku nante katahara itai desu. *It's ridiculous for him to preach hard work.*

mukappara o tateru   向かつ腹を立てる   *to lose one's temper*
[lit. to make a confrontational belly stand up]
あの人はすぐに向かつ腹を立てます。Ano hito wa sugu ni mukappara o tatemasu. *He loses his temper easily.*

---

harawata   腸   *intestines*
harawata ga chigireru   腸がちぎれる   *heartbroken*
[lit. One's intestines are torn.]
子供に死なれて、実に腸がちぎれる思いです。Kodomo ni

shinarete, jitsu ni harawata ga chigireru omoi desu.   *Since my child died, I've been completely heartbroken.*

harawata ga kakimushirareru   腸がかきむしられる
heartrending
[lit. to get one's intestines scratched]
腸がかきむしられる知らせを、友達から聞きました。
Harawata ga kakimushirareru shirase o, tomodachi kara kikimashita.   *I heard the heartrending news from my friend.*

harawata ga kusaru   腸が腐る   *morally corrupt*
[lit. One's intestines are rotten.]
彼は女性をだまして平気な、腸が腐った男です。Kare wa josei o damashite heiki na, harawata ga kusatta otoko desu.
He's a morally corrupt scoundrel who deceives women without any concern.

harawata ga miesuku   腸が見え透く   *Someone's motive is obvious.*
[lit. to see through someone's intestines]
彼女は親切な振りをしていても、腸が見え透いています。
Kanojo wa shinsetsu na furi o shite itemo, harawata ga miesuite imasu.   *She's pretending to be kind, but her motive is obvious.*

harawata ga niekurikaeru   腸が煮えくり返る   *to become infuriated*
[lit. One's intestines boil over.]
汚職の疑いをかけられて、腸が煮えくり返りました。
Oshoku no utagai o kakerarete, harawata ga niekurikaerimashita.   *I became infuriated because I was suspected of corruption.*

harawata o tatsu   腸を断つ   *to break one's heart*
[lit. to sever one's intestines]
そのニュースを聞いて、腸を断つ思いでした。Sono nyūsu o kiite, harawata o tatsu omoi deshita.   *I felt like my heart was breaking after hearing that news.*

hare　　晴れ　　*fine weather*
　hare no　　晴れの　　*best, formal*
　[lit. fine weather]
　晴れの場に、晴れ着を着て行きました。Hare no ba ni, haregi
　　o kite ikimashita.　*I wore my best dress for a formal occasion.*

　harebaresuru　　晴れ晴れする　　*to feel relieved*
　[lit. to become clear]
　期末試験が終わって、晴れ晴れした気持ちです。Kimatsu
　　shiken ga owatte, harebare shita kimochi desu.　*I feel relieved
　　at finishing the final exams.*

　haregamashii　　晴れがましい　　*radiant*
　[lit. feeling like fine weather]
　娘の結婚式で、両親は晴れがましそうでした。Musume no
　　kekkonshiki de, ryōshin wa haregamashisō deshita.　*The
　　parents looked radiant at their daughter's wedding.*

　haregi　　晴れ着　　*one's best clothes*
　[lit. fine-weather clothes]
　招待状によると、そのパーティーには晴れ着を着る必要が
　　ありそうです。Shōtaijō ni yoru to, sono pātī niwa haregi o
　　kiru hitsuyō ga arisō desu.　*According to the invitation, I may
　　need to wear my best clothes to the party.*

　hareru　　晴れる　　*to dissipate, to clear up*
　[lit. The weather becomes fine.]
　説明を聞いて、彼女に対する疑いが晴れました。Setsumei o
　　kiite, kanojo ni taisuru utagai ga haremashita.　*As I listened to
　　her explanation, my suspicions about her dissipated.*

　hareyaka na　　晴れやかな　　*bright, cheerful*
　[lit. like fine weather]
　部屋は、晴れやかな雰囲気にあふれていました。Heya wa,
　　hareyaka na fun-iki ni afurete imashita.　*The room was filled
　　with a cheerful atmosphere.*

haremono　　腫れ物　　*swelling*
　haremono ni fureru yō ni　　腫れ物に触るように

gingerly

[lit. like touching a swelling]

社長は非常に気短なので、腫れ物に触れるように接しています。 Shachō wa hijō ni kimijika nanode, haremono ni fureru yō ni sesshite imasu.   *Since the president is short-tempered, we're dealing with him gingerly.*

---

hari   針   *needle*

hari no aru   針のある   *accusatory, harsh*

[lit. There is a needle.]

妻は夫を針のある目つきで見つめました。 Tsuma wa otto o hari no aru metsuki de mitsumemashita.   *The wife stared at her husband with accusatory eyes.*

hari no mushiro ni suwaru omoi   針の筵に座る思い
to be painful (emotionally)

[lit. feeling like sitting on a mat made of needles]

全て自分の責任だと思うと、針の筵に座る思いです。 Subete jibun no sekinin da to omou to, hari no mushiro ni suwaru omoi desu.   *When I think of how it was all my fault, it's painful.*

hari o fukunda kotoba   針を含んだ言葉   *nasty tone*

[lit. words containing needles]

彼の機嫌が悪いのは、針を含んだ言葉から明らかでした。 Kare no kigen ga warui no wa, hari o fukunda kotoba kara akiraka deshita.   *It was obvious from his nasty tone that he was upset.*

---

hashi   箸   *chopsticks*

hashi ga susumu   箸が進む   *to eat a lot*

[lit. chopsticks to proceed]

素晴らしいご馳走で、箸が進みました。 Subarashii gochisō de, hashi ga susumimashita.   *Since it was a wonderful meal, I ate a lot.*

hashi nimo bō nimo kakaranai   箸にも棒にもかからない
no good, dubious

[lit. not making contact with even chopsticks or a stick]
彼は、箸にも棒にもかからない人です。Kare wa, hashi nimo
   bō nimo kakaranai hito desu.   *He's no good.*

hashi no ageoroshi   箸の上げ下ろし   *trivial matters*
[lit. the picking up and putting down of chopsticks]
彼女は、箸の上げ下ろしにも口うるさい人です。Kanojo wa
   hashi no ageoroshi nimo kuchiurusai hito desu.   *She criticizes
   everyone, even for trivial matters.*

hashi o toru   箸を取る   *to start eating*
[lit. to pick up chopsticks]
どうぞ、箸をお取り下さい。Dōzo, hashi o otori kudasai.
   Please begin.

hashi o tsukeru   箸をつける   *to eat*
[lit. to touch food with chopsticks]
あの外国人は、刺身に箸をつけませんでした。Ano
   gaikokujin wa, sashimi ni hashi o tsukemasen deshita.   *The
   foreigner didn't eat raw fish.*

---

hashi   橋   *bridge*
abunai hashi o wataru   危ない橋を渡る   *to take risks*
[lit. to cross a dangerous bridge]
金儲けのためには、危ない橋も渡りました。Kane mōke no
   tame niwa, abunai hashi mo watarimashita.   *I took risks to
   make big bucks.*

hashiwatashi   橋渡し   *mediation*
[lit. construction of a bridge]
経営者と組合の間には、橋渡しが必要でした。Keieisha to
   kumiai no aida niwa, hashiwatashi ga hitsuyō deshita.
   *Mediation between management and the labor union was
   necessary.*

---

hashigo   梯子   *ladder*
hashigo suru   梯子する   *to go bar-hopping*
[lit. to try a ladder]
夫は今晩もまた梯子をしているようです。Otto wa konban

mo mata hashigo o shite iru yō desu. *My husband may be out bar-hopping again tonight.*

---

hata 旗 *flag*

hata o ageru   旗を揚げる   *to start a business*
[lit. to hoist a flag]
彼は旗を揚げる準備をしています。Kare wa hata o ageru junbi o shite imasu. *He's preparing to start a business.*

hata o furu   旗を振る   *to lead*
[lit. to wave a flag]
彼女は消費者団体の旗を振っています。Kanojo wa shōhisha dantai no hata o futte imasu. *She's leading a consumer group.*

hata o maku   旗を巻く   *to withdraw, to close down*
[lit. to furl a flag]
シカゴに支店を出しましたが、三年で旗を巻きました。Shikago ni shiten o dashimashita ga, san nen de hata o makimashita. *We opened a branch office in Chicago but closed it down after three years.*

hataage   旗揚げ   *inauguration, beginning*
[lit. raising of a flag]
あの政治家は、新政党の旗揚げを目指しています。Ano seijika wa, shin seitō no hataage o mezashite imasu. *That politician is aiming at the inauguration of a new political party.*

hatafuri   旗振り   *leader*
[lit. a flagman]
彼は政治改革の旗振りです。Kare wa seiji kaikaku no hatafuri desu. *He is a leader for political reform.*

hitohata ageru   一旗揚げる   *to try one's fortune, to make it*
[lit. to hoist a flag]
彼は一旗揚げるために東京に来ました。Kare wa hitohata ageru tame ni Tōkyō ni kimashita. *He came to Tokyo to try his fortune.*

hatairo 旗色 *situation*

hatairo ga ii 旗色がいい *The odds of winning are favorable.*

[lit. The color of the banner is good.]

この選挙では、保守的な候補者の旗色がいいです。Kono senkyo dewa, hoshuteki na kōhosha no hatairo ga ii desu. *In this election, the odds of winning are in the conservative candidate's favor.*

hatairo ga warui 旗色が悪い *The odds of winning are unfavorable.*

[lit. The color of the banner is bad.]

販売競争では、わが社の旗色が悪いです。Hanbai kyōsō dewa, waga sha no hatairo ga warui desu. *In the sales competition, the chances of our company's winning are slim.*

hatairo o miru 旗色を見る *to sit on the fence*

[lit. to observe the color of the banner]

どちらの候補者を支持するか決める前、しばらく旗色を見ましょう。Dochira no kōhosha o shiji suru ka kimeru mae, shibaraku hatairo o mimashō. *Let's sit on the fence awhile before deciding which candidate to support.*

---

hatake 畑 *farm*

hatake ga chigau 畑が違う *outside one's specialty*

[lit. A farm is different.]

その企画は、畑が違うので苦労しました。Sono kikaku wa, hatake ga chigau node kurō shimashita. *I had a tough time with the project because it was outside my specialty.*

---

he 屁 *gas*

he demo nai 屁でもない *nothing, so easy*

[lit. not even gas]

そんなことするのは、屁でもない。Sonna koto suru nowa, he demo nai. *That's so easy for me to do.*

he no kappa   屁の河童   *cinch*

[lit. a river imp's gas]

マラソンなんて屁の河童だ。Marason nante he no kappa da.
Running a marathon is a cinch.

he tomo omowanai   屁とも思わない   *to think nothing*
    of something

[lit. to not even think it's gas]

あの生徒は、遅刻しても屁とも思いません。Ano seito wa,
    chikoku shitemo he tomo omoimasen. *That pupil thinks*
    nothing of being late for school.

herikutsu o koneru   屁理屈をこねる   *to quibble*

[lit. to knead gas-like logic]

彼は屁理屈をこねるので、誰も彼と話したがりません。
    Kare wa herikutsu o koneru node, daremo kare to
    hanashitagarimasen. *Since he quibbles, nobody wants to talk*
    to him.

---

hedate   隔て   *partition*

hedate no aru   隔てのある   *cold, distant*

[lit. There is a partition.]

彼女は隔てのある態度で、彼に応対しました。Kanojo wa
    hedate no aru taido de, kare ni ōtai shimashita. *She received*
    him coldly.

hedate o tsukeru   隔てをつける   *to discriminate*

[lit. to set up a partition]

着ている物によって、人に隔てをつけてはなりません。
    Kiteiru mono ni yotte, hito ni hedate o tsuketewa narimasen.
    You shouldn't discriminate against people because of what
    they're wearing.

---

heikō sen   平行線   *parallel lines*

heikō sen o tadoru   平行線をたどる   *There is no*
    progress.

[lit. to follow parallel lines]

交渉は平行線をたどりました。Kōshō wa heikō sen o

tadorimashita. *There was no progress in the negotiations.*

---

henji　返事　*answer, reply*
　futatsu henji de　二つ返事で　*eagerly, readily*
　[lit. with two answers]
　その申し出を、二つ返事で引き受けました。Sono mōshide
　o, futatsu henji de hikiukemashita. *I eagerly accepted the
　offer.*

　nama henji　生返事　*lukewarm reply*
　[lit. an uncooked answer]
　彼女を映画に誘いましたが、生返事しかしませんでした。
　Kanojo o eiga ni sasoimashita ga, nama henji shika shimasen
　deshita. *I invited her to a movie, but she gave me a lukewarm
　reply.*

---

henrin　片鱗　*part, glimpse*
　henrin o nozokaseru　片鱗をのぞかせる　*to show a
　glimpse of something*
　[lit. to show a bit of fish scale]
　この子は、音楽の才能の片鱗をのぞかせています。Kono ko
　wa, ongaku no sainō no henrin o nozokasete imasu. *This
　child is showing a glimpse of her musical talent.*

---

herazuguchi　減らず口　*bad loser's retort*
　herazuguchi o tataku　減らず口をたたく　*to retort
　defensively*
　[lit. to drum a never-ending mouth]
　減らず口をたたかないで、奥さんが正しいことを認めなさい。
　Herazuguchi o tatakanai de, okusan ga tadashii koto o
　mitomenasai. *Rather than retorting defensively, you should
　admit that your wife is right.*

---

heso　臍　*navel*
　heso ga cha o wakasu　臍が茶を沸かす　*laughable*
　[lit. One's navel boils tea.]
　彼が映画俳優になりたいなんて、臍が茶を沸かします。

Kare ga eiga haiyū ni naritai nante, heso ga cha o wakashimasu. *His wanting to become a movie actor is laughable.*

heso o mageru   へそを曲げる   *to sulk*
[lit. to twist one's navel]
彼女は演じたかった役を人に取られて、臍を曲げています。
Kanojo wa enjitakatta yaku o hito ni torarete, heso o magete imasu. *She's sulking because somebody got the role she wanted.*

hesokuri   臍繰り   *secret savings*
[lit. to reckon with one's own navel]
彼の奥さんはこの五年、臍繰りをしています。Kare no okusan wa kono go nen, hesokuri o shite imasu. *His wife has been secretly saving money for the last five years.*

hesomagari   へそ曲がり   *someone perverse*
[lit. a twisted navel]
彼はへそ曲がりだから、まともに話せません。Kare wa hesomagari dakara, matomo ni hanasemasen. *Since he's so perverse, I can't be straightforward with him.*

---

hi   日   *sun*
hi no ataru basho   日の当たる場所   *charmed position*
[lit. a sunny spot]
彼は、日の当たる場所から日の当たる場所へ渡ってきました。
Kare wa, hi no ataru basho kara hi no ataru basho e watatte kimashita. *He's been moving from one charmed position to another.*

hi no me o miru   日の目を見る   *to gain public recognition*
[lit. to see the eyes of the sun]
あの歌手は、やっと日の目を見ることが出来ました。Ano kashu wa, yatto hi no me o miru koto ga dekimashita. *That singer was finally able to gain public recognition.*

hinode no ikioi   日の出の勢い   *One's star is ascending.*

[lit. the vigor of the rising sun]

あの政治家は、近頃日の出の勢いです。Ano seijika wa, chikagoro hinode no ikioi desu. *Recently, that politician's star has been ascending.*

---

hi   火   *fire*

hi ga tsuku   火がつく   *to catch fire (figuratively)*
[lit. A fire starts.]
地震の後、政府の対応について論争に火がつきました。
Jishin no ato, seifu no taiō ni tsuite ronsō ni hi ga tsukimashita. *After the earthquake, the debate over the government's response caught fire.*

hi ni abura o sosogu   火に油を注ぐ   *to make things worse*
[lit. to pour oil over fire]
お父さんが怒っているから、火に油を注がないように黙っていなさい。Otōsan ga okotte iru kara, hi ni abura o sosoganai yō ni damatte inasai. *Since your father is angry, keep your mouth shut and don't make things worse.*

hi no deru yō na   火の出るような   *intense*
[lit. as if flames will come out]
二人は、火の出るような恋の末に結婚しました。Futari wa, hi no deru yō na koi no sue ni kekkon shimashita. *After an intense love affair, they got married.*

hi no kieta yō   火の消えたよう   *to be deserted, to stand still*
[lit. as if fire went out]
このビジネス街は、週末には火の消えたようになります。
Kono bijinesu gai wa, shūmatsu niwa hi no kieta yō ni narimasu. *This business district becomes deserted on the weekend.*

hi no tsuita yō   火の付いたよう   *frantic*
[lit. like catching fire]
年度末を控えて、経理部は今、火のついたような状態です。
Nendo matsu o hikaete, keiribu wa ima, hi no tsuita yō na jōtai

desu. *With the end of the fiscal year approaching, the accounting office is frantic.*

hi o fuku　　火を噴く　　*to erupt*
[lit. to spew fire]

製造業者の価格操作に、消費者の怒りが火を噴きました。
Seizō gyōsha no kakaku sōsa ni, shōhisha no ikari ga hi o fukimashita. *The consumers' anger at the manufacturers' price manipulation erupted.*

hi o miru yorimo akiraka　　火を見るよりも明らか　　*as plain as day*
[lit. clearer than seeing fire]

彼のビジネスが失敗することは、火を見るよりも明らかでした。Kare no bijinesu ga shippai suru koto wa, hi o miru yorimo akiraka deshita. *It was as plain as day that his business would fail.*

hi o tōsu　　火を通す　　*to heat food thoroughly*
[lit. to let heat go through]

その残り物は、火を通した方がおいしいです。Sono nokorimono wa, hi o tōshita hō ga oishii desu. *If you heat the leftovers thoroughly, they'll taste better.*

hi o tsukeru　　火をつける　　*to trigger something*
[lit. to set fire]

彼の頑固な意見が、口論の火をつけました。Kare no ganko na iken ga, kōron no hi o tsukemashita. *His headstrong opinion triggered the argument.*

hinokuruma　　火の車　　*to be in financial straits*
[lit. a wheel of fire]

わが家は、毎月火の車です。Wagaya wa, maitsuki hinokuruma desu. *Our family is in financial straits every month.*

hinote ga agaru　　火の手が上がる　　*to spark*
[lit. to burst into flame]

マスコミの無責任さに、批判の火の手が上がりました。
Masukomi no musekininsa ni, hihan no hinote ga agarimashita.

The media's irresponsibility has sparked criticism.

---

hibana　火花　*spark*
hibana o chirasu　火花を散らす　*to fight tooth and nail*
[lit. to scatter sparks]
この前の選挙では、候補者は互いに火花を散らしました。
Kono mae no senkyo dewa, kōhosha wa tagai ni hibana o
chirashimashita.　*In the last election, the candidates fought
among themselves tooth and nail.*

---

hibi　ひび　*crack*
hibi ga hairu　ひびが入る　*to go sour*
[lit. A crack appears.]
つまらないことが原因で、長年の友情にひびが入ってしま
いました。Tsumaranai koto ga gen-in de, naganen no yūjō ni
hibi ga haitte shimaimashita.　*Our long-term friendship went
sour over something insignificant.*

---

hibuta　火蓋　*lid of a musket pan*
hibuta o kiru　火蓋を切る　*to launch*
[lit. to open the lid of a musket pan]
政党が、増税についての論争の火蓋を切りました。Seitō ga,
zōzei ni tsuite no ronsō no hibuta o kirimashita.　*The political
parties launched a discussion about the tax increase.*

---

hidari　左　*left*
hidarikiki　左利き　*a drinker*
[lit. good with the left hand]
彼は左利きだから、ココアよりビールの方がいいでしょう。
Kare wa hidarikiki dakara, kokoa yori bīru no hō ga ii deshō.
Since he likes to drink, beer would be better than hot chocolate.

hidarimae　左前　*financial difficulty*
[lit. left side front]
あの店は左前で、今にも潰れそうです。Ano mise wa
hidarimae de, ima nimo tsuburesō desu.　*That store is losing
money, and it looks like it'll go under anytime.*

hidarimaki   左巻き   *nut, crackpot*
[lit. counterclockwise]

あの左巻きの言うことなんか、聞く必要ありません。Ano
hidarimaki no iu koto nanka, kiku hitsuyō arimasen.   *You
don't need to listen to what that crackpot says.*

hidariuchiwa   左うちわ   *easy life with no work*
[lit. a fan in one's left hand]

彼は親の金に頼って、左うちわで暮らしています。Kare wa
oya no kane ni tayotte, hidariuchiwa de kurashite imasu.   *He's
living an easy life relying on his parents' money.*

---

hiji   肘   *elbow*
hijideppō o kuwasu   肘鉄砲を食わす   *to rebuff, to snub*
[lit. to hit someone with an elbow gun]

彼は彼女にデートを申し込んで、肘鉄砲を食わされました。
Kare wa kanojo ni dēto o mōshikonde, hijideppō o
kuwasaremashita.   *He was rebuffed when he asked her for a
date.*

---

hikage   日陰   *shade*
hikage no mi   日陰の身   *someone in obscurity; social
outcast*
[lit. someone in shade]

今は日陰の身でも、努力すれば成功します。Ima wa hikage
no mi demo, doryoku sureba seikō shimasu.   *You may not be
known now, but if you work at it you can be successful.*

彼は汚職の疑いで辞職してから、日陰の身です。Kare wa
oshoku no utagai de jishoku shite kara, hikage no mi desu.
*He's been a social outcast since resigning from his job under
suspicion of corruption.*

---

hikari   光   *light*
oya no hikari   親の光   *the influential position of a parent*
[lit. the light of a parent]

彼女は親の光ではなく、自分で成功しました。Kanojo wa
oya no hikari dewa naku, jibun de seikō shimashita.   *She*

made it by herself, not as the daughter of an influential parent.

---

hike   引け   *defeat, closing*

hike o toranai   引けを取らない   *to compare favorably with someone*

[lit. not to get behind]

日本の歴史にかけては、誰にも引けを取りません。Nihon no rekishi ni kakete wa, dare nimo hike o torimasen. *My knowledge of Japanese history compares favorably with anyone's.*

hike o toru   引けを取る   *to be beaten*

[lit. to pick up a defeat]

橋の建設の入札では、競争相手に引けを取ってしまいました。Hashi no kensetsu no nyūsatsu dewa, kyōsō aite ni hike o totte shimaimashita. *We were beaten by our competitor in the bidding on the bridge construction.*

hikedoki   引け時   *quitting time*

[lit. the time for closing]

引け時までに、今の仕事を終えて下さい。Hikedoki made ni, ima no shigoto o oete kudasai. *Please finish your work by quitting time.*

hikeme   引け目   *inferiority*

[lit. the experience of a defeat]

他の出席者に比べて、自分の経験に引け目を感じました。Hoka no shussekisha ni kurabete, jibun no keiken ni hikeme o kanjimashita. *I felt inferior about my experience compared to that of the other participants.*

---

hikeshi   火消し   *fire fighter*

hikeshiyaku   火消し役   *troubleshooter*

[lit. the role of a fire fighter]

火消し役が要るなら、彼に頼みなさい。Hikeshiyaku ga iru nara, kare ni tanominasai. *If you need a troubleshooter, ask him.*

---

hiki   引き   *pull*

hikimokirazu   引きも切らず   *immediately*
[lit. without interrupting a pull]
出張から帰って、引きも切らずに新しい企画に手を付けま
  した。Shutchō kara kaette, hikimokirazu ni atarashii kikaku ni
  te o tsukemashita.   *Back from the business trip, I immediately
  undertook a new project.*

---

hiku   引く   *to pull, to retreat*

hiku ni hikenai   引くに引けない   *no choice but to stay
put*
[lit. not able to retreat]
私がその案の提案者なので、今さら引くに引けません。
  Watakushi ga sono an no teiansha nanode, imasara hiku ni
  hikemasen.   *Since I'm the one who proposed the plan, I have
  no choice but to stay put.*

hikute amata   引く手あまた   *many suitors*
[lit. a lot of pulling hands]
彼は引く手あまたで、どの仕事を選ぶか迷っています。
  Kare wa hikute amata de, dono shigoto o erabuka mayotte
  imasu.   *With many suitors after him with job offers, he's
  having trouble choosing one.*

---

hima   暇   *time*

hima ni akasete   暇に飽かせて   *using all one's free
time*
[lit. using time to the extent that one gets weary]
暇に飽かせて、小説をたくさん読んでいます。Hima ni
  akasete, shōsetsu o takusan yonde imasu.   *I've been using all
  my free time to read novels.*

hima o dasu   暇を出す   *to fire*
[lit. to give time]
あの店員は欠勤が多すぎるので、暇を出しました。Ano ten-
  in wa kekkin ga ōsugiru node, hima o dashimashita.   *Because
  that salesclerk was absent too often, I fired him.*

hima o nusumu   暇を盗む   *to make good use of one's free time*

[lit. to steal time]

暇を盗んで、コンピュ－タの勉強をしています。Hima o nusunde, konpyūta no benkyō o shite imasu. *To make good use of my free time, I'm studying computers.*

hima o saku   暇を割く   *to find time*

[lit. to cut time out]

忙しかったけれど、暇を割いて彼女の話を聞いてあげました。Isogashikatta keredo, hima o saite kanojo no hanashi o kiite agemashita. *Although I was busy, I found time to listen to her story.*

hima o tsubusu   暇をつぶす   *to kill time*

[lit. to squash time]

暇を潰すために、映画を見に行きました。Hima o tsubusu tame ni, eiga o mini ikimashita. *To kill time, I went to see a movie.*

himadoru   暇取る   *to take much time*

[lit. to take up time]

報告書は、調査に思ったより暇取りました。Hōkokusho wa, chōsa ni omotta yori himadorimashita. *The research for the report took much more time than I expected.*

---

hipparu   引っ張る   *to pull*

hipparidako   引っ張りだこ   *to be much sought after*

[lit. a kite being pulled]

あの弁護士は決して負けないので、ビジネス界で引っ張りだこです。Ano bengoshi wa kesshite makenai node, bijinesu kai de hipparidako desu. *Because that lawyer never loses a lawsuit, he's much sought after in the business world.*

---

hirou   拾う   *to pick up*

hiroimono   拾い物   *a lucky find*

[lit. a found article]

この間のみの市で買った絵は、本当に拾い物でした。Kono

aida nominoichi de katta e wa, hontō ni hiroimono deshita.
The painting I bought at the flea market was truly a lucky find.

hiroiyomi 拾い読み   *to skim through a book*
[lit. to pick up and read here and there]
面白い本でしたが、時間がないので拾い読みしました。
Omoshiroi hon deshita ga, jikan ga nai node hiroiyomi
shimashita. *Although the book was interesting, I didn't have much time, so I skimmed through it.*

---

hitai 額   *forehead*
  hitai ni ase shite hataraku 額に汗して働く   *to work hard*
[lit. to work with the sweat on one's forehead]
彼は車を買うために、額に汗して働きました。Kare wa
kuruma o kau tame ni, hitai ni ase shite hatarakimashita. *He worked hard to buy a car.*

  hitai o atsumeru 額を集める   *to huddle together, to put heads together*
[lit. to put people's foreheads together]
問題を急いで解決するために、額を集めて相談しました。
Mondai o isoide kaiketsu suru tame ni, hitai o atsumete sōdan
shimashita. *We put our heads together and conferred to solve the problem quickly.*

---

hito 人   *person*
  hito no ii 人の良い   *good-natured*
[lit. Someone is good.]
彼は人の良さから、みんなに好かれています。Kare wa hito
no yosa kara, minna ni sukarete imasu. *Everybody likes him for his good nature.*

  hito no warui 人の悪い   *bad-natured, unpleasant*
[lit. Someone is bad.]
彼女は人の悪さで知られています。Kanojo wa hito no warusa
de shirarete imasu. *She is known for her unpleasant personality.*

hito o kutta   人を食った   *contemptuous*
[lit. to have eaten a man]
彼の人を食った態度に、みんなが怒りました。Kare no hito
o kutta taido ni, minna ga okorimashita.   *Everyone got angry
at his contemptuous attitude.*

hito o miru mei   人を見る明   *good judge of character*
[lit. the wisdom to look at someone]
彼には人を見る明がないので、いつも苦労しています。
Kare niwa hito o miru mei ga nai node, itsumo kurō shite
imasu.   *Because he's not a good judge of character, he's
always in trouble.*

hitoatari   人当たり   *mannered*
[lit. touching someone]
彼は、人当たりがとても穏やかです。Kare wa, hitoatari ga
totemo odayaka desu.   *He is very gentle mannered.*

hitodenashi   人で無し   *brute*
[lit. not human]
彼は人で無しで、欲しい物を手に入れるには何事もためら
いません。Kare wa hitodenashi de, hoshii mono o te ni ireru
niwa nanigoto mo tameraimasen.   *He's such a brute that he'll
stop at nothing to get what he wants.*

hitogaki   人垣   *a throng*
[lit. a fence of people]
交通事故の現場には、すぐに人垣が出来ました。Kōtsū jiko
no genba niwa, sugu ni hitogaki ga dekimashita.   *A throng
immediately gathered at the site of the traffic accident.*

hitoichibai   人一倍   *much more than others*
[lit. twice as much as others]
彼は人一倍食べます。Kare wa hitoichibai tabemasu.   *He eats
much more than other people do.*

hitojichi   人質   *hostage*
[lit. a human pawn]
新聞の一面に、人質事件の記事が出ていました。Shinbun no
ichi men ni, hitojichi jiken no kiji ga dete imashita.   *The front*

*page of the newspaper had an article about the hostage
incident.*

hitome ni amaru   人目に余る   *excessive*
[lit. too much for one's eyes]
彼の最近の振る舞いは、人目に余ります。 Kare no saikin no
furumai wa, hitome ni amarimasu.   *His recent behavior is
excessive.*

hitome ni tsuku   人目に付く   *to attract attention*
[lit. to attach to people's eyes]
彼女の服装は、どこでも人目に付きます。 Kanojo no fukusō
wa, doko demo hitome ni tsukimasu.   *Her clothes attract
attention wherever she goes.*

hitome o habakaru   人目をはばかる   *shady*
[lit. to be afraid of people's eyes]
彼は、人目をはばかる商売をしているそうです。 Kare wa,
hitome o habakaru shōbai o shite iru sō desu.   *I hear that he's
in a shady business.*

hitome o nusunde   人目を盗んで   *covertly*
[lit. by stealing people's eyes]
人目を盗んで質屋へ行きました。 Hitome o nusunde shichiya e
ikimashita.   *I went to a pawnshop covertly.*

hitome o shinonde   人目を忍んで   *secretly*
[lit. to avoid people's eyes]
彼女と、人目を忍んでつき合っています。 Kanojo to, hitome
o shinonde tsukiatte imasu.   *I've been going out with her
secretly.*

hitonami hazureta   人並み外れた   *unusual*
[lit. beyond average people]
彼は、人並み外れた食欲を持っています。 Kare wa, hitonami
hazureta shokuyoku o motte imasu.   *He has an unusually
large appetite.*

hitonami sugureta   人並み優れた   *extraordinary*
[lit. surpassing average people]
彼は数学では、人並み優れた才能を持っています。 Kare wa

sūgaku dewa, hitonami sugureta sainō o motte imasu. *He has an extraordinary talent for mathematics.*

hitosawagase o suru   人騒がせをする   *to trigger a false alarm*
[lit. to disturb people]

先日は人騒がせをして、まことに申し訳ありませんでした。
Senjitsu wa hitosawagase o shite, makoto ni mōshiwake arimasen deshita. *I'm truly sorry for causing a false alarm the other day.*

hitozute ni   人伝に   *indirectly*
[lit. through someone]

人伝に、彼が離婚したのを知りました。Hitozute ni, kare ga rikon shita no o shirimashita. *I heard indirectly that he was divorced.*

---

hito   一   *one*

hitoashi osaki ni   一足お先に   *before someone*
[lit. one leg ahead]

一足お先に失礼します。Hitoashi osaki ni shitsurei shimasu. *Excuse me for leaving before you.*

hitoawa fukaseru   一泡吹かせる   *to get someone rattled*
[lit. to let someone foam at the mouth]

討論で、彼に一泡吹かせました。Tōron de, kare ni hitoawa fukasemashita. *I got him rattled in the debate.*

hitohada nugu   一肌脱ぐ   *to give someone some help*
[lit. to take off one's own skin]

彼が事業を始めるために、一肌脱いであげました。Kare ga jigyō o hajimeru tame ni, hitohada nuide agemashita. *I gave him some help starting his own business.*

hitohana sakaseru   一花咲かせる   *to attain success*
[lit. to let a flower bloom]

彼は不動産への投機で、一花咲かせました。Kare wa fudōsan e no tōki de, hitohana sakasemashita. *He attained success by speculating in real estate.*

hitohata ageru　　一旗揚げる　　　*to make it, to try one's fortune*
[lit. to raise a flag]
彼女はファッションの世界で一旗揚げるため、パリに行きました。Kanojo wa fasshon no sekai de hitohata ageru tame, Pari ni ikimashita.　*She went to Paris to make it in the fashion industry.*

hitohone oru　　一骨折る　　　*to make a special effort for someone*
[lit. to break a bone]
息子の就職のために、友達が一骨折ってくれました。
Musuko no shūshoku no tame ni, tomodachi ga hitohone otte kuremashita.　*My friend made a special effort to help my son find a job.*

hitoiki ireru　　一息入れる　　　*to take a short rest*
[lit. to let a breath in]
ここで一息入れましょうか。Koko de hitoiki iremashō ka.
Shall we take a short rest now?

hitoiki tsuku　　一息つく　　　*to have breathing space*
[lit. to take a breath]
中間試験が終わったので、ちょっと一息ついています。
Chūkan shiken ga owatta node, chotto hitoiki tsuite imasu.
With midterm exams over, I'm having a little breathing space.

hitokuchi noru　　一口乗る　　　*to join in something*
[lit. to take a mouthful]
この企画に、一口乗っていただきたいのですが。Kono kikaku ni, hitokuchi notte itadakitai no desu ga.　*We would like you to join in this project.*

hitokuse arisō na　　一癖有りそうな　　　*sinister-looking*
[lit. to appear to have a vice]
彼は一癖ありそうですが、実は親切で正直です。Kare wa hitokuse arisō desu ga, jitsu wa shinsetsu de shōjiki desu.　*He seems like a sinister person, but in reality, he's kind and honest.*

hitomebore   一目惚れ   *love at first sight*
[lit. love at a glance]
彼は、彼女に一目惚れしてしまいました。Kare wa, kanojo ni
   hitomebore shite shimaimashita.   *He fell in love with her at
   first sight.*

hitoshibai utsu   一芝居打つ   *to conspire*
[lit. to run a play]
彼は会議に混乱を起こそうと一芝居打ちましたが、失敗し
   ました。Kare wa kaigi ni konran o okosō to hitoshibai
   uchimashita ga, shippai shimashita.   *He conspired to create
   chaos in the meeting but failed.*

hitosujinawa dewa ikanai   一筋縄ではいかない   *to be
tough to deal with*
[lit. to be unable to handle with a piece of rope]
あの政治家は、一筋縄ではいかないという評判があります。
   Ano seijika wa, hitosujinawa dewa ikanai to iu hyōban ga
   arimasu.   *That politician has a reputation for being tough to
   deal with.*

hitotamari mo naku   一たまりもなく   *immediately*
[lit. without any holding]
大きいスーパーが出来ると、近くの小さい店は一たまりも
   なく潰れてしまいました。ōkii sūpā ga dekiru to, chikaku
   no chiisai mise wa hitotamari mo naku tsuburete
   shimaimashita.   *When the big supermarket opened, the small
   shops nearby immediately went bankrupt.*

hitotsubudane   一粒種   *only child*
[lit. a grain of seed]
隣の家では、息子を一粒種として甘やかしています。
   Tonari no ie dewa, musuko o hitotsubudane toshite
   amayakashite imasu.   *Our next door neighbors are indulging
   their son, an only child.*

hitoyaku kau   一役買う   *to offer one's service*
[lit. to buy a role]
隣近所の組織化に、一役買いました。Tonarikinjo no

107

soshikika ni, hitoyaku kaimashita. *I volunteered to take part in organizing our neighborhood.*

hitoyama ateru   一山当てる   *to strike it rich*
[lit. to guess a mountain]

彼女は、株で一山当てました。Kanojo wa, kabu de hitoyama atemashita. *She struck it rich in the stock market.*

hitoyama kosu   一山越す   *to pull through something difficult*
[lit. to go over a mountain]

論文を三つ提出して、今学期も一山越しました。Ronbun o mittsu teishutsu shite, kongakki mo hitoyama koshimashita. *By submitting three term papers, I pulled through this semester.*

---

hitomi   瞳   *pupil (eye)*
hitomi o korashite   瞳を凝らして   *intently*
[lit. by applying one's pupils]

彼女は芝居を瞳を凝らして見守りました。Kanojo wa shibai o hitomi o korashite mimamorimashita. *She watched the play intently.*

---

hitori   独り   *one person*
hitoriaruki   独り歩き   *independence*
[lit. a solitary walk]

彼は大学を出ましたが、まだ財政的に独り歩きできません。 Kare wa daigaku o demashita ga, mada zaiseiteki ni hitoriaruki dekimasen. *Although he graduated from college, he isn't financially independent yet.*

hitoributai   独り舞台   *unchallenged position*
[lit. alone on a stage]

外交政策の分野は、彼の独り舞台です。Gaikō seisaku no bun-ya wa, kare no hitoributai desu. *He holds an unchallenged position in the field of foreign policy.*

hitorigaten   独り合点   *to take something for granted*
[lit. to agree with oneself]

彼女は自分もパーティーに呼ばれたと独り合点しています。
Kanojo wa jibun mo pātī ni yobareta to hitorigaten shite imasu.
She took it for granted that she was also invited to the party.

hitorijime suru   独り占めする   *to monopolize someone or something*
[lit. to occupy by oneself]
彼は会社の車を独り占めしています。Kare wa kaisha no kuruma o hitorijime shite imasu. *He's monopolizing a company car.*

hitoriyogari   独り善がり   *self-complacency*
[lit. to make oneself good]
彼女は独り善がりで、人の気持ちなど決して考えません。
Kanojo wa hitoriyogari de, hito no kimochi nado kesshite kangaemasen. *She's self-complacent and never thinks about other people's feelings.*

hitorizumō   独り相撲   *to tilt at windmills*
[lit. to wrestle alone]
抗議運動は支持が殆ど無く、独り相撲に終わりました。
Kōgi undō wa shiji ga hotondo naku, hitorizumō ni owarimashita. *With little support, the protest movement ended up tilting at windmills.*

---

hiyameshi   冷や飯   *cold rice*
hiyameshi o kuu   冷や飯を食う   *to be in the doghouse*
[lit. to eat cold rice]
会社の方針に反対したため、一年冷や飯を食ってしまいました。Kaisha no hōshin ni hantai shita tame, ichi nen hiyameshi o kutte shimaimashita. *I was in the doghouse for a year for opposing company policies.*

---

hiyori   日和   *weather conditions*
hiyori o miru   日和を見る   *to see how the wind blows*
[lit. to check the weather]
彼はどの政党を支持するか、日和を見ています。Kare wa dono seitō o shiji suru ka, hiyori o mite imasu. *He's waiting*

to see how the wind blows before deciding which party to support.

---

hiza   膝   *knee*

hiza o kussuru   膝を屈する   *to yield*
[lit. to bend one's knees]
政府は、国民の反対に膝を屈しました。Seifu wa, kokumin no hantai ni hiza o kusshimashita.   *The government yielded to the objections of the people.*

hiza o majieru   膝を交える   *to have an intimate talk*
[lit. to mingle each other's knees]
母と娘は、膝を交えて話し合いました。Haha to musume wa, hiza o majiete hanashiaimashita.   *The mother and daughter had an intimate talk.*

hiza o noridasu   膝を乗り出す   *to show great interest*
[lit. to make one's knees go forward]
彼女の話に、全員が膝を乗り出して聞きました。Kanojo no hanashi ni, zen-in ga hiza o noridashite kikimashita. *Everybody listened to her story with great interest.*

hiza o tadasu   膝を正す   *to sit upright*
[lit. to straighten one's knees]
先生の話を、膝を正して聞きました。Sensei no hanashi o, hiza o tadashite kikimashita.   *We listened attentively to the talk by our teacher.*

hiza o tataku   膝を叩く   *to agree, to be impressed*
[lit. to hit one's knees]
彼の提案に、出席者はみんな膝を叩きました。Kare no teian ni, shussekisha wa minna hiza o tatakimashita.   *All the attendees agreed to his proposal.*

hiza o tsukiawaseru   膝を突き合わせる   *to have a heart-to-heart talk*
[lit. to get knee to knee]
私たちは、夜遅くまで膝を突き合わせて話し合いました。Watakushitachi wa, yoru osoku made hiza o tsukiawasete

hanashiaimashita. *We had a heart-to-heart talk till late at night.*

hiza o utsu   膝を打つ   *to agree, to be impressed*
[lit. to hit one's knees]
彼女の名案に膝を打ちました。Kanojo no meian ni hiza o uchimashita.   *I was impressed with her wonderful idea.*

hizazume danpan   膝詰め談判   *to press demands for something*
[lit. parley knee to knee]
組合は会社と、賃上げについて膝詰め談判しました。
Kumiai wa kaisha to, chin-age ni tsuite hizazume danpan shimashita.   *The labor union pressed demands for a wage increase with the company.*

---

hochō   歩調   *pace, step*
hochō ga au   歩調が合う   *to get along well with someone*
[lit. One's steps fit with another's.]
彼女と私は、いつも歩調が合います。Kanojo to watakushi wa, itsumo hochō ga aimasu.   *She and I always get along well.*

hochō o awaseru   歩調を合わせる   *to join forces*
[lit. to adjust one's steps]
野党各党は、政府に反対するために歩調を合わせました。
Yatō kakutō wa, seifu ni hantai suru tame ni hochō o awasemashita.   *The minority parties joined forces to confront the government.*

---

hogo   ほご   *waste paper*
hogo ni suru   ほごにする   *to scrap, to discard*
[lit. to throw waste paper away]
彼女は約束をほごにしました。Kanojo wa yakusoku o hogo ni shimashita.   *She broke her promise.*

---

hoko   矛   *halberd*
hoko o osameru   矛を収める   *to stop fighting*
[lit. to sheathe the halberd]

矛を収めて、長年の訴訟の和解をしました。Hoko o osamete, naganen no soshō no wakai o shimashita. *I stopped fighting and settled the longstanding lawsuit out of court.*

hokosaki ga niburu　　矛先が鈍る　　*to lose momentum, to be deflated*

[lit. The tip of a halberd becomes dull.]

彼がすぐ謝ったので、怒りの矛先が鈍ってしまいました。Kare ga sugu ayamatta node, ikari no hokosaki ga nibutte shimaimashita. *Since he apologized immediately, my anger was deflated.*

hokosaki o tenjiru　　矛先を転じる　　*to change the focus of attack*

[lit. to turn the tip of a halberd]

彼は不満の矛先を、小売店から製造会社に転じました。Kare wa fuman no hokosaki o, kouriten kara seizō gaisha ni tenjimashita. *He switched the focus of his dissatisfaction from the retailer to the manufacturer.*

---

hon　　本　　*real, exact, true*

hongoshi o ireru　　本腰を入れる　　*to get down to serious business*

[lit. to apply one's hip fully]

大学の入試が近付いて、勉強に本腰を入れています。Daigaku no nyūshi ga chikazuite, benkyō ni hongoshi o irete imasu. *With entrance exams starting soon, I've gotten down to serious studying.*

honne o haku　　本音を吐く　　*to reveal one's true intentions*

[lit. to vomit one's true tune]

相次ぐ質問に答えながら、彼はとうとう本音を吐いてしまいました。Aitsugu shitsumon ni kotaenagara, kare wa tōtō honne o haite shimaimashita. *Answering successive questions, he finally revealed what he really wanted.*

---

hone　　骨　　*bone*

hone ga aru　　骨がある　　*to have strong convictions*

[lit. to have bones]

彼は骨があるので、意見もしっかりしています。Kare wa
   hone ga aru node, iken mo shikkari shite imasu.   *Since he's a
   man of strong convictions, his opinion is unshakable.*

hone ga oreru   骨が折れる   *to be tough*

[lit. One's bones break.]

この仕事は、思ったより骨が折れます。Kono shigoto wa,
   omotta yori hone ga oremasu.   *This job is tougher than you
   think.*

hone made shaburu   骨までしゃぶる   *to exploit
   someone totally*

[lit. to even suck someone's bones]

彼は彼女の骨までしゃぶった後、別の女性と結婚しました。
   Kare wa kanojo no hone made shabutta ato, betsu no josei to
   kekkon shimashita.   *After totally exploiting her, he married
   another woman.*

hone ni kizande   骨に刻んで   *absolutely*

[lit. by etching something on one's bone]

私の警告を、骨に刻んで覚えておきなさい。Watakushi no
   keikoku o, hone ni kizande oboete okinasai.   *You should
   absolutely heed my warning.*

hone no zui made   骨の髄まで   *profoundly*

[lit. deep into one's bone marrow]

この間の苦い経験は、骨の髄まで染み込んでいます。Kono
   aida no nigai keiken wa, hone no zui made shimikonde imasu.
   *The bitter experience I had the other day affected me
   profoundly.*

hone o oru   骨を折る   *to make an extra effort*

[lit. to break one's bones]

交渉を決着させるために、骨を折りました。Kōshō o
   ketchaku saseru tame ni, hone o orimashita.   *I made an extra
   effort to conclude the negotiations.*

hone o uzumeru   骨を埋める   *to make a place one's
   last home*

[lit. to bury one's own bones]

彼はそこに骨を埋めるつもりで、フランスに行きました。

Kare wa soko ni hone o uzumeru tsumori de, Furansu ni ikimashita. *He went to France intending to make it his last home.*

honenashi   骨無し   *spineless*

[lit. having no bones]

彼は骨無しで、いざというときには役に立ちません。Kare wa honenashi de, iza to iu toki niwa yaku ni tachimasen. *Since he's spineless, he isn't effective in a crisis.*

honenuki ni suru   骨抜きにする   *to water something down*

[lit. to debone]

私の提案は、すっかり骨抜きにされてしまいました。

Watakushi no teian wa, sukkari honenuki ni sarete shimaimashita. *It's regrettable that my proposal was totally watered down.*

honeorizon   骨折り損   *wasting one's time and energy*

[lit. no return for breaking one's own bones]

彼女を助けてあげようとしましたが、骨折り損に終わりました。Kanojo o tasukete ageyō to shimashita ga, honeorizon ni owarimashita. *Although I tried to help her, I ended up wasting my time and energy.*

honeoshimi   骨惜しみ   *unwilling*

[lit. stingy with one's bones]

彼の骨惜しみする態度は、理解できません。Kare no honeoshimi suru taido wa, rikai dekimasen. *I don't understand his unwilling attitude.*

honeppoi   骨っぽい   *to have firm convictions*

[lit. bony]

彼は骨っぽい男です。Kare wa honeppoi otoko desu. *He's a man of strong convictions.*

honeyasume   骨休め   *rest*

[lit. letting one's bones rest]

最近は働き過ぎで、骨休めが必要です。Saikin wa

hatarakisugi de, honeyasume ga hitsuyō desu.   *I need a rest because I've been working too much.*

---

honemi   骨身   *flesh and bones*
  honemi ni kotaeru   骨身にこたえる   *to affect someone deeply*
  [lit. to affect one's flesh and bones]
  彼女の助言は、骨身にこたえずにはいられませんでした。
  Kanojo no jogen wa, honemi ni kotaezu niwa iraremasen deshita.   *Her advice affected me deeply.*

  honemi ni shimite   骨身にしみて   *deeply*
  [lit. to penetrate one's bones]
  あの人の忠告は、今でも骨身にしみて感じています。Ano hito no chūkoku wa, ima demo honemi ni shimite kanjite imasu.   *Even now, his advice affects me deeply.*

  honemi o kezuru   骨身を削る   *to go through tremendous hardships*
  [lit. to plane one's own flesh and bones]
  若いときには、骨身を削る苦労も気にかけませんでした。
  Wakai toki niwa, honemi o kezuru kurō mo ki ni kakemasen deshita.   *When I was young, I didn't mind going through tremendous hardships.*

  honemi o oshimazuni   骨身を惜しまずに   *diligently*
  [lit. without sparing one's flesh and bones]
  彼のためなら、骨身を惜しまず働きます。Kare no tame nara, honemi o oshimazu hatarakimasu.   *If it's for him, I'll work extremely hard.*

---

hoo   頬   *cheek*
  hoo ga yurumu   頬がゆるむ   *to smile*
  [lit. One's cheeks get loose.]
  素晴らしい知らせを聞いて、頬がゆるまずにはいられませんでした。Subarashii shirase o kiite, hoo ga yurumazu niwa iraremasen deshita.   *I couldn't stop smiling at hearing the wonderful news.*

hoo o fukuramaseru   頬を膨らませる   *to sulk*
[lit. to puff one's cheeks]
子供はお母さんがおもちゃを買ってくれないので、頬を膨らませています。Kodomo wa okāsan ga omocha o katte kurenai node, hoo o fukuramasete imasu. *The child is sulking because his mother won't buy him a toy.*

hoo o tsuneru   頬をつねる   *to make sure that one's good luck is real*
[lit. to pinch one's cheek]
宝くじに当たって、頬をつねりました。Takarakuji ni atatte, hoo o tsunerimashita. *When I won the lottery, I pinched myself to make sure it was real.*

hookaburi o suru   頬被りをする   *to feign ignorance*
[lit. to cover one's cheeks with a towel]
隣の家の両親は、子供の悪戯に頬被りをしています。
Tonari no ie no ryōshin wa, kodomo no itazura ni hookaburi o shite imasu. *The parents next door are feigning ignorance of their child's mischief.*

---

hoshi   星   *star*
hoshi ga wareru   星が割れる   *to find out who the culprit is*
[lit. A star cracks.]
先月の銀行強盗の星が割れました。Sengetsu no ginkō gōtō no hoshi ga waremashita. *The police found out who the culprit was in last month's bank robbery.*

hoshi o ageru   星を挙げる   *to arrest a criminal*
[lit. to catch a star]
殺人現場のすぐ近くで、警官は星を挙げました。Satsujin genba no sugu chikaku de, keikan wa hoshi o agemashita. *The police arrested the criminal right near the murder scene.*

hoshi o kasegu   星を稼ぐ   *to win, to gain favor*
[lit. to earn a star]
私のひいきの力士は、今場所は毎日星を稼いでいます。
Watakushi no hiiki no rikishi wa, konbasho wa mainichi hoshi

o kaseide imasu.   *My favorite sumo wrestler has been winning every day in this tournament.*

hoshimawari   星回り   *luck, fortune*
[lit. a cycle of one's star]
今年は星回りがよくて、いい事が次々に起こっています。
Kotoshi wa hoshimawari ga yokute, ii koto ga tsugitsugi ni okotte imasu.   *It's a lucky year for me, and good things are happening one after the other.*

---

hotoke   仏   *Buddha*
hotoke ni naru   仏になる   *to die*
[lit. to become a Buddha]
あの人は、去年仏になったそうです。Ano hito wa, kyonen hotoke ni natta sō desu.   *I hear that he died last year.*

hotoke no kao mo sando   仏の顔も三度   *limits to one's patience*
[lit. the Buddha's face for three times but no more]
また締め切りに間に合わなかったね。仏の顔も三度だよ。
Mata shimekiri ni ma ni awanakatta ne. Hotoke no kao mo sando da yo.   *You missed the deadline again. I'm running out of patience.*

hotokegokoro   仏心   *mercy*
[lit. the Buddha's mind]
彼は、仏心で部下の失策をかばってあげました。Kare wa, hotokegokoro de buka no shissaku o kabatte agemashita.   *He mercifully defended his subordinate's mistake.*

hotokekusai   仏臭い   *preachy*
[lit. smelling like the Buddha]
彼の意見は、いつも仏臭いです。Kare no iken wa, itsumo hotokekusai desu.   *His opinions always sound preachy.*

---

hozo   臍   *navel*
hozo o kamu   臍を噛む   *to regret deeply*
[lit. to gnaw one's own navel]
住宅ローンを拒否されて、もっと貯金しなかったことに臍

を噛みました。Jūtaku rōn o kyohi sarete, motto chokin
shinakatta koto ni hozo o kamimashita.　*When my mortgage
application was rejected, I deeply regretted that I hadn't saved more.*

hozo o katameru　臍を固める　*to resolve*
[lit. to harden one's own navel]
会社を辞めて独立する臍を固めました。Kaisha o yamete
dokuritsu suru hozo o katamemashita.　*I resolved to quit the
company and become self-employed.*

---

hyaku　百　*one hundred*
hyaku mo shōchi　百も承知　*to be fully aware*
[lit. to know even a hundred]
それに危険が伴うことは、百も承知です。Sore ni kiken ga
tomonau koto wa, hyaku mo shōchi desu.　*I'm fully aware
that it involves some danger.*

hyakusen renma no shi　百戦錬磨の士　*veteran*
[lit. a skilled soldier through a hundred wars]
市場開拓では、彼は百戦錬磨の士です。Shijō kaitaku dewa,
kare wa hyakusen renma no shi desu.　*He's a battle-hardened
veteran in market development.*

---

hyōzan　氷山　*iceberg*
hyōzan no ikkaku　氷山の一角　*the tip of the iceberg*
[lit. the tip of the iceberg]
統計の麻薬使用者の数は、氷山の一角に過ぎません。Tōkei
no mayaku shiyōsha no kazu wa, hyōzan no ikkaku ni
sugimasen.　*The number of drug users in the statistics is
merely the tip of the iceberg.*

I

i　意　*mind, will*
i ni kaisanai　意に介さない　*to not mind*

[lit. to not put one's mind in between]
彼女はどんな用事を頼まれても、意に介しません。Kanojo
  wa donna yōji o tanomaretemo, i ni kaishimasen. *She doesn't
  mind being asked to run any errand.*

i ni mitanai   意に満たない   *unsatisfactory*
[lit. to not fill someone's will]
そんな言い訳では意に満ちません。Sonna iiwake dewa i ni
  michimasen. *Such an excuse is unsatisfactory.*

i o kumu   意を汲む   *to read someone's mind*
[lit. to scoop up someone's mind]
彼女の意を汲んで、それをしてあげました。Kanojo no i o
  kunde, sore o shite agemashita. *I did it for her by reading her
  mind.*

---

ibara   茨   *thorn*
  ibara no michi o tadoru   茨の道をたどる   *to have a
  tough life*
  [lit. to follow a thorny road]
  彼は今は茨の道をたどっています。Kare wa ima wa ibara no
  michi o tadotte imasu. *He's having a tough life right now.*

---

ichi   一   *one*
  ichi ka bachi ka yattemiru   一か八かやってみる   *to
  put all one's eggs in one basket*
  [lit. to try, whether it's one or eight]
  一か八か、ジャンクボンドに投資してみました。 Ichi ka
  bachi ka, janku bondo ni tōshi shite mimashita. *I put all my
  eggs in one basket and invested in junk bonds.*

  ichi kara jū made   一から十まで   *thoroughly*
  [lit. from one to ten]
  彼には一から十まで説明したのに、まだ分かりませんでした。
  kare niwa ichi kara jū made setsumei shita noni, mada
  wakarimasen deshita. *Although I explained it to him
  thoroughly, he still didn't understand it.*

  ichi mo ni mo naku   一も二もなく   *readily*

[lit. without one or two]

彼女は、私の意見に一も二もなく賛成しました。Kanojo wa, watakushi no iken ni ichi mo ni mo naku sansei shimashita. *She readily agreed with my opinion.*

ichijitsu no chō   一日の長   *to be better and more experienced*

[lit. the merit of one day]

市場分析にかけては、彼女は彼より一日の長があります。 Shijō bunseki ni kakete wa, kanojo wa kare yori ichijitsu no chō ga arimasu. *For market analysis, she's better and more experienced than he is.*

ichimai kamu   一枚噛む   *to take part in something*

[lit. to bite a sheet of paper]

この企画には、私も一枚噛んでいます。Kono kikaku niwa, watakushi mo ichimai kande imasu. *I'm taking part in this project.*

ichimoku oku   一目置く   *to take one's hat off to someone*

[lit. to place one's own *go* stone first]

彼女の親孝行には、一目置いています。Kanojo no oya kōkō niwa, ichimoku oite imasu. *I take my hat off to her for her devotion to her parents.*

ichimyaku tsūjiru   一脈通じる   *to have something in common*

[lit. to understand someone's heartbeat]

政治については、私と彼には一脈通じるものがあります。 Seiji ni tsuite wa, watakushi to kare niwa ichimyaku tsūjiru mono ga arimasu. *He and I have something in common as far as politics is concerned.*

ichiyoku o ninau   一翼を担う   *to assume an important role*

[lit. to carry one wing on one's shoulder]

彼は政治改革運動で一翼を担って忙しいです。Kare wa seiji kaikaku undō de ichiyoku o ninatte isogashii desu. *He's busy assuming an important role in the political reform movement.*

ikka o nasu   一家を成す   *to establish oneself as an authority*
[lit. to form a family]
彼は物理の分野で一家を成しています。 Kare wa butsuri no bun-ya de ikka o nashite imasu.   *He's an acknowledged authority in the field of physics.*

ikkan no owari   一巻の終わり   *end*
[lit. the end of the volume of a story]
彼の人生の夢は、事業の失敗で一巻の終わりとなりました。 Kare no jinsei no yume wa, jigyō no shippai de ikkan no owari to narimashita.   *His lifelong dream ended with the failure of his business.*

ippai kuwasu   一杯食わす   *to fool someone, to pull a fast one*
[lit. to make someone eat a bowl of food]
彼に一杯食わされて、返ってくる当てがないお金を貸してしまいました。 Kare ni ippai kuwasarete, kaette kuru ate ga nai okane o kashite shimaimashita.   *I was fooled and lent him money I would never get back.*

ippon toru   一本取る   *to score a point*
[lit. to pick up a piece]
国会の審議で、野党は政府から一本取りました。 Kokkai no shingi de, yatō wa seifu kara ippon torimashita.   *In the Diet session, the minority parties scored a point over the government.*

ippondachi   一本立ち   *self-supporting*
[lit. standing alone]
大学は卒業したけれど、まだ一本立ちできません。 Daigaku wa sotsugyō shita keredo, mada ippondachi dekimasen. *Although I graduated from a university, I can't support myself yet.*

ipponjōshi   一本調子   *monotonous*
[lit. the same tune]

一本調子の生活に飽き飽きしています。Ipponjōshi no
　seikatsu ni akiaki shite imasu.　*I'm bored with my monotonous
　life.*

ipponyari　　一本槍　　*nothing but . . .*
[lit. one spear]
最近は勉強一本槍の毎日です。Saikin wa benkyō ipponyari no
　mainichi desu.　*Recently it's been nothing but study, day in
　and day out.*

issatsu ireru　　一札入れる　　*to give someone a signed
　document*
[lit. to bring in a sheet of paper]
お金は貸して上げるけど、一札入れて下さい。Okane wa
　kashite ageru kedo, issatsu irete kudasai.　*I'll lend you money,
　but give me a signed document.*

isseki mōkeru　　一席設ける　　*to arrange a party*
[lit. to set up a seat]
大切な顧客のために、一席設けました。Taisetsu na kokyaku
　no tame ni, isseki mōkemashita.　*I arranged a party for our
　important clients.*

isseki o tōjiru　　一石を投じる　　*to create a stir*
[lit. to throw a stone]
彼の発言は、学会に一石を投じました。Kare no hatsugen wa,
　gakkai ni isseki o tōjimashita.　*His speech created a stir in
　academic circles.*

issen o kakusuru　　一線を画する　　*to be on opposite sides*
[lit. to draw a line]
環境問題については、彼の意見と一線を画しています。
　Kankyō mondai ni tsuite wa, kare no iken to issen o kakushite
　imasu.　*On environmental issues, he and I are on opposite
　sides.*

isshi midarezu　　一糸乱れず　　*in unison*
[lit. not even a piece of thread out of place]
野党は一糸乱れずに団結して、政府と対立しました。Yatō
　wa isshi midarezu ni danketsu shite, seifu to tairitsu shimashita.

In unison the minority parties confronted the government.

isshi o mukuiru   一矢を報いる   *to retaliate*
[lit. to return an arrow]

いつも負けているチームに勝って、一矢を報いました。
Itsumo makete iru chīmu ni katte, isshi o mukuimashita. *We retaliated by defeating the team which had been beating us.*

---

ido   井戸   *well*
idobata kaigi   井戸端会議   *gossiping (by a group of women)*
[lit. a well-side conference]

彼女たちは、毎日昼休みに井戸端会議を開いています。
Kanojotachi wa, mainichi hiruyasumi ni idobata kaigi o hiraite imasu. *These.women are gossiping during lunch break every day.*

---

ii   いい   *good, fine, nice*
ii kao   いい顔   *big shot*
[lit. a good face]

彼は地元ではいい顔です。Kare wa jimoto dewa ii kao desu.
He's a big shot in his hometown.

ii ko ni naru   いい子になる
to gain credit at others' expense
[lit. to become a good child]

彼はいつも上役の前では、いい子になろうとします。Kare wa itsumo uwayaku no mae dewa, ii ko ni narō to shimasu.
He always tries to gain credit at other's expense in front of the boss.

ii tsura no kawa   いい面の皮   *Serves (one) right!*
[lit. good facial skin]

彼は汚職で首になったそうですね。いい面の皮ですよ。
Kare wa oshoku de kubi ni natta sō desu ne. Ii tsura no kawa desu yo. *I hear he was fired for corruption. Serves him right!*

---

ikari   怒り   *anger*

---

ikari o kau   怒りを買う   *to make someone angry*
[lit. to buy someone's anger]

毎晩帰宅が非常に遅くなって、妻の怒りを買ってしまい
ました。Maiban kitaku ga hijō ni osokunatte, tsuma no ikari o
katte shimaimashita. *I regret that I made my wife angry by
returning very late every night.*

ikari o maneku   怒りを招く   *to trigger someone's anger*
[lit. to invite someone's anger]

政府の無能が、国民の怒りを招いています。Seifu no munō
ga, kokumin no ikari o maneite imasu. *The government's
incompetency has triggered the people's anger.*

---

iki   息   *breathing*

iki ga au   息が合う   *to be in perfect tune with each other*
[lit. Each other's breathing is in harmony.]

彼女と私は、何をやっても息が合います。Kanojo to
watakushi wa, nani o yattemo iki ga aimasu. *Whatever we do,
she and I are in perfect tune with each other.*

iki ga kakaru   息がかかる   *under the patronage of
someone*
[lit. Someone's breathing covers you.]

彼には、社長の息がかかっているそうです。Kare niwa,
shachō no iki ga kakatte iru sō desu. *I hear he's under the
patronage of the president.*

iki ga kireru   息が切れる   *to run out of steam, to ebb*
[lit. to be out of breath]

彼の指導力は、一年たつと息が切れてきました。Kare no
shidōryoku wa, ichi nen tatsu to iki ga kirete kimashita. *His
leadership began to run out of steam after one year.*

iki ga nagai   息が長い   *long-lasting*
[lit. Breathing is deep.]

彼女の作家活動は息が長く、ベストセラーを何冊も書きま
した。Kanojo no sakka katsudō wa iki ga nagaku, besuto serā
o nansatsu mo kakimashita. *She's had a long career as a
writer, and she's written many bestsellers.*

iki ga tsumaru   息が詰まる   *nervous, to not be able to relax*
[lit. hard to breathe]
パーティーには先生も来ていたので、息が詰まりました。
Pātī niwa sensei mo kite ita node, iki ga tsumarimashita.
I couldn't relax at the party because my teacher was there too.

iki mo tsukasezu   息もつかせず   *rapidly*
[lit. without letting someone breathe]
教授は息もつかせず学生に質問を投げかけました。Kyōju
  wa iki mo tsukasezu gakusei ni shitsumon o nagekakemashita.
  The professor rapidly hurled questions at her students.

iki o fukikaesu   息を吹き返す   *to revive*
[lit. to breathe again]
あの会社は、新しい経営陣を入れて息を吹き返しました。
  Ano kaisha wa, atarashii keieijin o irete iki o fukikaeshimashita.
  *With the introduction of the new management team, that
  company revived.*

iki o hikitoru   息を引き取る   *to die*
[lit. to withdraw one's breathing]
彼は長い病気の末、息を引き取りました。Kare wa nagai
  byōki no sue iki o hikitorimashita.   *He died after a long
  illness.*

iki o korashite   息を凝らして   *intently*
[lit. by concentrating one's own breath]
私たちは息を凝らして、彼女の話を聞きました。
  Watakushitachi wa iki o korashite, kanojo no hanashi o
  kikimashita.   *We listened to her story intently.*

iki o koroshite   息を殺して   *expectantly*
[lit. by killing one's own breath]
その村の人全員が、息を殺して首相の到着を待ちました。
  Sono mura no hito zen-in ga, iki o koroshite shushō no tōchaku
  o machimashita.   *All the villagers waited expectantly for the
  arrival of the prime minister.*

iki o nomu   息を呑む   *to be astonished*

[lit. to swallow one's own breath]

景色のあまりの美しさに息を呑みました。 Keshiki no amari no utsukushisa ni iki o nomimashita. *I was astonished at the extreme beauty of the scenery.*

iki o nuku   息を抜く   *to relax*
[lit. to draw a breath]
仕事が忙しくて、息を抜く暇もありません。 Shigoto ga isogashikute, iki o nuku hima mo arimasen. *I have no time to relax because I'm busy with work.*

iki o tsuku   息をつく   *to breathe a sigh of relief*
[lit. to take a breath]
大切な試験が終わって、息をつきました。 Taisetsu na shiken ga owatte, iki o tsukimashita. *With the big exam over, I breathed a sigh of relief.*

iki o tsumete   息を詰めて   *attentively*
[lit. by holding one's breath]
学生は、試験の結果を息を詰めて聞きました。 Gakusei wa, shiken no kekka o iki o tsumete kikimashita. *The students listened attentively to the results of the exam.*

ikinuki o suru   息抜きをする   *to take a breather*
[lit. to draw a breath]
仕事の息抜きをするために、妻と旅行しました。 Shigoto no ikinuki o suru tame ni, tsuma to ryokō shimashita. *I went on a trip with my wife to take a breather from work.*

ikizumaru yō na   息詰まるような   *thrilling*
[lit. like choking]
今日見た映画には、息詰まるような場面がいくつもありました。 Kyō mita eiga niwa, ikizumaru yō na bamen ga ikutsu mo arimashita. *There were many thrilling scenes in the movie I saw today.*

---

imo   芋   *potato*
imo o arau yō   芋を洗うよう   *to be very crowded*
[lit. like washing potaoes]

昨日は祭日で、デパートは芋を洗うようでした。Kinō wa saijitsu de, depāto wa imo o arau yō deshita.   *Yesterday was a holiday, and the department store was very crowded.*

---

in   陰   *behind, back*
  in ni komoru   陰にこもる   *to be pent up*
  [lit. to keep it in the back]
  彼には不満が陰にこもっているようです。Kare niwa fuman ga in ni komotte iru yō desu.   *He seems to have some pent-up discontent.*

---

inga   因果   *cause and effect*
  inga o fukumeru   因果を含める   *to persuade someone to accept his or her fate*
  [lit. to include cause and effect]
  嫌がる友達に因果を含めて、奥さんに謝らせました。Iyagaru tomodachi ni inga o fukumete, okusan ni ayamarasemashita.   *I persuaded my reluctant friend to accept his fate and apologize to his wife.*

---

inochi   命   *life*
  inochi no oya   命の親   *savior*
  [lit. the parent of someone's life]
  失業中の私に仕事をくれた彼は、命の親です。Shitsugyō chū no watakushi ni shigoto o kureta kare wa inochi no oya desu.   *He is my savior because he gave me a job when I was unemployed.*

  inochi no sentaku   命の洗濯   *diversion*
  [lit. laundering of life]
  命の洗濯として、一週間温泉に行きました。Inochi no sentaku to shite, isshūkan onsen ni ikimashita.   *As a diversion, I went to a hot springs resort for a week.*

  inochi no tsuna   命の綱   *lifeblood*
  [lit. a rope for life]
  輸出産業は、日本にとって命の綱です。Yushutsu sangyō wa,

Nihon ni totte inochi no tsuna desu.   *The export industries are Japan's lifeblood.*

inochishirazu   命知らず   *reckless*
[lit. not knowing one's own life]
彼は命知らずに車を運転します。
Kare wa inochishirazu ni kuruma o unten shimasu.   *He drives a car recklessly.*

inu   犬   *dog*

inu mo kuwanai   犬も食わない   *Nobody takes it seriously.*
[lit. Even a dog won't eat.]
君たちはつまらないことで口論しているけれど、犬も食わ
ないよ。Kimitachi wa tsumaranai koto de kōron shite iru keredo, inu mo kuwanai yo.   *You're arguing over something trivial, so nobody will take it seriously.*

inu to saru   犬と猿   *to be on bad terms*
[lit. a dog and a monkey]
彼らは犬と猿で、会うといつも口げんかになります。
Karera wa inu to saru de, au to itsumo kuchigenka ni narimasu. *They're on bad terms, and they quarrel whenever they meet.*

inujinisuru   犬死にする   *to die in vain*
[lit. to die like a dog]
彼の死は、全くの犬死にでした。Kare no shi wa, mattaku no inujini deshita.   *He died in vain.*

iro   色   *color*

iro ga aseru   色があせる   *to lose attractiveness*
[lit. The color fades.]
あの政治家の人気は、二年で色があせてしまいました。
Ano seijika no ninki wa, ninen de iro ga asete shimaimashita. *Within two years, the politician lost popularity.*

iro o nasu   色をなす   *to turn red with anger*
[lit. to turn color]
友達の親切な助言なのに、彼はそれを聞いて色をなしました。

Tomodachi no shinsetsu na jogen nanoni, kare wa sore o kiite iro o nashimashita.   *His friend's advice was meant well, but hearing it, he turned red with anger.*

iro o tsukeru   色を付ける   *to throw in something extra*
[lit. to color something]
もう少し色を付けてくれたら、それを買ってもいいです。
Mō sukoshi iro o tsukete kuretara, sore o kattemo ii desu.   *If you throw in something extra, I'll buy it.*

iro o ushinau   色を失う   *to lose one's composure*
[lit. to lose color]
突然の悲しい知らせに、色を失ってしまいました。
Totsuzen no kanashii shirase ni, iro o ushinatte shimaimashita. *Hearing the sudden sad news, I lost my composure.*

irojikake   色仕掛け   *pretense of love*
[lit. a trick of color]
彼は色仕掛けで、彼女から借金することに成功しました。
Kare wa irojikake de, kanojo kara shakkin suru koto ni seikō shimashita.   *Under the pretense of love, he succeeded in borrowing money from her.*

iromegane de miru   色眼鏡で見る   *to have biased opinions*
[lit. to see things through tinted eyeglasses]
彼女には、何事も色眼鏡で見る傾向があります。Kanojo niwa, nanigoto mo iromegane de miru keikō ga arimasu.   *She tends to have biased opinions.*

iromeku   色めく   *to get excited*
[lit. to become colorful]
町の人はみんな、今お祭りで色めいています。Machi no hito wa minna, ima omatsuri de iromeite imasu.   *All the townspeople are excited about the festival taking place now.*

ironaoshi   色直し   *bride's changing clothes during the wedding reception*
[lit. a change of color]
花嫁は、披露宴で何度色直しをしましたか。Hanayome wa,

hirōen de nando ironaoshi o shimashita ka.   *How often did the bride change her clothes during the wedding reception?*

irowake   色分け   *classification*
[lit. a separation of color]
応募者を、まず特技によって色分けしました。
Ōbosha o, mazu tokugi ni yotte irowake shimashita.
First we classified the applicants according to their special skills.

---

isha   医者   *doctor*
yabuisha   薮医者   *incompetent doctor*
[lit. a bush doctor]
あの病院は、薮医者が多いという噂があります。Ano byōin wa, yabuisha ga ōi to iu uwasa ga arimasu.   *There's a rumor that the hospital has many incompetent doctors.*

---

ishi   石   *stone*
ishi ni kajiritsuitemo   石にかじりついても   *no matter what*
[lit. even biting into a stone]
石にかじりついても、願いを遂げるつもりです。Ishi ni kajiritsuitemo, negai o togeru tsumori desu.   *I intend to make my wish come true no matter what.*

ishiatama   石頭   *someone inflexible*
[lit. a stone head]
彼は石頭だから、それをいくら説明しても無駄です。Kare wa ishiatama dakara, sore o ikura setsumei shitemo muda desu.   *Because he's inflexible, it doesn't matter how much you explain it to him.*

---

ita   板   *board*
ita ni tsuku   板につく   *to get used to something*
[lit. to belong to a board]
二番目の子供が産まれて、彼の父親ぶりも板につきました。
Nibanme no kodomo ga umarete, kare no chichioya buri mo ita ni tsukimashita.   *With his second child, he's gotten used to being a father.*

itabasami   板挟み   *in a fix, torn*
[lit. to be squeezed between boards]
彼は、義理と人情の板挟みになっています。Kare wa, giri to
ninjō no itabasami ni natte imasu. *He's torn between his
sympathy and his sense of duty.*

tateita ni mizu   立て板に水   *glibly*
[lit. like water running on a standing board]
彼は立て板に水のように話します。Kare wa tateita ni mizu no
yō ni hanashimasu. *He's a glib talker.*

---

itachi   鼬   *weasel*
itachigokko   鼬ごっこ   *to be in a vicious circle*
[lit. weasels' play]
物価と賃金の上昇の鼬ごっこが起こっています。Bukka to
chingin no jōshō no itachigokko ga okotte imasu. *The
vicious circle between the increase in prices and in wages has
begun.*

---

itai   痛い   *painful*
itai me ni au   痛い目にあう   *to have a bitter experience*
[lit. to encounter a painful eye]
彼女を信用したために、痛い目にあいました。Kanojo o
shin-yō shita tame ni, itai me ni aimashita. *Because I trusted
her, I had a bitter experience.*

itakumo kayukumo nai   痛くも痒くもない   *to not
affect one at all*
[lit. neither painful nor itchy]
彼が私をいくら批判しても、痛くも痒くもありません。
Kare ga watakushi o ikura hihan shitemo, itakumo kayukumo
arimasen. *Even if he criticizes me a lot, it doesn't affect me at
all.*

itashi kayushi   痛し痒し   *in a quandary*
[lit. painful and itchy at the same time]
昇進はしたけれど、出張が増えて痛し痒しです。Shōshin
wa shita keredo, shutchō ga fuete itashi kayushi desu.

Although I was promoted, I'm in a quandary because I have to make more business trips.

---

ito   糸   *thread*

ito o hiku   糸を引く   *to manipulate*

[lit. to pull thread]

この抗議運動は、ある政党が糸を引いているそうです。
   Kono kōgi undō wa, aru seitō ga ito o hiite iru sō desu.   *It's said that a certain political party is manipulating this protest movement.*

itoguchi   糸口   *clue, first step*

[lit. the end of thread]

それが、問題解決の糸口になりました。Sore ga, mondai kaiketsu no itoguchi ni narimashita.   *That turned out to be the first step toward solving the problem.*

---

iya   否、嫌   *no*

iya demo ō demo   否でも応でも   *like it or not*

[lit. if it's yes or no]

否でも応でも、会議には出席しなければなりません。Iya demo ō demo, kaigi niwa shusseki shinakereba narimasen.   *Like it or not, you must attend the meeting.*

iya to iu hodo   嫌というほど   *enough*

[lit. to the extent that one says no]

昨日の晩は、嫌というほど鮨を食べました。Kinō no ban wa, iya to iu hodo sushi o tabemashita.   *Last night I ate enough sushi.*

J

---

ja   蛇   *snake*

ja no michi wa hebi   蛇の道は蛇   *It takes one to know one.*

[lit. Snakes know snakes' paths.]

蛇の道は蛇だから、彼が何をたくらんでいるか分かります。

Ja no michi wa hebi dakara, kare ga nani o takurande iru ka wakarimasu.   *Because it takes one to know one, I understand what he's plotting.*

---

ji   時   *hour*

jikan o kasegu   時間を稼ぐ   *to buy time, to get an extension of time*

[lit. to earn time]

病気を理由に、締め切りまでの時間を稼ぎました。Byōki o riyū ni, shimekiri made no jikan o kasegimashita.   *By pleading illness, I got the deadline extended.*

jiryū ni noru   時流に乗る   *to be trendy*

[lit. to ride on the flow of the times]

あの店は時流に乗って、若い人たちの間で人気があります。 Ano mise wa jiryū ni notte, wakai hitotachi no aida de ninki ga arimasu.   *Because that shop is trendy, it's popular among young people.*

---

ji   地   *ground*

ji de iku   地でいく   *to behave naturally*

[lit. to go with the ground]

どんな集まりか知りませんが、私は地でいくつもりです。 Donna atsumari ka shirimasen ga, watakushi wa ji de iku tsumori desu.   *I don't know what kind of gathering it's going to be, but I'll just behave naturally.*

jidanda o fumu   地団駄を踏む   *to be mortified*

[lit. to stamp on the ground]

彼は自分の提案が採用されなくて、地団駄を踏みました。 Kare wa jibun no teian ga saiyō sarenakute, jidanda o fumimashita.   *He was mortified that his suggestion wasn't adopted.*

---

ji   自   *self*

ji ta tomo ni yurusu   自他ともに許す   *acknowledged*

[lit. to be accepted by both oneself and others]

彼女は自他ともに許す、社会問題の権威です。Kanojo wa ji

ta tomo ni yurusu, shakai mondai no ken-i desu. *She's the acknowledged authority on social issues.*

jibara o kiru　自腹を切る　*to pay out of one's own pocket*

[lit. to cut one's own belly]

出張で、洗濯代は自腹を切りました。Shutchō de, sentaku dai wa jibara o kirimashita. *On the business trip, I paid my laundry costs out of my own pocket.*

jigajisan suru　自画自賛する　*to praise one's own achievement*

[lit. to praise one's own painting]

彼女は自分の報告書を自画自賛しています。Kanojo wa jibun no hōkokusho o jigajisan shite imasu. *She's praising her own report.*

---

jigane　地金　*core metal*

jigane o dasu　地金を出す　*to reveal one's true colors*

[lit. to show core metal]

彼女は話している内に、地金を出してしまいました。 Kanojo wa hanashite iru uchi ni, jigane o dashite shimaimashita. *While talking, she unintentionally revealed her true colors.*

---

jigoku　地獄　*hell*

jigoku de hotoke　地獄で仏　*A friend in need (is a friend indeed).*

[lit. meeting the Buddha in hell]

私の車が故障したそのときにフレッドが車で通りかかって、正に地獄で仏でした。Watakushi no kuruma ga koshō shita sono toki ni Fureddo ga kuruma de tōri kakatte, masa ni jigoku de hotoke deshita. *Fred was truly "a friend in need" when he drove by just as my car broke down.*

jigokumimi　地獄耳　*to have a nose for news*

[lit. hellish ears]

彼は地獄耳だから、気をつけなさい。Kare wa jigokumimi

dakara, ki o tsukenasai. *Be careful around him: he has a nose for news.*

---

jo 序 *order*

jo no kuchi   序の口   *beginning, start*

[lit. the lowest class in the sumo tournament]

このくらいの湿気はまだ序の口で、これからもっと高くなります。Kono kurai no shikke wa mada jo no kuchi de, kore kara motto takaku narimasu. *This humidity is just the beginning; it will get much higher from now on.*

---

jō 情 *feeling*

jō ga fukai   情が深い   *warm-hearted*

[lit. One's feeling is deep.]

彼女は情が深いので、誰からも好かれます。Kanojo wa jō ga fukai node, dare kara mo sukaremasu. *Because she's warm-hearted, she's well liked.*

jō ga usui   情が薄い   *cold-hearted*

[lit. One's feeling is thin.]

彼は情が薄くて、人の気持ちを理解しようとしません。Kare wa jō ga usukute, hito no kimochi o rikai shiyō to shimasen. *He's cold-hearted and doesn't try to understand other people's feelings.*

jō ga utsuru   情が移る   *to become attached to someone or to an animal*

[lit. One's feeling shifts.]

友達の猫を一週間預かっていたら、情が移ってしまいました。Tomodachi no neko o isshūkan azukatte itara, jō ga utsutte shimaimashita. *While I was keeping my friend's cat for a week, I got attached to it.*

jō ni moroi   情にもろい   *soft-hearted*

[lit. sensitive to someone's feelings.]

彼は情にもろいので、借金に来る人がたくさんいます。Kare wa jō ni moroi node, shakkin ni kuru hito ga takusan imasu. *Since he's soft-hearted, many people come to him to*

135

borrow money.

---

jūbako   重箱   *stack of lacquer boxes*
  jūbako no sumi o hojikuru   重箱の隅をほじくる   *to*
    be very fussy
  [lit. to pick a corner of a lacquer box]
  彼は、重箱の隅をほじくるような男です。Kare wa, jūbako
    no sumi o hojikuru yō na otoko desu.   *He' a very fussy guy.*

---

jūhachi   十八   *eighteen*
  jūhachiban   十八番   *one's forte*
  [lit. the eighteenth]
  ピアノ演奏が、彼女の十八番です。Piano ensō ga, kanojo no
    jūhachiban desu.   *Playing the piano is her forte.*

---

jūnin   十人   *ten people*
  jūnin toiro   十人十色   *It takes all kinds.*
  [lit. ten people with ten different colors]
  会議では違った意見がたくさんありましたが、それも十人
    十色だからです。Kaigi dewa chigatta iken ga takusan
    arimashita ga, sore mo jūnin toiro dakara desu.   *There were so*
    many different opinions in the meeting; but as they say, "It
    takes all kinds."

  jūninnami   十人並み   *average, ordinary*
  [lit. just like ten other people]
  彼には、十人並みの才能しかありません。Kare niwa,
    jūninnami no sainō shika arimasen.   *He has only average*
    talent.

---

jutsu   術   *tactic*
  jutchū ni ochiiru   術中に陥る   *to fall into a trap*
  [lit. to fall into a tactic]
  上司の術中に陥り、土曜出勤の約束をしてしまいました。
    Jōshi no jutchū ni ochiiri, doyō shukkin no yakusoku o shite
    shimaimashita.   *I fell into my boss's trap and promised to*
    come to work on Saturday.

K

ka 蚊 *mosquito*
  ka ga naku yō na koe de 蚊が鳴くような声で *in a whisper*
  [lit. with a voice like a mosquito's buzzing]
  彼は蚊が鳴くような声で、秘密を打ち明けました。Kare wa ka ga naku yō na koe de, himitsu o uchiakemashita. *He confided his secret to me in a whisper.*

kaban 鞄 *bag, briefcase*
  kabanmochi 鞄持ち *assistant, secretary*
  [lit. someone carrying a briefcase]
  彼は顧問のように振る舞っているけれど、実は鞄持ちに過ぎません。Kare wa komon no yō ni furumatte iru keredo, jitsu wa kabanmochi ni sugimasen. *He's pretending to be an advisor, but actually he's only an assistant.*

kabe 壁 *wall*
  kabe ni tsukiataru 壁に突き当たる *to hit a snag, to be bogged down*
  [lit. to run into a wall]
  貿易交渉は、壁に突き当たっています。Bōeki kōshō wa, kabe ni tsukiatatte imasu. *The trade negotiations are bogged down.*

kabi 黴 *mold*
  kabi ga haeru 黴が生える *to become antiquated*
  [lit. Mold grows.]
  彼の考えは、黴が生えています。Kare no kangae wa, kabi ga haete imasu. *His ideas have become antiquated.*

kabu 株 *stock*
  kabu ga agaru 株が上がる *to gain respect*
  [lit. One's stock goes up.]
  大切な契約をいくつも取って、社内での株が上がりました。

Taisetsu na keiyaku o ikutsu mo totte, shanai de no kabu ga agarimashita.   *I gained respect in the company by winning many important contracts.*

okabu o ubawareru   お株を奪われる   *to be outdone by someone*
[lit. One's stock is robbed.]
彼は歌が得意ですが、昨日は同僚にお株を奪われてしまいました。 Kare wa uta ga tokui desu ga, kinō wa dōryō ni okabu o ubawarete shimaimashita.   *He sings well, but he was outdone by his colleague yesterday.*

---

kabuto   兜   *helmet*
kabuto o nugu   兜を脱ぐ   *to admit defeat*
[lit. to take a helmet off]
市場調査の分野で、競争会社に兜を脱ぎました。 Shijō chōsa no bun-ya de, kyōsō gaisha ni kabuto o nugimashita. *We admitted defeat to our competitor in the field of market research.*

---

kachi   勝ち   *victory*
kachi ni jōjiru   勝ちに乗じる   *to follow up a victory*
[lit. to ride on a victory]
共和党は選挙での勝ちに乗じて、法案を次々に提出しました。 Kyōwatō wa senkyo deno kachi ni jōjite, hōan o tsugitsugi ni teishutsu shimashita.   *To follow up their election victory, the Republicans introduced successive bills.*

---

kado   角   *corner, angle*
kado ga tasu   角が立つ   *to aggravate*
[lit. Angles stand up.]
角が立たないように、言葉遣いに気をつけなさい。 Kado ga tatanai yō ni, kotobazukai ni ki o tsukenasai.   *Pay attention to what you say, and don't aggravate anyone.*

kado ga toreru   角が取れる   *to mellow*
[lit. Angles come off.]
社長も角が取れて、話しやすくなりました。 Shachō mo

kado ga torete, hanashiyasuku narimashita.   *The president has
mellowed, and it has become easier to talk to him.*

kadoban ni tatsu   角番に立つ   *to face a critical phase*
[lit. to stand at the corner of a board]
彼は大学を卒業できるかできないか、角番に立っています。
Kare wa daigaku o sotsugyō dekiru ka dekinai ka, kadoban ni
tatte imasu.   *He's facing a critical phase: whether or not he
can graduate from college.*

me ni kado o tatete   目に角を立てて   *with eyes glaring*
[lit. by making one's eyes angled]
彼女は目に角を立てて、私を見つめました。 Kanojo wa me
ni kado o tatete, watakushi o mitsumemashita.   *She stared at
me with eyes glaring.*

---

kage   陰   *shade*
  kage de ito o hiku   陰で糸を引く   *to control behind the
  scenes*
  [lit. to pull a string in the shade]
  あの政治派閥は、彼が陰で糸を引いています。 Ano seiji
  habatsu wa, kare ga kage de ito o hiite imasu.   *He is
  controlling the political faction behind the scenes.*

  kage ni nari hinata ni nari   陰になり日向になり   *both
  openly and discreetly*
  [lit. both in the shade and the sun]
  彼女は陰になり日向になり、私の経歴を助けてくれました。
  Kanojo wa kage ni nari hinata ni nari, watakushi no keireki o
  tasukete kuremashita.   *She supported my career both openly
  and discreetly.*

  kageguchi o tataku   陰口をたたく   *to stab someone in
  the back*
  [lit. to drum up backbites]
  彼がいくら陰口をたたいても、私の信用は落ちません。
  Kare ga ikura kageguchi o tataitemo, watakushi no shin-yō wa
  ochimasen.   *No matter how much he stabs me in the back, my
  reputation won't suffer.*

---

kagehinata ga aru   陰日向がある   *to be two-faced*
[lit. to have both the shady and the sunny spot]
彼女には何事にも陰日向があるので、信用できません。
　　Kanojo niwa nanigoto nimo kagehinata ga aru node, shin-yō
　　dekimasen.   *I can't trust her; she's two-faced about
　　everything.*

---

kage   影   *shadow, silhouette*
  kage ga sasu   影が差す   *to go wrong*
  [lit. A shadow covers something.]
  二人の関係に影が差し始めたのは、誰の目にも明らかでした。
　　Futari no kankei ni kage ga sashihajimeta nowa, dare no me ni
　　mo akiraka deshita.   *It was clear that the couple's
　　relationship began to sour.*

  kage ga usui   影が薄い   *to take a back seat*
  [lit. One's shadow is light.]
  新しい技術が導入されて、熟練工の影が薄くなりました。
　　Atarashii gijutsu ga dōnyū sarete, jukurenkō no kage ga usuku
　　narimashita.   *With the introduction of new technology, the
　　skilled workers took back seats.*

  kage mo katachi mo nai   影も形もない   *to be
  nonexistent*
  [lit. There is no shape or shadow.]
  去年すごく流行った歌手は、今年は陰も形もありません。
　　Kyonen sugoku hayatta kashu wa, kotoshi wa kage mo katachi
　　mo arimasen.   *This year we haven't heard a thing about the
　　singer who was extremely popular last year.*

  kage o hisomeru   影を潜める   *to lie low*
  [lit. to conceal one's shadow]
  あの政治家は落選して以来、影を潜めています。Ano seijika
　　wa rakusen shite irai, kage o hisomete imasu.   *That politician
　　has been lying low since losing the election.*

  miru kage mo nai   見る影もない   *to be down and out*
  [lit. There isn't even a shadow to look at.]
  彼は大金持ちでしたが、今は見る影もありません。

Kare wa ōganemochi deshita ga, ima wa miru kage mo arimasen. *He was an extremely wealthy man, but now he's down and out.*

kaji   舵   *helm*

kaji o toru   舵をとる   *to be at the helm*

[lit. to steer]

この会社では、社長の代わりに息子が舵を取っています。
Kono kaisha dewa, shachō no kawari ni musuko ga kaji o totte imasu. *Instead of the president, his son is at the helm of this company.*

kakeru   駆ける   *to run*

kakedashi   駆け出し   *greenhorn*

[lit. someone who is starting to run]

彼女は弁護士としては、まだ駆け出しです。Kanojo wa bengoshi toshite wa, mada kakedashi desu. *As a lawyer, she's still a greenhorn.*

kakeochisuru   駆け落ちする   *to elope*

[lit. to run and drop out]

親が結婚に反対したので、彼女とボーイフレンドは駆け落ちしました。Oya ga kekkon ni hantai shita node, kanojo to bōifurendo wa kakeochi shimashita. *Since her parents opposed the marriage, she and her boyfriend eloped.*

kama   鎌   *sickle*

kama o kakeru   鎌をかける   *to ask leading questions*

[lit. to apply a sickle]

彼女は人の秘密を聞き出すため、鎌をかけるのが上手です。Kanojo wa hito no himitsu o kikidasu tame, kama o kakeru no ga jōzu desu. *She's good at asking leading questions to find out other people's secrets.*

kami   紙   *paper*

kami hitoe no sa   紙一重の差   *slight difference, paper-thin margin*

[lit. the difference of the thickness of a sheet of paper]

私が支持する候補者は、紙一重の差で勝てて幸運でした。
Watakushi ga shiji suru kōhosha wa, kami hitoe no sa de katete
kōun deshita.　*The candidate I supported was lucky to win by
a paper-thin margin.*

---

kami　　　神　　　*god*
　　kamiwaza　　　神業　　　*superhuman feat*
　　[lit. the work of a god]
彼の発明は、まさに神業でした。Kare no hatsumei wa, masa
　　ni kamiwaza deshita.　*His invention was truly a superhuman
　　feat.*

---

kaminari　　　雷　　　*thunder*
　　kaminari o otosu　　　雷を落とす　　　*to explode at someone*
　　[lit. to drop thunder]
弟がテレビばかり見ているので、父が雷を落としました。
　　Otōto ga terebi bakari mite iru node, chichi ga kaminari o
　　otoshimashita.　*My father exploded at my younger brother
　　because he does nothing but watch TV.*

　　kaminari oyaji　　　雷親父　　　*snarling old man*
　　[lit. a thundering old man]
彼はよく怒るので、みんなは陰で雷親父と呼んでいます。
　　Kare wa yoku okoru node, minna wa kage de kaminari oyaji to
　　yonde imasu.　*Since he easily gets angry, everyone calls him a
　　snarling old man behind his back.*

---

kamo　　　鴨　　　*duck*
　　ii kamo　　　いい鴨　　　*sucker*
　　[lit. a good duck]
値切り方を知らなかったため、海外旅行でいい鴨になって
　　しまいました。Negirikata o shiranakatta tame, Kaigai ryokō
　　de ii kamo ni natte shimaimashita.　*I was a sucker for
　　merchants on my trip abroad since I didn't know how to
　　haggle.*

　　kamo ni suru　　　鴨にする　　　*to victimize someone*

[lit. to make a duck of someone]

彼は消費者を鴨にして、安物を高額で売りつけました。

Kare wa shōhisha o kamo ni shite, yasumono o kōgaku de uritsukemashita. *He victimized consumers, selling them cheap products at high prices.*

---

kamu 噛む *to bite, chew*

kande fukumeru yō ni 噛んで含めるように *carefully and repeatedly*

[lit. like chewing something and holding it in one's mouth]

先生は、それを生徒に噛んで含めるように説明しました。

Sensei wa, sore o seito ni kande fukumeru yō ni setsumei shimashita. *The teacher explained it to the pupils carefully and repeatedly.*

kande hakidasu yō ni 噛んで吐き出すように *disgustedly*

[lit. like biting something and then spitting it out]

彼女は噛んで吐き出すように、自分の誤りを認めました。

Kanojo wa kande hakidasu yō ni, jibun no ayamari o mitomemashita. *Disgustedly, she admitted her mistake.*

---

kan 間 *space*

kan ippatsu de 間一髪で *narrowly*

[lit. with the breadth of a hair]

締め切りは、間一髪で間に合いました。Shimekiri wa, kan ippatsu de maniaimashita. *I narrowly met the deadline.*

---

kanban 看板 *signboard*

kanban ga naku 看板が泣く *to be shameful to one's reputation*

[lit. A signboard cries.]

そんな品質が悪いものを売ると、看板が泣きますよ。Sonna hinshitsu ga warui mono o uru to, kanban ga nakimasu yo. *It's shameful for the store's good name to sell such poor-quality products.*

kanban o nurikaeru 看板を塗り替える *to change*

[lit. to repaint a signboard]

彼女は医者の看板を塗り替えて、小説家になりま
  した。Kanojo wa isha no kanban o nurikaete, shōsetsuka ni
  narimashita. *She changed her occupation from doctor to
  novelist.*

kanban o orosu   看板を下ろす   *to close a shop*
[lit. to take a signboard down]

近くにスーパーができて、駅前の肉屋は看板を下ろしました。
Chikaku ni sūpā ga dekite, ekimae no nikuya wa kanban o
  oroshimashita. *The butcher near the station closed his shop
  after a supermarket had opened nearby.*

kanbandaore   看板倒れ   *showy but little substance*
[lit. falling of a signboard]

政府の実行計画は看板倒れでした。Seifu no jikkō keikaku wa
  kanbandaore deshita. *The action plan by the government was
  showy, but it had little substance.*

---

kane   金   *money*

kane ga mono o iu   金が物を言う   *Money talks.*
[lit. Money talks.]

選挙運動では、金がものを言うと言われています。Senkyo
  undō dewa, kane ga mono o iu to iwarete imasu. *They say
  money talks in election campaigns.*

kane ga unaru   金がうなる   *to have lots of money*
[lit. Money is humming.]

彼女の家には、金がうなっています。Kanojo no ie niwa,
  kane ga unatte imasu. *Her family has lots of money.*

kane ni akasu   金に飽かす   *to pour in unlimited
  amounts of money*
[lit. to make someone bored with money]

彼は金に飽かせて、土地を買いまくりました。Kare wa kane
  ni akasete, tochi o kaimakurimashita. *He kept buying pieces
  of land by pouring in unlimited amounts of money.*

kane ni itome o tsukenai   金に糸目をつけない   *Money*

is no object.

[lit. to not attach strings to money]

彼は絵画収集のためには、金に糸目をつけません。Kare wa kaiga shūshū no tame niwa, kane ni itome o tsukemasen. *When he collects paintings, money is no object.*

kane no naru ki   金のなる木   *source of unlimited money*

[lit. a tree that bears money]

彼女にとって、お母さんは金のなる木です。Kanojo ni totte, okāsan wa kane no nari ki desu. *For her, her mother is a source of unlimited money.*

kane o nekasu   金を寝かす   *to let money sit idle*

[lit. to make money sleep]

金を寝かして置くよりも、株に長期投資した方がいいですよ。Kane o nekashite oku yori mo, kabu ni chōki tōshi shita hō ga ii desu yo. *It's better to invest in stocks for a long term rather than letting money sit idle.*

kane o nigiraseru   金を握らせる   *to grease someone's palm*

[lit. to let someone grasp money]

彼は医者に金を握らせて、病院の個室をもらいました。Kare wa isha ni kane o nigirasete, byōin no koshitsu o moraimashita. *He got a private room in the hospital by greasing the palm of a doctor.*

kanezuku de   金ずくで   *by sheer force of money*

[lit. totally by money]

彼女は金ずくで、その会社を買い取りました。Kanojo wa kanezuku de sono kaisha o kaitorimashita. *She purchased the company by sheer force of money.*

---

kane   鉦   *bell*

kane ya taiko de sagasu   鉦や太鼓で探す   *to search for someone or something actively*

[lit. to search for someone or something with a bell and a drum]

新しくできた野球のチームは、監督を鉦や太鼓で探して

いています。Atarashiku dekita yakyū no chīmu wa, kantoku o
kane ya taiko de sagashite imasu. *The newly organized
baseball team is actively searching for a manager.*

---

kankei   関係   *relation*
  sankaku kankei   三角関係   *love triangle*
  [lit. a triangular relation]
  彼は今、三角関係で悩んでいます。Kare wa ima, sankaku
    kankei de nayande imasu. *He's suffering in a love triangle
    now.*

---

kanmuri   冠   *crown*
  kanmuri o mageru   冠を曲げる   *to get upset*
  [lit. to tilt a crown]
  私が結婚記念日を忘れたので、妻は冠を曲げました。
    Watakushi ga kekkon kinenbi o wasureta node, tsuma wa
    kanmuri o magemashita. *My wife got upset when I forgot our
    wedding anniversary.*

---

kanshin   歓心   *favor*
  kanshin o kau   歓心を買う   *to curry favor with someone*
  [lit. to buy someone favor]
  得意先をゴルフに招待して、歓心を買いました。Tokuisaki
    o gorufu ni shōtai shite, kanshin o kaimashita. *I curried favor
    with the clients by inviting them to play golf.*

---

kantan   肝胆   *liver and gall*
  kantan aiterasu   肝胆相照らす   *to be close friends*
  [lit. to compare each other's liver and gall]
  彼とは肝胆相照らす仲なので、何でも打ち明けられます。
  Kare to wa kantan aiterasu naka nanode, nandemo
    uchiakeraremasu. *Because we're close friends, I can confide
    in him about anything.*

  kantan o hiraku   肝胆を開く   *to unburden one's
  heart to someone*

[lit. to open up one's liver and gall]

彼女には悩みがあるけれど、肝胆を開く相手がいません。

Kanojo niwa nayami ga aru keredo, kantan o hiraku aite ga imasen.   *Although she has major problems, she doesn't have anyone to whom she can unburden her heart.*

---

kao   顔   *face*

kao ga au   顔が合う   *to come across someone*

[lit. Faces meet.]

彼女と、思いがけないところで顔が合いました。Kanojo to, omoigakenai tokoro de kao ga aimashita.   *I came across her in an unexpected place.*

kao ga hiroi   顔が広い   *to know many people*

[lit. One's face is wide.]

彼は顔が広いので、仕事探しの相談に行きました。Kare wa kao ga hiroi node, shigoto sagashi no sōdan ni ikimashita. *Since he knows many people, I went to confer with him before job hunting.*

kao ga kiku   顔が利く   *to be influential*

[lit. One's face is effective.]

彼は財界で顔が利きます。Kare wa zaikai de kao ga kikimasu. *He's influential in business circles.*

kao ga sorou   顔が揃う   *to have everybody present*

[lit. All faces gather.]

顔が揃ったので、会議を始めましょう。Kao ga sorotta node, kaigi o hajimemashō.   *We have everybody here, so let's start the meeting.*

kao ga tatsu   顔が立つ   *to save one's honor*

[lit. One's face stands up.]

約束を無事に果たせて、顔が立ちました。Yakusoku o buji ni hatasete, kao ga tachimashita.   *I saved my reputation when I fulfilled my promise without any problems.*

kao ga tsubureru   顔が潰れる   *to lose face*

[lit. One's face falls to pieces.]

担当した企画の結果が思わしくなくて、顔が潰れました。
Tantō shita kikaku no kekka ga omowashiku nakute, kao ga
tsuburemashita.   *I lost face when the project I took charge of
didn't turn out well.*

kao ga ureru   顔が売れる   *to be widely known*
[lit. One's face is selling.]
彼女は新進の作家として、顔が売れています。 Kanojo wa
shinshin no sakka to shite, kao ga urete imasu.   *She has
become widely known as a rising novelist.*

kao kara hi ga deru   顔から火が出る   *to blush*
[lit. Flame comes out of one's face.]
宿題を持ってくるのを忘れて、顔から火が出ました。
Shukudai o motte kuru no o wasurete, kao kara hi ga
demashita.   *I blushed because I forgot to bring my homework
with me.*

kao ni doro o nuru   顔に泥を塗る   *to disgrace oneself*
[lit. to put mud on one's face]
その政治家はインタビューで失言して、自らの顔に泥を塗
りました。 Sono seijika wa intabyū de shitsugen shite,
mizukara no kao ni doro o nurimashita.   *The politician
disgraced himself by making a gaffe during an interview.*

kao o awaseru   顔を合わせる   *to meet*
[lit. to put faces together]
あのチームとは、最終戦でまた顔を合わせることになりそ
うです。 Ano chīmu to wa, saishū sen de mata kao o awaseru
koto ni narisō desu.   *It seems as if we'll meet that team again
in the final game.*

kao o dasu   顔を出す   *to show up*
[lit. to stick one's face out]
その集まりには行きたくなくても、顔を出すべきです。
Sono atsumari ni wa ikitaku nakutemo, kao o dasu beki desu.
*Even if you may not want to go to the gathering, you ought to
show up.*

kao o kasu   顔を貸す   *to give time*

[lit. to lend one's face]

ちょっと話ししたいことがあるので、顔を貸してくれませんか。
Chotto hanashishitai koto ga aru node, kao o kashite kuremasen ka.   *Can you spare a moment? I have something I want to talk to you about.*

kao o kumoraseru   顔を曇らせる   *to look glum*
[lit. to make one's face cloudy]
父は景気後退の長続きに、顔を曇らせています。Chichi wa keiki kōtai no nagatsuzuki ni, kao o kumorasete imasu.   *My father is looking glum because of the long recession.*

kao o miseru   顔を見せる   *to visit*
[lit. to show one's face]
叔母は、最近顔を見せていません。Oba wa, saikin kao o misete imasen.   *My aunt hasn't visited us recently.*

kao o tateru   顔を立てる   *to let someone save face*
[lit. to make someone's face stand]
彼女の顔を立てて、彼女ではなく私が謝りました。Kanojo no kao o tatete, kanojo dewa naku watakushi ga ayamarimashita.   *To let her save face, I apologized rather than letting her do it.*

kao o tsunagu   顔をつなぐ   *to keep one's presence known*
[lit. to connect one's face]
顔をつなぐために、一週間に一度同じバーで飲んでいます。
Kao o tsunagu tame ni, isshūkan ni ichido onaji bā de nonde imasu.   *I drink once a week at the same bar to keep on as a regular customer.*

kaobure   顔触れ   *cast, lineup*
[lit. faces coming in contact with each other]
今度の内閣の顔触れは素晴らしいです。Kondo no naikaku no kaobure wa subarashii desu.   *The lineup of the new cabinet is wonderful.*

kaodashi   顔出し   *token appearance*
[lit. sticking out of one's face]

顔出しだけで結構ですから、是非パーティーに来て下さい。

Kaodashi dake de kekkō desu kara, zehi pātī ni kite kudasai.

Please come to the party; even if it's a token appearance, it's quite all right.

kaoiro o ukagau 顔色をうかがう *to study someone's mood*

[lit. to observe the color of someone's face]

彼女は何かする前、いつも上司の顔色をうかがいます。

Kanojo wa nanika suru mae, itsumo jōshi no kaoiro o ukagaimasu. *She always studies the boss's mood before doing anything.*

kaomake suru 顔負けする *to be shocked at something*

[lit. to lose one's face]

彼の図々しさには顔負けです。kare no zūzūshisa niwa kaomake desu. *I'm shocked at his impertinent manner.*

kaomise 顔見せ *debut*

[lit. showing one's face]

このコンサートで、彼女は芸能界に顔見せしました。Kono konsāto de, kanojo wa geinō kai ni kaomise shimashita. *The concert was her debut in the entertainment business.*

kaomuke dekinai 顔向け出来ない *to be too ashamed to see someone*

[lit. to be unable to turn a face to someone]

大学の入学試験に落ちてしまって、家族に顔向けできません。

Daigaku no nyūgaku shiken ni ochite shimatte, kazoku ni kaomuke dekimasen. *I'm too ashamed to face my family because I failed my college entrance exams.*

kaoyaku 顔役 *man of influence*

[lit. the role of a face]

彼がこの村の顔役です。

Kare ga kono mura no kaoyaku desu.

He's the man of influence in this village.

ōkina kao o suru 大きな顔をする *to act like a big deal*

[lit. to make a big face]

彼は大きな顔をしているけれど、実は課長に過ぎません。
Kare wa ōkina kao o shite iru keredo, jitsu wa kachō ni
sugimasen.   *He's acting like a big deal, but he is, in fact, just
a section chief.*

shoppai kao   しょっぱい顔   *sullen face*
[lit. a salty face]

父はしょっぱい顔をしながら、兄に車を貸しました。
Chichi wa shoppai kao o shinagara, ani ni kuruma o
kashimashita.   *With a sullen face, my father lent his car to my
older brother.*

suzushii kao o suru   涼しい顔をする   *to look
nonchalant*
[lit. to make a cool face]

彼女はみんなに心配をかけながら、全く涼しい顔をしてい
ます。Kanojo wa minna ni shinpai o kakenagara, mattaku
suzushii kao o shite imasu.   *Although she caused everybody to
worry, she looks totally nonchalant.*

wagamonogao   我が物顔   *to be egoistic*
[lit. to behave as if it's one's own]

共同作業なのに、彼女は我が物顔に振る舞っています。
Kyōdō sagyō nanomi, kanojo wa wagamonogao ni furumatte
imasu.   *Although it's a joint operation, she is lording it over
everyone.*

---

kara   殻   *shell*
kara ni tojikomoru   殻に閉じこもる   *to withdraw into
oneself*
[lit. to keep oneself in shells]

彼は引退して以来、殻に閉じこもっています。Kare wa intai
shite irai, kara ni tojikomotte imasu.   *He has withdrawn into
himself since his retirement.*

---

kara   空   *empty*
karaibari   空威張り   *bluff*
[lit. an empty boast]

あれは空威張りだから、気にしなくていいですよ。
Are wa karaibari dakara, ki ni shinakute ii desu yo.
That's a bluff, so you shouldn't pay any attention to it.

karasawagi   空騒ぎ   *much ado about nothing*
[lit. an empty fuss]
大したこと無いのに、みんなが空騒ぎしています。Taishita
koto nai noni, minna ga karasawagi shite imasu.   *Although it's
not a big deal, everybody is making much ado about nothing.*

---

karada   体   *body*
karada ga aku   体が空く   *to have free time*
[lit. One's body is free.]
今は忙しいけれど、来週体が空きます。Ima wa isogashii
keredo, raishū karada ga akimasu.   *I'm busy right now, but I'll
have free time next week.*

karada ga iu koto o kikanai   体が言うことを聞かない
to be physically impossible
[lit. One's body does not listen to what it is told to do.]
富士山に登りたくても、体が言うことを聞きません。
Fujisan ni noboritakutemo, karada ga iu koto o kikimasen.
*Although I want to climb Mt. Fuji, it's physically impossible for
me.*

karada ga tsuzuku   体が続く   *to be in good health*
[lit. One's body continues.]
体が続く限り、引退するつもりはありません。Karada ga
tsuzuku kagiri, intai suru tsumori wa arimasen.   *I have no
intention of retiring as long as I'm in good health.*

karada o haru   体を張る   *to devote one's life to
something*
[lit. to spread one's own body]
彼は体を張って、新しい事業を始めました。Kare wa karada
o hatte, atarashii jigyō o hajimemashita.   *He started a new
business, devoting his life to it.*

karada o kona ni suru   体を粉にする   *to work very hard*

[lit. to turn one's body into powder]

彼は体を粉にして働いて、自分の家を手に入れました。

Kare wa karada o kona ni shite hataraite, jibun no ie o te ni iremashita. *He bought his own house by working very hard.*

karada o kowasu　体を壊す　*to ruin one's health*

[lit. to destroy one's health]

彼女は働きすぎて、体を壊してしまいました。Kanojo wa hatarakisugite, karada o kowashite shimaimashita. *She ruined her health by working too hard.*

---

karai　辛い　*hot, pungent*

karatō　辛党　*drinker*

[lit. a partisan of things hot]

彼は辛党で、特にビールが好きです。Kare wa karatō de, toku ni bīru ga suki desu. *He is a drinker and especially likes beer.*

---

kasa　笠　*bamboo hat*

kasa ni kiru　笠に着る　*to exploit someone's influence*

[lit. to wear something like a bamboo hat]

彼女はお父さんが社長なのを笠に着て、態度が大きいです。

Kanojo wa otōsan ga shachō nano o kasa ni kite, taido ga ōkii desu. *Exploiting her father's influence, the company president's daughter is arrogant.*

---

kasa　嵩　*bulk*

kasa ni kakaru　嵩にかかる　*to be arrogant*

[lit. to put bulk on something]

彼は嵩にかかって、自分の意見を主張しました。Kare wa kasa ni kakatte, jibun no iken o shuchō shimashita. *He pushed his own opinions arrogantly.*

---

kata　肩　*shoulder*

kata de iki o suru　肩で息する　*to gasp for breath*

[lit. to breathe through one's shoulder]

テニスをした後、肩で息をしなければなりませんでした。

Tenisu o shita ato, kata de iki o shinakereba narimasendeshita.
After playing tennis, I had to gasp for breath.

kata de kaze o kiru   肩で風を切る   *to swagger around*
[lit. to cut wind with shoulders]
彼は課長になって以来、肩で風を切っています。Kare wa
　kachō ni natte irai, kata de kaze o kitte imasu.　*He has been
　swaggering around since he advanced to section chief.*

kata ga haru   肩が張る   *to be tense*
[lit. One's shoulders get stiff.]
出張は社長と一緒だったため、肩が張りました。Shutchō
　wa shachō to issho datta tame, kata ga harimashita.　*I was
　tense because the business trip was with the president.*

kata ga karukunaru   肩が軽くなる   *to feel relieved*
[lit. One's shoulders become light.]
子供たちが大学を卒業して、肩が軽くなりました。
　Kodomotachi ga daigaku o sotsugyō shite, kata ga karuku
　narimashita.　*I feel relieved that all my children graduated
　from college.*

kata ga koru   肩が凝る   *to get a stiff neck*
[lit. One's shoulders get stiff.]
締め切り続きで、肩が凝りました。Shimekiri tsuzuki de, kata
　ga korimashita.　*With the deadlines coming one after another,
　I got a stiff neck.*

kata no ni ga oriru   肩の荷がおりる   *to feel relieved*
[lit. A load of packages on one's shoulders comes down.]
約束を果たして、肩の荷がおりました。Yakusoku o
　hatashite, kata no ni ga orimashita.　*I felt relieved at fulfilling
　my promise.*

kata o hogusu   肩をほぐす   *to relax*
[lit. to loosen one's shoulders]
彼女はご主人が無事なことを聞いて、肩をほぐしました。
　Kanojo wa goshujin ga buji na koto o kiite, kata o
　hogushimashita.　*She relaxed on hearing that her husband
　was safe.*

kata o ikaraseru　　　肩を怒らせる　　*to get angry*
[lit. to make one's own shoulders stiffen]
彼は肩を怒らせて、息子を非難しました。Kare wa kata o
　ikarasete, musuko o hinan shimashita.　*He angrily accused his
　son.*

kata o ireru　　　肩を入れる　　*to back someone or something*
[lit. to put one's shoulders in]
彼女は長いこと、女性問題に肩を入れています。Kanojo wa
　nagai koto josei mondai ni kata o irete imasu.　*She has been
　backing women's issues for a long time.*

kata o motsu　　　肩を持つ　　*to take sides with someone*
[lit. to hold someone's shoulders]
昨日父と母が口論したとき、母の肩を持ちました。Kinō
　chichi to haha ga kōron shita toki, haha no kata o
　mochimashita.　*I took sides with Mother when she and Father
　had an argument yesterday.*

kata o naraberu　　　肩を並べる　　*to equal, to rival*
[lit. to put shoulders side by side]
スキーが上手になって、指導員と肩を並べるようになりま
　した。Sukī ga jōzu ni natte, shidōin to kata o naraberu yō ni
　narimashita.　*My skiing has become good enough to rival that
　of any instructor.*

kata o otosu　　　肩を落とす　　*to feel dejected*
[lit. to drop one's shoulders]
彼は結婚の申し込みを断られて、肩を落としています。
　Kare wa kekkon no mōshikomi o kotowararete, kata o otoshite
　imasu.　*He's feeling dejected because his marriage proposal
　was rejected.*

kata o sobiyakasu　　　肩をそびやかす　　*to swell with pride*
[lit. to perk up one's shoulders]
彼は課長になって、肩をそびやかしています。Kare wa
　kachō ni natte, kata o sobiyakashite imasu.　*He is swelling
　with pride at becoming a section chief.*

katagaki　　　肩書き　　*title*

[lit. writing on a shoulder]

彼の会社での肩書きは何ですか。 Kare no kaisha deno katagaki wa nan desu ka. *What is his title in his company?*

katagawari   肩代わり   *to assume someone else's responsibilities*

[lit. switching one's shoulders with someone else's]

私はいま妹の肩代わりで、借金を支払っています。 Watakushi wa ima imōto no katagawari de, shakkin o shiharatte imasu. *I'm now assuming my younger sister's responsibilities by paying her debts.*

katami ga hiroi   肩身が広い   *to be proud of someone or something*

[lit. One's body and shoulders are wide.]

娘が医者になって、肩身が広い思いです。 Musume ga isha ni natte, katami ga hiroi omoi desu. *I am proud of my daughter's becoming a medical doctor.*

katami ga semai   肩身が狭い   *to be ashamed to face someone*

[lit. One's body and shoulders are narrow.]

約束を破って、友達に対して肩身が狭いです。 Yakusoku o yabutte, tomodachi ni taishite katami ga semai desu. *I'm ashamed to face my friends, because I broke my promise to them.*

katasukashi o kuwaseru   肩すかしを食わせる   *to parry*

[lit. to pull one's shoulder away from someone]

彼女の質問に肩すかしを食わせました。 Kanojo no shitsumon ni katasukashi o kuwasemashita. *I parried her question.*

kata   片   *one side*

katabō o katsugu   片棒を担ぐ   *to take part in something (bad)*

[lit. to carry one end of a pole]

彼は、その会社の乗っ取りの片棒を担ぎました。 Kare wa, sono kaisha no nottori no katabō o katsugimashita. *He took part in the hostile takeover of that company.*

katahada nugu   片肌脱ぐ   *to help someone in particular*
[lit. to bare one shoulder]
あなたのためなら、片肌脱ぎましょう。Anata no tame nara,
katahada nugimashō.   *I'll help only because it's you.*

katahara itai   片腹痛い   *ridiculous, absurd*
[lit. One side of one's abdomen hurts.]
嘘つきの彼女が私を嘘つきと呼ぶなんて、片腹痛いです。
Usotsuki no kanojo ga watakushi o usotsuki to yobu nante,
katahara itai desu.   *It's ridiculous for her to call me a liar
when she's the liar.*

kataiji o haru   片意地を張る   *to be obstinate*
[lit. to stick with a one-sided will]
彼は意見の間違いを認める代わりに、まだ片意地を張っ
ています。Kare wa iken no machigai o mitomeru kawari ni,
mada kataiji o hatte imasu.   *Instead of admitting that his
opinion was wrong, he's still obstinate.*

kataomoi   片思い   *unrequited love*
[lit. one-sided thinking]
彼は片思いで悩んでいます。Kare wa kataomoi de nayande
imasu.   *He is agonizing over his unrequited love.*

katateochi   片手落ち   *unfair, partial*
[lit. one hand dropping]
交渉の分裂で、こちら側だけを非難するのは肩手落ちです。
Kōshō no bunretsu de, kochiragawa dake o hinan suru no wa
katateochi desu.   *It's unfair to blame only this side for the
breakdown of the negotiations.*

kataude   片腕   *right-hand man*
[lit. one arm]
彼は私の片腕です。Kare wa watakushi no kataude desu.   *He
is my right-hand man.*

---

kata   型、形   *form, shape, mold*
kata ni hamatta   型にはまった   *conventional*
[lit. to fit into a mold]

彼の演説は型にはまっていて、面白くありませんでした。
Kare no enzetsu wa kata ni hamatte ite, omoshiroku arimasen deshita. *His speech wasn't interesting because it was too conventional.*

kata ni torawareru　型にとらわれる　*conventional*
[lit. to be captured by a form]
彼の絵は型にとらわれすぎていて、面白くありません。
Kare no e wa kata ni torawaresugite ite, omoshiroku arimasen. *Because her paintings are too conventional, they're not interesting.*

katanashi　形無し　*disgrace*
[lit. no shape]
テニスが自慢の彼も、息子に負けて形無しでした。Tenisu ga jiman no kare mo, musuko ni makete katanashi deshita. *He was proud of his tennis, but he lost face by losing the game to his son.*

katayaburi no　型破りの　*unconventional*
[lit. of breaking a form]
彼女は、型破りの政治家です。Kanojo wa, katayaburi no seijika desu. *She is an unconventional politician.*

---

katazu　固唾　*saliva*
katazu o nomu　固唾を呑む　*to hold one's breath, breathtakingly*
[lit. to swallow one's saliva]
その庭は、固唾を呑むほどの美しさでした。Sono niwa wa, katazu o nomu hodo no utsukushisa deshita. *That garden was breathtakingly beautiful.*

---

katsu　活　*life*
katsu o ireru　活を入れる　*to cheer someone up*
[lit. to put life back in]
彼は最近元気がないので、活を入れました。Kare wa saikin genki ga nai node, katsu o iremashita. *Since he seemed to have lost heart recently, I cheered him up.*

---

kayui   痒い   *itchy*

  kayui tokoro ni te ga todoku   痒いところに手が届く

    to be very attentive

  [lit. Someone's hand reaches one's itchy spot.]

  今度の旅行先では、痒いところに手が届く待遇を受けました。

    Kondo no ryokō saki dewa, kayui tokoro ni te ga todoku taigū
    o ukemashita.   *Where we went on the last trip, we received*
    very attentive treatment.

---

kaze   風   *wind*

  kazamuki ga warui   風向きが悪い   *to be in bad mood*

  [lit. The wind direction is bad.]

  今晩は、父の風向きが悪いです。 Konban wa, chichi no
    kazamuki ga warui desu.   *My father is in a bad mood tonight.*

  kaze no fukimawashi   風の吹き回し   *for some reason*
    or other

  [lit. swirling of wind]

  どうした風の吹き回しか、突然叔母が訪ねてきました。 Dō
    shita kaze no fukimawashi ka, totsuzen oba ga tazunete
    kimashita.   *For some reason or other, my aunt unexpectedly*
    came to visit us.

  kaze no tayori   風の便り   *rumor*

  [lit. a message by wind]

  風の便りに聞くと、彼女は去年離婚したそうです。 Kaze no
    tayori ni kiku to, kanojo wa kyonen rikon shita sō desu.
    Rumor has it that she was divorced last year.

  kazeatari ga tsuyoi   風当たりが強い   *strong criticism*
    to mount

  [lit. The wind strongly blows onto someone or something.]

  政府の経済政策に対する風当たりが強まっています。 Seifu
    no keizai seisaku ni taisuru kazeatari ga tsuyomatte imasu.
    Strong criticism of the government's economic policy is
    mounting.

---

ke   毛   *hair, fur*

ke no haeta yō na   毛の生えたような   *to be not much*
better than someone or something
[lit. like hair coming out]
彼は、素人に毛の生えたような歌手にすぎません。Kare wa,
shirōto ni ke no haeta yō na kashu ni sugimasen. *Simply put,*
he's not much better than an amateur singer.

keiro no kawatta   毛色の変わった   *strange, unusual*
[lit. The hair color is different.]
彼女の経歴は、毛色が変わっています。Kanojo no keireki
wa, keiro ga kawatte imasu. *Her background is unusual.*

kenami no ii   毛並みのいい   *to be from a good family*
[lit. The coat of hair is good.]
彼の毛並みがいい事は、会ってすぐに分かりました。Kare
no kenami ga ii koto wa, atte sugu ni wakarimashita. *When*
we met, I knew immediately that he was from a good family.

kechi   けち   *bad luck*
kechi o tsukeru   けちを付ける   *to find fault with*
something
[lit. to attach bad luck]
彼は、みんなが賛成した計画にけちを付けました。Kare wa,
minna ga sansei shita keikaku ni kechi o tsukemashita. *He*
found fault with the plan everybody else agreed on.

keijū   軽重   *weight*
keijū o hakaru   軽重を計る   *to consider something*
carefully
[lit. to measure weight]
契約は、その軽重を計ってから合意するべきです。Keiyaku
wa, sono keijū o hakatte kara gōi suru beki desu. *You should*
agree on the contract only after considering it carefully.

keisan   計算   *calculation*
keisan ni ireru   計算に入れる   *to take something into*
account

[lit. to include something in the calculations]

ある程度の遅れは、予定の計算に入れてあります。Aru teido no okure wa, yotei no keisan ni irete arimasu. *When planning the schedule, we've taken into account a certain amount of delay.*

---

kejime けじめ *difference*

kejime o tsukeru けじめをつける *to distinguish*

[lit. to attach a difference]

仕事と遊びのけじめをつけなさい。Shigoto to asobi no kejime o tsukenasai. *You should distinguish between work and play.*

---

kekki 血気 *vigor*

kekki ni hayaru 血気にはやる *to be rash*

[lit. to be eager with vigor]

彼らは血気にはやって行動したため、戦略に欠けていました。 Karera wa kekki ni hayatte kōdō shita tame, senryaku ni kakete imashita. *Because they acted rashly, they were short on strategy.*

kekkizakari 血気盛り *young and vigorous*

[lit. to be at the peak of vigor]

彼は血気盛りだけに、妥協の価値を知りません。Kare wa kekkizakari dake ni, dakyō no kachi o shirimasen. *Since he's still young and vigorous, he doesn't know the value of compromise.*

---

kemu, kemuri 煙 *smoke*

kemu ni maku 煙に巻く *to be evasive*

[lit. to wrap something in smoke]

彼はどんな質問をされても、相手を煙に巻くのが上手です。 Kare wa donna shitsumon o saretemo, aite o kemu ni maku no ga jōzu desu. *No matter what kind of questions they ask, he's skilled at being evasive.*

kemuri ni naru 煙になる *to waste, to dissipate*

[lit. to become smoke]

努力しましたが、結果は煙になってしまいました。
Doryoku shimashita ga, kekka wa kemuri ni natte shimaimashita.
I tried hard, but my efforts were wasted.

kemutagaru   煙たがる   *to keep someone at a distance*
[lit. to be sensitive to smoke]
彼は議論好きなので、みんなが煙たがっています。Kare wa
  gironzuki nanode, minna ga kemutagatte imasu.   *Because he's
  argumentative, everybody keeps him at a distance.*

---

ken   犬   *dog*
ken-en no naka   犬猿の仲   *to be on bad terms*
[lit. relations between a dog and a monkey]
彼と彼女は犬猿の仲です。Kare to kanojo wa ken-en no naka
  desu.   *He and she are on bad terms.*

---

keta   桁   *unit, figure*
keta ga chigau   桁が違う   *to be no match*
[lit. The unit is different.]
彼のお金の使い方は、普通の人とは桁が違います。Kare no
  okane no tsukaikata wa, futsū no hito towa keta ga chigaimasu.
  The way he spends money is no match for ordinary people.

ketachigai no   桁違いの   *extraordinary*
[lit. a different unit]
彼女は桁違いの金持ちです。Kanojo wa ketachigai no
  kanemochi desu.   *She is extraordinarily rich.*

ketahazure no   桁はずれの   *unusual*
[lit. off the units]
彼女は、桁はずれの才能を持ったピアニストです。Kanojo
  wa, ketahazure no sainō o motta pianisuto desu.   *She is an
  unusually talented pianist.*

---

ki   気   *mind, feeling, intention, mood, attention,
  sensation*
ki ga aru   気がある   *to be interested in someone or
  something*

[lit. There are feelings.]

彼女は私に気があるようです。 Kanojo wa watakushi ni ki ga aru yō desu. *She seems to be interested in me.*

ki ga chiru   気が散る   *to be distracted*

[lit. One's mind scatters.]

テレビの音に気が散って、仕事に集中できません。 Terebi no oto ni ki ga chitte, shigoto ni shūchū dekimasen. *I can't concentrate on my work because I'm distracted by the noise of the TV.*

ki ga hareru   気が晴れる   *to feel relieved*

[lit. One's feelings are cleared.]

試験期間が終わって、気が晴れました。 Shiken kikan ga owatte, ki ga haremashita. *I felt relieved because the exam period was over.*

ki ga haritsumeru   気が張りつめる   *to be fully alert*

[lit. One's attention stretches to the full extent.]

気が張りつめていたので、全然疲れを覚えませんでした。 Ki ga haritsumete ita node, zenzen tsukare o oboemasen deshita. *Since I was fully alert, I didn't feel tired at all.*

ki ga hayai   気が早い   *to be hasty*

[lit. One's feelings are fast.]

彼は気が早すぎるので、結論には信用が置けません。 Kare wa ki ga hayasugiru node, ketsuron niwa shin-yō ga okemasen. *Since he's too hasty, we can't really trust his conclusions.*

ki ga hikeru   気が引ける   *to feel ashamed*

[lit. One's feeling is pulling oneself backward.]

私の意見でそうなったために、気が引けます。 Watakushi no iken de sō natta tame ni, ki ga hikemasu. *I feel ashamed because my opinion led to that result.*

ki ga ki de nai   気が気でない   *to be anxious*

[lit. One's feeling is not materializing.]

試験の結果に、気が気ではありません。 Shiken no kekka ni, ki ga ki de dewa arimasen. *I'm very anxious about the results of the exam.*

ki ga kiku   気が利く   *to be sensible*
[lit. One's sensitivity is effective.]
彼女は気が利くので、何を頼んでも安心です。Kanojo wa ki
  ga kiku node, nani o tanondemo anshin desu.   *Since she's
  sensible, you can count on her when you ask her to do
  something.*

ki ga magireru   気が紛れる   *to be distracted*
[lit. One's intention is indistinguishable.]
気が紛れて、発表の準備を忘れました。Ki ga magirete,
  happyō no junbi o wasuremashita.   *Because I was distracted, I
  forgot to prepare for my oral report.*

ki ga meiru   気が滅入る   *to get depressed*
[lit. One's feelings go down.]
将来のことを考えると、気が滅入ります。Shōrai no koto o
  kangaeru to, ki ga meirimasu.   *If I think about the future, I get
  depressed.*

ki ga momeru   気がもめる   *to be anxious*
[lit. The feeling is rubbed.]
息子の将来については、気がもめます。Musuko no shōrai ni
  tsuite wa, ki ga momemasu.   *I feel anxious about my son's
  future.*

ki ga nai   気がない   *to be not interested in someone or
  something*
[lit. One's feelings don't exist.]
山登りには、あまり気がありません。Yamanobori niwa,
  amari ki ga arimasen.   *I'm not much interested in mountain
  climbing.*

ki ga okenai   気が置けない   *to feel very close to
  someone*
[lit. no way to keep distance between persons' feelings]
彼とは、気が置けない仲です。Kare to wa, ki ga okenai naka
  desu.   *He and I are very close.*

ki ga ōkii   気が大きい   *to be generous*
[lit. One's heart is big.]

彼は気が大きいから、何を頼んでも引き受けてくれます。
Kare wa ki ga ōkii kara, nani o tanondemo hikiukete kuremasu.
Since he's generous, he'll do whatever you ask.

ki ga omoi   気が重い   *to be depressing*
[lit. One's heart is heavy.]
この週末は働かなければならないので、気が重いです。
Kono shūmatsu wa hatarakanakereba naranai node, ki ga omoi
desu.   *It's depressing to have to work during the weekend.*

ki ga sasu   気が差す   *to feel guilty*
[lit. One's feeling fills.]
約束を守れなくて、気が差します。Yakusoku o
mamorenakute, ki ga sashimasu.   *I feel guilty because I
couldn't keep my promise.*

ki ga seku   気が急く   *to be too anxious*
[lit. One's feelings are in a hurry.]
気が急いて、試験はあまり出来ませんでした。Ki ga seite,
shiken wa amari dekimasen deshita.   *I was too anxious, so I
didn't do well on the exam.*

ki ga sumu   気が済む   *to feel justified*
[lit. One's feelings end.]
私が正しいことを証明するまでは、気が済みません。
Watakushi ga tadashii koto o shōmei suru made wa, ki ga
sumimasen.   *I won't feel justified until I prove that I'm right.*

ki ga susumanai   気が進まない   *to be not in the mood*
[lit. One's feeling doesn't proceed.]
パーティーに誘われましたが、気が進みません。Pātī ni
sasowaremashita ga, ki ga susumimasen.   *I was invited to a
party, but I'm not in the mood.*

ki ga tatte iru   気が立っている   *to be on edge*
[lit. One's feelings are standing.]
彼は仕事がはかどらないので、気が立っています。Kare wa
shigoto ga hakadoranai node, ki ga tatte imasu.   *He's on edge
because his work isn't progressing much.*

ki ga togameru   気が咎める   *to feel guilty*

[lit. One's feelings accuse oneself.]

昨日は妻の誕生日を忘れてしまい、気が咎めました。Kinō
　wa tsuma no tanjōbi o wasurete shimai, ki ga togamemashita.
　I felt guilty because I forgot my wife's birthday yesterday.

ki ga tōkunaru yō　　気が遠くなるよう　　　*to feel
overwhelmed*

[lit. like fainting]

明日しなければならないことを考えると、気が遠くなるよ
　うです。Ashita shinakereba naranai koto o kangaeru to, ki ga
　tōkunaru yō desu.　*When I think about everything I have to do
　tomorrow, I feel overwhelmed.*

ki ga tsuku　　気がつく　　　*to be attentive*

[lit. to become aware of something]

新しい秘書は、よく気がつきます。Atarashii hisho wa, yoku
　ki ga tsukimasu.　*The new secretary is very attentive.*

ki ni iru　　気に入る　　　*to be pleased with someone or
something*

[lit. to enter into one's mind]

昨日行ったレストランがとても気に入りました。Kinō itta
　resutoran ga totemo ki ni irimashita.　*I was very pleased with
　the restaurant we went to yesterday.*

ki ni kakaru　　気にかかる　　　*to be anxious about someone
or something*

[lit. Something hangs in one's mind.]

旅行中、残してきた子供のことが気にかかりました。
　Ryokō chū, nokoshite kita kodomo no koto ga ki ni
　kakarimashita.　*During the trip, we were anxious about our
　children at home.*

ki ni kuwanai　　気に食わない　　　*to detest*

[lit. to not suit one's feelings]

私は、彼女の人生に対する態度が気に食いません。
　Watakushi wa, kanojo no jinsei ni taisuru taido ga ki ni
　kuimasen.　*I detest her attitude toward life.*

ki ni naru　　気になる　　　*to feel uneasy*

[lit. to come to one's feelings]

先週受けた就職の面接の結果が気になります。Senshū uketa shūshoku no mensetsu no kekka ga ki ni narimasu.　*I feel uneasy about the results of the job interview I had last week.*

ki ni sawaru　　気に障る　　*to offend*

[lit. to interfere with someone's feelings]

彼女は人の気に障ることを平気でよく言います。Kanojo wa hito no ki ni sawaru koto o heiki de yoku iimasu.　*Without any hesitation, she often says things that offend others.*

ki ni suru　　気にする　　*to be anxious about someone or something*

[lit. to be mindful]

最初のデートの後、彼は彼女がどう思ったか気にしています。 Saisho no dēto no ato, kare wa kanojo ga dō omottaka ki ni shite imasu.　*Since their first date, he has been anxious about how she felt about him.*

ki ni yamu　　気に病む　　*to be worried*

[lit. to be sick to one's heart]

彼は娘の将来をひどく気に病んでいます。Kare wa musume no shōrai o hidoku ki ni yande imasu.　*He is extremely worried about his daughter's future.*

ki o haku　　気を吐く　　*to be elated*

[lit. to spew one's sensation out]

彼は株で大儲けして気を吐いています。Kare wa kabu de ōmōke shite ki o haite imasu.　*He's elated at making a large profit on the stock market.*

ki o hiku　　気を引く　　*to attract*

[lit. to pull someone's attention]

彼女の気を引くことに成功しました。Kanojo no ki o hiku koto ni seikō shimashita.　*I succeeded in attracting her.*

ki o ireru　　気を入れる　　*to pour one's energy*

[lit. to put one's feelings into something]

遊びより、勉強にもっと気を入れなさい。Asobi yori, benkyō ni motto ki o irenasai.　*You should pour more energy into studying than playing.*

ki o kikasu   気を利かす   *to be considerate*
[lit. to make one's mind work]
母に気を利かせて、お使いをしてあげました。Haha ni ki o
   kikasete, otsukai o shite agemashita.   *To be considerate of my
   mother, I did errands for her.*

ki o kubaru   気を配る   *to be attentive to someone or
   something*
[lit. to deliver one's attention]
彼女は子供の教育に、非常に気を配っています。Kanojo wa
   kodomo no kyōiku ni, hijō ni ki o kubatte imasu.   *She is
   extremely attentive to her children's education.*

ki o kusarasu   気を腐らす   *to be depressed*
[lit. to let one's feelings rot]
彼は計画が思い通りにいかなくて、気を腐らせています。
   Kare wa keikaku ga omoidōri ni ikanakute, ki o kusarasete
   imasu.   *He has been depressed because the plan didn't go as
   he expected.*

ki o mawashisugiru   気を回しすぎる   *to be overly
   concerned*
[lit. to spin one's mind too much]
彼女は街の犯罪について、気を回しすぎます。Kanojo wa
   machi no hanzai ni tsuite, ki o mawashisugimasu.   *She is
   overly concerned about street crime.*

ki o momu   気を揉む   *to be anxious*
[lit. to rub one's feelings]
試験の結果については、気を揉む必要はありません。
   Shiken no kekka ni tsuite wa, ki o momu hitsuyō wa arimasen.
   You don't need to be anxious about the results of the exam.

ki o motaseru   気を持たせる   *to raise someone's hopes*
[lit. to let someone have one's feelings]
お金を貸す件では、彼に気を持たせるつもりはありません
   でした。Okane o kasu ken dewa, kare ni ki o motaseru
   tsumori wa arimasen deshita.   *I didn't have any intention of*

raising his hopes that I would lend him money.

ki o nomareru 気を呑まれる *to be overwhelmed*
[lit. to get one's mind swallowed]
交渉で、相手側の頑固さに気を呑まれました。 Kōshō de,
aitegawa no gankosa ni ki o nomaremashita. *We were
overwhelmed by the stubbornness of our counterpart in the
negotiations.*

ki o otosu 気を落とす *to be disappointed*
[lit. to drop one's mood]
ボーナスが期待していたより少なくて、気を落としました。
Bōnasu ga kitai shite ita yori sukunakute, ki o otoshimashita.
*I was disappointed because the bonus was less than I had
expected.*

ki o torareru 気を取られる *to be distracted by
someone or something*
[lit. to have one's attention taken away]
締め切りに気を取られて、映画を楽しめませんでした。
Shimekiri ni ki o torarete, eiga o tanoshimemasen deshita. *I
couldn't enjoy the movie because I was distracted by the
deadline.*

ki o torinaosu 気を取り直す *to pull oneself together*
[lit. to take one's own feelings up again]
火事で全てを失いましたが、気を取り直してまた働き始め
ました。 Kaji de subete o ushinaimashita ga, ki o torinaoshite
mata hatarakihajimemashita. *I lost everything in a fire but
pulled myself together and started over again.*

ki o tsukau 気を遣う *to worry*
[lit. to spend one's own mind]
彼女は何事にも気を遣いすぎます。
Kanojo wa nanigoto nimo ki o tsukaisugimasu.
She worries too much about everything.

ki o waruku suru 気を悪くする *to take offense*
[lit. to make one's own feelings bad]
彼は私が冗談で言ったことに、気を悪くしました。 Kare wa

watakushi ga jōdan de itta koto ni, ki o waruku shimashita.
He took offense at what I meant as a joke.

ki o yokusuru   気をよくする   *to feel good*
[lit. to make one's own feelings good]
彼は息子が有名大学に入学するので、気をよくしています。
Kare wa musuko ga yūmei daigaku ni nyūgaku suru node, ki o
   yoku shite imasu.   *He's feeling good because his son is going
   to a famous university.*

ki o yurusu   気を許す   *to let one's guard down*
[lit. to let one's mind trust]
彼女に気を許したため、苦い経験をしました。Kanojo ni ki
   o yurushita tame, nigai keiken o shimashita.   *I had a bitter
   experience because I let my guard down with her.*

kibarashi   気晴らし   *for a change of pace*
[lit. clearing one's mind]
先週は忙しかったので、週末に気晴らしにテニスをしました。
Senshū wa isogashikatta node, shūmatsu ni kibarashi ni tenisu
   o shimashita.   *Since last week was busy, for a change of pace
   I played tennis on the weekend.*

kibaru   気張る   *to exert oneself*
[lit. to stretch one's intention]
彼は大学入試のため、気張って勉強しています。Kare wa
   daigaku nyūshi no tame, kibatte benkyō shite imasu.   *He's
   exerting himself to study for the college entrance exams.*

kiokure suru   気後れする   *to feel timid*
[lit. One's mind gets behind.]
今日は大勢の前で演説しなければならず、気後れしました。
Kyō wa ōzei no mae de enzetsu shinakereba narazu, kiokure
   shimashita.   *Today I felt timid because I had to give a speech
   in front of a lot of people.*

kiyasui   気安い   *to be willing, to be friendly*
[lit. One's mind is easy.]
彼は気安く何でもやってくれます。Kare wa kiyasuku
   nandemo yatte kuremasu.   *He does anything for you willingly.*

ki   機   *chance*

ki ga jukusu   機が熟す   *The opportunity has come.*
[lit. A chance ripens.]
会社を辞めて独立する機が熟しました。 Kaisha o yamete
dokuritsu suru ki ga jukushimashita.   *The opportunity has
come to quit the company and start my own business.*

ki ni jōjiru   機に乗じる   *to take advantage of an
opportunity*
[lit. to ride on a chance]
円高の機に乗じて、家族を連れて海外旅行に行きました。
En daka no ki ni jōjite, kazoku o tsurete kaigai ryokō ni
ikimashita.   *Taking advantage of the strong yen, I traveled
abroad with my family.*

---

ki   木   *tree*

ki de hana o kukuru yō na   木で鼻をくくるような
curt
[lit. like rubbing a nose with a piece of wood]
彼に借金を申し込みましたが、木で鼻をくくるような返事
でした。 Kare ni shakkin o mōshikomimashita ga, ki de hana
o kukuru yō na henji deshita.   *I asked him for a loan, but he
gave me a curt response.*

ki ni take o tsugu   木に竹を接ぐ   *to not mix, to not be
natural*
[lit. to graft a bamboo to a tree]
その政治連合は、最初から木に竹を接ぐようなものでした。
Sono seiji rengō wa, saisho kara ki ni take o tsugu yō na mono
deshita.   *That political coalition was not natural to begin
with.*

---

kiai   気合い   *spirit*

kiai o ireru   気合いを入れる   *to reprimand someone*
[lit. to put spirit into someone]
息子は最近あまり勉強しないので、気合いを入れました。
Musuko wa saikin amari benkyō shinai node, kiai o iremashita.

I reprimanded my son for not studying much recently.

kibisu　きびす　*heel*
kibisu o kaesu　きびすを返す　*to turn back*
[lit. to turn one's heels]
その件については、今更きびすを返すわけにはいきません。
Sono ken ni tsuite wa, imasara kibisu o kaesu wake niwa
ikimaen.　*I can't turn back from my position on that subject at
such a late date.*

kibisu o sessuru yō ni　きびすを接するように　*one
after another*
[lit. by touching one heel with another]
日本各地で、地震がきびすを接するように起こっています。
Nihon kakuchi de, jishin ga kibisu o sessuru yō ni okotte
imasu.　*There are earthquakes one after another all over
Japan.*

kibone　気骨　*mental strain*
kibone ga oreru　気骨が折れる　*to be stressful*
[lit. One's mind and bones break.]
義母が来ているので、多少気骨が折れます。Gibo ga kite iru
node, tashō kibone ga oremasu.　*Because my mother-in-law is
staying with us, it's somewhat stressful.*

kidō　軌道　*orbit*
kidō ni noru　軌道に乗る　*to get on track*
[lit. to get on an orbit]
長期計画が、やっと軌道に乗り始めました。Chōki keikaku
ga, yatto kidō ni norihajimemashita.　*The long-term plan
finally started to get on track.*

kigen　機嫌　*mood*
gokigen ga naname　ご機嫌が斜め　*to be in a bad
temper*
[lit. Someone's mood is oblique.]
妻はご機嫌が斜めなので、うっかり口を利くと危ないです。

Tsuma wa gokigen ga naname nanode, ukkari kuchi o kiku to abunai desu.   *Because my wife is in a bad temper, it's dangerous if I say something casually.*

gokigentori   ご機嫌取り   *flattering*
[lit. making someone's mood good]
彼はいつも部長のご機嫌取りをしています。Kare wa itsumo buchō no gokigentori o shite imasu.   *He's always flattering the department chief.*

---

kiiroi   黄色い   *yellow*
kiiroi koe   黄色い声   *screeching voice*
[lit. a yellow voice]
人気の歌手が出てくると、ファンは黄色い声を上げました。
Ninki no kashu ga dete kuru to, fan wa kiiroi koe o agemashita. *When the popular singer appeared, his fans started screeching.*

---

kikotsu   気骨   *spirit*
kikotsu ga aru   気骨がある   *to be gutsy*
[lit. to have a mind and bones]
彼は静かだけれど、とても気骨があります。Kare wa shizuka da keredo, totemo kikotsu ga arimasu.   *He is quiet but very gutsy.*

---

kiku   聞く   *to hear, to listen*
kikimimi o tateru   聞き耳を立てる   *to be all ears*
[lit. to make listening ears stand up]
彼女は娘のボーイフレンドとの電話に、聞き耳を立てました。
Kanojo wa musume no bōifurendo tono denwa ni, kikimimi o tatemashita.   *She was all ears during her daughter's phone conversation with her boyfriend.*

kikishi ni masaru   聞きしに勝る   *to exceed one's expectations*
[lit. to surpass what one has heard]
彼の歌は、聞きしに勝るすばらしさでした。Kare no uta wa, kikishi ni masaru subarashisa deshita.   *His singing exceeded my expectations.*

---

kikoeyogashi ni   聞こえよがしに   *saying something negative intentionally within someone's earshot*
[lit. as if wishing for something to be heard]
彼女は聞こえよがしに、私の悪口を言っています。Kanojo
wa kikoeyogashi ni, watakushi no warukuchi o itte imasu.
She's intentionally badmouthing me within my earshot.

---

kiku   利く   *to be effective*
kiita fū na   利いた風な   *presumptuous*
[lit. as if effective]
彼はこの会社で新しいのに、利いた風な口を利いています。
Kare wa kono kaisha de atarashii noni, kiita fū na kuchi o kiite
imasu.   *Although he's new in the company, he's making
presumptuous statements.*

---

kime   肌理   *texture*
kime no komakai   肌理の細かい   *detailed*
[lit. finely textured]
彼は、肌理の細かい企画が得意ではありません。Kare wa
kime no komakai kikaku ga tokui dewa arimasen.   *He is not
good at detailed planning.*

---

kimo   肝   *liver*
dogimo o nukareru   度肝を抜かれる   *to be
dumbfounded*
[lit. One's liver gets extracted.]
息子に突然結婚すると言われ、度肝を抜かれました。
Musuko ni totsuzen kekkon suru to iware, dogimo o
nukaremashita.   *I was dumbfounded by my son's sudden
announcement that he was getting married.*

kimo ga futoi   肝が太い   *bold, plucky*
[lit. One's liver is thick.]
彼は肝が太いので、いざというときに頼りになります。
Kare wa kimo ga futoi node, iza to iu toki ni tayori
ni narimasu.   *Because he's plucky, you can rely on him
during an emergency.*

kimo ga suwaru   肝が据わる   *to have nerves of iron*
[lit. One's liver settles firmly.]
彼はあらゆる経験を積んできただけに、肝が据わっています。
　Kare wa arayuru keiken o tsunde kita dake ni, kimo ga suwatte imasu.   *Because he's had all sorts of experience, he has nerves of iron.*

kimo ni meijiru   肝に銘じる   *to take something to heart*
[lit. to chisel something into one's liver]
その助言を肝に銘じて、同じ間違いをしないことを誓います。
　Sono jogen o kimo ni meijite, onaji machigai o shinai koto o chikaimasu.   *I promise that I'll take your advice to heart and won't make the same mistake again!*

kimo o hiyasu   肝を冷やす   *to be scared*
[lit. to chill one's liver]
大切な面会の約束に遅れそうになって、肝を冷やしました。
　Taisetsu na menkai no yakusoku ni okuresō ni natte, kimo o hiyashimashita.   *I was scared that I would be late for an important appointment.*

kimo o sueru   肝を据える   *to be resolved*
[lit. to set one's liver firmly]
どんな結果でもそれを受け入れようと肝を据えました。
　Donna kekka demo sore o ukeireyō to kimo o suemashita.   *I was resolved to accept whatever the outcome would be.*

kimo o tsubusu   肝を潰す   *to be flabbergasted*
[lit. to smash one's own liver]
彼女のあまりにも図々しい態度に、肝を潰しました。
　Kanojo no amari nimo zūzūshii taido ni, kimo o tsubushimashita.   *I was flabbergasted by her extremely cheeky attitude.*

kimoiri   肝煎り   *good offices, sponsorship*
[lit. roasting of a liver]
地元の政治家の肝煎りで、東京で仕事を見つけることが出来ました。Jimoto no seijika no kimoiri de, Tōkyō de shigoto o mitsukeru koto ga dekimashita.   *Because of the good offices*

of the local politician, I was able to find a job in Tokyo.

---

kimochi   気持ち   *feeling, frame of mind*
  kimochi o kumu   気持ちを汲む   *to sense someone's feelings*
[lit. to scoop up someone's feelings]
彼女の罪の意識を汲んで、今度の失敗は大目に見てあげました。 Kanojo no tsumi no ishiki o kunde, kondo no shippai wa ōme ni mite agemashita. *Sensing her feelings of guilt, I overlooked her mistake this time.*

---

kimyaku   気脈   *blood vessel*
  kimyaku o tsūjiru   気脈を通じる   *to conspire with someone/others*
[lit. to connect one's blood vessels with others']
あの組合の幹部は、会社側と気脈を通じているそうです。 Ano kumiai no kanbu wa, kaishagawa to kimyaku o tsūjite iru sō desu. *That senior labor union official is said to be conspiring with management.*

---

kiru   切る   *to cut*
  kiremono   切れ者   *capable person*
[lit. someone who can cut things]
彼は切れ者だから、大切な仕事も任せられます。 Kare wa kiremono dakara, taisetsu na shigoto mo makaseraremasu. *Since he's capable, you can trust him with important work.*

  kittemo kirenai   切っても切れない   *to be closely bound to someone*
[lit. to be not able to cut even if someone tries]
彼らは、切っても切れない仲です。 Karera wa kittemo kirenai naka desu. *They are closely bound to each other.*

---

kisei   気勢   *spirit, vigor*
  kisei o ageru   気勢を上げる   *to be elated*
[lit. to raise spirits]
わが社の売り上げが競争相手のを抜いたので、気勢を上げ

ました。Waga sha no uriage ga kyōsō aite no o nuita node, kisei o agemashita. *We were elated because our sales surpassed our competitor's.*

kinsen   琴線   *koto (Japanese harp) strings*
  kinsen ni fureru   琴線に触れる   *to tug at one's heartstrings*
[lit. to touch *koto* strings]
彼女の優しい言葉が、私の心の琴線に触れました。Kanojo no yasashii kotoba ga, watakushi no kokoro no kinsen ni furemashita. *Her gentle words tugged at my heartstrings.*

kinteki   金的   *golden bull's-eye*
  kinteki o itomeru   金的を射止める   *to hit the jackpot*
[lit. to hit the golden bull's-eye]
彼は社長の娘と結婚して、金的を射止めました。Kare wa shachō no musume to kekkon shite, kinteki o itomemashita. *He hit the jackpot by marrying the company president's daughter.*

kirin   麒麟   *giraffe*
  kirinji   麒麟児   *prodigy*
[lit. a giraffe child]
あの女の子は、麒麟児のピアニストです。Ano onna no ko wa, kirinji no pianisuto desu. *That girl is a prodigy as a pianist.*

kitsune   狐   *fox*
  kitsune ni tsumamareta yō   狐につままれたよう   *to be puzzled*
[lit. like being fooled by a fox]
駄目だと思った試験に受かって、狐につままれたような気がしました。 Dame da to omotta shiken ni ukatte, kitsune ni tsumamareta yō na ki ga shimashita. *I was puzzled when I passed the exam which I thought I had failed.*

  kitsune no yomeiri   狐の嫁入り   *rain while the sun is shining*

[lit. a fox's wedding]
ピクニックに行こうとしたら、狐の嫁入りでした。

Pikunikku ni ikō to shitara, kitsune no yomeiri deshita.   *Just as we were about to go on a picnic, it started raining while the sun was shining.*

kitsune to tanuki no bakashiai   狐と狸の化かし合い
to try to outfox each other

[lit. A fox and a raccoon dog are trying to bewitch each other.]
あの二人は昇進を争って、狐と狸の化かし合いをしています。

Ano futari wa shōshin o arasotte, kitsune to tanuki no bakashiai o shite imasu.   *Those two are competing for a promotion and trying to outfox each other.*

---

kō   紅   *red*

kō itten   紅一点   *only one woman among men*

[lit. one red spot]
討論会の出席者としては、彼女が紅一点でした。Tōronkai no shussekisha to shite wa, kanojo ga kō itten deshita.   *As for the participants in the debate, she was the only woman among the men.*

---

kobana   小鼻   *wings of a nose*

kobana o ugomekasu   小鼻をうごめかす   *to have a swelled head*

[lit. to move the wings of one's nose incessantly]
彼は高級車を買って、小鼻をうごめかしています。Kare wa kōkyūsha o katte, kobana o ugomekashite imasu.   *He bought an expensive car, and he has a swelled head.*

---

koe   声   *voice*

koe ga kakaru   声が掛かる   *to be asked*

[lit. Someone's voice approaches.]
友達から、映画に行かないかと声が掛かりました。

Tomodachi kara, eiga ni ikanaika to koe ga kakarimashita.   *I was asked by my friend if I would like to go to a movie with him.*

---

koe o furishiboru   声を振り絞る   *to strain one's voice*
[lit. to wring out one's voice]
候補者は声を振り絞って、街頭の人々に投票を頼みました。
   Kōhosha wa koe o furishibotte, gaitō no hitobito ni tōhyō o
   tanomimashita.   *Straining his voice, the candidate asked
   people in the street to vote for him.*

koe o hazumasete   声を弾ませて   *in a lively tone of
   voice*
[lit. by making one's voice bounce]
彼女は新婚旅行について、声を弾ませて話しました。
   Kanojo wa shinkon ryokō ni tsuite, koe o hazumasete
   hanashimashita.   *She talked about her honeymoon in a lively
   tone of voice.*

koe o hisomeru   声を潜める   *to lower one's voice*
[lit. to hide one's voice]
医者は患者の奥さんに、声を潜めて診断の結果を告げました。
   Isha wa kanja no okusan ni, koe o hisomete shindan no kekka o
   tsugemashita.   *Lowering her voice, the doctor told the
   patient's wife the diagnosis.*

koe o korosu   声を殺す   *to whisper*
[lit. to kill one's own voice]
彼は声を殺して秘密を打ち明けました。Kare wa koe o
   koroshite himitsu o uchiakemashita.   *In a whisper, he
   revealed a secret to me.*

koe o kumoraseru   声を曇らせる   *to murmur sadly*
[lit. to make one's voice cloudy]
父は叔母の病気を聞いて、声を曇らせました。 Chichi wa
   oba no byōki o kiite, koe o kumorasemashita.   *On hearing
   about my aunt's illness, my father murmured sadly.*

koe o nomu   声を呑む   *to become speechless*
[lit. to swallow one's own voice]
地震の結果のあまりのひどさに声を呑みました。Jishin no
   kekka no amari no hidosa ni koe o nomimashita.   *I became
   speechless at the terrible results of the earthquake.*

koe o otosu   声を落とす   *to lower one's voice*
[lit. to drop one's voice]

彼は声を落として、故人の思い出を語りました。Kare wa koe o otoshite, kojin no omoide o katarimashita. *He lowered his voice and talked about his memories of the deceased.*

koe o tateru   声を立てる   *to raise one's voice*
[lit. to let one's voice stand up]

先生は声を立てて、学生に警告しました。Sensei wa koe o tatete gakusei ni keikoku shimashita. *Raising his voice, the teacher warned the students.*

okoegakari de   お声掛かりで   *at someone's command*
[lit. with the request of an honorable voice]

社長のお声掛かりで、新事業計画に着手しました。 Shachō no okoegakari de, shin jigyō keikaku ni chakushu shimashita. *At the president's command, we embarked on the new business plan.*

ubugoe o ageru   産声を上げる   *to be born*
[lit. A newborn baby cries at birth.]

ハイテクの分野で、沢山の会社が毎日産声を上げています。 Haiteku no bun-ya de, takusan no kaisha ga mainichi ubugoe o agete imasu. *Many companies are being born every day in the field of advanced technology.*

---

kōjin   後塵   *dust kicked up backward*
kōjin o haisuru   後塵を拝する   *to play second fiddle*
[lit. to get covered with dust kicked up backward by someone]

顧客の開拓では、彼の後塵を拝しています。Kokyaku no kaitaku dewa, kare no kōjin o haishite imasu. *I'm playing second fiddle to him in client development.*

---

kokoro   心   *mind, heart, feeling, intention, will*
kokoro ga kayou   心が通う   *to understand each other perfectly*
[lit. Feelings circulate between persons.]

彼女と私は、心が通っています。Kanojo to watakushi wa,
   kokoro ga kayotte imasu.   *She and I understand each other
   perfectly.*

kokoro ga komoru   心がこもる   *to be considerate, to be
   thoughtful*
[lit. One's heart is put into something.]
彼の助言には、とても心がこもっていました。Kare no
   jogen niwa, totemo kokoro ga komotte imashita.   *His advice
   to me was very thoughtful.*

kokoro ga odoru   心が躍る   *to get excited*
[lit. One's heart jumps.]
来週の旅行のことを考えると、心が躍ります。Raishū no
   ryokō no koto o kangaeru to, kokoro ga odorimasu.   *I get
   exited when I think about the trip next week.*

kokoro ga sawagu   心が騒ぐ   *to feel uneasy*
[lit. One's heart gets agitated.]
父に何度電話しても通じないので、心が騒ぎました。
   Chichi ni nando denwa shitemo tsūjinai node, kokoro ga
   sawagimashita.   *Since there was no answer no matter how
   many times I called my father, I felt uneasy.*

kokoro ga ugoku   心が動く   *to be tempted*
[lit. One's heart moves.]
ゴルフに誘われると、忙しくても心が動きます。Gorufu ni
   sasowareru to, isogashikutemo kokoro ga ugokimasu.   *If I'm
   asked to play golf, I'm tempted to go even if I'm busy.*

kokoro ni egaku   心に描く   *to imagine, to picture*
[lit. to paint a picture in one's mind]
将来の成功を心に描いて、一生懸命働きました。Shōrai no
   seikō o kokoro ni egaite, isshōkenmei hatarakimashita.
   Picturing my future success, I worked very hard.

kokoro ni kanau   心にかなう   *to suit one's taste*
[lit. to fit one's feelings]
家は買いたいけれど、心にかなうのを見つけるのに苦労し
   ています。Ie wa kaitai keredo, kokoro ni kanau no o

mitsukeru noni kurō shite imasu. *I'd like to buy a house, but I'm having trouble finding one that suits my taste.*

kokoro ni kizamu   心に刻む   *to remember*
[lit. to engrave something on one's heart]
私の言ったことを、よく心に刻んでおきなさい。Watakushi no itta koto o yoku kokoro ni kizande okinasai. *You should remember what I said.*

kokoro ni tomeru   心に留める   *to keep something in mind*
[lit. to make something remain in one's mind]
子供の教育については、いつも心に留めています。Kodomo no kyōiku ni tsuite wa, itsumo kokoro ni tomete imasu. *I'm always keeping my children's education in mind.*

kokoro o awaseru   心を合わせる   *to cooperate, to unite*
[lit. to put people's minds together]
意見の違いはありましたが、心を合わせて目的を遂げました。Iken no chigai wa arimashita ga, kokoro o awasete mokuteki o togemashita. *We had differences of opinion, but we cooperated and achieved our goal.*

kokoro o irekaeru   心を入れ替える   *to change one's habits*
[lit. to replace one's mind]
大学へ行きたかったら、心を入れ替えてもっと勉強しなさい。Daigaku e ikitakattara, kokoro o irekaete motto benkyō shinasai. *If you want to go to college, you should change your habits and study harder.*

kokoro o itameru   心を痛める   *to worry*
[lit. to make one's heart hurt]
彼女は子供の将来について、心を痛めています。Kanojo wa kodomo no shōrai ni tsuite, kokoro o itamete imasu. *She's worrying about her child's future.*

kokoro o kubaru   心を配る   *to be attentive*
[lit. to arrange one's mind]
あの店の店員は、客によく心を配ります。Ano mise no ten-

in wa, kyaku ni yoku kokoro o kubarimasu. *The clerks at that shop are quite attentive to the customers.*

kokoro o kudaku　心を砕く　　*to rack one's brains*
[lit. to grind one's mind]
契約を成立させるために、心を砕いています。Keiyaku o seiritsu saseru tame ni, kokoro o kudaite imasu. *I'm racking my brains to conclude the contract.*

kokoro o kumu　心を汲む　　*to sense*
[lit. to scoop up someone's feelings]
彼の孤独な心を汲んで、夕食に誘いました。Kare no kodoku na kokoro o kunde, yūshoku ni sasoimashita. *Sensing his loneliness, I invited him for dinner.*

kokoro o oni ni suru　心を鬼にする　　*to steel oneself*
[lit. to make one's mind a devil]
心を鬼にして、社員に一時雇用を伝えました。Kokoro o oni ni shite, shain ni ichiji kaiko o tsutaemashita. *Steeling myself, I told the employees about the temporary layoff.*

kokoro o ubawareru　心を奪われる　　*to be captivated*
[lit. to get one's heart stolen]
彼の話に、すっかり心を奪われました。Kare no hanashi ni, sukkari kokoro o ubawaremashita. *I was totally captivated by his story.*

kokoro o utsu　心を打つ　　*to touch someone's heart*
[lit. to hit someone's heart]
彼女の親への献身は、人々の心を打ちました。Kanojo no oya e no kenshin wa, hitobito no kokoro o uchimashita. *Her devotion to her parents touched everyone's heart.*

kokoro o yoseru　心を寄せる　　*to be interested in someone*
[lit. to draw one's heart up to someone]
彼は、彼女に心を寄せているようです。Kare wa, kanojo ni kokoro o yosete iru yō desu. *He seems to be interested in her.*

kokoro o yurusu　心を許す　　*to trust*
[lit. to set one's mind free]

彼女とは長いつき合いで、すっかり心を許しています。
Kanojo towa nagai tsukiai de, sukkari kokoro o yurushite
imasu. *I have been friendly with her for a long time, and I
trust her totally.*

kokoroatari　　心当たり　　*clue, hint*
[lit. a guess by one's mind]
彼がどこに行ったか、全く心当たりがありません。Kare ga
doko ni ittaka, mattaku kokoroatari ga arimasen. *I don't have
a clue as to where he went.*

kokorobosoi　　心細い　　*to feel uneasy*
[lit. One's heart is thin.]
その問題に一人で取り組むのは、ちょっと心細いです。
Sono mondai ni hitori de torikumu no wa, chotto kokorobosoi
desu. *I feel a bit uneasy tackling the problem alone.*

kokoroegao de　　心得顔で　　*knowingly*
[lit. with the face of knowledge]
彼女は心得顔で、私を見つめました。Kanojo wa kokoroegao
de watakushi o mitsumemashita. *She looked at me knowingly.*

kokorogamae　　心構え　　*being prepared for something*
[lit. a mental frame]
いつでも責任を取って辞める心構えです。Itsu demo sekinin
o totte yameru kokorogamae desu. *I'm prepared to bear the
responsibility and quit anytime.*

kokorogurushii　　心苦しい　　*to feel sorry for something*
[lit. One's heart is painful.]
彼女につらい思いをさせて、心苦しいです。Kanojo ni tsurai
omoi o sasete kokorogurushii desu. *I feel sorry for
tormenting her.*

kokoronarazumo　　心ならずも　　*against one's will*
[lit. with one's heart not proving something]
店員の滑らかな話に、心ならずもそれを買ってしまいました。
Ten-in no nameraka na hanashi ni, kokoronarazumo sore o
katte shimaimashita. *Because of the clerk's smooth talk, I
ended up buying it against my will.*

kokoronokori   心残り   *regret*
[lit. One's heart remains.]
学生の時にもっと勉強しなかったのが、いま心残りです。
　Gakusei no toki ni motto benkyō shinakatta no ga, ima
　kokoronokori desu.   *I now regret that I didn't study harder
　when I was a student.*

kokorookinaku   心置きなく   *without hesitation*
[lit. without leaving one's heart]
言いたいことは、どうぞ心置きなくおっしゃって下さい。
　Iitai koto wa, dōzo kokorookinaku osshatte kudasai.   *Please
　say whatever you'd like to say without hesitation.*

kokoroyukumade   心ゆくまで   *to one's heart's content*
[lit. as far as one's heart goes]
昨日の晩は、友達と心ゆくまで話し合いました。Kinō no
　ban wa, tomodachi to kokoroyukumade hanashiaimashita.
　Last night, I talked with my friends to my heart's content.

kokorozukushi   心尽くし   *kind, thoughtful*
[lit. exerting one's heart]
お母さんの心尽くしの助言も、彼には効き目がありません
　でした。Okāsan no kokorozukushi no jogen mo, kare niwa
　kikime ga arimasen deshita.   *Even his mother's kind advice
　didn't have any effect on him.*

tegokoro o kuwaeru   手心を加える   *to go easy on
someone*
[lit. to hand one's feelings to someone]
彼は大失敗をしたけれど、初めてだったので手心を加えま
　した。Kare wa daishippai o shita keredo, hajimete datta node
　tegokoro o kuwaemashita.   *Although he made a big mistake,
　since it was his first one, I went easy on him.*

---

komimi   小耳   *inside an ear*
komimi ni hasamu   小耳にはさむ   *to happen to hear*
[lit. to put something into an ear]
彼女がこの夏結婚することを、小耳にはさみました。
　Kanojo ga kono natsu kekkon suru koto o, komimi ni

hasamimashita. *I happened to hear that she would get married this summer.*

---

kon 根 *root, stamina*

kon ga tsukiru 根が尽きる *to have no more patience for something*
[lit. A root comes to an end.]

娘の不精な生活には、根が尽きました。Musume no bushō na seikatsu niwa, kon ga tsukimashita. *I have no more patience for my daughter's life of laziness.*

kon o tsumeru 根を詰める *to concentrate one's energy*
[lit. to pack stamina]

来週の試験のために、根を詰めて勉強しています。Raishū no shiken no tame ni, kon o tsumete benkyō shite imasu. *I'm concentrating my energy and studying hard for the exam next week.*

konkurabe 根比べ *a waiting game*
[lit. competition for stamina]

彼らは妥協を拒否して、根比べをしています。Karera wa dakyō o kyohi shite, konkurabe o shite imasu. *By rejecting a compromise, they're playing a waiting game.*

---

kōnō 効能 *effectiveness*

kōnōgaki o naraberu 効能書きを並べる *to sing the praises of something*
[lit. to display a statement of effectiveness]

政府はしきりに、新政策の効能書きを並べています。Seifu wa shikirini, shin seisaku no kōnōgaki o narabete imasu. *The government is eagerly singing the praises of the new policy.*

---

koshi 腰 *hip, waist*

koshi ga hikui 腰が低い *modest, humble, courteous*
[lit. One's waist is low.]

彼は、誰に対しても腰が低いです。Kare wa, dare ni taishite mo koshi ga hikui desu. *He is courteous to everyone.*

koshi ga omoi   腰が重い   *to be slow getting started*
[lit. One's waist is heavy.]
彼は有能ですが、欠点は何事にも腰が重いことです。Kare
wa yūnō desu ga, ketten wa nanigoto nimo koshi ga omoi koto
desu. *He's a capable person, but his shortcoming is that he's
slow getting started.*

koshi ga tsuyoi   腰が強い   *to be strong-willed*
[lit. One's waist is strong.]
彼女は腰が強いから、この困難も克服できるでしょう。
Kanojo wa koshi ga tsuyoi kara, kono konnan mo kokufuku
dekiru deshō. *Since she's strong-willed, she'll overcome her
current difficulties.*

koshi ga yowai   腰が弱い   *to be weak-kneed*
[lit. One's waist is weak.]
彼は腰が弱いので、交渉に関わるのは不向きです。Kare wa
koshi ga yowai node, kōshō ni kakawaru no wa fumuki desu.
*Because he's weak-kneed, he's not suitable for engaging in
negotiations.*

koshi o ageru   腰を上げる   *to take action*
[lit. to pick up one's hips]
女性問題について、政府がやっと腰を上げました。Josei
mondai ni tsuite, seifu ga yatto koshi o agemashita. *The
government finally took action on the women's issues.*

koshi o nukasu   腰を抜かす   *to be scared stiff*
[lit. to leave out one's hips]
彼女は蛇を見て、腰を抜かしました。 Kanojo wa hebi o
mite, koshi o nukashimashita. *She was scared stiff at seeing a
snake.*

koshi o ochitsukeru   腰を落ち着ける   *to settle down*
[lit. to make one's hips stay]
彼は結婚して以来、腰を落ち着けました。
Kare wa kekkon shite irai, koshi o ochitsukemashita.
He's settled down since his marriage.

koshi o oru   腰を折る   *to interrupt, to spoil a story*

[lit. to break someone's hips]

彼女はよく人の話の腰を折るので、友達が出来ません。
Kanojo wa yoku hito no hanashi no koshi o oru node,
tomodachi ga dekimasen. *Because she often interrupts other
people's conversation, she can't make friends.*

koshi o sueru   腰を据える   *to buckle down*
[lit. to steady one's hips]

来月から腰を据えて、論文を書き始めます。 Raigetsu kara
koshi o suete, ronbun o kakihajimemasu. *I'll buckle down
and start writing my thesis starting next month.*

hongoshi o ireru   本腰を入れる   *to apply oneself
diligently*
[lit. to apply one's hips fully]

仕事に本腰を入れないと、首になりますよ。 Shigoto ni
hongoshi o irenai to, kubi ni narimasu yo. *If you don't apply
yourself more diligently to your work, you'll be fired.*

koshikudake ni naru   腰砕けになる   *to fall through in
the middle of something*
[lit. One's hips break.]

彼の計画は、準備の途中で腰砕けになってしまいました。
Kare no keikaku wa, junbi no tochū de koshikudake ni natte
shimaimashita. *His plan fell through in the middle of the
preparations.*

koshinuke   腰抜け   *coward*
[lit. One's hips are gone.]

彼は、上司の言うことなら何でも賛成してしまう腰抜けです。
Kare wa, jōshi no iu koto nara nandemo sansei shite shimau
koshinuke desu. *He's a coward who agrees with everything
the boss says.*

nigegoshi ni naru   逃げ腰になる   *to get ready to back
out*
[lit. to fall into fleeing hips]

彼は、約束した仕事から逃げ腰になっています。 Kare wa,
yakusoku shita shigoto kara nigegoshi ni natte imasu. *He's*

getting ready to back out of the work he promised to do.

yowagoshi   弱腰   *timid*
[lit. weak hips]

そんな弱腰の態度では、厳しい相手と交渉できませんよ。
Sonna yowagoshi no taido dewa, kibishii aite to kōshō
dekimasen yo.   *If you have such a timid attitude, you can't
negotiate with a tough counterpart.*

---

koshikake   腰掛け   *chair, stool*
    koshikake shigoto   腰掛け仕事   *transient work*
[lit. short-term work while sitting on a chair]

腰掛け仕事のつもりなら、採用できません。 Koshikake
shigoto no tsumori nara, saiyō dekimasen.   *If you're intending
this to be transient work, we can't hire you.*

---

koto   事   *thing, something, matter, affair, fact, event,
accident*
    koto ga koto dakara   事が事だから   *under the
circumstances*
[lit. as something matters]

事が事だから、この際あなたの頼みを引き受けましょう。
Koto ga koto dakara, kono sai anata no tanomi o hikiukemashō.
Under the circumstances, I'll grant your request.

koto o aradateru   事を荒立てる   *to worsen something*
[lit. to make something rough]

そんなささいなことで、事を荒立てないようにしましょう。
Sonna sasai na koto de, koto o aradatenai yō ni shimashō.
Let's not worsen the situation because of such trivial things.

koto o kamaeru   事を構える   *to create controversy*
[lit. to set something up]

彼は機会を見つけては、事を構えたがります。 Kare wa kikai
o mitsukete wa, koto o kamaetagarimasu.   *He looks for
opportunities to create controversy.*

koto o konomu hito   事を好む人   *troublemaker*
[lit. to prefer an incident]

事を好む人たちが待っているから、あそこに着いたら気を
つけなさい。 Koto o konomu hitotachi ga matte iru kara,
asoko ni tsuitara ki o tsukenasai.   *Since those troublemakers
are waiting for you, be careful once you get there.*

kotomonage ni   事も無げに   *casually*
[lit. as if there isn't anything]
彼女は事も無げに彼との約束を破りました。 Kanojo wa
kotomonage ni kare to no yakusoku o yaburimashita.   *She
casually broke her promise to him.*

kotokireru   事切れる   *to pass away*
[lit. Something expires.]
父は家族全員が見守る中で事切れました。 Chichi wa kazoku
zen-in ga mimamoru naka de kotokiremashita.   *My father died
with the entire family looking on.*

kotonaki o eru   事なきを得る   *to save the day*
[lit. to have no accident]
子守がいるとき母が来てくれて、事なきを得ました。
Komori ga iru toki haha ga kite kurete, kotonaki o emashita.
*When we needed a baby sitter, my mother saved the day by
coming over to our house.*

kotoniyoru to   事によると   *might*
[lit. depending on something]
事によると、雨が降るかも知れません。 Kotoniyoru to, ame
ga furu kamo shiremasen.   *It might rain.*

kotoyosete   事寄せて   *under pretense of something*
[lit. by putting something closer]
彼は仕事に事寄せて、一日に何度も彼女に会いに行きます。
Kare wa shigoto ni kotoyosete, ichinichi ni nando mo kanojo ni
ai ni ikimasu.   *Under pretense of work, he goes to see her
many times a day.*

ōgoto   大事   *serious matter*
[lit. a big thing]
それがそんなに大事とは知りませんでした。 Sore ga sonna
ōgoto towa shirimasen deshita.   *I didn't know it was such a*

serious matter.

tadagoto dewa nai   只事ではない   *out of the ordinary, serious*

[lit. It's not something free.]

彼の声から、事態はただ事では無いことが分かりました。
Kare no koe kara, jitai wa tadagoto dewa nai koto ga wakarimashita.   *From his voice, I understood that the situation was out of the ordinary.*

---

kotoba   言葉   *language, speech, term, word*

kotoba ni amaeru   言葉に甘える   *to accept someone's kind offer*

[lit. to presume upon someone's words]

お言葉に甘えて、ご馳走になります。Okotoba ni amaete, gochisō ni narimasu.   *I'll accept your kind offer of a meal.*

kotoba ni amaru   言葉に余る   *beyond description*

[lit. too much for words]

その庭の美しさは言葉に余りました。Sono niwa no utsukushisa wa kotoba ni amarimashita. *The beauty of the garden was beyond description.*

kotoba ni kado ga aru   言葉に角がある   *to speak harshly*

[lit. There are angles in speech.]

彼の顔は平静でしたが、言葉に角がありました。 Kare no kao wa heisei deshita ga, kotoba ni kado ga arimashita. *His face was calm, but he spoke harshly.*

kotoba no aya   言葉の綾   *figure of speech*

[lit. the twill of speech]

彼が言ったことは言葉の綾で、あなたを非難したわけではありません。Kare ga itta koto wa kotoba no aya de, anata o hinan shita wake dewa arimasen. *What he said was a figure of speech, and he didn't mean to criticize you.*

kotoba o kaesu   言葉を返す   *to talk back*

[lit. to return words]

彼は自分の過ちを認める代わりに、いつも言葉を返します。
  Kare wa jibun no ayamachi o mitomeru kawari ni, itsumo
  kotoba o kaeshimasu.   *Instead of admitting his mistakes, he
  always talks back.*

kotoba o kazaru   言葉を飾る   *to use flowery language*
[lit. to decorate one's words]
彼女は言葉を飾るのは上手でも、話の内容はまあまあです。
  Kanojo wa kotoba o kazaru no wa jōzu demo, hanashi no naiyō
  wa māmā desu.   *Although she's good at using flowery
  language, the content of her talk is mediocre.*

kotoba o nigosu   言葉を濁す   *to speak vaguely*
[lit. to make one's words muddy]
彼は過去について聞かれて、言葉を濁しました。Kare wa
  kako ni tsuite kikarete, kotoba o nigoshimashita.   *When he
  was asked about his past, he spoke vaguely.*

kotoba o tsukushite   言葉を尽くして   *at length*
[lit. by exhausting one's words]
彼は言葉を尽くして、彼女の許しを乞いました。Kare wa
  kotoba o tsukushite, kanojo no yurushi o koimashita.   *He
  begged her forgiveness at length.*

kotobajiri o toraeru   言葉尻をとらえる   *to pick apart
someone's words*
[lit. to catch the buttocks of someone's words]
彼は人の言葉尻をとらえて、議論を始める癖があります。
  Kare wa hito no kotobajiri o toraete, giron o hajimeru kuse ga
  arimasu.   *He has the habit of starting arguments by picking
  apart other people's words.*

toge no aru kotoba   刺のある言葉   *harsh language*
[lit. words with thorns]
刺のある言葉から、彼女の機嫌が悪いことが分かりました。
  Toge no aru kotoba kara, kanojo no kigen ga warui koto ga
  wakarimashita.   *I knew from her harsh language that she was
  upset.*

urikotoba ni kaikotoba   売り言葉に買い言葉

exchanging verbal insults

[lit. buying words for selling words]

売り言葉に買い言葉から、喧嘩が始まりました。Urikotoba ni kaikotoba kara, kenka ga hajimarimashita. *After exchanging verbal insults, they started fighting.*

---

kotsu 骨 *bone*

kotsuniku no arasoi 骨肉の争い *domestic strife*

[lit. the fight between bones and flesh]

あの家族は、遺産相続をめぐって骨肉の争いを繰り広げています。Ano kazoku wa, isan sōzoku o megutte kotsuniku no arasoi o kurihirogete imasu. *That family is engaged in domestic strife over the inheritance.*

---

ku 苦 *suffering*

kuhai o nameru 苦杯をなめる *to be beaten*

[lit. to lick a bitter cup]

公共事業契約の入札で、苦杯をなめました。Kōkyō jigyō keiyaku no nyūsatsu de, kuhai o namemashita. *We were beaten in our bid for the public works contract.*

---

kū 空 *emptiness*

kū ni kisuru 空に帰する *to come to nothing*

[lit. to return to emptiness]

司法試験に落ちて、彼の努力は空に帰してしまいました。Shihō shiken ni ochite, kare no doryoku wa kū ni kishite shimaimashita. *His efforts came to nothing when he failed the bar exam.*

---

kubi 首 *neck, head, dismissal*

kubi ga abunai 首が危ない *to face dismissal*

[lit. Someone's neck is in danger.]

社内に、彼の首が危ないという噂があります。Shanai ni, kare no kubi ga abunai to iu uwasa ga arimasu. *There's a rumor in the company that he's facing dismissal.*

kubi ga tobu 首が飛ぶ *to be fired*

[lit. A head flies.]

汚職事件で、幹部官僚の首がたくさん飛びました。Oshoku jiken de, kanbu kanryō no kubi ga takusan tobimashita. *With the corruption incident, many senior government officials were fired.*

kubi ga mawaranai   首が回らない   *to be up to one's ears in debt*

[lit. A neck doesn't turn.]

借金で首が回りません。Shakkin de kubi ga mawarimasen. *I'm up to my ears in debt.*

kubi ga tsunagaru   首がつながる   *to hold on to one's job*

[lit. A neck is intact.]

支店長の計らいで、首がつながりました。Shitenchō no hakarai de, kubi ga tsunagarimashita. *Thanks to the branch manager's discretion, I held on to my job.*

kubi ni naru   首になる   *to be fired*

[lit. to be reduced to a neck]

彼は上司と言い争って、首になりました。Kare wa jōshi to iiarasotte, kubi ni narimashita. *He was fired after quarreling with his boss.*

kubi ni suru   首にする   *to fire someone*

[lit. to result in the loss of a neck]

彼女は全く働く気がないので、首にしました。Kanojo wa mattaku hataraku ki ga nai node, kubi ni shimashita. *Because she wasn't willing to work at all, I fired her.*

kubi o hineru   首をひねる   *to wonder*

[lit. to let one's head lean to one side]

彼女は娘の将来について首をひねっています。Kanojo wa musume no shōrai ni tsuite kubi o hinette imasu. *She's wondering about her daughter's future.*

kubi o kashigeru   首を傾げる   *to be skeptical*

[lit. to cock one's head]

みんなは彼の話に首を傾げました。Minna wa kare no hanashi

ni kubi o kashigemashita.   *Everybody was skeptical of his story.*

kubi o kiru   首を切る   *to fire someone*
[lit. to cut someone's head off]
不景気でも、社員の首は切りたくありません。Fukeiki
   demo, shain no kubi wa kiritaku arimasen.   *In spite of the
   recession, I don't want to fire any employees.*

kubi o nagaku shite matsu   首を長くして待つ   *to look
   forward to something*
[lit. to wait for something by stretching one's neck]
母は父が出張から帰るのを、首を長くして待っています。
   Haha wa chichi ga shutchō kara kaeru no o, kubi o nagakushite
   matte imasu.   *My mother is looking forward to my father's
   return from the business trip.*

kubi o soroeru   首を揃える   *to gather*
[lit. to put heads in order]
参加者全員が首を揃えるまで、待ちましょう。Sankasha
   zen-in ga kubi o soroeru made, machimashō.   *Let's wait till
   all the participants gather.*

kubi o sugekaeru   首をすげ替える   *to replace someone*
[lit. to change a head]
重役会は社長の首をすげ替えました。Jūyakukai wa shachō
   no kubi o sugekaemashita.   *The board of directors replaced
   the president.*

kubi o tate ni furu   首を縦に振る   *to say yes*
[lit. to shake one's head vertically]
先生は、学生の要望にやっと首を振りました。 Sensei wa,
   gakusei no yōbō ni yatto kubi o tate ni furimashita.   *The
   teacher finally said yes to the students' request.*

kubi o tsukkomu   首を突っ込む   *to stick one's nose
   into something*
[lit. to thrust one's neck into something]
彼は何にでも首を突っ込みたがります。Kare wa nani ni
   demo kubi o tsukkomitagarimasu.   *He wants to stick his nose
   into everything.*

kubi o yoko ni furu   首を横に振る   *to say no*
[lit. to shake one's head horizontally]
彼女は結婚の申し込みに、首を横に振りました。Kanojo wa
   kekkon no mōshikomi ni, kubi o yoko ni furimashita.   *She*
   said no to the marriage proposal.

kubippiki de   首っ引きで   *with the constant help of*
something
[lit. by pulling one's neck to something]
手引き書と首っ引きで、オートバイを組み立てています。
   Tebikisho to kubippiki de, ōtobai o kumitatete imasu.   *I'm*
   assembling a motorcycle with the constant help of the
   manual.

kubittake   首っ丈   *to be head over heels in love*
[lit. one's entire head]
彼は彼女に首っ丈です。Kare wa kanojo ni kubittake desu.
He's head over heels in love with her.

nekubi o kaku   寝首を掻く   *to stab someone in the back*
[lit. to cut a sleeping head off]
彼は出世のためなら、人の寝首を掻くのもためらいません。
   Kare wa shusse no tame nara, hito no nekubi o kaku no mo
   tameraimasen.   *He doesn't hesitate to stab people in the back*
   to promote his own success.

---

kuchi   口   *mouth, job, word, lips*
kuchi ga hiagaru   口が干上がる   *to fall on hard times*
financially
[lit. One's mouth dries up.]
失業して、口が干上がってしまいました。Shitsugyō shite,
   kuchi ga hiagatte shimaimashita.   *When I lost my job, I fell on*
   hard times financially.

kuchi ga heranai   口が減らない   *to be never at loss for*
words
[lit. One's words never diminish.]
それがどんな状況でも、彼女は口が減りません。Sore ga

donna jōkyō demo, kanojo wa kuchi ga herimasen.   *Under any circumstances, she's never at loss for words.*

kuchi ga hogureru   口がほぐれる   *to loosen up and start to talk*
[lit. One's mouth gets loose.]
彼女の口がやっとほぐれました。Kanojo no kuchi ga yatto hoguremashita.   *Finally, she loosened up and started to talk.*

kuchi ga kakaru   口が掛かる   *to be offered a position*
[lit. A job is dangled.]
夫に、大学から教授の口が掛かりました。Otto ni, daigaku kara kyōju no kuchi ga kakarimashita.   *My husband was offered a professorship by a university.*

kuchi ga karui hito   口が軽い人   *blabbermouth*
[lit. A mouth is light.]
彼は口が軽いから、個人的なことは話せません。Kare wa kuchi ga karui kara, kojinteki na koto wa hanasemasen.   *Since he's a blabbermouth, I don't tell him anything personal.*

kuchi ga katai   口が堅い   *tight-lipped*
[lit. A mouth is hard.]
彼女は口が堅いから、秘密を話しても安心です。Kanojo wa kuchi ga katai kara, himitsu o hanashitemo anshin desu.
Because she's tight-lipped, I feel comfortable telling her a secret.

kuchi ga koeru   口が肥える   *to be a gourmet*
[lit. A mouth gets enriched.]
彼は口が肥えているので、素晴らしいレストランをたくさん知っています。Kare wa kuchi ga koete iru node, subarashii resutoran o takusan shitte imasu.   *Since he's a gourmet, he knows many great restaurants.*

kuchi ga kusattemo   口が腐っても   *no matter what*
[lit. even if one's mouth rots]
口が腐っても、人の悪口は言いません。Kuchi ga kusattemo, hito no warukuchi wa iimasen.   *No matter what, I won't badmouth other people.*

kuchi ga omoi   口が重い   *man of few words*
[lit. A mouth is heavy.]
あの作家は口が重いので、インタビューするのが大変です。
Ano sakka wa kuchi ga omoi node, intabyū suru no ga taihen
desu.   *Because that novelist is a man of few words, it's
difficult to interview him.*

kuchi ga saketemo   口が裂けても   *no matter what*
[lit. even if one's mouth is torn]
口が裂けても、その秘密は守ります。Kuchi ga saketemo,
sono himitsu wa mamorimasu.   *No matter what, I'll keep the
secret.*

kuchi ga suberu   口が滑る   *to make a slip of the tongue*
[lit. a mouth slips.]
口が滑って、彼女に余計なことを言ってしまいました。
Kuchi ga subette, kanojo ni yokei na koto o itte shimaimashita.
*I regret that I made a slip of the tongue and said too much to
her.*

kuchi ga sugiru   口が過ぎる   *to say things one is not
supposed to say to someone*
[lit. Words are excessive.]
父と口論したとき、口が過ぎてしまいました。Chichi to
kōron shita toki, kuchi ga sugite shimaimashita.   *During the
quarrel with my father, I said things one isn't supposed to say
to one's father.*

kuchi ga suppakunaru hodo   口が酸っぱくなるほど
repeatedly
[lit. to the extent that one's mouth gets sour]
彼には口が酸っぱくなるほど説明したのに、まだ分かって
いません。Kare niwa kuchi ga suppakunaru hodo setsumei
shita noni, mada wakatte imasen.   *Although I explained it to
him repeatedly, he still doesn't understand.*

kuchi ga umai   口がうまい   *smooth-talking*
[lit. A mouth is skillful.]
彼女は口がうまいから、気をつけなさい。Kanojo wa kuchi

ga umai kara, ki o tsukenasai. *Be careful, because she's a
smooth talker.*

kuchi ga urusai   口がうるさい   *to be particular about
something*
[lit. A mouth is noisy.]
彼は何事にも口がうるさいので、みんなが敬遠します。
  Kare wa nanigoto nimo kuchi ga urusai node, minna ga keien
  shimasu. *Because he's particular about everything,
  everybody avoids him.*

kuchi ga warui   口が悪い   *to have a sharp tongue*
[lit. A mouth is bad.]
彼は口が悪いかも知れないけれど、悪気はありません。
  Kare wa kuchi ga warui kamo shirenai keredo, warugi wa
  arimasen. *He may have a sharp tongue, but he doesn't have
  malicious intentions.*

kuchi kara saki ni umareru   口から先に生まれる   *to
not know when to shut up*
[lit. to be born mouth-first]
彼は口から先に生まれたような人で、話がいつも長引きます。
  Kare wa kuchi kara saki ni umareta yō na hito de, hanashi ga
  itsumo nagabikimasu. *Since he doesn't know when to shut up,
  his conversation always drags on.*

kuchi ni au   口に合う   *to suit one's taste*
[lit. to fit someone's mouth]
おいしそうな料理でしたが、口に合いませんでした。
  Oishisō na ryōri deshita ga, kuchi ni aimasen deshita. *It
  looked like a delicious dish, but it didn't suit my taste.*

kuchi ni dasu   口に出す   *to utter*
[lit. to let something out of one's mouth]
彼女の秘密を口に出してしまいました。Kanojo no himitsu o
  kuchi ni dashite shimaimashita. *Accidentally, I uttered her
  secret.*

kuchi ni noboru   口に上る   *to be mentioned*
[lit. to come up to one's mouth]

候補者として、彼の名前が最近よく口に上っています。
Kōhosha to shite, kare no namae ga saikin yoku kuchi ni
nobotte imasu. *His name has been mentioned often as a
candidate recently.*

kuchi ni suru 口にする *to speak of something*
[lit. to make something into words]
彼は自分の過去について、決して口にしません。Kare wa
jibun no kako nitsuite, kesshite kuchi ni shimasen. *He never
speaks of his past.*

kuchi o dasu 口を出す *to meddle with something*
[lit. to put words out]
そのことには、口を出さないで下さい。Sono koto niwa,
kuchi o dasanai de kudasai. *Please don't meddle with that.*

kuchi o hasamu 口を挟む *to interrupt while others are
talking*
[lit. to insert one's words]
彼女は、人の話に口を挟む癖があります。Kanojo wa, hito
no hanshi ni kuchi o hasamu kuse ga arimasu. *She has a habit
of interrupting while other people are talking.*

kuchi o hiraku 口を開く *to start talking*
[lit. to open one's mouth]
彼はやっと口を開きました。Kare wa yatto kuchi o
hirakimashita. *He finally started talking.*

kuchi o kiku 口をきく *to speak to someone*
[lit. to make one's words effective]
息子とは、この一ヶ月口をきいていません。Musuko towa,
kono ikkagetsu kuchi o kiite imasen. *I haven't spoken to my
son for a month.*

kuchi o kiru 口を切る *to be the first one to speak*
[lit. to cut one's words out]
家族の集まりでは、祖父がまず口を切りました。Kazoku no
atsumari dewa, sofu ga mazu kuchi o kirimashita. *The
grandfather was the first one to speak at the family gathering.*

kuchi o kiwamete   口を極めて   *outspokenly*
[lit. by making one's words extreme]
彼は口を極めて政府を批判しました。Kare wa kuchi o
  kiwamete seifu o hihan shimashita.   *He criticized the
  government outspokenly.*

kuchi o nuguu   口を拭う   *to pretend not to know
  something*
[lit. to wipe one's mouth]
彼女は友達がカンニングしたことについて、口を拭ってい
  ます。Kanojo wa tomodachi ga kanningu shita koto nitsuite,
  kuchi o nugutte imasu.   *She's pretending not to know that her
  friend cheated on the exam.*

kuchi o soroete   口を揃えて   *unanimously*
[lit. by putting mouths in order]
母の考えに、家族全員が口を揃えて賛成しました。Haha no
  kangae ni, kazoku zen-in ga kuchi o soroete sansei shimashita.
  *All of us in the family unanimously agreed with our mother's
  idea.*

kuchi o suppaku shite   口を酸っぱくして   *repeatedly*
[lit. by making one's mouth sour]
彼女に口を酸っぱくして警告しましたが、効き目がありま
  せんでした。Kanojo ni kuchi o suppaku shite keikoku
  shimashita ga, kikime ga arimasen deshita.   *Although I
  repeatedly warned her, it had no effect on her.*

kuchi o togarasu   口を尖らす   *to get upset*
[lit. to purse one's lips]
彼女はすぐ口を尖らします。Kanojo wa sugu kuchi o
  togarashimasu.   *She gets upset easily.*

kuchi o waru   口を割る   *to confess*
[lit. to split one's mouth open]
容疑者は、逮捕されるとすぐに口を割りました。Yōgisha
  wa, taiho sareru to sugu ni kuchi o warimashita.   *The suspect
  confessed immediately when he was arrested.*

kuchibashiru   口走る   *to blurt out*
[lit. to run one's mouth]
あの候補者は、競争相手について事実無根のことを口走っ
  ています。 Ano kōhosha wa, kyōsō aite ni tsuite jijitsumukon
  no koto o kuchibashitte imasu.   *That candidate is blurting out
  something unfounded about his opponent.*

kuchidome suru   口止めする   *to hush someone up*
[lit. to stop someone's mouth]
彼女を口止めするため、高い贈り物を上げねばなりません
  でした。 Kanojo o kuchidome suru tame, takai okurimono o
  ageneba narimasen deshita.   *I had to give her an expensive
  gift to hush her up.*

kuchigitanai   口汚い   *foul-mouthed*
[lit. One's mouth is dirty.]
彼は口汚いので、両親に紹介できません。 Kare wa
  kuchigitanai node, ryōshin ni shōkai dekimasen.   *Because
  he's foul-mouthed, I can't introduce him to my parents.*

kuchigomoru   口ごもる   *to hem and haw*
[lit. to let words stay in one's mouth]
彼女は彼の求婚に口ごもりました。 Kanojo wa kare no
  kyūkon ni kuchigomorimashita.   *She hemmed and hawed at
  his marriage proposal.*

kuchigotae suru   口答えする   *to talk back*
[lit. to answer with one's words]
彼は人からの助言に、必ず口答えします。 Kare wa hito kara
  no jogen ni, kanarazu kuchigotae shimasu.   *He habitually
  talks back to people who give him advice.*

kuchiguruma ni noseru   口車に乗せる   *to cajole
someone into doing something*
[lit. to give someone a ride on the wheels of words]
彼女を口車に乗せて、私の宿題をやらせました。 Kanojo o
  kuchiguruma ni nosete, watakushi no shukudai o
  yarasemashita.   *I cajoled her into doing my homework.*

kuchihabattai   口幅ったい   *impertinent*
[lit. one's mouth being too wide]
口幅ったいかも知れませんが、もっと丁寧に話すべきです。
Kuchihabattai kamoshiremasen ga, motto teinei ni hanasu beki
desu.   *This may sound impertinent, but you should speak more
politely.*

kuchihatchō tehatchō   口八丁手八丁   *to be eloquent
and talented on the surface*
[lit. eight mouths and eight hands]
彼は口八丁手八丁だけれど、いい大統領になるかどうか分
かりません。Kare wa kuchihatchō tehatchō da keredo,
ii daitōryō ni naru ka dō ka wakarimasen.   *He's eloquent and
talented on the surface, but I don't know if he'd be a good
president.*

kuchikomi   口コミ   *word-of-mouth*
[lit. communication by mouths]
彼女の東京での成功は、口コミで故郷の町中に広がりました。
Kanojo no Tōkyō de no seikō wa, kuchikomi de kokyō no
machijū ni hirogarimashita.   *Her success in Tokyo spread by
word-of-mouth all over her hometown.*

kuchisaki dake no   口先だけの   *empty*
[lit. only with the tip of a mouth]
口先だけの約束なら、しない方がましです。Kuchisaki dake
no yakusoku nara, shinai hō ga mashi desu.   *If it's an empty
promise, it's better not to make it.*

kuchisaki no umai   口先のうまい   *smooth-talking*
[lit. being good at the tip of a mouth]
母親は娘に、口先のうまい男には気をつけなさいと言いま
した。Hahaoya wa musume ni, kuchisaki no umai otoko niwa
ki o tsukenasai to iimashita.   *The mother told her daughter to
be careful of smooth-talking men.*

kuchiura o awaseru   口裏を合わせる   *to prearrange a*

story so as not to contradict each other later
[lit. to adjust the lining of the words]

彼と彼女は結婚の危機を否定するときに矛盾しないように、
口裏を合わせました。Kare to kanojo wa kekkon no kiki o
hitei suru toki ni mujun shinai yō ni, kuchiura o awasemashita.
*He and she prearranged a story so as not to contradict each
other when denying their marriage was in crisis.*

kuchiyakamashii   口やかましい   *nagging*
[lit. One's mouth is noisy.]

父は口やかましいので、そばにいるとくつろげません。
Chichi wa kuchiyakamashii node, soba ni iru to
kutsurogemasen. *Because my father is a nag, I can't relax
around him.*

kuchiyakusoku   口約束   *verbal commitment*
[lit. a word of promise]

彼女の口約束は信用できません。Kanojo no kuchiyakusoku
wa shin-yō dekimasen. *I can't trust her verbal commitment.*

kuchiyogoshi   口汚し   *just a morsel (food)*
[lit. something to dirty someone's food]

ほんの口汚しですが¹、どうぞ召し上がってください。
Honno kuchiyogoshi desu ga, dōzo meshiagatte kudasai. *It's
only a morsel, but please eat it.*

kuchizoe   口添え   *recommendation*
[lit. to lend one's words to someone]

叔父の口添えで、クラブの会員になれました。Oji no
kuchizoe de, kurabu no kaiin ni naremashita. *I was able to
become a member of the club because of my uncle's
recommendation.*

mudaguchi o tataku   無駄口を叩く   *to chatter idly*
[lit. to drum up wasteful words]

友達と電話で無駄口を叩いているより、本を読みなさい。
Tomodachi to denwa de mudaguchi o tataite iru yori, hon o
yominasai. *Read books rather than chattering idly on the
phone with your friends.*

nikumareguchi o tataku   憎まれ口を叩く   *to say nasty things*

[lit. to drum up the words that will cause hatred]

彼は、誰にも憎まれ口を叩くので知られています。Kare wa, dare nimo nikumareguchi o tataku node shirarete imasu. *He's known to say nasty things to everyone.*

ōguchi o tataku   大口を叩く   *to talk big*

[lit. to drum up one's own words]

彼は、将来首相になると大口を叩いています。Kare wa, shōrai shushō ni naru to ōguchi o tataite imasu. *He's talking big, saying that he'll become prime minister in the future.*

---

kuchibashi   嘴   *beak*

kuchibashi ga kiiroi   嘴が黄色い   *to be a greenhorn*

[lit. One's beak is yellow.]

彼女は嘴が黄色いのに、自分では専門家だと思っています。Kanojo wa kuchibashi ga kiiroi noni, jibun dewa senmonka da to omotte imasu. *Although she's a greenhorn, she thinks of herself as an expert.*

kuchibashi o ireru   嘴を入れる   *to poke one's nose into others' affairs*

[lit. to insert one's beak into something]

人のことに嘴を入れたがるのが、彼の欠点です。Hito no koto ni kuchibashi o iretagaru no ga, kare no ketten desu. *His eagerness to poke his nose into others' affairs is his weakness.*

---

kuchibi   口火   *fuse*

kuchibi o kiru   口火を切る   *to be the first to do something*

[lit. to ignite a fuse]

この環境問題で口火を切ったのが彼女です。Kono kankyō mondai de kuchibi o kitta no ga kanojo desu. *She's the one who started this environmental issue.*

---

kuchibiru   唇   *lip*

kuchibiru o kamu   唇を嚙む   *to endure*
[lit. to bite one's own lips]
不当な批判に、唇を嚙みました。Futō na hinan ni, kuchibiru o kamimashita.   *I endured the unjust accusation.*

kuda   管   *tube*
kuda o maku   管を巻く   *to blather about someone or something over drinks*
[lit. to wind a tube around something]
友達は、彼の上役について管を巻きました。Tomodachi wa kare no uwayaku ni tsuite kuda o makimashita.   *My friend blathered about his boss over drinks.*

kugi   釘   *nail*
kugi o sasu   釘をさす   *to remind someone of something*
[lit. to drive a nail]
来週必ず論文を提出するように、学生に釘をさしました。Raishū kanarazu ronbun o teishutsu suru yō ni, gakusei ni kugi o sashimashita.   *I reminded the students to submit their papers without exception next week.*

kujū   苦汁   *bitter juice*
kujū o nameru   苦汁を嘗める   *to have a bitter experience*
[lit. to lick bitter juice]
去年は失業の苦汁を嘗めました。Kyonen wa shitsugyō no kujū o namemashita.   *Last year I had the bitter experience of being unemployed.*

kumo   雲   *cloud*
kumo o tsukamu yō na   雲をつかむような   *vague*
[lit. like grasping a cloud]
彼女は、彼の雲をつかむような計画に大金を投資しました。Kanojo wa, kare no kumo o tsukamu yō na keikaku ni taikin o tōshi shimashita.   *She invested a large sum of money in his vague plan.*

kumogakuresuru　雲隠れする　　*to drop out of sight*
[lit. to hide behind the clouds]
彼はマスコミの追求を避けて、雲隠れしています。Kare wa
　masukomi no tsuikyū o sakete, kumogakure shite imasu.
　He's dropped out of sight to avoid inquiries by the media.

kumoyuki o miru　雲行きを見る　　*to be still deciding*
[lit. to see the movement of clouds]
彼女は立候補するかどうか、雲行きを見ています。Kanojo
　wa rikkōho suru ka dō ka, kumoyuki o mite imasu.　*She's still
　deciding whether to run for election or not.*

---

kumo　蜘蛛　*spider*
kumo no ko o chirasu yō ni　蜘蛛の子を散らすように
　in all directions
[lit. like scattering baby spiders]
夕立が始まって、人々は蜘蛛の子を散らすように走り出し
　ました。Yūdachi ga hajimatte, hitobito wa kumo no ko o
　chirasu yō ni hashiridashimashita.　*When the shower started,
　people started running in all directions.*

---

kusa　草　*grass*
kusa no ne o wakete sagasu　草の根を分けて探す　*to
　search thoroughly*
[lit. to look for something even by separating roots of grass]
彼女はいなくなった猫を、草の根を分けて探しました。
　Kanojo wa inakunatta neko o, kusa no ne o wakete
　sagashimashita.　*She searched thoroughly for her missing cat.*

kusaba no kage de naku　草葉の陰で泣く　*to turn over
　in one's grave*
[lit. to cry in the shade of grass and leaves]
そんなことをすると、お父さんが草葉の陰で泣きますよ。
　Sonna koto o suru to, otōsan ga kusaba no kage de nakimasu
　yo.　*If you do that, your father will turn over in his grave.*

---

kusai　臭い　*bad-smelling*

kusai meshi o kuu 　臭い飯を食う　 *to be behind bars, to be in jail*

[lit. to eat bad-smelling rice]

彼はいま、臭い飯を食っています。Kare wa ima kusai meshi o kutte imasu. *He's behind bars now.*

kusai mono ni futa o suru 　臭い物に蓋をする　 *to cover things up*

[lit. to put a lid on a smelly thing]

国民は、政府の臭いものに蓋をするような態度を批判しています。Kokumin wa, seifu no kusai mono ni futa o suru yō na taido o hihan shite imasu. *The people are criticizing the government's propensity to cover things up.*

---

kusaru 　腐る　 *to rot*

kusaru hodo 　腐るほど　 *great number of something*

[lit. to the extent that things will rot]

彼女は、ドレスを腐るほど持っています。Kanojo wa, doresu o kusaru hodo motte imasu. *She has a great number of dresses.*

---

kutabireru 　くたびれる　 *to get tired*

kutabiremōke 　くたびれ儲け　 *to come up empty-handed*

[lit. to earn tiredness]

仕事を探しに行きましたが、くたびれ儲けでした。Shigoto o sagashini ikimashita ga, kutabiremōke deshita. *Although I went to look for a job, I came up empty-handed.*

---

kuu 　食う　 *to eat*

kuitarinai 　食い足りない　 *to be dissatisfied with something*

[lit. to not have eaten enough]

彼女の説明は、食い足りませんでした。Kanojo no setsumei wa, kuitarimasen deshita. *I was dissatisfied with her explanation.*

kutte kakaru 　食って掛かる　 *to challenge*

[lit. to set about eating]

彼は駐車違反の券を渡されて、警官に食って掛かりました。
Kare wa chūsha ihan no ken o watasarete, keikan ni kutte
kakarimashita. *When he was handed a ticket for a parking
violation, he challenged the policeman.*

kuuka kuwareruka   食うか食われるか   *life-or-death*
[lit. to eat or be eaten]

与党と野党は、食うか食われるかの闘争を繰り広げています。
Yotō to yatō wa, kuuka kuwareruka no tōsō o kurihirogete
imasu. *The majority and minority parties are engaged in a
life-or-death struggle.*

kuwasemono   食わせ物   *fake*
[lit. something to make someone eat]

彼女は食わせ物だから、気をつけなさい。Kanojo wa
kuwasemono dakara, ki o tsukenasai. *Be careful of her
because she's a fake.*

ippai kuwaseru   一杯食わせる   *to play a trick on
someone*
[lit. to make someone eat whatever is offered]

競争相手に一杯食わせることに成功しました。Kyōsō aite ni
ippai kuwaseru koto ni seikō shimashita. *We succeeded in
playing a trick on our competitor.*

kuzu   屑   *waste*
ningen no kuzu   人間の屑   *good-for-nothing*
[lit. a waste of a human being]

彼女は人間の屑です。Kanojo wa ningen no kuzu desu. *She is
a good-for-nothing.*

kyo   虚   *void*
kyo ni jōjiru   虚に乗じる   *to catch someone off guard*
[lit. to ride on someone's void]

今度の入札は、相手の虚に乗じて勝つことが出来ました。
Kondo no nyūsatsu wa, aite no kyo ni jōjite katsu koto ga
dekimashita. *We won the bidding by catching our competitor*

off guard.

---

kyō   恐   *to be scared*
  kyōsaika   恐妻家   *a henpecked husband*
[lit. a husband who is scared of his wife]
彼は恐妻家です。Kare wa kyōsaika desu.   *He's a henpecked husband.*

M

---

ma   間   *space, time, timing*
  ma ga warui   間が悪い   *to be embarrassed*
[lit. The timing is bad.]
授業中の居眠りを先生に見られて、間が悪い思いをしました。
  Jugyō chū no inemuri o sensei ni mirarete, ma ga warui omoi o
  shimashita.   *I felt embarrassed because the teacher saw me
  dozing during class.*

  ma ga motenai   間が持てない   *to be unable to fill the
  silences*
[lit. to be unable to hold space]
初めてのデートで、間が持てなくて困りました。Hajimete
  no dēto de, ma ga motenakute komarimashita.   *I had a tough
  time on the first date because I couldn't fill the silence.*

  manuke   間抜け   *blockhead*
[lit. someone with no sense of timing]
彼女は間抜けだから、何かするといつも失敗があります。
  Kanojo wa manuke dakara, nanika suru to itsumo shippai ga
  arimasu.   *Since she's a blockhead, whenever she does
  something, there's a mistake .*

---

ma   魔   *devil*
  ma gasasu   魔がさす   *The devil made (one) do it.*
[lit. to be dictated by a devil]

魔が差して、言うべきでないことを言ってしまってすみま
せん。Ma ga sashite, iu beki de nai koto o itte shimatte
sumimasen.   *I shouldn't have said that; the devil made me do
it.*

---

ma   真   *truth*
ma ni ukeru   真に受ける   *to accept something as true*
[lit. to receive something as being true]
彼女の話を真に受けて、同情してしまいました。Kanojo no
hanashi o ma ni ukete, dōjō shite shimaimashita.   *I regret that
I sympathized with her by believing her story.*

---

magaru   曲がる   *to curve*
magarinari ni mo   曲がりなりにも   *at least*
[lit. even with a curve]
曲がりなりにも、コンピュータは使うことが出来ます。
Magarinari ni mo, konpyūta wa tsukau koto ga dekimasu.   *At
least I can use a computer.*

---

maikyo   枚挙   *enumeration*
maikyo ni itoma ga nai   枚挙にいとまがない   *to be
too numerous to mention*
[lit. to be too busy to count something one by one]
彼は、枚挙にいとまがないほどの沢山の賞を受けています。
Kare wa, maikyo ni itoma ga nai hodo no takusan no shō o
ukete imasu.   *He received so many awards they were too
numerous to mention.*

---

makka   真っ赤   *deep red*
makka na uso   真っ赤な嘘   *outright lie*
[lit. a deep red lie]
彼女のいいわけは、真っ赤な嘘であることがすぐ分かりま
した。Kanojo no iiwake wa, makka na uso dearu koto ga sugu
wakarimashita.   *I immediately knew that her excuse was an
outright lie.*

makkō　抹香　*incense*

makkō kusai　抹香臭い　*preachy*

[lit. smelling like incense]

彼の話はいつも抹香臭いので、みんなが彼を避けています。

Kare no hanashi wa itsumo makkō kusai node, minna ga kare o sakete imasu.　*Because he's always preachy, everybody avoids him.*

maku　巻く　*to wrap something*

makizoe o kuu　巻き添えを食う　*to get mixed up in trouble*

[lit. to be wrapped and thrown into something]

会社の権力争いの巻き添えを食って、首になってしまいました。Kaisha no kenryoku arasoi no makizoe o kutte, kubi ni natte shimaimashita.　*I got fired after getting mixed up in the power struggle in the company.*

makura　枕　*pillow*

makura o takaku shite nemuru　枕を高くして眠る　*to sleep peacefully*

[lit. to sleep by making one's pillow higher]

借金を払い終わったので、枕を高くして眠れます。Shakkin o haraiowatta node, makura o takaku shite nemuremasu. *Because I finished repaying the debt, I can start sleeping peacefully.*

manaita　まな板　*cutting board*

manaita ni noseru　まな板に載せる　*to take up something for discussion*

[lit. to put something on a cutting board]

次の会議では、来年の計画をまな板に載せるつもりです。Tsugi no kaigi dewa, rainen no keikaku o manaita ni noseru tsumori desu.　*In the next meeting, we'll take up the plans for next year.*

marui　丸い　*round*

maruku osameru   丸く収める   *to settle something amicably*

[lit. to finish roundly]

彼女との口論を、丸く収めることが出来ました。Kanojo to no kōron o, maruku osameru koto ga dekimashita.   *I was able to settle the quarrel with her amicably.*

---

masseki   末席   *lowest seat*

masseki o kegasu   末席を汚す   *to have the honor of being present at something*

[lit. to dirty the lowest seat]

今日は、委員会の会議の末席を汚させていただきます。 Kyō wa, iinkai no kaigi no masseki o kegasasete itadakimasu. *I'm honored to be present at the committee meeting today.*

---

mata   股   *thigh*

futamata kakeru   二股かける   *to get involved in two things at the same time*

[lit. to put each thigh on a different thing]

彼女はクラブ活動では、テニスと水泳に二股かけています。 Kanojo wa kurabu katsudō dewa, tenisu to suiei ni futamata kakete imasu.   *In extracurricular activities, she's involved in both tennis and swimming.*

---

mato   的   *target*

mato o shiboru   的を絞る   *to focus*

[lit. to squeeze a target]

会議の話題として、新製品開発に的を絞りました。Kaigi no wadai toshite, shin seihin kaihatsu ni mato o shiborimashita. *For the subject of the meeting, we focused on the development of a new product.*

matohazure   的外れ   *irrelevant*

[lit. off-target]

彼女の質問は、全く的外れでした。Kanojo no shitsumon wa, mattaku matohazure deshita.   *Her question was totally irrelevant.*

matsu　待つ　*to wait*

　mattanashi　待った無し　*now or never*

　[lit. without a wait]

　わが社は今、待った無しの状態に直面しています。Waga
　　sha wa ima, mattanashi no jōtai ni chokumen shite imasu.
　　Our company is facing a "now or never" situation.

---

mawaru　回る　*to go around*

　mawarikudoi　回りくどい　*to beat around the bush*

　[lit. to go around tediously]

　彼の話し方は回りくどいので、聞いているといらいらします。
　　Kare no hanashikata wa mawarikudoi node, kiite iru to iraira
　　shimasu.　*Because he always beats around the bush, it's
　　irritating to listen to him.*

　mawashimono　回し者　*spy*

　[lit. someone who goes around]

　あの店員は、競争相手の店の回し者という噂があります。
　　Ano ten-in wa kyōsō aite no mise no mawashimono to iu
　　uwasa ga arimasu.　*There's a rumor that the salesclerk over
　　there is a spy for a competing store.*

---

mayu　眉　*eyebrows*

　mayu ni tsuba o nuru　眉に唾を塗る　*to take
　something with a grain of salt*

　[lit. to put saliva on one's eyebrows]

　彼女の話は、眉に唾を塗って聞かねばなりません。Kanojo
　　no hanashi wa, mayu ni tsuba o nutte kikaneba narimasen.
　　You should take her story with a grain of salt.

　mayu o hisomeru　眉をひそめる　*to frown on
　something*

　[lit. to knit one's eyebrows]

　彼は、妹の人生に対する態度に眉をひそめました。
　　Kare wa, imōto no jinsei ni taisuru taido ni mayu o
　　hisomemashita.　*He frowned on his younger sister's attitude
　　toward life.*

mayu o kumoraseru   眉を曇らせる   *to be concerned*
[lit. to make one's eyebrows cloudy]
彼女の話を聞いて、眉を曇らせました。Kanojo no hanashi o
  kiite, mayu o kumorasemashita.   *After hearing her story, I
  was concerned about it.*

mayutsubamono   眉唾物   *fake*
[lit. something which causes one to put saliva on one's eyebrows]
彼女の話は、全くの眉唾物です。Kanojo no hanashi wa,
  mattaku no mayutsubamono desu.   *Her story is a total fake.*

---

me   芽   *bud*
  me ga deru   芽が出る   *to begin to prosper*
  [lit. A bud begins to come out.]
  彼女の商売は、やっと芽が出始めました。Kanojo no shōbai
    wa, yatto me ga dehajimemashita.   *Her business has finally
    begun to prosper.*

  mebaeru   芽生える   *to emerge*
  [lit. to start a bud]
  彼に学者になりたい気持ちが芽生えたのは、昔のことです。
    Kare ni gakusha ni naritai kimochi ga mebaeta no wa, mukashi
    no koto desu.   *It was long ago that his desire to become a
    scholar emerged.*

---

me   目   *eye*
  me ga kiku   目が利く   *to have a critical eye for
    something*
  [lit. One's eye is effective.]
  彼女は中国の骨董品に目が利きます。Kanojo wa Chūgoku no
    kottōhin ni me ga kikimasu.   *She has a critical eye for
    Chinese antiques.*

  me ga koeru   目が肥える   *to be a good judge of
    someone or something*
  [lit. One's eyes grow fertile.]
  彼は、新入社員を見る目が肥えています。Kare wa shinnyū
    shain o miru me ga koete imasu.   *He's a good judge of new*

employees in the company.

me ga kuramu　　目がくらむ　　*to be dazzled by something*
[lit. One's eyes grow dizzy.]

彼は金に目がくらんで、会社の秘密を漏らしてしまいました。
　Kare wa kane ni me ga kurande, kaisha no himitsu o morashite
　shimaimashita.　*Dazzled by money, he leaked the company*
　secrets.

me ga nai　　目がない・　　*to be extremely fond of something*
[lit. no eyes]

彼はゴルフに目がありません。Kare wa gorufu ni me ga
　arimasen.　*He's extremely fond of playing golf.*

me ga mawaru yō ni isogashii　　目が回るように忙しい
　to be as busy as a bee
[lit. to be so busy as to feel dizzy]

今は会計年度末なので、目が回るように忙しいです。Ima
　wa kaikei nendo matsu nanode, me ga mawaru yō ni isogashii
　desu.　*Because it's the end of the fiscal year now, we're as*
　busy as bees.

me ga saeru　　目が冴える　　*to be wide awake*
[lit. One's eyes are clear.]

夕べは目が冴えて、午前二時まで眠れませんでした。Yūbe
　wa me ga saete, gozen niji made nemuremasen deshita.　*I was*
　wide awake last night and couldn't fall asleep till two in the
　morning.

me ga sameru　　目が覚める　　*to come to one's senses*
[lit. to become awake]

彼はやっと目が覚めて、悪い仲間との縁を切りました。
　Kare wa yatto me ga samete, warui nakama to no en o
　kirimashita.　*He finally came to his senses and severed*
　relations with his no-good friends.

me ga takai　　目が高い　　*to have an expert eye for*
　something
[lit. One's eyes are high.]

彼女は、美術に対する目が高いです。Kanojo wa, bijutsu ni

taisuru me ga takai desu.   *She has an expert eye for art.*

me ga tobideru   目が飛び出る   *to be shocked at an exorbitant price*
[lit. One's eyes pop out.]

そのレストランの勘定があまりにも高かったので、目が飛び出ました。Sono resutoran no kanjō ga amari nimo takakatta node, me ga tobidemashita.   *I was shocked at the exorbitant check at the restaurant.*

me ga todoku   目が届く   *to be attentive to someone*
[lit. One's eyes reach someone.]

あの店では、客一人一人に対する目が届いています。Ano mise dewa, kyaku hitorihitori ni taisuru me ga todoite imasu. *In that store, they're attentive to each customer.*

me kara hana ni nukeru yō na   目から鼻に抜けるような   *sharp, intelligent*
[lit. like something passing through one's eyes to the nose]

彼は、目から鼻に抜けるような人です。Kare wa, me kara hana ni nukeru yō na hito desu.   *He's very sharp.*

me kara hi ga deru   目から火が出る   *to see stars*
[lit. Sparks come out of one's eyes.]

ドアに頭をぶつけて、目から火が出ました。Doa ni atama o butsukete, me kara hi ga demashita.   *I saw stars when I hit my head against a door.*

me kara uroko ga ochiru   目から鱗が落ちる   *to see the light*
[lit. The scales drop from one's eyes.]

彼は間違っていると思っていたけれど、話してみて、目から鱗が落ちました。Kare wa machigatte iru to omotte ita keredo, hanashite mite, me kara uroko ga ochimashita. *Although I had thought he was wrong, after talking with him, I saw the light .*

me mo aterarenai   目も当てられない   *too terrible to look at*
[lit. to be unable to even cast one's eyes]

交通事故の現場は、目も当てられないほどのひどさでした。
Kōtsū jiko no genba wa, me mo aterarenai hodo no hidosa
deshita.   *The scene of the traffic accident was too terrible to
look at.*

me mo kurenai   目もくれない   *to ignore someone or
something*
[lit. not even to cast one's eyes]
彼女は、親の忠告には目もくれません。Kanojo wa, oya no
chūkoku niwa me mo kuremasen.   *She ignores her parents'
advice.*

me ni amaru   目に余る   *to be intolerable*
[lit. to be excessive to one's eyes]
彼の最近の言動は目に余ります。Kare no saikin no gendō wa
me ni amarimasu.   *His recent speech and conduct are
intolerable.*

me ni hairu   目に入る   *to come across someone or
something*
[lit. to enter into one's eyes]
ギフトの買い物をしていると、きれいなセーターが目に入
りました。Gifuto no kaimono o shite iru to, kirei na sētā ga
me ni hairimashita.   *While gift shopping, I came across a
beautiful sweater.*

me ni fureru   目に触れる   *to attract one's attention*
[lit. to touch one's eyes]
デパートでは、外国製品があちこちで目に触れました。
Depāto dewa, gaikoku seihin ga achi kochi de me ni
furemashita.   *Foreign products attracted my attention here
and there in the department store.*

me ni iretemo itakunai   目に入れても痛くない   *to be
the apple of one's eye*
[lit. Even if one puts a child in one's eye, it does't hurt.]
初孫は、目に入れても痛くありません。Hatsumago wa, me
ni iretemo itaku arimasen.   *My first grandchild is the apple of
my eye.*

me ni kado o tateru　　目に角を立てる　　*to get angry*
[lit. to make one's eyes angular]
彼はつまらないことなのに、目に角を立てました。Kare wa
　　tsumaranai koto nanoni, me ni kado o tatemashita.　　*Although
　　it was such a trivial matter, he got angry.*

me ni mieru　　目に見える　　*to be obvious*
[lit. to be able to see something with one's own eyes]
選挙は、すでに結果が目に見えています。Senkyo wa, sude
　　ni kekka ga me ni miete imasu.　　*The election results are
　　already obvious.*

me ni miete　　目に見えて　　*visibly*
[lit. being visible in one's eyes]
近頃彼女は、目に見えて幸せそうです。Chikagoro kanojo
　　wa, me ni miete shiawase sō desu.　　*Nowadays, she looks
　　visibly happy.*

me ni mieteiru　　目に見えている　　*to be a foregone
conclusion*
[lit. to have been visible]
彼が首になることは、目に見えていました。Kare ga kubi ni
　　naru koto wa, me ni miete imashita.　　*It was a foregone
　　conclusion that he would be fired.*

me ni mono iwaseru　　目に物言わせる　　*to give someone
a look*
[lit. to let one's eyes speak]
父は目に物言わせて、兄の態度を戒めました。Chichi wa me
　　ni mono iwasete, ani no taido o imashimemashita.　　*Giving him
　　a look, my father chided my older brother for his attitude.*

me ni mono miseru　　目に物見せる　　*to teach someone a
lesson*
[lit. to show someone's eyes something]
この前の仕返しに、彼に目に物を見せてやりました。Kono
　　mae no shikaeshi ni, kare ni me ni mono o misete yarimashita.
　　*I taught him a lesson to retaliate for what he did to me last
　　time.*

me ni suru   目にする   *to notice*
[lit. to make one's eyes see]
最近は、ここでも外国の高級車をよく目にしています。
　　Saikin wa, koko demo gaikoku no kōkyūsha o yoku me ni shite
　　imasu.   *Recently, I've been noticing many expensive foreign
　　cars here.*

me ni tomaru   目に留まる   *to catch someone's eye*
[lit. to stay with one's eyes]
彼女の素晴らしい才能が、私の目に留まりました。Kanojo
　　no subarashii sainō ga, watakushi no me ni tomarimashita.
　　Her great talent caught my eye.

me ni tsuku   目に付く   *to be noticeable*
[lit. to attach to someone's eyes]
会議での彼の影響力は、全く目に付きませんでした。Kaigi
　　de no kare no eikyōryoku wa, mattaku me ni tsukimasen
　　deshita.   *His influence was not at all noticeable at the
　　conference.*

me ni ukabu   目に浮かぶ   *to flash in front of one's eyes*
[lit. something to float in one's eyes]
母と話しているとき、古里のことが目に浮かびました。
　　Haha to hanashite iru toki, furusato no koto ga me ni
　　ukabimashita.   *When I was talking to my mother, my
　　hometown flashed in front of my eyes.*

me no doku   目の毒   *to be too much of a temptation*
[lit. poison for one's eyes]
ダイエット中なので、甘い物は目の毒です。Daietto chū
　　nanode, amai mono wa me no doku desu.   *Since I'm on diet,
　　sweets are too much of a temptation.*

me no iro o kaeru   目の色を変える   *to have a serious
look, to look serious*
[lit. to change one's eye color]
彼女は目の色を変えて、一生懸命働いています。Kanojo wa
　　me no iro o kaete, isshōkenmei hataraite imasu.   *She's
　　working hard with a serious look on her face.*

me no hoyō   目の保養   *feast for one's eyes*
[lit. recreation for one's eyes]
素晴らしい美術品を見て、目の保養になりました。
Subarashii bijutsuhin o mite, me no hoyō ni narimashita. *It was a feast for my eyes to see the great art objects.*

me no kataki ni suru   目の敵にする   *to always show animosity toward someone*
[lit. to make someone an enemy of one's eyes]
なぜ彼が私を目の敵にするのか、分かりません。Naze kare ga watakushi o me no kataki ni suru no ka, wakarimasen. *I don't know why he always shows animosity toward me.*

me no kuroi uchi   目の黒いうち   *while alive*
[lit. while one's eyes are still black]
彼女は目の黒い内に、孫の顔を見たがっています。Kanojo wa me no kuroi uchi ni, mago no kao o mitagatte imasu. *She wants to see the face of a grandchild while she's still alive.*

me no mae ga kurakunaru   目の前が暗くなる   *to feel depressed*
[lit. The front of one's eyes gets dark.]
夫が失業して、目の前が暗くなりました。Otto ga shitsugyō shite, me no mae ga kurakunarimashita. *I felt depressed because my husband lost his job.*

me no ue no tankobu   目の上のたんこぶ   *constant hindrance*
[lit. a swelling above one's eye]
彼は私の昇進にとって、目の上のたんこぶです。Kare wa watakushi no shōshin ni totte, me no ue no tankobu desu. *He's a constant hindrance to my promotion.*

me o hanasu   目を離す   *to take one's eyes off someone or something*
[lit. to let one's eyes go]
空港でちょっと目を離した隙に、荷物を盗まれてしまいました。Kūkō de chotto me o hanashita suki ni, nimotsu o nusumarete shimaimashita. *The moment I took my eyes off my*

luggage at the airport, it was stolen.

me o hikarasu　目を光らす　*to keep a sharp eye on something*

[lit. to shine one's eyes]

マスコミは、政治汚職に目を光らせています。　Masukomi wa, seiji oshoku ni me o hikarasete imasu.　*The media is keeping a sharp eye on political corruption.*

me o hiku　目を引く　*to draw someone's attention*

[lit. to pull someone's eyes toward something]

彼女の演説は、ひときわ出席者の目を引きました。　Kanojo no enzetsu wa, hitokiwa shussekisha no me o hikimashita.　*Her speech particularly drew the participants' attention.*

me o hiraku　目を開く　*to realize*

[lit. to open one's eyes]

彼は、辛抱の大切さにやっと目を開きました。　Kare wa, shinbō no taisetsusa ni yatto me o hirakimashita.　*He finally realized the importance of patience.*

me o hosomeru　目を細める　*One's eyes light up.*

[lit. to make one's eyes narrow]

彼女はボーイフレンドからプレゼントをもらって、目を細めました。　Kanojo wa bōifurendo kara purezento o moratte, me o hosomemashita.　*Her eyes lit up when she received a gift from her boyfriend.*

me o kakeru　目をかける　*to be partial to someone*

[lit. to set one's eyes on someone]

彼はまじめでよく働くので、目をかけています。　Kare wa majime de yoku hataraku node, me o kakete imasu.　*I'm partial to him because he's serious and works hard.*

me o korasu　目を凝らす　*to strain one's eyes*

[lit. to apply one's eyes to something]

彼女は目を凝らして、息子のバイオリン演奏を見守りました。　Kanojo wa me o korashite, musuko no baiorin ensō o mimamorimashita.　*Straining her eyes, she watched her son play the violin.*

___

me o kubaru   目を配る   *to watch carefully*
[lit. to distribute one's eyes]

先生は試験中、不正がないように目を配りました。Sensei
wa shiken chū, fusei ga nai yō ni me o kubarimashita.   *During
the exam, the teacher watched carefully so that there would be
no cheating.*

me o maruku suru   目を丸くする   *to stare in wonder*
[lit. to make one's eyes round]

彼の豪華な家に、友達はみんな目を丸くしました。Kare no
gōka na ie ni, tomodachi wa minna me o marukushimashita.
All his friends stared in wonder at his gorgeous house.

me o mawasu   目を回す   *to be stunned*
[lit. to faint]

彼女のけち加減には、目を回しました。Kanojo no kechi
kagen niwa, me o mawashimashita.   *I was stunned by the
degree of her stinginess.*

me o miharu   目を見張る   *to be amazed*
[lit. to stretch one's eyes open]

彼の習字の見事さに目を見張りました。Kare no shūji no
migotosa ni me o miharimashita.   *We were amazed at his
great calligraphy.*

me o muite   目をむいて   *with eyes glaring*
[lit. by peeling one's eyes]

彼は、目をむいて同僚を非難しました。Kare wa, me o muite
dōryō o hinan shimashita.   *With eyes glaring, he accused his
colleagues.*

me o nusunde   目を盗んで   *behind someone's back*
[lit. by stealing someone's eyes]

彼は仕事中、ボスの目を盗んでコンピュータゲームをして
います。Kare wa shigoto chū, bosu no me o nusunde
konpyūta gēmu o shite imasu.   *He's playing computer games
on the job behind the boss's back.*

me o otosu   目を落とす   *to cast one's eyes down*
[lit. to drop one's eyes]

彼女は試験の結果にがっかりして、目を落としました。
Kanojo wa shiken no kekka ni gakkari shite, me o
otoshimashita.   *Disappointed at the test results, she cast her
eyes down.*

me o sankaku ni suru   目を三角にする   *to look angrily
at someone*
[lit. to make one's eyes triangular]
父は目を三角にして、姉をしかりました。Chichi wa me o
sankaku ni shite, ane o shikarimashita.   *Looking angrily at my
older sister, my father scolded her.*

me o sara no yō ni shite   目を皿のようにして   *with
saucer eyes, with one's eyes peeled*
[lit. by making one's eyes like saucers]
落とした財布を目を皿のようにして探したけれど、見つか
りませんでした。Otoshita saifu o me o sara no yō ni shite
sagashita keredo, mitsukarimasen deshita.   *I kept my eyes
peeled for my lost wallet, but I couldn't find it.*

me o shirokuro saseru   目を白黒させる   *to roll one's
eyes in bewilderment*
[lit. to make one's eyes black and white]
彼女はそれを聞いて、目を白黒させました。Kanojo wa sore
o kiite, me o shirokuro sasemashita.   *When she heard the
story, she rolled her eyes in bewilderment.*

me o sosogu   目を注ぐ   *to look at something carefully*
[lit. to pour one's eyes over something]
父はテレビでの首相の演説に、目を注いでいました。
Chichi wa terebi de no shushō no enzetsu ni, me o sosoide
imashita.   *My father was watching the prime minister's
speech on TV carefully.*

me o tōsu   目を通す   *to look through something*
[lit. to let one's eyes go through something]
毎朝、三つの新聞に目を通します。Maiasa, mittsu no shinbun
ni me o tōshimasu.   *I look through three newspapers every
morning.*

me o tsuburu 　目をつぶる 　*to wink at someone's fault or mistake*

[lit. to close one's eyes]

事情が分かるので、今度の彼の失敗に目をつぶることにしました。Jijō ga wakaru node, kondo no kare no shippai ni me o tsuburu koto ni shimashita. *Because I understood the circumstances, I decided to wink at his mistake this time.*

me o tsukeru 　目をつける 　*to focus on someone or something*

[lit. to attach one's eyes to someone or something]

会社は雇用のため、志願者の誠実な人柄に目を付けています。Kaisha wa koyō no tame, shigansha no seijitsu na hitogara ni me o tsukete imasu. *For hiring, our company is focusing on candidates who show sincerity.*

me o ubawareru 　目を奪われる 　*to be dazzled*

[lit. to get one's eyes stolen]

その景色の美しさに、目を奪われました。Sono keshiki no utsukushisa ni, me o ubawaremashita. *I was dazzled by the beauty of the scenery.*

meboshi o tsukeru 　目星をつける 　*to make an educated guess*

[lit. to attach an estimate]

それを誰がしたか、目星はついています。Sore o dare ga shita ka, meboshi wa tsuite imasu. *I've already made an educated guess about who did it.*

medama shōhin 　目玉商品 　*loss leader*

[lit. eyeball goods]

あのスーパーの今週の目玉商品はステーキです。Ano sūpā no konshū no medama shōhin wa sutēki desu. *This week the loss leader at that supermarket is steak.*

megao de shiraseru 　目顔で知らせる 　*to give someone a meaningful look*

[lit. to let someone know something through the expression in one's eyes]

彼女は私に同意していることを、目顔で知らせてくれました。
Kanojo wa watakushi ni dōi shite iru koto o, megao de
shirasete kuremashita.   *She gave me a meaningful look that
signaled she agreed with me.*

megashira ga atsukunaru   目頭が熱くなる   *One's
eyes fill with tears.*
[lit. The inside corners of one's eyes get hot.]
感動的な話を聞いて、彼は目頭が熱くなりました。
Kandōteki na hanashi o kiite, kare wa megashira ga atsuku
narimashita.   *When he heard the moving story, his eyes filled
with tears.*

mehana ga tsuku   目鼻がつく   *to be almost complete*
[lit. Eyes and a nose are attached.]
目標達成の目鼻がつきました。Mokuhyō tassei no mehana ga
tsukimashita.   *Achieving our goal is almost complete.*

mejiri o sageru   目尻を下げる   *to be pleased with
something*
[lit. to lower the outside corners of one's eyes]
彼はレポートを先生に誉められて、目尻を下げました。
Kare wa repōto o sensei ni homerarete, mejiri o sagemashita.
He was pleased with his teacher's praising his report.

mekujira o tateru   めくじらを立てる   *to nitpick*
[lit. to make the outside corners of one's eyes stand up]
彼女はいつも何でもめくじらを立てるので、つき合いにく
いです。Kanojo wa itsumo nandemo mekujira o tateru node,
tsukiainikui desu.   *Because she always nitpicks, it's difficult
to be friendly with her.*

mekuso hanakuso o warau   目糞鼻糞を笑う   *the pot
calling the kettle black*
[lit. Eye mucus laughs at nose snot.]
彼は彼女を批判しているけれど、それは「目糞鼻糞を笑う」
ようなものです。Kare wa kanojo o hihan shite iru keredo,
sore wa "mekuso hanakuso o warau" yō na mono desu.   *He's
criticizing her, but it's like the pot calling the kettle black.*

mesaki ga kiku   目先が利く   *to have foresight*
[lit. to have an effect on something before one's eyes]
彼女は目先が利くので、変化への対応も上手です。Kanojo
   wa mesaki ga kiku node, henka e no taiō mo jōzu desu.   *Since
   she has foresight, she's good at dealing with change.*

mesaki o kaeru   目先を変える   *to do something for a
   change*
[lit. to change something before one's eyes]
今回は目先を変えて、顧客をカントリークラブで接待しま
   した。Konkai wa mesaki o kaete, kokyaku o kantorī kurabu
   de settai shimashita.   *This time, for a change, we entertained
   our clients at the country club.*

meyasu ga tsuku   目安がつく   *to get a general idea*
[lit. to attain a measurement]
やっと、問題解決の目安がつきました。Yatto, mondai
   kaiketsu no meyasu ga tsukimashita.   *Finally, we got a
   general idea of how to solve the problem.*

ōme ni miru   大目に見る   *to give someone a break*
[lit. to look at someone or something with big eyes]
彼の間違いは初めてなので、大目に見てあげることにしま
   した。Kare no machigai wa hajimete nanode, ōme ni mite
   ageru koto ni shimashita.   *Since it was his first mistake, I
   decided to give him a break.*

ōmedama o kuu   大目玉を食う   *to be scolded severely*
[lit. to eat a big eyeball]
彼女はまた宿題をしなかったので、先生に大目玉を食いま
   した。Kanojo wa mata shukudai o shinakatta node, sensei ni
   ōmedama o kuimashita.   *Because she didn't do her
   homework again, she was scolded severely by the teacher.*

shirime ni kakeru   尻目にかける   *to disregard
   someone or something*
[lit. to catch someone or something with the bottom of one's eye]
彼女は親の願いを尻目にかけて、彼とデートしています。
   Kanojo wa oya no negai o shirime ni kakete, kare to dēto shite

imasu.   *She's dating him disregarding her parents' wishes.*

shiroi me de miru   白い目で見る   *to look at someone disdainfully*

[lit. to look at someone with white eyes]

彼は自分の利益しか考えないので、みんなが白い目で見ています。Kare wa jibun no rieki shika kangaenai node, minna ga shiroi me de mite imasu.   *Because he thinks only of his own interests, everyone looks at him disdainfully.*

---

megane   眼鏡   *eyeglasses*

megane ni kanau   眼鏡にかなう   *to pass a test*

[lit. to suit someone's eyeglasses]

彼女は、彼が両親の眼鏡にかなって喜んでいます。Kanojo wa, kare ga ryōshin no megane ni kanatte yorokonde imasu. *She's delighted that he passed her parents' test.*

---

meian   明暗   *light and darkness*

meian o wakeru   明暗を分ける   *to determine the outcome of something*

[lit. to divide light and darkness]

選手のサイズが、試合の結果の明暗を分けました。Senshu no saizu ga, shiai no kekka no meian o wakemashita.   *The size of the players determined the outcome of the game.*

---

mekki   めっき   *plating, gilding*

mekki ga hageru   めっきがはげる   *to reveal one's true colors*

[lit. The plating comes off.]

彼は進歩派を装っていましたが、彼の投票からメッキがはげてしまいました。Kare wa shinpoha o yosootte imashita ga, kare no tōhyō kara mekki ga hagete shimaimashita. *Although he was pretending to be a liberal, his vote revealed his true colors.*

---

men   面   *face*

men to mukatte   面と向かって   *to someone's face*

[lit. by facing someone's face]

彼女は彼に面と向かって、嘘つきだと非難しました。

    Kanojo wa kare ni men to mukatte, usotsuki da to hinan
    shimashita.   *She accused him to his face of being a liar.*

---

menboku   面目   *honor, appearance*

  menboku o hodokosu   面目を施す   *to maintain one's
  honor*

[lit. to perform one's honor]

企画の成功で、彼は担当者としての面目を施しました。

    Kikaku no seikō de, kare wa tantōsha to shite no menboku o
    hodokoshimashita.   *With the success of the project, he
    maintained his honor as the person in charge.*

  menboku o isshin suru   面目を一新する   *to undergo a
  complete change*

[lit. to make an appearance totally new]

我が社はリストラをして、面目を一新しました。 Waga sha

    wa risutora o shite, menboku o isshin shimashita.   *Our
    company underwent a complete change by restructuring.*

  menboku o ushinau   面目を失う   *to lose face*

[lit. to lose one's honor]

約束を果たせなくて、面目を失ってしまいました。

    Yakusoku o hatasenakute, menboku o ushinatte shimaimashita.
    Because I couldn't fulfill my promise, I lost face.

  menbokunai   面目ない   *to be ashamed of oneself*

[lit. no honor]

大切な会議に遅れて、面目ありませんでした。 Taisetsu na

    kaigi ni okurete, menboku arimasen deshita.   *I was ashamed
    of myself for being late to such an important meeting.*

---

mesu   メス   *surgical knife*

  mesu o ireru   メスを入れる   *to take drastic measures
  (for a cure)*

[lit. to insert a surgical knife into something]

警察は、組織犯罪にメスを入れるべきです。 Keisatsu wa,

soshiki hanzai ni mesu o ireru beki desu. *The police should take drastic measures against organized crime.*

---

mētoru　　メートル　　*meter*
　mētoru o ageru　　メートルを上げる　　*to become high-spirited over drinks*
　[lit. to run the meter]
　昨日の晩、彼は友達とバーでメートルを上げました。Kinō no ban, kare wa tomodachi to bā de mētoru o agemashita. *Last night, he and his friends became high-spirited over drinks at a bar.*

---

mi　　実　　*fruit*
　mi o musubu　　実を結ぶ　　*to pay off*
　[lit. to bear fruit]
　長年の努力が、やっと実を結びました。Naganen no doryoku ga, yatto mi o musubimashita. *All my efforts for many years finally paid off.*

---

mi　　身　　*body, oneself, container*
　mi ga hairu　　身が入る　　*to accomplish something*
　[lit. One's body is into something.]
　今日は、仕事にとても身が入りました。Kyō wa, shigoto ni totemo mi ga hairimashita. *I accomplished a lot of work today.*

　mi ga motanai　　身が持たない　　*to be unable to maintain one's health*
　[lit. One's body can't last.]
　仕事の圧力がこれ以上続くと、身が持たなくなります。Shigoto no atsuryoku ga kore ijō tsuzuku to, mi ga motanaku narimasu. *If the pressure on the job continues, I can't maintain my health.*

　mi mo futa mo nai　　身も蓋もない　　*to be brutally frank*
　[lit. There's neither a container nor a lid.]
　彼の意見は、身も蓋もありませんでした。Kare no iken wa, mi mo futa mo arimasen deshita. *His opinion was brutally*

frank.

mi ni amaru 身に余る   *undeserved*
[lit. excessive to one's body]
わが身に余る光栄を感謝いたします。Waga mi ni amaru kōei o kansha itashimasu. *I'd like to thank you for the undeserved honor bestowed upon me.*

mi ni oboe ga nai 身に覚えがない   *to have nothing to do with something*
[lit. no memory for oneself]
私がしたと言われていますが、身に覚えがありません。Watakushi ga shita to iwarete imasu ga, mi ni oboe ga arimasen. *Although they say I did it, I had nothing to do with it.*

mi ni shimiru 身に染みる   *to feel deeply*
[lit. to penetrate one's body]
彼女の親切が身に染みました。Kanojo no shinsetsu ga mi ni shimimashita. *I felt her kindness deeply.*

mi ni tsukeru 身につける   *to master, to acquire*
[lit. to add something to one's body]
一年で、スペイン語を身につけました。Ichi nen de, Supeingo o mi ni tsukemashita. *I mastered Spanish in one year.*

mi ni tsumasareru 身につまされる   *to deeply sympathize with someone*
[lit. to affect one's body]
彼の苦労が身につまされます。Kare no kurō ga mi ni tsumasaremasu. *I deeply sympathize with him over his hardship.*

mi o hiku 身を引く   *to leave something, to get out of something*
[lit. to pull one's own body]
彼女は芸能界から身を引きました。Kanojo wa geinō kai kara mi o hikimashita. *She left the entertainment world.*

mi o katameru 身を固める   *to get married*

231

[lit. to solidify one's body]

彼は、高校の級友と身を固める決心をしました。Kare wa, kōkō no kyūyū to mi o katameru kesshin o shimashita. *He decided to get married to his high-school classmate.*

mi o kirareru omoi   身を切られる思い   *to feel great pain*

[lit. to feel as if one's body is slashed]

彼は妻に先立たれて、身を切られる思いをしました。Kare wa tsuma ni sakidatarete, mi o kirareru omoi o shimashita. *When his wife died, he felt great pain.*

mi o kogasu   身を焦がす   *to be consumed with love for someone*

[lit. to scorch one's own body]

彼女は妻子ある男性との恋に、身を焦がしています。Kanojo wa saishi aru dansei to no koi ni, mi o kogashite imasu. *She's consumed with love for a man who has a wife and children.*

mi o ko ni suru   身を粉にする   *to work one's fingers to the bone*

[lit. to make one's own body into powder]

彼は新車を買うため、身を粉にして働いています。Kare wa shinsha o kau tame, mi o ko ni shite hataraite imasu. *He's working his fingers to the bone to buy a new car.*

mi o mochikuzusu   身を持ち崩す   *to ruin one's life by indulging in something*

[lit. to worsen one's own body]

彼は酒と女で身を持ち崩しました。Kare wa sake to onna de mi o mochikuzushimashita. *He ruined his life by indulging in women and liquor.*

mi o tateru   身を立てる   *to make a career*

[lit. to make one's own body stand up]

彼女は、女優として身を立てる決心をしました。Kanojo wa, joyū toshite mi o tateru kesshin o shimashita. *She decided to make a career as an actress.*

232

mi o tōjiru   身を投じる   *to enter something*
[lit. to throw one's own body into something]
彼は実業界から政治に身を投じました。Kare wa jitsugyōkai
   kara seiji ni mi o tōjimashita.   *He entered politics from the
   business world.*

mi o yoseru   身を寄せる   *to go to live with someone*
[lit. to bring oneself close to someone]
失業中は、兄の所へ身を寄せていました。Shitsugyō chū wa,
   ani no tokoro e mi o yosete imashita.   *While I was
   unemployed, I went to live with my older brother.*

minohodo shirazu   身の程知らず   *conceited*
[lit. to not know the degree of oneself]
彼は身の程知らずで、呼ばれない会議に出てきて意見を述
   べました。Kare wa minohodo shirazu de, yobarenai kaigi ni
   dete kite iken o nobemashita.   *He's so conceited that he came
   to the meeting uninvited and gave his opinions.*

minoke ga yodatsu   身の毛がよだつ   *hair-raising*
[lit. One's body hair stands up.]
身の毛がよだつ怪談をテレビで見ました。Minoke ga
   yodatsu kaidan o terebi de mimashita.   *We watched a hair-
   raising ghost story on TV.*

---

michi   道   *way, road, course*
michi ga hirakeru   道が開ける   *the prospect for
something to become possible*
[lit. A road opens.]
社長の命令で、妥協の道が開けました。Shachō no meirei de,
   dakyō no michi ga hirakemashita.   *The prospect for a
   compromise became possible with the president's order.*

michi o ayamaru   道を誤る   *to take a wrong turn*
[lit. to take a wrong road]
彼はいい先生でしたが、道を誤って賭事に熱中しています。
   Kare wa ii sensei deshita ga, michi o ayamatte kakegoto ni
   netchū shite imasu.   *He was a good teacher, but he took a
   wrong turn, and he's now absorbed in gambling.*

michi o tsukeru　　道を付ける　　*to pave the way*
[lit. to cut a path]
彼は、地震の研究に道を付けた人です。Kare wa, jishin no
　　kenkyū ni michi o tsuketa hito desu.　*He's the one who paved
　　the way for the research on earthquakes.*

michikusa o kuu　　道草を食う　　*to fool around on the
way*
[lit. to eat grass on the roadside]
学校が終わったら、道草を食わないでまっすぐうちに帰っ
　　てきなさい。Gakkō ga owattara, michikusa o kuwanaide
　　massugu uchi ni kaette kinasai.　*Don't fool around after
　　school, and come straight back home.*

midokoro　　見所　　*merit*
midokoro no aru　　見所のある　　*promising*
[lit. There's merit.]
彼は見所のある若者です。Kare wa midokoro no aru
　　wakamono desu.　*He's a promising young man.*

migaki　　磨き　　*polish*
migaki o kakeru　　磨きをかける　　*to improve*
[lit. to polish something]
夏休みの間、テニスに磨きをかけました。Natsu yasumi no
　　aida, tenisu ni migaki o kakemashita.　*During the summer
　　recess, I improved my tennis skills.*

migi　　右　　*right*
migi e narae　　右へ倣え　　*to follow suit*
[lit. Right, dress!]
彼が賛成するとみんな右へ倣えで、その案はすぐ採用され
　　ました。Kare ga sansei suru to minna migi e narae de, sono
　　an wa sugu saiyō saremashita.　*The plan was quickly
　　approved because everyone followed suit when he favored it.*

migi kara hidari ni　　右から左に　　*immediately (after
receiving money or something)*

[lit. from right to left]

彼女はお金をもらうと、右から左に使ってしまいます。

Kanojo wa okane o morau to, migi kara hidari ni tsukatte shimaimasu. *When she gets money, she immediately spends it all.*

migi ni deru mono ga nai   右に出る者がない   *the best*

[lit. There's nobody on the right side.]

冗談にかけては、彼の右にでる人はいません。Jōdan ni kakete wa, kare no migi ni deru hito wa imasen. *When it comes to jokes, he's the best.*

migi to ieba hidari   右と言えば左   *to contradict everyone*

[lit. Someone says "left" when you say "right."]

彼女は右と言えば左というので、みんなが彼女を避けます。

Kanojo wa migi to ieba hidari to iu node, minna ga kanojo o sakemasu. *Since she contradicts everyone, everyone avoids her.*

migiude   右腕   *right-hand man*

[lit. a right arm]

彼は有力な政治家の右腕として知られています。Kare wa, yūryoku na seijika no migiude to shite shirarete imasu. *He's known as the influential politician's right-hand man.*

---

mikake   見掛け   *appearance*

mikakedaoshi   見掛け倒し   *deceptive image*

[lit. An appearance is upset.]

彼女はインテリぶっていますが、実は見かけ倒しです。

Kanojo wa interi butte imasu ga, jitsu wa mikakedaoshi desu. *She's pretending to be an intellectual, but it's really a deceptive image.*

---

mikka   三日   *three days*

mikka ni agezu   三日に上げず   *frequently*

[lit. without a three-day interval]

彼はホステスに会うため、三日に上げずバーに顔を出して

います。Kare wa hosutesu ni au tame, mikka ni agezu bā ni kao o dashite imasu.   *He has been showing up at the bar frequently to see the hostess.*

mikkabōzu   三日坊主   *to be unable to stick with anything*
[lit. a Buddhist priest for only three days]
彼女は何をしても三日坊主です。Kanojo wa nani o shitemo mikkabōzu desu.   *No matter what she does, she can't stick with anything.*

---

mikoshi   神輿   *portable shrine*
mikoshi o ageru   神輿を上げる   *to finally take action*
[lit. to raise a portable shrine]
政府は、やっと政治改革の神輿を上げました。Seifu wa, yatto seiji kaikaku no mikoshi o agemashita.   *The government finally took action for political reform.*

mikoshi o katsugu   神輿を担ぐ   *to cajole someone*
[lit. to carry a portable shrine]
彼の神輿を担いで、宴会の準備の責任を引き受けさせました。Kare no mikoshi o katsuide, enkai no junbi no sekinin o hikiukesasemashita.   *We cajoled him into taking charge of the preparations for the party.*

mikoshi o sueru   神輿を据える   *to stay too long*
[lit. to lay a portable shrine down]
彼がうちに来ると神輿を据えるので、妻が嫌がります。Kare ga uchi ni kuru to mikoshi o sueru node, tsuma ga iyagarimasu.   *Because he always stays too long when he visits us, my wife isn't crazy about him.*

---

mimi   耳   *ear*
mimi ga hayai   耳が早い   *to have big ears*
[lit. One's ears are fast.]
彼女は耳が早いので、近所の噂は全部知っています。
Kanojo wa mimi ga hayai node, kinjo no uwasa wa zenbu shitte imasu.   *Because she has big ears, she knows all the*

neighborhood gossip.

mimi ga itai   耳が痛い   *to make one's ears burn*
[lit. One's ears hurt.]
彼が私の間違いを指摘するのを聞いて、耳が痛かったです。
Kare ga watakushi no machigai o shiteki suru no o kiite, mimi
ga itakatta desu.   *Listening to his pointing out my mistakes
made my ears burn.*

mimi ga koeru   耳が肥える   *to have an ear for
something*
[lit. One's ears get enriched.]
彼女は親が音楽家なので、耳が肥えています。Kanojo wa
oya ga ongakuka nanode, mimi ga koete imasu.   *Because her
parents are musicians, she has an ear for music.*

mimi ni hairu   耳に入る   *to learn*
[lit. Something enters into one's ear.]
彼女に赤ちゃんが生まれたというニュースが耳に入りました。
Kanojo ni akachan ga umareta to iu nyūsu ga mimi ni
hairimashita.   *I learned the news that she had a baby.*

mimi ni hasamu   耳にはさむ   *to get wind of something*
[lit. to put something into one's ear]
彼が結婚したという噂を耳にはさみました。Kare ga kekkon
shita to iu uwasa o mimi ni hasamimashita.   *I got wind of the
rumor that he got married.*

mimi ni ireru   耳に入れる   *to tell someone something*
[lit. to put something into someone's ear]
耳に入れたいことがあるので、お目に掛かりたいのですが。
Mimi ni iretai koto ga aru node, ome ni kakaritai no desu ga.
I'd like to see you because I have something to tell you.

mimi ni nokoru   耳に残る   *to linger in one's ear*
[lit. Something remains in one's ear.]
彼女の言ったことが、今でも耳に残っています。Kanojo no
itta koto ga, ima demo mimi ni nokotte imasu.   *What she said
to me is still lingering in my ear.*

mimi ni suru   耳にする   *to happen to hear something*

[lit. to reach one's ear]

彼が近いうちに社長になるという噂を耳にしました。Kare ga chikai uchi ni shachō ni naru to iu uwasa o mimi ni shimashita. *I happened to hear a rumor that he would become president soon.*

mimi ni tako ga dekiru　耳にたこができる　*to be sick and tired of hearing something*

[lit. A callus grows in one's ear.]

彼女の苦情は、耳にたこができるほど聞きました。Kanojo no kujō wa, mimi ni tako ga dekiru hodo kikimashita. *I'm sick and tired of hearing her complaints.*

mimi ni tomaru　耳に留まる　*to draw one's attention*

[lit. Something stays in one's ear.]

彼の意見が耳に留まりました。Kare no iken ga mimi ni tomarimashita. *His remarks drew my attention.*

mimi ni tsuku　耳に付く　*to bother someone (noise)*

[lit. Noise sticks to one's ear.]

テレビの音が耳について、勉強に集中できません。Terebi no oto ga mimi ni tsuite, benkyō ni shūchū dekimasen. *With the noise of the TV bothering me, I can't concentrate on my studying.*

mimi o kasanai　耳を貸さない　*to turn a deaf ear to something*

[lit. to not lend one's ear to something]

彼女は、両親の忠告に耳を貸しませんでした。Kanojo wa, ryōshin no chūkoku ni mimi o kashimasen deshita. *She turned a deaf ear to her parents' advice.*

mimi o katamukeru　耳を傾ける　*to listen carefully*

[lit. to lean one's ear toward something]

父は、ラジオのニュース番組に耳を傾けていました。 Chichi wa, rajio no nyūsu bangumi ni mimi o katamukete imashita. *My father was listening carefully to the news program on the radio.*

mimi o sobadateru　耳をそばだてる　*to prick up one's*

ears

[lit. to make one's ears stand up high]

同僚の内緒話に耳をそばだてました。 Dōryō no naisho banashi ni mimi o sobadatemashita. *I pricked up my ears at the whispering among my colleagues.*

mimi o soroete   耳を揃えて   *in full*

[lit. by arranging the border of bills neatly]

返済日の前に、借金を耳を揃えて返しました。 Hensaibi no mae ni, shakkin o mimi o soroete kaeshimashita. *I paid back the debt in full before the due date.*

mimi o sumasu   耳を澄ます   *to be all ears*

[lit. to make one's ears clear]

社員は、社長の話に耳を澄ませました。 Shain wa, shachō no hanashi ni mimi o sumasemashita. *The employees were all ears during the president's speech.*

mimi o utagau   耳を疑う   *to be unable to believe one's ears*

[lit. to doubt one's own ears]

彼が死んだと聞いたとき、耳を疑いました。 Kare ga shinda to kiita toki, mimi o utagaimashita. *When I heard that he had died, I couldn't believe my ears.*

mimiuchi suru   耳打ちする   *to whisper into someone's ear*

[lit. to tap someone's ear]

お母さんが子供に何か耳打ちすると、子供は泣き止みました。 Okāsan ga kodomo ni nanika mimiuchi suru to, kodomo wa nakiyamimashita. *When the mother whispered something into her child's ear, he stopped crying.*

mimiyori na   耳寄りな   *worth listening to*

[lit. coming nearer to one's ears]

それは会社にとって、耳寄りな情報です。 Sore wa kaisha ni totte, mimiyori na jōhō desu. *This information is worth listening to for the company.*

mimizawari   耳障り   *grating*

[lit. to be offensive to one's ears]

彼女の声は、実に耳障りでした。Kanojo no koe wa, jitsu ni mimizawari deshita. *Her voice was truly grating.*

nemimi ni mizu   寝耳に水   *bolt out of the blue*
[lit. water into the ear of someone sleeping]

上司が突然会社を辞めたというニュースは、寝耳に水でした。
Jōshi ga totsuzen kaisha o yameta to iu nyūsu wa, nemimi ni mizu deshita. *The news that my boss suddenly quit the company was a bolt out of the blue.*

---

miru   見る   *to see, to look at*

miru kage mo nai   見る影もない   *down and out*
[lit. There's no shadow to look at.]

昔は大金持ちだった彼も、今は見る影もありません。
Mukashi wa ōganemochi datta kare mo, ima wa miru kage mo arimasen. *He was very rich before, but he's down and out now.*

miru me ga aru   見る目がある   *to have an eye for something*
[lit. to have eyes to look at something]

彼女には、個人の才能を見る目があります。Kanojo niwa, kojin no sainō o miru me ga arimasu. *She has an eye for judging someone's talent.*

miru me ga nai   見る目がない   *to be a poor judge of something*
[lit. to not have eyes to look at something]

彼には、女性を見る目がありません。Kare niwa, josei o miru me ga arimasen. *He's a poor judge of women.*

miru ni mikaneru   見るに見かねる   *to be unable to stand watching something*
[lit. to be unable to just look at something]

彼の料理の仕方を見るに見かねて、手伝いました。Kare no ryōri no shikata o miru ni mikanete, tetsudaimashita. *Because I couldn't stand watching the way he was cooking, I helped him.*

mirukarani   見るからに   *to just glance at something*
[lit. from a look]
あの子は、見るからに頭がいいのが分かります。Ano ko
wa, mirukarani atama ga ii no ga wakarimasu.   *Just glancing
at that child, I know that she's intelligent.*

mite minu furi o suru   見て見ぬ振りをする   *to look
the other way*
[lit. to pretend to not see anything]
友達がうそをつくのを、見て見ぬ振りをしました。
Tomodachi ga uso o tsuku no o, mite minu furi o shimashita.
While my friend lied, I looked the other way.

---

mise   店   *shop*
mise o haru   店を張る   *to open a store*
[lit. to spread a shop]
彼女は去年、銀座に店を張りました。Kanojo wa kyonen,
Ginza ni mise o harimashita.   *She opened a store in Ginza last
year.*

mise o tatamu   店を畳む   *to close a store*
[lit. to fold a shop]
彼は融資を受けられなくて、店を畳まねばなりませんでした。
Kare wa yūshi o ukerarenakute, mise o tatamaneba narimasen
deshita.   *Because he couldn't get a loan, he had to close his
store.*

---

miso   味噌   *bean paste*
miso   味噌   *the beauty of something*
[lit. bean paste]
この製品は使いやすい。そこが味噌です。Kono seihin wa
tsukaiyasui. Soko ga miso desu.   *This product is easy to use.
That's the beauty of it.*

miso o tsukeru   味噌をつける   *to make a mess of
something*
[lit. to spread bean paste on something]
今度担当した事業計画では、味噌をつけてしまいました。

Kondo tantō shita jigyō keikaku dewa, miso o tsukete shimaimashita.   *I made a mess of the recent business plan I was in charge of.*

---

mizu   水   *water*

mizu ga awanai   水があわない   *to not agree with someone or something*

[lit. The water doesn't suit someone.]

彼には、大阪の水があいませんでした。Kare niwa, Ōsaka no mizu ga aimasen deshita.   *Osaka didn't agree with him.*

mizu mo morasanu   水も漏らさぬ   *airtight*

[lit. to not even leak water]

テロ行為を防ぐため、警察は水も漏らさぬ警戒をしています。Tero kōi o fusegu tame, keisatsu wa mizu mo morasanu keikai o shite imasu.   *The police are keeping an airtight guard against terrorist acts.*

mizu ni nagasu   水に流す   *to let bygones be bygones*

[lit. to flush something in water]

彼らは過去を水に流して、またつき合うことにしました。Karera wa kako o mizu ni nagashite, mata tsukiau koto ni shimashita.   *They decided to resume their relationship and let bygones be bygones.*

mizu no awa ni naru   水の泡になる   *to go down the drain*

[lit. to become a water bubble]

交渉が決裂して、これまでの努力が水の泡になりました。Kōshō ga ketsuretsu shite, kore made no doryoku ga mizu no awa ni narimashita.   *With the negotiations breaking down, all our efforts until now have gone down the drain.*

mizu mo shitataru yō na   水も滴るような   *breathtaking (person)*

[lit. as if water will drip]

彼は、水も滴るような美人と結婚しました。Kare wa, mizu mo shitataru yō na bijin to kekkon shimashita.   *He married a woman of breathtaking beauty.*

mizu o akeru   水をあける   *to open a lead*
[lit. to open water]
我が社は市場占有率で、競争相手に大きく水をあけています。
  Waga sha wa shijō sen-yū ritsu de, kyōsō aite ni ōkiku mizu o
  akete imasu.   *Our company has opened a wide lead over our
  competitors for market share.*

mizu o mukeru   水を向ける   *to entice someone*
[lit. to offer water]
彼女に水を向けて、秘密を話させました。Kanojo ni mizu o
  mukete, himitsu o hanasasemashita.   *I enticed her into
  revealing her secret.*

mizu o sasu   水を差す   *to throw cold water on
  something*
[lit. to pour water]
彼女は、夫の熱意に水を差しました。Kanojo wa, otto no
  netsui ni mizu o sashimashita.   *She threw cold water on her
  husband's enthusiasm.*

mizu o utta yō ni shizuka   水を打ったように静か   *so
  quiet you could hear a pin drop*
[lit. as quiet as if water were sprinkled]
彼女が話し始めると、会場は水を打ったように静かになり
ました。Kanojo ga hanashihajimeru to, kaijō wa mizu o utta
  yō ni shizuka ni narimashita.   *When she started talking, the
  room became so quiet you could hear a pin drop.*

mizu to abura   水と油   *to never mix, to not get along*
[lit. water and oil]
彼と彼女は、水と油です。
Kare to kanojo wa, nizu to abura desu.
He and she don't get along with each other.

mizugiwadatta   水際立った   *brilliant, striking*
[lit. standing at the water's edge]
彼女の水際だった演技に、観客は深く感動しました。
  Kanojo no mizugiwadatta engi ni, kankyaku wa fukaku kandō
  shimashita.   *The audience was deeply impressed by her*

brilliant performance.

mizuirazu de   水入らずで   *all by oneself*
[lit. without the interference of water]
妻と私は、週末を水入らずで過ごしました。Tsuma to
watakushi wa shūmatsu o mizuirazu de sugoshimashita.   *My
wife and I spent the weekend all by ourselves.*

mizukakeron   水掛け論   *endless dispute*
[lit. an argument like dumping water on each other]
彼らの議論は、水掛け論に発展しました。Karera no giron
wa, mizukakeron ni hatten shimashita.   *Their discussion
developed into an endless dispute.*

mizukusai   水臭い   *distant, unfriendly, too formal*
[lit. to smell like water]
そんな水臭い話し方は止めよう。Sonna mizukusai
hanashikata wa yameyō.   *Let's stop speaking so formally.*

mizumashi suru   水増しする   *to pad something*
[lit. to add water]
この請求書には、水増しした疑いがあります。Kono
seikyūsho niwa, mizumashi shita utagai ga arimasu.   *I have a
suspicion that they padded this bill.*

mizumono   水物   *an uncertain affair*
[lit. a watery thing]
選挙は水物だといわれています。Senkyo wa mizumono da to
iwarete imasu.   *They say that an election is an uncertain
affair.*

mizushōbai   水商売   *the entertainment business
(including bartenders, bar hostesses, waiters, and so forth)*
[lit. the water business]
彼女は、水商売から足を洗って結婚しました。Kanojo wa,
mizushōbai kara ashi o aratte kekkon shimashita.   *She quit the
entertainment business and got married.*

yobimizu   呼び水   *trigger*
[lit. priming water]
公共事業投資が呼び水になって、景気回復が始まりました。

Kōkyō jigyō tōshi ga yobimizu ni natte, keiki kaifuku ga hajimarimashita. *With the investment in public works as a trigger, the ecomonic recovery has begun.*

---

moku   黙   *silence*
  mokusatsu suru   黙殺する   *to deliberately ignore something*
  [lit. to kill something silently]
  学校側は、学生の要請を黙殺しました。Gakkōgawa wa, gakusei no yōsei o mokusatsu shimashita. *The school administration ignored the students' requests.*

---

momu   揉む   *to rub*
  momikesu   揉み消す   *to hush something up*
  [lit. to rub and put out something]
  政府は、汚職の噂を揉み消すのに必死です。Seifu wa oshoku no uwasa o momikesu no ni hisshi desu. *The government is making frantic efforts to hush up the rumor of corruption.*

---

mon   門   *gate*
  mongen   門限   *curfew*
  [lit. time restriction at a gate]
  この寄宿舎の門限は午後十時です。Kono kishukusha no mongen wa gogo jūji desu. *The curfew for this dormitory is ten p.m.*

  monzenbarai o kuu   門前払いを食う   *to be turned away at a door*
  [lit. to be gotten rid of in front of a gate]
  有名な作家に会いに行きましたが、門前払いを食いました。Yūmei na sakka ni aini ikimashita ga, monzenbarai o kuimashita. *I went to see the famous novelist, but I was turned away at the door.*

---

mono   物   *thing, matter*
  mono ga wakaru   物が分かる   *to be sensible*

[lit. to understand things]

私の両親は、物がよく分かります。Watakushi no ryōshin wa, mono ga yoku wakarimasu. *My parents are very sensible.*

mono ni suru　物にする　*to obtain*

[lit. to make something one's own]

やっと、興味のあった骨董の壺を物にしました。Yatto, kyōmi no atta kottō no tsubo o mono ni shimashita. *I finally obtained the antique jar I was interested in.*

mono ni naru　物になる　*to amount to something*

[lit. to become something]

彼は将来、物になるでしょう。Kare wa shōrai, mono ni naru deshō. *He may amount to something in the future.*

mono no hazumi de　物の弾みで　*propelled by the circumstances*

[lit. by the bounce of a thing]

物の弾みで、言ってはいけないことを言ってしまいました。Mono no hazumi de, ittewa ikenai koto o itte shimaimashita. *Propelled by the circumstances, I said something I shouldn't have said.*

mono no kazu dewa nai　物の数ではない　*to be insignificant*

[lit. to count a number of things for nothing]

彼の脅かしなど、物の数ではありません。Kare no odokashi nado, mono no kazu dewa arimasen. *His threat is insignificant to me.*

mono o iu　物を言う　*to matter, to count*

[lit. to say things]

最近の仕事環境で、物を言っているのがコンピュータの知識です。Saikin no shigoto kankyō de, mono o itte iru no ga konpyūta no chishiki desu. *In the current work environment, it's the knowledge of computers that counts.*

mono o iwasete　物をいわせて　*by sheer force of something*

[lit. by resorting to something]

与党は、数に物を言わせて審議を打ち切りました。Yotō wa, kazu ni mono o iwasete shingi o uchikirimashita. *The majority party cut off the deliberations by sheer force of numbers.*

mono tomo sezu ni   物ともせずに   *refusing to give in to something*
[lit. by not making a big deal of something]
彼は病気を物ともせずに、仕事を続けました。Kare wa byōki o mono tomo sezu ni, shigoto o tsuzukemashita. *He kept working, refusing to give in to his illness.*

mono tomo shinai   物ともしない   *to defy something*
[lit. to not make something a concern]
彼女は、先生の警告を物ともしませんでした。Kanojo wa, sensei no keikoku o mono tomo shimasen deshita. *She defied her teacher's warning.*

mono wa iiyō   物は言いよう   *It's important how you say it.*
[lit. The way of saying things matters.]
物は言いようだから、言葉に気をつけなさい。Mono wa ii yō dakara, kotoba ni ki o tsukenasai. *Since it's important how you say it, you'd better watch your mouth.*

mono wa kangaeyō   物は考えよう   *Look on the bright side.*
[lit. The way of thinking about things matters.]
物は考えようで、雨の週末は読書にいいです。Mono wa kangaeyō de, ame no shūmatsu wa dokusho ni ii desu. *Look on the bright side: a rainy weekend is good for reading.*

mono wa sōdan   物は相談   *It helps to talk things over.*
[lit. Consultation is a thing of significance.]
物は相談なので、仕事について教授と話しました。Mono wa sōdan nanode, shigoto ni tsuite kyōju to hanashimashita. *I spoke with the professor about my job because it helps to talk things over.*

mono wa tameshi   物は試し   *You won't know unless you try.*

[lit. Trying has significance.]

物は試しだから、宝くじの券を買ってみました。Mono wa tameshi dakara, takarakuji no ken o katte mimashita. *Since you won't know unless you try, I bought lottery tickets.*

monogusa 物臭 *lazy*
[lit. smelling of things]

彼は物臭だから、用事を頼んでも無駄ですよ。Kare wa monogusa dakara, yōji o tanondemo muda desu yo. *Because he's lazy, asking him to do an errand is a waste of time.*

monoii o tsukeru 物言いをつける *to object to something*
[lit. to have a thing to say]

彼女は、彼の計画に物言いをつけました。Kanojo wa, kare no keikaku ni monoii o tsukemashita. *She objected to his plan.*

monomonoshii 物々しい *elaborate*
[lit. like something on top of something]

警察は首脳会談のため、物々しい警戒をしています。Keisatsu wa shunō kaidan no tame, monomonoshii keikai o shiteimasu. *The police are on an elaborate alert for the leaders' conference.*

monooji shinai 物怖じしない *to not flinch*
[lit. to not fear things]

彼は誰の前でも物怖じしません。Kare wa dare no mae demo monooji shimasen. *He doesn't flinch in front of anyone.*

monotarinai 物足りない *to be unsatisfactory*
[lit. to lack something]

彼女にとって、彼はボーイフレンドとして物足りませんでした。Kanojo ni totte, kare wa bōifurendo toshite monotarimasen deshita. *For her, he was unsatisfactory as a boyfriend.*

monowakare ni naru 物別れになる *to end in failure*
[lit. to come to scatter things]

交渉は物別れになりました。Kōshō wa monowakare ni
narimashita.   *The negotiations ended in failure.*

monowakari ga ii   物わかりがいい   *considerate*
[lit. good at understanding things]
彼女に人気があるのは、とても物わかりがいいからです。
　Kanojo ni ninki ga aru no wa, totemo monowakari ga ii kara
　desu.   *The reason for her popularity is that she's very
　considerate.*

monowarai   物笑い   *laughingstock*
[lit. a laughing matter]
彼はいつも見当違いの質問をするので、物笑いになつてい
　ます。Kare wa itsumo kentōchigai no shitsumon o suru node,
　monowarai ni natte imasu.   *Because he always asks irrelevant
　questions, he has become a laughingstock.*

monozuki   物好き   *inquisitive*
[lit. liking things]
彼女は物好きで、何にでも手を付けようとします。Kanojo
　wa monozuki de, nani ni demo te o tsukeyō to shimasu.
　*Because she's inquisitive, she tries to get involved with
　everything.*

---

moto   元   *origin, source, principal*
moto mo ko mo nai   元も子もない   *to lose everything*
[lit. There's neither the principal nor the interest.]
地震による被害のため、元も子もなくなってしまいました。
　Jishin ni yoru higai no tame, moto mo ko mo nakunatte
　shimaimashita.   *I lost everything because of the earthquake
　damage.*

---

mōtō   毛頭   *bit*
mōtō nai   毛頭無い   *not at all*
[lit. no hair or head]
彼女を疑う気持ちは毛頭ありません。Kanojo o utagau
　kimochi wa mōtō arimasen.   *I have no intention at all of
　doubting her.*

---

motsu　持つ　*to have, to carry*

mochiaji o ikasu　持ち味を生かす　*to make the most of one's talents*

[lit. to make good use of one's taste]

会社は社員の持ち味を生かすため、人事再編成を行いました。
    Kaisha wa shain no mochiaji o ikasu tame, jinji saihensei o
    okonaimashita. *The company carried out a personnel
    reorganization to make the most of the employees' talents.*

mochitsu motaretsu　持ちつ持たれつ　*give and take*

[lit. to carry someone and to be carried by someone]

彼とは、持ちつ持たれつの仲です。Kare to wa, mochitsu
    motaretsu no naka desu. *I have a give-and-take relationship
    with him.*

moteamasu　持て余す　*to not know what to do with something*

[lit. to have an excess of something]

彼女は子供が大きくなってから、時間を持て余しています。
    Kanojo wa kodomo ga ōkiku natte kara, jikan o moteamashite
    imasu. *Since her children are grown, she doesn't know what
    to do with her time.*

mottekoi no　持ってこいの　*just right*

[lit. by bringing someone or something in]

彼はその仕事には持ってこいです。Kare wa sono shigoto
    niwa mottekoi desu. *He's just the right person for that job.*

motte mawatta　持って回った　*roundabout*

[lit. carrying something around]

彼女は持って回った言い方で、結婚の申し込みを断りました。
    Kanojo wa motte mawatta iikata de, kekkon no mōshikomi o
    kotowarimashita. *She turned down the marriage proposal
    with a roundabout way of speaking.*

---

mottomo　尤も　*true*

mottomorashii　尤もらしい　*plausible*

[lit. to seem to be true]

彼の言い訳は尤もらしいけれど、本当かどうかは分かりません。 Kare no iiwake wa mottomorashii keredo, hontō ka dō ka wa wakarimasen. *Although his excuse sounds plausible, I don't know if it's true or not.*

---

mu　無　*nothing*

mu ni kisuru　無に帰する　*to be wasted*
[lit. to return to nothing]

雨で試合が中止になったため、激しい練習が無に帰しました。 Ame de shiai ga chūshi ni natta tame, hageshii renshū ga mu ni kishimashita. *Since the game was canceled because of rain, our rigorous practice was wasted.*

mu ni suru　無にする　*to waste something*
[lit. to make something nothing]

人の親切を無にするものではありません。 Hito no shinsetsu o mu ni suru mono dewa arimasen. *You should know better than to waste other people's kindness.*

---

muda　無駄　*waste*

mudaashi o fumu　無駄足を踏む　*to waste a trip*
[lit. to tread wasteful steps]

叔父に借金をしに行きましたが、断られて無駄足を踏みました。 Oji ni shakkin o shini ikimashita ga, kotowararete mudaashi o fumimashita. *I wasted a trip to my uncle's when he turned down my request for a loan.*

mudabone o oru　無駄骨を折る　*to waste one's efforts*
[lit. to break one's bones wastefully]

彼女を説得しようとしましたが、無駄骨を折る結果に終わりました。 Kanojo o settoku shiyō to shimashita ga, mudabone o oru kekka ni owarimashita. *I tried to persuade her but ended up wasting my efforts.*

mudaguchi o tataku　無駄口を叩く　*to chatter aimlessly*
[lit. to sound a wasteful mouth]

無駄口を叩いているより勉強しなさい。 Mudaguchi o tataite

iru yori benkyō shinasai. *You should study instead of chattering aimlessly.*

---

mukō   向こう   *opposite side*

mukō ni mawasu   向こうに回す   *to take someone on*
[lit. to send someone around to the opposite side]
彼は専門家を向こうに回して、対立的な見解を述べました。
Kare wa senmonka o mukō ni mawashite, tairitsuteki na kenkai o nobemashita. *Taking on the specialist, he stated the opposing view.*

mukō o haru   向こうを張る   *to compete*
[lit. to set against an opposite side]
地元の商店は新しいスーパーの向こうを張って、バーゲンセールを行っています。Jimoto no shōten wa atarashii sūpā no mukō o hatte, bāgensēru o okonatte imasu. *The local stores are holding a bargain sale, competing with the new supermarket.*

mukōmizu na   向こう見ずな   *reckless*
[lit. not looking at the opposite side]
彼の向こう見ずな言動を、お母さんはとても心配しています。
Kare no mukōmizu na gendō o, okāsan wa totemo shinpai shite imasu. *His mother is gravely concerned about his reckless speech and behavior.*

---

muna   胸   *chest*

munasawagi ga suru   胸騒ぎがする   *to feel uneasy*
[lit. One's chest becomes agitated.]
夫の帰宅がとても遅いので胸騒ぎがしましたが、無事でした。
Otto no kitaku ga totemo osoi node munasawagi ga shimashita ga, buji deshita. *I felt uneasy when my husband was very late returning home, but he was okay.*

munazanyō suru   胸算用する   *to figure on something*
[lit. to calculate something in one's own chest]
彼は、来年は課長になれると胸算用しています。
Kare wa, rainen wa kachō ni nareru to munazanyō shite imasu.

He figures on becoming a section chief next year.

---

mune   胸   *chest*

mune ga hareru   胸が晴れる   *to feel relieved*
[lit. One's chest is cleared.]
私に対する疑いが解けて、胸が晴れました。Watakushi ni taisuru utagai ga tokete, mune ga haremashita.   *I felt relieved because I was cleared of suspicion.*

mune ga harisakeru   胸が張り裂ける   *to tear one apart*
[lit. One's chest bursts.]
深い悲しみで、胸が張り裂けました。Fukai kanashimi de, mune ga harisakemashita.   *My grief tore me apart.*

mune ga hazumu   胸が弾む   *to get excited*
[lit. One's chest bounces.]
この夏の旅行のことを考えると、いつも胸が弾みます。Kono natsu no ryokō no koto o kangaeru to, itsumo mune ga hazumimasu.   *Whenever I think about our trip next summer, I get excited.*

mune ga ippai ni naru   胸が一杯になる   *to get a lump in one's throat*
[lit. One's chest becomes full.]
彼女の悲しい話を聞いて、胸が一杯になりました。Kanojo no kanashii hanashi o kiite, mune ga ippai ni narimashita.   *I got a lump in my throat hearing her sad story.*

mune ga suku   胸がすく   *to be relieved*
[lit. One's chest becomes cleared.]
借金を返し終わって、胸がすきました。Shakkin o kaeshiowatte, mune ga sukimashita.   *I'm relieved at having paid back the entire debt.*

mune ga tsumaru   胸が詰まる   *to be choked up*
[lit. One's chest gets clogged.]
胸が詰まって、言葉がでませんでした。Mune ga tsumatte, kotoba ga demasen deshita.   *Because I was choked up, I*

253

couldn't utter a word.

mune ni himeru   胸に秘める   *to keep something to
   oneself*
[lit. to conceal something in one's chest]
彼女は、いつか女優になる夢を胸に秘めていました。
   Kanojo wa, itsuka joyū ni naru yume o mune ni himete
   imashita.   *She kept her dream of becoming an actress
   someday to herself.*

mune ni kotaeru   胸に応える   *to hit one very hard*
[lit. Something responds to one's chest.]
父の訓戒が胸に応えました。Chichi no kunkai ga mune ni
   kotaemashita.   *My father's admonition hit me very hard.*

mune ni osameru   胸に納める   *to keep something to
   oneself*
[lit. to put something away in one's chest]
あなたの秘密は、私の胸だけに納めておきます。Anata no
   himitsu wa, watakushi no mune dake ni osamete okimasu.   *I'll
   keep your secret just to myself.*

mune ni semaru   胸に迫る   *to be filled with emotion*
[lit. Emotion compels one's chest.]
大学の卒業式で、喜びが胸に迫りました。Daigaku no
   sotsugyō shiki de, yorokobi ga mune ni semarimashita.   *I was
   filled with joy at the college graduation ceremony.*

mune ni ukabu   胸に浮かぶ   *to flash across one's mind*
[lit. Something floats in one's chest.]
素晴らしい考えが胸に浮かびました。Subarashii kangae ga
   mune ni ukabimashita.   *A wonderful idea flashed across my
   mind.*

mune o fukuramaseru   胸を膨らませる   *to have high
   hopes (about something)*
[lit. to expand one's chest]
彼は、成功の期待に胸を膨らませています。Kare wa, seikō
   no kitai ni mune o fukuramasete imasu.   *He has high hopes
   that he'll be successful.*

mune o hatte   胸を張つて   *with one's head held high*
[lit. to throw out one's chest]
自分が正しいなら、胸を張つてそう言いなさい。 Jibun ga
tadashii nara, mune o hatte sō iinasai.   *If you're right, say so*
with your head held high.

mune o hazumasete   胸を弾ませて   *excitedly*
[lit. by bouncing one's chest]
彼女は胸を弾ませて、プレゼントを開けました。 Kanojo wa
mune o hazumasete purezento o akemashita.   *She opened the*
gift excitedly.

mune o itameru   胸を痛める   *to be worried about*
something
[lit. to hurt one's own chest]
彼女は娘の将来について、胸を痛めています。 Kanojo wa
musume no shōrai ni tsuite, mune o itamete imasu.   *She is*
worried about her daughter's future.

mune o kogasu   胸を焦がす   *to pine away with love for*
someone
[lit. to scorch one's chest]
彼は、その女性に胸を焦がしています。 Kare wa, sono josei
ni mune o kogashite imasu.   *He's pining away with love for*
that woman.

mune o nadeorosu   胸をなで下ろす   *to feel relieved*
[lit. to pat one's own chest down]
彼女は赤ちゃんの高熱が下がって、胸をなで下ろしました。
Kanojo wa akachan no kōnetsu ga sagatte, mune o
nadeoroshimashita.   *When her baby's high fever went down,*
she felt relieved.

mune o odoraseru   胸を躍らせる   *to be excited*
[lit. to make one's chest jump]
彼はいい知らせを受けて、胸を躍らせました。 Kare wa ii
shirase o ukete, mune o odorasemashita.   *He was excited at*
receiving good news.

mune o shimetsukeru   胸を締め付ける   *to break one's*

255

heart

[lit. to squeeze one's chest]

彼の悲しい話は、聞く人の胸を締め付けました。Kare no kanashii hanashi wa, kiku hito no mune o shimetsukemashita. *His sad story broke the listeners' hearts.*

mune o sorasu   胸を反らす   *to pride oneself on something*

[lit. to bend one's chest backward]

彼女は司法試験に受かって、胸を反らせました。Kanojo wa shihō shiken ni ukatte, mune o sorasemashita. *She prides herself on having passed the bar exam.*

mune o tokimekasu   胸をときめかす   *to get excited at something*

[lit. to make one's chest throb]

子供たちは、明日ディズニーランドへ行くので、胸をときめかしています。Kodomotachi wa, ashita Dizunīrando e iku node, mune o tokimekasete imasu. *My children are getting excited at going to Disneyland tomorrow.*

mune o tsukareru   胸を突かれる   *to be stunned*

[lit. to get stabbed in one's chest]

私に対する突然の批判に、胸を突かれました。Watakushi ni taisuru totsuzen no hihan ni, mune o tsukaremashita. *I was stunned by the sudden criticism of me.*

mune o utsu   胸を打つ   *to deeply move someone*

[lit. to hit someone's chest]

彼女の親切に胸を打たれました。Kanojo no shinsetsu ni mune o utaremashita. *I was deeply moved by her kindness.*

---

mushi   虫   *insect, worm*

mushi ga ii   虫がいい   *to take too much for granted*

[lit. One's worm is good.]

虫がいいことばかり言っていないで働きなさい。Mushi ga ii koto bakari itte inaide hatarakinasai. *You should work instead of taking too much for granted.*

mushi ga sukanai   虫が好かない   *to dislike someone*
[lit. An insect doesn't like someone.]
彼は虫が好かないけれど、才能があることは認めます。
   Kare wa mushi ga sukanai keredo, sainō ga aru koto wa
   mitomemasu. *Although I dislike him, I admit that he has
   talent.*

mushi ga tsuku   虫が付く   *(a young woman) to have a
no-good man as a lover*
[lit. An insect holds on to a young woman.]
娘に悪い虫が付いたようで心配です。 Musume ni warui
   mushi ga tsuita yō de shinpai desu. *I'm concerned that my
   daughter seems to have a no-good man as a lover.*

mushi mo korosanai   虫も殺さない   *wouldn't hurt a fly*
[lit. wouldn't kill an insect]
彼女は虫も殺さないような顔をしていますが、実は手ごわ
   い交渉相手です。 Kanojo wa mushi mo korosanai yō na kao
   o shite imasu ga, jitsu wa tegowai kōshō aite desu. *Although
   she looks as if she wouldn't hurt a fly, she's actually a tough
   counterpart in the negotiations.*

mushi no idokoro ga warui   虫の居所が悪い   *to be in
a bad mood*
[lit. The location of the worm is bad.]
父はこの週末、虫の居所が悪いです。 Chichi wa kono
   shūmatsu, mushi no idokoro ga warui desu. *My father has
   been in a bad mood this weekend.*

mushi no iki   虫の息   *to be at death's door*
[lit. an insect's breathing]
私が駆けつけたとき、祖父はすでに虫の息でした。
   Watakushi ga kaketsuketa toki, sofu wa sude ni mushi no iki
   deshita. *When I rushed in, Grandfather was already at
   death's door.*

mushi no shirase   虫の知らせ   *premonition*
[lit. the news brought by an insect]
彼が急死する直前に遺書を書いたのは、虫の知らせかも知

れません。 Kare ga kyūshi suru chokuzen ni isho o kaita no wa, mushi no shirase kamo shiremasen. *It could have been a premonition that made him write a will just before his sudden death.*

mushi no sukanai　虫の好かない　　*disgusting, repulsive*
[lit. disliked even by an insect]
娘が、虫の好かない男とつき合っています。 Musume ga, mushi no sukanai otoko to tsukiatte imasu. *My daughter is dating a repulsive guy.*

mushizu ga hashiru　虫酸が走る　　*to give someone the creeps*
[lit. Insect acid runs through one's body.]
彼の名前を聞いただけで、虫酸が走ります。 Kare no namae o kiita dake de, mushizu ga hashirimasu. *Just hearing his name gives me the creeps.*

nigamushi o kamitsubushita yō na　苦虫を嚙み潰したような　*sour*
[lit. like biting into a bitter worm]
彼女は失業して、苦虫を嚙み潰したような顔をしています。 Kanojo wa shitsugyō shite, nigamushi o kamitsubushita yō na kao o shite imasu. *She's been looking sour since she lost her job.*

---

musu　蒸す　*to steam*
mushikaesu　蒸し返す　*to raise an issue again*
[lit. to steam the same thing over again]
彼女は問題を蒸し返そうとしましたが、成功しませんでした。 Kanojo wa mondai o mushikaesō to shimashita ga, seikō shimasen deshita. *Although she tried to raise the issue again, she was unsuccessful.*

---

muyō　無用　*unworthiness*
muyō no chōbutsu　無用の長物　*white elephant*
[lit. a long, unworthy item]
コンピュータを買って以来、古いタイプライターは無用の

長物になりました。Konpyūta o katte irai, furui taipuraitā wa muyō no chōbutsu ni narimashita.   *Since we bought a computer, our old typewriter has become a white elephant.*

---

myaku   脈   *pulse*
  myaku ga aru   脈がある   *There's a ray of hope.*
  [lit. There's a pulse.]
  まだ脈がありそうなので、彼女をもう一度デートに誘ってみます。Mada myaku ga arisō nanode, kanojo o mō ichido dēto ni sasotte mimasu.   *Because there still seems to be a ray of hope, I'll ask her again for a date.*

N

---

na   名   *name*
  na ga tōru   名が通る   *well-known*
  [lit. One's name passes through.]
  彼は世界で名が通っているファッションデザイナーです。Kare wa sekai de na ga tōtte iru fasshon dezainā desu.   *He's a well-known fashion designer worldwide.*

  na ga ureru   名が売れる   *to be famous*
  [lit. One's name is selling.]
  彼女は名が売れるようになるまで、ずいぶん苦労しました。Kanojo wa na ga ureru yō ni naru made, zuibun kurō shimashita.   *Until she became famous, she went through real hardships.*

  na mo nai   名も無い   *unknown, obscure*
  [lit. There's not even a name.]
  名も無い歌手の歌が、突然はやり始めました。Na mo nai kashu no uta ga, totsuzen hayarihajimemashita.   *A song by an obscure singer has suddenly become popular.*

  na ni shi ou   名にし負う   *famous*
  [lit. carrying one's name on the back]

彼女は世界でも名にし負うピアニストで、素晴らしい
   コンサートでした。Kanojo wa sekai demo na ni shi ou
pianisuto de, subarashii konsāto deshita. *She's a
world-famous pianist, and her concert was wonderful.*

na no tōtta   名の通った   *well-known*
[lit. One's name passes through.]
夕べ、名の通った小説家と会う機会がありました。Yūbe, na
no tōtta shōsetsuka to au kikai ga arimashita. *Last night I had
an opportunity to meet a well-known novelist.*

na o ageru   名を挙げる   *to become famous*
[lit. to raise one's own name]
彼は、数学の天才として名を挙げています。Kare wa,
sūgaku no tensai to shite na o agete imasu. *He has become
famous as a mathematical genius.*

na o haseru   名を馳せる   *to be well-known*
[lit. to make one's name run]
彼は、偉大な実業家として名を馳せています。Kare wa, idai
na jitsugyōka to shite na o hasete imasu. *He is well-known as
a great industrialist.*

na o karite   名を借りて   *under the pretense of
something*
[lit. by borrowing the name of something]
政府は赤字財政削減に名を借りて、増税しました。Seifu wa
akaji zaisei sakugen ni na o karite, zōzei shimashita. *The
government raised taxes under the pretense of reducing the
deficit.*

na o kegasu   名を汚す   *to disgrace a reputation*
[lit. to soil one's name]
先生は万引で捕まって、学校の名を汚してしまいました。
Sensei wa manbiki de tsukamatte, gakkō no na o kegashite
shimaimashita. *The teacher disgraced the school's reputation
by being caught shoplifting.*

na o nasu   名を成す   *to become famous*
[lit. to achieve one's name]

友達は、ゴルフのプロとして名を成しています。Tomodachi wa, gorufu no puro toshite na o nashite imasu. *My friend has become famous as a professional golfer.*

na o nokosu　名を残す　　*to make one's name immortal*
[lit. to leave one's name]
彼女は、偉大なオペラ歌手として名を残しました。Kanojo wa, idai na opera kashu toshite na o nokoshimashita. *She made her name immortal as a great opera singer.*

na o oshimu　名を惜しむ　　*to protect one's reputation*
[lit. to value one's name]
彼は教授としての名を惜しんで、非難に反論しました。
Kare wa kyōju toshite no na o oshinde, hinan ni hanron shimashita. *To protect his reputation as a professor, he refuted the accusations.*

nanori o ageru　名乗りを上げる　　*to announce something*
[lit. to give one's name to take part in something]
彼は、知事選挙の候補者として名乗りを上げました。Kare wa, chiji senkyo no kōhosha toshite nanori o agemashita. *He announced his candidacy for the gubernatorial election.*

---

nagai　長い　　*long*
nagai me de miru　長い目で見る　　*to take a long-range view*
[lit. to look at something with long eyes]
この株は、長い目で見ればいい投資になるでしょう。Kono kabu wa, nagai me de mireba ii tōshi ni naru deshō. *If you take the long-range view, these stocks will be a good investment.*

---

nagare　流れ　　*stream, flow*
nagare o kumu　流れを汲む　　*to belong to something*
[lit. to scoop up water from the stream]
彼女の花の生け方は、伝統的な流派の流れを汲んでいます。
Kanojo no hana no ikekata wa, dentōteki na ryūha no nagare o

kunde imasu. *Her style of flower arrangement belongs to a traditional school.*

---

naka 仲 *relations*

naka ni hairu 仲に入る *to mediate*
[lit. to let oneself into relations]
友達と奥さんの仲に入って、口論を収めました。Tomodachi to okusan no naka ni haitte kōron o osamemashita. *By mediating for my friend and his wife, I settled their quarrel.*

naka o saku 仲を裂く *to drive a wedge between the two*
[lit. to split relations]
彼は、二人の仲を裂こうとたくらんでいます。Kare wa, futari no naka o sakō to takurande imasu. *He's plotting to drive a wedge between the two.*

---

naku 泣く *to cry*

naki o ireru 泣きを入れる *to beg for mercy*
[lit. to bring along one's crying]
学生は先生に泣きを入れて、試験を一週間延ばしてもらいました。Gakusei wa sensei ni naki o irete, shiken o isshūkan nobashite moraimashita. *The students begged the teacher for mercy and got the exam postponed for a week.*

naki o miru 泣きを見る *to find oneself in a fix*
[lit. to see one's own crying]
彼女は投機に買った土地の値段が下がって、泣きを見ました。Kanojo wa tōki ni katta tochi no nedan ga sagatte, naki o mimashita. *Because the price of the land she bought for speculation went down, she found herself in a fix.*

nakidokoro 泣き所 *Achilles' heel*
[lit. a spot for crying]
彼は仕事が出来ますが、英語が話せないのが泣き所です。Kare wa shigoto ga dekimasu ga, eigo ga hanasenai no ga nakidokoro desu. *He's an able worker, but his Achilles' heel is that he can't speak English.*

nakigoto o naraberu　　泣き言を並べる　　*to make idle complaints*

[lit. to display crying speech]

彼女はよく泣き言を並べるので、みんなが彼女を避けよう
とします。Kanojo wa yoku nakigoto o naraberu node, minna
ga kanojo o sakeyō to shimasu.　*Because she frequently makes
idle complaints, everybody tries to avoid her.*

nakineiri suru　　泣き寝入りする　　*to have to accept something*

[lit. to cry oneself to sleep]

会社の決定は不当だったけれど、泣き寝入りするしかあり
ませんでした。Kaisha no kettei wa futō datta keredo,
nakineiri suru shika arimasen deshita.　*Although the
company's decision was unfair, I had to accept it.*

nakiotosu　　泣き落とす　　*to pull at someone's heartstrings*

[lit. to secure someone by crying]

妻を泣き落として、毎月の小遣いを増やしてもらいました。
Tsuma o nakiotoshite, maitsuki no kozukai o fuyashite
moraimashita.　*I got my monthly allowance increased by
pulling at my wife's heartstrings.*

---

naku　　鳴く　　*to chirp*

nakazu tobazu　　鳴かず飛ばず　　*to be inactive*

[lit. no chirping or flying]

私が好きな女優は、この三年間鳴かず飛ばずです。
Watakushi ga suki na joyū wa, kono san nen kan nakazu tobazu
desu.　*The actress I like has been inactive for the last three
years.*

---

nama　　生　　*raw, uncooked*

namakajiri no　　生かじりの　　*superficial knowledge of something*

[lit. nibbling at something uncooked]

彼は生かじりの経済学しか知らないのに、専門家気取りです。
Kare wa namakajiri no keizaigaku shika shiranai noni, senmonka
kidori desu.　*Although he has only a superficial knowledge of*

economics, he poses as an expert.

---

nameru　嘗める　*to lick*

namete kakaru　嘗めてかかる　*to take someone or something lightly*

[lit. to lick someone for something]

彼は彼女を嘗めてかかったので、討論では負けてしまいました。Kare wa kanojo o namete kakatta node, tōron dewa makete shimaimashita.　*Because he took her lightly, he lost to her in a debate.*

---

nami　波　*wave*

nami ni noru　波に乗る　*to ride the crest of something*

[lit. to ride on the waves]

彼女の商売は、時代の波に乗って繁盛しています。Kanojo no shōbai wa, jidai no nami ni notte hanjō shite imasu.　*Her business is flourishing by riding the crest of the times.*

namikaze ga tatsu　波風が立つ　*Troubles arise.*
(interpersonal)

[lit. Waves and wind rise.]

結婚して一年後には、二人の間に波風が立ち始めました。Kekkon shite ichi nen go niwa, futari no aida ni namikaze ga tachihajimemashita.　*One year after the wedding, troubles began to arise between them.*

---

namida　涙　*tear*

namida ni kureru　涙に暮れる　*to cry one's eyes out*

[lit. It gets dark because of tears.]

彼は失恋した後一週間、涙に暮れていました。Kare wa shitsuren shita ato isshūkan, namida ni kurete imashita.　*After he lost his love, he cried his eyes out for a week.*

namida ni shizumu　涙に沈む　*to be dissolved in tears*

[lit. to submerge oneself in tears]

彼女は赤ちゃんを事故で亡くして、涙に沈んでいます。Kanojo wa akachan o jiko de nakushite, namida ni shizunde imasu.　*She is still dissolved in tears at having lost her baby in an accident.*

namida o furutte   涙を振るつて   *by repressing one's feelings*

[lit. by shaking one's tears off]

彼は涙を振るつて、同僚の横領を上司に告げました。Kare wa namida o furutte, dōryō no ōryō o jōshi ni tsugemashita. *Repressing his feelings, he reported his colleague's embezzlement to the boss.*

namida o moyōsu   涙を催す   *to be moved to tears*

[lit. to feel the urge for tears]

彼女の年老いた親への献身に、涙を催しました。Kanojo no toshi oita oya e no kenshin ni, namida o moyōshimashita. *I was moved to tears by her total devotion to her elderly parents.*

namida o nomu   涙を飲む   *to suppress one's chagrin*

[lit. to drink one's own tears]

彼はみんなの前で涙を飲んで、自らの失敗を認めました。Kare wa minna no mae de namida o nonde, mizukara no shippai o mitomemashita. *He suppressed his chagrin and admitted his mistakes in front of everyone*

namida o sasou   涙を誘う   *to move to tears*

[lit. to invite tears]

夕べ見た映画は、見る人の涙を誘いました。Yūbe mita eiga wa, miru hito no namida o sasoimashita. *The movie we saw last night moved the audience to tears.*

namidakin   涙金   *a small amount of consolation money*

[lit. tear money]

政府は地震の犠牲者に、取りあえず涙金を配りました。Seifu wa jishin no giseisha ni, toriaezu namidakin o kubarimashita. *The government hastily distributed a small amount of money to the earthquake victims.*

namidamoroi   涙もろい   *to be easily moved to tears*

[lit. to be susceptible to tears]

母は涙もろくて、テレビ番組を見てはよく泣いています。Haha wa namidamorokute, terebi bangumi o mite wa yoku naite imasu. *My mother is easily moved to tears and often cries while watching TV programs.*

---

nan 難 *difficulty, fault*

nankuse o tsukeru 難癖をつける *to find fault with someone or something*

[lit. to apply criticism to someone or something]

あの評論家は、彼女の素晴らしい演技に難癖をつけました。Ano hyōronka wa, kanojo no subarashii engi ni nankuse o tsukemashita. *That critic found fault with her wonderful acting.*

nanshoku o shimesu 難色を示す *to express disapproval*

[lit. to show a difficult color]

学校は、学生の要求に難色を示しました。Gakkō wa, gakusei no yōkyū ni nanshoku o shimeshimashita. *The school expressed its disapproval of the students' demands.*

---

nani 何 *what, something, anything, thing*

nani ga nandemo 何が何でも *no matter what*

[lit. even if something amounts to anything]

この仕事は、何が何でも今週中に終えるつもりです。Kono shigoto wa, nani ga nandemo konshū chū ni oeru tsumori desu. *No matter what, I intend to finish the work this week.*

nani ka ni tsukete 何かにつけて *one way or another*

[lit. by taking advantage of anything]

彼女は何かにつけて、人を批判します。Kanojo wa nanika ni tsukete, hito o hihan shimasu. *She criticizes others one way or another.*

nani kara nani made 何から何まで *everything*

[lit. anything from the beginning to the end]

アメリカに旅行して、何から何まで楽しみました。Amerika ni ryokō shite, nani kara nani made tanoshimimashita. *I made a trip to the United States and enjoyed everything.*

nani kuwanu kao 何食わぬ顔 *completely innocent look*

[lit. the face of someone who didn't eat anything]

彼は、何食わぬ顔でうそをつきます。Kare wa, nani kuwanu kao de uso o tsukimasu.   *He lies with a completely innocent look.*

nani wa sate oki   何はさておき   *first of all*

[lit. by putting things aside]

子供が生まれたとき、何はさておき両親に電話しました。Kodomo ga umareta toki, nani wa sate oki ryōshin ni denwa shimashita.   *When the baby was born, first of all, I called my parents.*

nani wa tomo are   何はともあれ   *anyway*

[lit. whatever a thing may be]

問題がたくさんありましたが、何はともあれ研究を終えました。Mondai ga takusan arimashita ga, nani wa tomo are kenkyū o oemashita.   *Although there were many problems, we finished the research anyway.*

nani ya ka ya   何やかや   *with one thing or another*

[lit. for this thing or for that thing]

彼は何やかやと言い訳を作って、私によく会いに来ます。Kare wa nani ya kaya to iiwake o tsukutte, watakushi ni yoku aini kimasu.   *He comes to see me often with one excuse or another.*

---

narabu   並ぶ   *to line up*

narabu mono ga inai   並ぶ者がいない   *to be second to none*

[lit. There's nobody who can line up with someone.]

英語にかけては、社内で彼女に並ぶ者がいません。Eigo ni kakete wa, shanai de kanojo ni narabu mono ga imasen.   *When it comes to English, in the company, she's second to none.*

---

nareru   慣れる   *to get familiar with someone or something*

nareai 慣れ合い   *cozy relationship*
[lit. familiarity with each other]
この会社では、管理職と組合幹部の慣れ合いが⁵目立ちます。
  Kono kaisha dewa, kanrishoku to kumiai kanbu no nareai ga
  medachimasu.   *In this company, the cozy relationship between
  management and the senior labor union officials is
  conspicuous.*

naresome 馴れ初め   *the beginning of love*
[lit. the start of getting familiar with each other]
彼らの馴れ初めは、去年の暮れのパーティーでした。
  Karera no naresome wa, kyonen no kure no pātī deshita.   *The
  beginning of their love was at a party at the end of last year.*

nari 鳴り   *ringing*
nari o hisomeru 鳴りを潜める   *to keep a low profile*
[lit. to hide the ringing]
あの映画スターは交通事故を起こして以来、鳴りを潜めて
  います。Ano eiga sutā wa kōtsū jiko o okoshite irai, nari o
  hisomete imasu.   *That movie star has kept a low profile since
  he caused a traffic accident.*

nari o shizumete 鳴りを静めて   *with hushed attention*
[lit. by making the ringing quiet]
社員は、鳴りを静めて社長の話を聞きました。Shain wa,
  nari o shizumete shachō no hanashi o kikimashita.   *The
  company employees listened to the president's speech with
  hushed attention.*

narimonoiri de 鳴り物入りで   *with a lot of fanfare*
[lit. with gongs and drums]
政府は鳴り物入りで、新経済政策を促進しています。
  Seifu wa narimonoiri de, shin keizai seisaku o sokushin shite
  imasu.   *The government is promoting the new economic
  policy with a lot of fanfare.*

nariagaru 成り上がる   *to rise to something
suddenly*

---

narikin 成金 *nouveau riche*
[lit. rising suddenly to become rich]
彼は成金で、ロールスロイスを十台持っています。 Kare wa
  narikin de, Rōrusuroisu o jū dai motte imasu. *He's nouveau
  riche and owns ten Rolls Royces.*

---

nashi 梨 *pear, none*
nashi no tsubute 梨の礫 *to not have heard from
  someone*
[lit. no reaction to thrown stones]
色々な会社に履歴書を送ったけれど、梨の礫です。 Iroiro na
  kaisha ni rirekisho o okutta keredo, nashi no tsubute desu.
  *Although I sent many companies my résumé, I haven't heard
  from them.*

---

nawa 縄 *rope*
nawabari arasoi 縄張り争い *territorial dispute*
[lit. a quarrel over a roped-off place]
政党は選挙民をめぐって、縄張り争いを行っています。
  Seitō wa senkyomin o megutte, nawabari arasoi o okonatte
  imasu. *The political parties are engaging in territorial
  disputes over constituents.*

---

ne 根 *root*
ne ga fukai 根が深い *to be deep-rooted*
[lit. The root is deep.]
米に対する国民の感情は、想像以上に根が深いです。 Kome
  ni taisuru kokumin no kanjō wa, sōzō ijō ni ne ga fukai desu.
  *Japanese feelings about rice are deep-rooted beyond
  imagination.*

ne mo ha mo nai 根も葉もない *to be completely
  groundless*
[lit. There are no leaves or roots.]
我が社が倒産するという噂には、根も葉もありません。
  Waga sha ga tōsan suru to iu uwasa niwa, ne mo ha mo

arimasen. *The rumor that our company will go under is completely groundless.*

ne ni motsu   根に持つ   *to hold a grudge against someone*

[lit. to have something at one's root]

彼女は私が言ったことを根に持って、口を聞きません。

Kanojo wa watakushi ga itta koto o ne ni motte, kuchi o kikimasen. *She holds a grudge against me for what I said and doesn't speak to me.*

ne o orosu   根を下ろす   *to take root in something*

[lit. to lower a root]

環境問題が、地域社会に根を下ろしました。Kankyō mondai ga, chiiki shakai ni ne o oroshimashita. *The environmental issues took root in the local community.*

ne wa   根は   *deep down*

[lit. as for a root]

彼はぶっきらぼうだけれど、根は優しい人です。Kare wa bukkirabō dakeredo, ne wa yasashii hito desu. *Although he is abrupt, deep down he is gentle.*

nehori hahori   根掘り葉掘り   *in great detail*

[lit. by digging roots and by digging leaves]

母は私の旅行計画について、根ほり葉ほり聞きました。

Haha wa watakushi no ryokō keikaku ni tsuite, nehori hahori kikimashita. *My mother asked me about my travel plans in great detail.*

nemawashi o suru   根回しをする   *to lay the groundwork*

[lit. to dig around the roots]

彼は、首相になるための根回しをしています。

Kare wa, shushō ni naru tame no nemawashi o shite imasu. He is laying the groundwork for becoming prime minister.

---

ne   音   *sound*

ne o ageru   音を上げる   *to whine*

[lit. to make sounds]

宿題の量が多いので、学生は音を上げています。 Shukudai no ryō ga ōi node, gakusei wa ne o agete imasu. *The students are whining because of a lot of homework.*

---

ne　値　*price*
ne ga haru　値が張る　*to be quite expensive*

[lit. A price stretches.]

このドレスは、デザイナー物なので値が張りました。 Kono doresu wa, dezainā mono nanode ne ga harimashita. *Since it was a designer dress, it was quite expensive.*

---

negau　願う　*to wish*
negattari kanattari　願ったりかなったり　*It's a wish come true.*

[lit. wishing something which then becomes reality]

この契約書にサインしていただければ、願ったりかなったりです。 Kono keiyakusho ni sain shite itadakereba, negattari kanattari desu. *If you'd sign this contract, it would be a wish come true.*

negattemonai　願ってもない　*couldn't ask for something better*

[lit. Besides this, there won't be anything even if one wishes.]

先週の特売は、新しいスーツを買うための願ってもない機会でした。 Senshū no tokubai wa, atarashii sūtsu o kau tame no negattemonai kikai deshita. *I couldn't have asked for a better opportunity to buy a new suit than last week's sale.*

---

neji　ネジ　*screw*
neji o maku　ネジを巻く　*to rouse someone to do something*

[lit. to tighten a screw]

もっと一生懸命練習するように、監督は選手のネジを巻きました。 Motto isshōkenmei renshū suru yō ni, kantoku wa senshu no neji o makimashita.

The manager roused the players to practice much harder.

---

neko 猫 *cat*

neko mo shakushi mo 猫も杓子も *every Tom, Dick and Harry*

[lit. also a cat and a ladle]

最近は、猫も杓子もスキューバダイビングをしています。 Saikin wa, neko mo shakushi mo sukyūbadaibingu o shite imasu. *Nowadays, every Tom, Dick and Harry is doing scuba diving.*

neko ni katsuobushi 猫に鰹節 *like trusting a wolf to guard sheep*

[lit. trusting a cat to guard a dried bonito]

彼女にケーキ屋を任せるなんて、猫に鰹節というものです。 Kanojo ni kēki ya o makaseru nante, neko ni katsuobushi to iu mono desu. *Letting her manage a cake shop is like trusting a wolf to guard sheep.*

neko ni koban 猫に小判 *casting (one's) pearls before swine*

[lit. gold coins to a cat]

彼にクラシック音楽のコンサートの券を上げても、猫に小判です。 Kare ni kurashikku ongaku no konsāto no ken o agetemo, neko ni koban desu. *Giving him a ticket for a classical music concert is like casting pearls before swine.*

neko no hitai 猫の額 *a very small area*

[lit. a cat's forehead]

東京では、猫の額ほどの土地でも価値があります。Tōkyō dewa, neko no hitai hodo no tochi demo kachi ga arimasu. *In Tokyo, even a very small piece of land is valuable.*

neko no me no yō ni kawaru 猫の目のように変わる *to change much too often*

[lit. to change like the eyes of a cat]

政府の経済政策は、猫の目のように変わります。Seifu no keizai seisaku wa, neko no me no yō ni kawarimasu. *The government's economic policy changes much too often.*

neko no te mo karitai   猫の手も借りたい   *to wish one could be two people*
[lit. to want to borrow a cat's paws]
昨日は引っ越しで、猫の手も借りたいほどの忙しさでした。
Kinō wa hikkoshi de, neko no te mo karitai hodo no isogashisa deshita.   *When I moved yesterday, I was so busy that I wished I could be two people.*

neko o kaburu   猫をかぶる   *to feign innocence*
[lit. to put a cat over oneself]
彼女はボーイフレンドの前では、猫をかぶっています。
Kanojo wa bōifurendo no mae de wa, neko o kabutte imasu.
She's feigning innocence in front of her boyfriend.

nekobaba suru   猫糞する   *to pocket something sneakily*
[lit. A cat defecates.]
彼は、地震の犠牲者のために集めた寄付金を猫糞していました。Kare wa, jishin no giseisha no tame ni atsumeta kifukin o nekobaba shite imashita.   *He was pocketing the donations he was collecting for the earthquake victims.*

nekonadegoe   猫撫で声   *wheedling tone of voice*
[lit. one's voice when one pets a cat]
息子は猫撫で声で、マウンテンバイクをねだりました。
Musuko wa nekonadegoe de, maunten baiku o nedarimashita.
In a wheedling tone of voice, my son asked for a mountain bicycle.

---

neru   寝る   *to sleep*
negaeri o utsu   寝返りを打つ   *to doublecross someone*
[lit. to roll over while sleeping]
彼は寝返りを打って、特許をライバル会社に売ってしまいました。Kare wa negaeri o utte, tokkyo o raibaru gaisha ni utte shimaimashita.   *He doublecrossed us and sold his patent to our rival company.*

netemo sametemo   寝ても覚めても   *all the time*
[lit. asleep or awake]
夫は、寝ても覚めても仕事のことばかり考えています。

Otto wa, netemo sametemo shigoto no koto bakari kangaete imasu.   *My husband thinks only about his work all the time.*

nezame ga warui   寝覚めが悪い   *to be conscience-stricken*

[lit. to be bad at waking from sleep]

彼女にしたことを思い返すと、寝覚めが悪いです。 Kanojo ni shita koto o omoikaesu to, nezame ga warui desu.   *I'm conscience-stricken when I recall what I did to her.*

---

netsu   熱   *heat, temperature, fever*

netsu ga sameru   熱が冷める   *One's enthusiasm fades.*

[lit. One's fever cools.]

彼の野球に対する熱が冷めたようです。 Kare no yakyū ni taisuru netsu ga sameta yō desu.   *His enthusiasm for baseball seems to have faded.*

netsu o ageru   熱を上げる   *to be insane about someone or something*

[lit. to make one's temperature higher for someone or something]

彼女は彼に熱を上げています。 Kanojo wa kare ni netsu o agete imasu.   *She is insane about him.*

---

nen   念   *sense, idea, attention*

nen o ireru   念を入れる   *to take special care with something*

[lit. to put one's attention to something]

お客を夕食に呼んだので、念を入れて料理しました。
Okyaku o yūshoku ni yonda node, nen o irete ryōri shimashita. *Because we invited guests for dinner, I took special care with the cooking.*

nen o osu   念を押す   *to make sure of something*

[lit. to press someone's attention]

教授は学生が論文の提出を忘れないように、念を押しました。
Kyōju wa gakusei ga ronbun no teishutsu o wasurenai yō ni, nen o oshimashita.   *The professor made sure that the students wouldn't forget to submit their papers.*

nentō ni oku   念頭に置く   *to keep something in mind*
[lit. to place something in one's idea]
安全を念頭に置いて、車を買うつもりです。 Anzen o nentō
  ni oite, kuruma o kau tsumori desu. *We intend to buy a car
  keeping safety in mind.*

---

nen   年   *year*
nenki ga haitte iru   年季が入っている   *veteran*
[lit. Years and seasons are put in.]
彼は政治で年季が入っているので、話がいつも面白いです。
  Kare wa seiji de nenki ga haitte iru node, hanashi ga itsumo
  omoshiroi desu. *Because he's a veteran of politics, what he
  says is always interesting.*

---

nengu   年貢   *land-tax*
nengu no osamedoki   年貢の納めどき   *The game is
  about over.*
[lit. It's about time to pay one's land-tax.]
そろそろ年貢の納め時で、首になるより引退するつもりです。
  Sorosoro nengu no osamedoki de, kubi ni naru yori intai suru
  tsumori desu. *The game is about over, and I intend to retire
  rather than being fired.*

---

ni   二   *two, second*
ni no ku ga tsugenai   二の句が継げない   *to be
  dumbfounded*
[lit. to be unable to follow with the second word]
彼の恥知らずな行いには、二の句が継げませんでした。
  Kare no hajishirazu na okonai niwa, ni no ku ga tsugemasen
  deshita. *I was dumbfounded at his shameless behavior.*

ni no mai o enjiru   二の舞を演じる   *to repeat
  someone's mistakes*
[lit. to perform the second dance]
株の投機で損して、父の二の舞を演じてしまいました。
  Kabu no tōki de son shite, chichi no ni no mai o enjite
  shimaimashita. *I repeated my father's mistakes by losing*

275

money in stock speculation.

ni no tsugi ni suru　　二の次にする　　*to put something off*
[lit. to make something secondary]
バカンスは二の次にして、今は仕事に集中しています。
Bakansu wa ni no tsugi ni shite, ima wa shigoto ni shūchū shite imasu.　*By putting my vacation off, I'm concentrating on my work now.*

nibansenji　　二番煎じ　　*an imitation, a rehash*
[lit. brewing tea for the second time using the same tea leaves]
彼の意見は、新聞の社説の二番煎じに過ぎません。Kare no iken wa, shinbun no shasetsu no nibansenji ni sugimasen.　*His opinion is just a rehash of the newspaper editorial.*

---

ni　　荷　　*load*
ni ga kachisugiru　　荷が勝ちすぎる　　*to be too heavy a load*
[lit. The load wins.]
その仕事は、私には荷が勝ちすぎます。Sono shigoto wa, watakushi niwa ni ga kachisugimasu.　*That job is too heavy a load for me.*

ni ga oriru　　荷が下りる　　*A great weight has been lifted.*
[lit. A load comes off.]
報告書を書き終わって、荷が下りました。Hōkokusho o kaki owatte, ni ga orimashita.　*A great weight has been lifted because I finished writing the report.*

---

nieru　　煮える　　*to boil*
niekiranai　　煮え切らない　　*lukewarm*
[lit. to not reach the boiling point]
年末のボーナスについて、会社は煮えきらない返事を繰り返しています。Nenmatsu no bōnasu ni tsuite, kaisha wa niekiranai henji o kurikaeshite imasu.　*The company is repeating lukewarm responses about the year-end bonus.*

nieyu o nomasareru　　煮え湯を飲まされる　　*to be*

burned badly
[lit. to be forced to drink boiling water]
彼が私の信用を裏切ったため、煮え湯を飲まされる思いで
した。 Kare ga watakushi no shin-yō o uragitta tame, nieyu o
nomasareru omoi deshita.   *I was burned badly because he
betrayed my trust.*

---

nigeru   逃げる   *to run away, to flee*
   nige o utsu   逃げを打つ   *to dodge*
[lit. to set out to flee]
彼女は時間が無いからと、私の依頼に逃げを打ちました。
Kanojo wa jikan ga nai kara to, watakushi no irai ni nige o
uchimashita.   *She dodged my request by saying that she
wouldn't have time.*

---

nirami   睨み   *glare*
   nirami o kikaseru   睨みを利かせる   *to exert one's
   authority*
[lit. to make use of one's glare]
あの評論家は、文壇で睨みを利かせています。 Ano
hyōronka wa, bundan de nirami o kikasete imasu.   *That critic
is exerting his authority over the literary world.*

---

niru   似る   *to resemble*
   nitari yottari   似たり寄ったり   *to be much the same*
[lit. resembling and drawing near something]
みんなの意見が似たり寄ったりで、目立つものがありませ
んでした。 Minna no iken ga nitari yottari de, medatsu mono
ga arimasen deshita.   *Since everyone's opinion was much the
same, there was nothing outstanding.*

   nitemo nitsukanu   似ても似つかぬ   *to be not at all like
   someone*
[lit. to not resemble a bit]
息子は高校中退で、学者のお父さんとは似ても似ついてい
ません。 Musuko wa kōkō chūtai de, gakusha no otōsan towa
nitemo nitsuite imasen.

*The son is a high-school dropout and not at all like his father,
who is a scholar.*

---

niru   煮る   *to boil*
nitemo yaitemo kuenai   煮ても焼いても食えない
  crafty
[lit. to be unable to eat it even if you boil it or grill it]
彼は煮ても焼いても食えない男だと言う評判があります。
  Kare wa nitemo yaitemo kuenai otoko da to iu hyōban ga
  arimasu.   *He has a reputation as a crafty fellow.*

---

nishi   西   *west*
nishi mo higashi mo wakaranai   西も東も分からない
  to not know what's what
[lit. to not know east or west]
彼女は大学を卒業したのに、西も東も分かりません。
  Kanojo wa daigaku o sotsugyō shita noni, nishi mo higashi mo
  wakarimasen.   *Although she graduated from a university, she
  doesn't know what's what.*

---

nishiki   錦   *gorgeous (Japanese) brocade*
nishiki no mihata   錦の御旗   *just cause*
[lit. a brocaded banner]
会社はリストラを錦の御旗にして、早期退職を強要してい
  ます。Kaisha wa risutora o nishiki no mihata ni shite, sōki
  taishoku o kyōyō shite imasu.   *Companies are forcing early
  retirement using restructuring as just cause.*

nishiki o kazaru   錦を飾る   *to return home in glory*
[lit. to decorate one's home with gorgeous brocade]
彼はプロ野球の選手になって、故郷に錦を飾りました。
  Kare wa puro yakyū no senshu ni natte, kokyō ni nishiki o
  kazarimashita.   *He became a professional baseball player and
  returned home in glory.*

---

niwaka   にわか   *sudden*
niwakajikomi   にわか仕込み   *cram*

[lit. suddenly trained]

外国に行くので、お茶とお花をにわか仕込みしています。

    Gaikoku ni iku node, ocha to ohana o niwakajikomi shite imasu.   *Since I'm going overseas, I'm cramming for tea ceremony and flower arrangement.*

---

nobetsu   のべつ   *always*

nobetsu makunashi ni   のべつ幕なしに   *incessantly*

[lit. always without dropping curtains]

パーティーのあいだ中、彼はのべつ幕なしに仕事の話を続けました。Pātī no aida jū, kare wa nobetsu makunashi ni shigoto no hanashi o tsuzukemashita.   *He talked incessantly about job-related things throughout the party.*

---

nodo   喉   *throat*

nodo kara te ga deru hodo hoshii   喉から手が出るほどほしい   *to want something badly*

[lit. like a hand coming out of one's throat]

彼女は、喉から手がでるほどピアノが欲しいです。Kanojo wa, nodo kara te ga deru hodo piano ga hoshii desu.   *She wants a piano so badly it hurts.*

---

nomu   呑む   *to receive someone*

nonde kakaru   呑んでかかる   *to make light of someone*

[lit. to set about receiving someone]

ベテランの政治家は、選挙運動で若い挑戦者を呑んでかかりました。Beteran no seijika wa, senkyo undō de wakai chōsensha o nonde kakarimashita.   *The veteran politician made light of the young challenger in the election campaign.*

---

noppiki   退っ引き   *retreat*

noppiki naranai   退っ引きならない   *unavoidable*

[lit. to be unable to retreat]

退っ引きならない事情があって、仕事にいけませんでした。Noppiki naranai jijō ga atte, shigoto ni ikemasen deshita. *Because of unavoidable circumstances, I couldn't go to work.*

noren   暖簾   *curtain with a shop sign, room-dividing curtain*

  noren o wakeru   暖簾を分ける   *to let someone open a branch of one's shop*

[lit. to distribute a curtain displaying a shop sign]

近所の寿司屋は、息子に暖簾を分けました。Kinjo no sushiya wa, musuko ni noren o wakemashita. *The sushi shop owner in our neighborhood let his son open a branch of the shop.*

  noren ni udeoshi   暖簾に腕押し   *like beating the air*

[lit. pushing a room-dividing curtain with one's arms]

彼女にデートを申し込みましたが、暖簾に腕押しでした。Kanojo ni dēto o mōshikomimashita ga, noren ni udeoshi deshita. *I asked her for a date, but it was like beating the air.*

---

noru   伸る   *to stretch*

  noruka soruka   伸るか反るか   *sink or swim*

[lit. stretch or bend]

伸るか反るか、とにかくやってみます。Noruka soruka, tonikaku yatte mimasu. *Sink or swim, I'll try anyway.*

---

noshi   熨斗   *noshi (a gift ornament)*

  noshi o tsukete   熨斗を付けて   *gladly*

[lit. by attaching a gift ornament]

こんな古いテレビでよかったら、熨斗をつけてさしあげます。Konna furui terebi de yokattara, noshi o tsukete sashiagemasu. *If you don't mind that the TV is old, I'll give it to you gladly.*

---

nozomi   望み   *hope*

  nozomi o takusu   望みを託す   *to pin one's hopes on someone or something*

[lit. to leave one's hopes with someone or something]

コンピュータを買うため、大きなボーナスに望みを託しています。Konpyūta o kau tame, ōkina bōnasu ni nozomi o takushite imasu. *I'm pinning my hopes on a big bonus so I can buy a computer.*

nuka 糠 *rice bran*
  nuka ni kugi 糠に釘 *to have no effect on someone*
  [lit. to drive a nail into rice bran]
  彼女への注意は全く糠に釘で、相変わらず浪費を続けてい
  ます。Kanojo e no chūi wa mattaku nuka ni kugi de,
  aikawarazu rōhi o tsuzukete imasu. *My warnings had no
  effect on her, and she has been wasting money as usual.*

---

nureru 濡れる *to get wet*
  nureginu o kiserareru 濡れ衣を着せられる *to be
  falsely accused*
  [lit. to be forced to put on wet clothes]
  彼女は万引きの濡れ衣を着せられました。Kanojo wa
  manbiki no nureginu o kiseraremashita. *She was falsely
  accused of shoplifting.*

  nurete de awa 濡れ手で粟 *to make easy profits*
  [lit. to grasp millet with a wet hand]
  猛暑のために、ビール会社が濡れ手で粟の大儲けをしました。
  Mosho no tame ni, birugaisha ga nurete de awa no ōmōke o
  shimashita. *Because of the extremely hot summer, beer
  companies made easy profits.*

O

o 尾 *tail*
  ohire o tsukeru 尾ひれを付ける *to exaggerate*
  [lit. to add a tail and fins]
  彼は話しに尾ひれを付けるので、どこまで正確か分かりま
  せん。Kare wa hanashi ni ohire o tsukeru node, doko made
  seikaku ka wakarimasen. *Because he exaggerates, you don't
  know how accurate his stories are.*

  oha uchikarasu 尾羽打ち枯らす *to be down and out*
  [lit. One's tail feathers and wings wither.]

彼は賭事のために、尾羽打ち枯らしています。Kare wa
kakegoto no tame ni, oha uchikarashite imasu.　*He's down
and out because of gambling.*

---

okado　　お門　　*gate*
　okado chigai　　お門違い　　*barking up the wrong tree*
　[lit. the wrong gate]
　彼を非難するのは、お門違いです。それは、彼のせいでは
　ないんですから。Kare o hinan suru nowa, okadochigai desu.
　Sore wa, kare no sei dewa naindesu kara.　*You're barking up
　the wrong tree by blaming him. It isn't his fault.*

---

oku　　奥　　*depth, interior*
　oku no te　　奥の手　　*ace in the hole*
　[lit. a deep hand]
　弁護士は奥の手を使って、二者間の和解を達成しました。
　Bengoshi wa oku no te o tsukatte, ni sha kan no wakai o tassei
　shimashita.　*Using his ace in the hole, the lawyer achieved an
　amicable settlement between the two companies.*

　okuba ni mono ga hasamatta yō　　奥歯に物が挟まったよう
　mealy-mouthed
　[lit. as if something were stuck between the back teeth]
　奥歯に物が挟まったような言い方をしないで、はっきり言
　って下さい。Okuba ni mono ga hasamatta yō na iikata o
　shinaide, hakkiri itte kudasai.　*Don't be mealy-mouthed.
　Please tell me what you think.*

---

okubi　　おくび　　*belch*
　okubi nimo dasanai　　おくびにも出さない　　*to not give
　the slightest indication*
　[lit. to not show something even in a belch]
　彼女は社長の姪であることを、おくびにも出しませんでした。
　Kanojo wa shachō no mei de aru koto o, okubi nimo
　dashimasen deshita.　*She never gave the slightest indication
　that she was the president's niece.*

---

omoi   思い   *thought, feelings*

omoi o harasu   思いを晴らす   *to pay off old scores*
[lit. to clear one's feelings]
去年負けたチームに思いを晴らすため、今一生懸命練習し
ています。Kyonen maketa chīmu ni omoi o harasu tame, ima
isshōkenmei renshū shite imasu.   *We're practicing hard to
pay off old scores with the team that beat us last year.*

omoi o haseru   思いを馳せる   *to think of someone or
something*
[lit. to make one's thoughts run]
彼は出張中も、家族のことに思いを馳せています。Kare wa
shutchō chū mo, kazoku no koto ni omoi o hasete imasu.
He's thinking of his family even during a business trip.

omoi o kakeru   思いをかける   *to give one's heart to
someone*
[lit. to set one's feelings on someone]
彼女は、友達のお兄さんに思いをかけました。Kanojo wa,
tomodachi no oniisan ni omoi o kakemashita.   *She gave her
heart to her friend's older brother.*

omoi o yoseru   思いを寄せる   *to take a fancy to
someone*
[lit. to let one's feelings come closer to someone]
彼はよく行くバーのホステスに、思いを寄せています。
Kare wa yoku iku bā no hosutesu ni, omoi o yosete imasu.
He's taken a fancy to the hostess at a bar where he often goes.

---

omoki   重き   *weight*

omoki o nasu   重きをなす   *to carry weight*
[lit. to achieve weight]
彼女は心理学の分野で、重きをなしています。Kanojo wa
shinrigaku no bun-ya de, omoki o nashite imasu.   *She carries
weight in the field of psychology.*

omoki o oku   重きを置く   *to emphasize something*
[lit. to place weight on something]
この会社は、先端技術の応用に重きを置いています。Kono

kaisha wa, sentan gijutsu no ōyō ni omoki o oite imasu. *This company is emphasizing the application of advanced technologies.*

---

omote   表   *surface, outside, front*
  omote o kazaru   表を飾る   *to keep up appearances*
  [lit. to decorate the exterior]
あの会社は表を飾っているけれど、実は倒産寸前です。
Ano kaisha wa omote o kazatte iru keredo, jitsu wa tōsan sunzen desu. *That company is keeping up appearances, but it's actually just about to go under.*

  omotekanban   表看板   *main occupation*
  [lit. a front signboard]
彼女の表看板は医者ですが、詩人としても知られています。
Kanojo no omotekanban wa isha desu ga, shijin toshite mo shirarete imasu. *Her main occupation is practicing medicine, but she's also known as a poet.*

---

on   恩   *kindness, favor, debt of gratitude*
  on ni kiseru   恩に着せる   *to demand thanks*
  [lit. to make someone wear one's favor]
彼に何かしてもらうと恩に着せるので、気軽に頼めません。
Kare ni nanika shite morau to on ni kiseru node, kigaru ni tanomemasen. *Because he demands thanks for whatever he does, you can't ask him to do anything lightly.*

  on ni kiru   恩に着る   *to be deeply grateful*
  [lit. to wear the favor given by someone]
病気の時、彼女が一週間も世話してくれたので、恩に着ています。Byōki no toki, kanojo ga isshūkan mo sewa shite kureta node, on ni kite imasu. *Because she took care of me for a week when I was sick, I'm deeply grateful to her.*

  on o uru   恩を売る   *to try to gain someone's gratitude*
  [lit. to sell gratitude to someone]
彼は機会を見つけては、友達に恩を売ろうとします。
Kare wa kikai o mitsukete wa, tomodachi ni on o urō to

shimasu. *He tries to gain his friends' gratitude at every opportunity.*

---

oni   鬼   *devil, demon*

oni no inu ma ni sentaku   鬼の居ぬ間に洗濯   *When the cat's away, the mice will play; to relax while someone of authority is away*

[lit. to do laundry while the demon is away]

お父さんが出張中だから、鬼の居ぬ間に洗濯しましょう。 Otōsan ga shutchō chū dakara, oni no inu ma ni sentaku shimashō. *Since Dad is away on a business trip, let's goof off.*

oni ni kanabō   鬼に金棒   *doubly powerful, effective, or productive*

[lit. to arm a demon with an iron rod]

彼はインテリだし、勉強さえすれば鬼に金棒です。Kare wa interi dashi, benkyō sae sureba oni ni kanabō desu. *Since he's intelligent, if he'd only study, he'd be doubly productive.*

oni no kubi demo totta yō ni   鬼の首でも取ったように   *as if one were a conquering hero*

[lit. as if he had beheaded a demon]

彼はゴルフで私に勝っただけで、鬼の首でもとったように大喜びしています。Kare wa gorugu de watakushi ni katta dake de, oni no kubi demo totta yō ni ōyorokobi shite imasu. *He's as overjoyed as a conquering hero at having beaten me at golf.*

---

osae   抑さえ   *weight*

osae ga kiku   抑さえが効く   *to keep something in order*

[lit. One's weight is effective.]

人事部では、課長の抑えが効いています。Jinjibu dewa, kachō no osae ga kiite imasu. *The section chief is keeping the personnel department in order.*

---

oshi   押し   *push*

oshi ga kiku   押しが利く   *to carry weight*

[lit. One's push is effective.]

あの政治家は、国際貿易の舞台でも押しが利いています。
Ano seijika wa, kokusai bōeki no butai demo oshi ga kiite
imasu.   *That politician carries weight in the arena of
international trade.*

oshi ga tsuyoi   押しが強い   *pushy*

[lit. One's push is strong.]

彼女は押しが強くて、何でも自分の思うことを通そうとし
ます。Kanojo wa oshi ga tsuyokute, nandemo jibun no omou
koto o tōsō to shimasu.   *Because she's pushy, she tries to have
everything her way.*

oshi mo osaremo senu   押しも押されもせぬ
recognized

[lit. not pushing or being pushed]

彼は、世界で押しも押されもせぬ実業家です。Kare wa,
sekai de oshi mo osaremo senu jitsugyōka desu.   *He's a
globally-recognized industrialist.*

oshi no itte de   押しの一手で   *doggedly*

[lit. nothing but purely pushing]

彼は押しの一手で、彼女に結婚を申し込みました。Kare wa
oshi no itte de, kanojo ni kekkon o mōshikomimashita.   *He
doggedly asked her to marry him.*

osuna osuna   押すな押すな   *to be jam-packed*

[lit. Don't push, don't push.]

祭日のため、デパートは押すな押すなのにぎわいでした。
Saijitsu no tame, depāto wa osuna osuna no nigiwai deshita.
Because of a holiday, the department store was jam-packed.

---

oto   音   *sound*

oto ni kiku   音に聞く   *famous*

[lit. to hear someone or something's sounds]

昨日レストランで、音に聞く作家を見ました。Kinō
resutoran de, oto ni kiku sakka o mimashita.   *Yesterday, I saw
a famous novelist at a restaurant.*

otoko   男   *man, manliness*

   otoko ga sutaru   男が廃る   *to lose one's manly honor*

   [lit. One's manliness diminishes.]

   そんな卑怯な手段に訴えるなら、男が廃れますよ。Sonna hikyō na shudan ni uttaeru nara, otoko ga sutaremasu yo. *If you resort to such cowardly means, you'll lose your manly honor.*

   otoko o ageru   男を上げる   *to earn a reputation for manliness*

   [lit. to raise one's manliness]

   彼は子供を火事から救って、男を上げました。Kare wa kodomo o kaji kara sukutte, otoko o agemashita. *He earned a reputation for manliness by rescuing a child from a fire.*

P

pin   ピン   *one, the top, the beginning*

   pin kara kiri made   ピンから切りまで   *to run the whole gamut*

   [lit. from the top to the bottom]

   候補者にはピンからキリまであるので、投票の際には気をつけるべきです。Kōhosha niwa pin kara kiri made aru node, tōhyō no sai niwa ki o tsukeru beki desu. *The candidates run the whole gamut, so you should be careful when you vote.*

   pinhanesuru   ピンはねする   *to skim money*

   [lit. set the top aside]

   彼が契約金の三割をピンはねしていたのを、知りませんでした。Kare ga keiyakukin no san wari o pinhaneshite ita no o, shirimasen deshita. *I didn't know he was skimming 30 percent off my contract money.*

R

---

rachi   埒   *picket fence, bounds*

rachi ga akanai   埒があかない   *to get nowhere*

[lit. A picket fence does not open.]

彼にいくら妥協の必要を説明しても、埒があきませんでした。
Kare ni ikura dakyō no hitsuyō o setsumei shitemo, rachi ga
akimasen deshita.   *No matter how much I explained to him the
need for a compromise, it got nowhere.*

rachi mo nai   埒もない   *silly*

[lit. no bounds]

彼女は埒もない話を、長々と話し続けました。Kanojo wa
rachi mo nai hanashi o, naganaga to hanashitsuzukemashita.
She kept talking her silly talk for a long time.

---

rappa   ラッパ   *trumpet*

rappa o fuku   ラッパを吹く   *to blow one's own horn*

[lit. to blow a trumpet]

彼は自分の実績について、いつもラッパを吹いています。
Kare wa jibun no jisseki ni tsuite, itsumo rappa o fuite imasu.
*He is always blowing his own horn about his past
performance.*

---

ri   理   *reason, principle, truth*

ri mo hi mo naku   理も非もなく   *by any means*

[lit. with no principles or wrongs]

彼女は理も非も無く、金儲けに熱中しています。Kanojo wa
ri mo hi mo naku, kanemōke ni netchū shite imasu.   *She's
engrossed in making money by any means.*

ri no tōzen   理の当然   *matter of course*

[lit. right on principle]

彼が怒ったのは、理の当然でした。Kare ga okotta no wa, ri
no tōzen deshita.   *His anger was a matter of course.*

---

rō   労   *labor, trouble, effort*

rō o ta to suru   労を多とする   *to appreciate someone's efforts*

[lit. to find that someone's labor was extensive]

社長は、社員の労を多としました。 Shachō wa, shain no rō o ta to shimashita. *The president appreciated his employees' efforts.*

rō o toru   労を取る   *to take the trouble to do something*

[lit. to take up troubles]

教授は、私のために推薦状を書く労を取って下さいました。 Kyōju wa, watakushi no tame ni suisen jō o kaku rō o totte kudasaimashita. *The professor took the trouble to write a letter of recommendation for me.*

---

romei   露命   *life fragile like dew*

romei o tsunagu   露命をつなぐ   *to live from hand to mouth*

[lit. to sustain a dew-like fragile life]

失業中は、持ち物を売って露命をつなぎました。 Shitsugyō chū wa, mochimono o utte romei o tsunagimashita. *When I was unemployed, we lived from hand to mouth by selling our possessions.*

---

rotō   路頭   *roadside*

rotō ni mayou   路頭に迷う   *to end up in the street, to become homeless*

[lit. to get lost at the roadside]

不景気が続いて、路頭に迷う人がでてきました。 Fukeiki ga tsuzuite, rotō ni mayou hito ga detekimashita. *Because of the lasting recession, people have begun to end up in the street.*

---

ron   論   *argument*

ron o matanai   論を待たない   *to be beyond question*

[lit. to be needless to argue]

彼女が腕の立つ弁護士であることは、論を待ちません。 Kanojo ga ude no tatsu bengoshi de aru koto wa, ron o machimasen. *That she's a capable lawyer is beyond question.*

ryū 竜 *dragon*

ryūtō dabi ni owaru 竜頭蛇尾に終わる *to peter out*
[lit. to start with a dragon's head and end with a snake's tail]
会社の拡張計画は、二年後には竜頭蛇尾に終わりました。
　　Kaisha no kakuchō keikaku wa, ni nen go ni wa ryūtō dabi ni
　　owarimashita. *The company expansion plan petered out after
　　two years.*

ryūin 溜飲 *gastric juices*

ryūin ga sagaru 溜飲が下がる *to feel great satisfaction*
[lit. Gastric juices go down.]
同僚に言いたいことを全部言って、溜飲が下がりました。
　　Dōryō ni iitai koto o zenbu itte, ryūin ga sagarimashita. *When
　　I said everything I wanted to say to my colleagues, I felt great
　　satisfaction.*

ryūbi 柳眉 *beautiful eyebrows*

ryūbi o sakadateru 柳眉を逆立てる *(for a beautiful
　　woman) to glare angrily*
[lit. to make one's beautiful eyebrows stand up]
彼女は上司との仲を怪しまれて、柳眉を逆立てました。
　　Kanojo wa jōshi to no naka o ayashimarete, ryūbi o
　　sakadatemashita. *When her relationship with her boss was
　　called into question, she glared angrily.*

S

saba 鯖 *mackerel*

saba o yomu 鯖を読む *to cheat at counting*
[lit. to count the number of mackerels]
デモの主催者は、参加者の数の鯖を読みました。Demo no
　　shusaisha wa, sankasha no kazu no saba o yomimashita. *The
　　organizer of the demonstration cheated at counting the number
　　of participants.*

---

saihai 采配   *command baton*
   saihai o furu 采配を振る   *to take charge of something*
   [lit. to swing a command baton]
   レストランの経営の采配を振っているのは、奥さんの方
     です。Resutoran no keiei no saihai o futte iru no wa, okusan
     no hō desu.   *She is the one who takes charge of the*
     restaurant's business.

---

saifu 財布   *wallet, purse*
   saifu no soko o hataku 財布の底をはたく   *to spend*
   all one's money
   [lit. to tap the bottom of one's wallet]
   財布の底をはたいて、コンピュータを買いました。Saifu no
     soko o hataite, konpyūta o kaimashita.   *I spent all my money*
     on a computer.

   saifu no himo o nigiru 財布の紐を握る   *to control a*
   budget
   [lit. to grip purse strings]
   わが家では、妻が財布の紐を握っています。Wagaya dewa,
     tsuma ga saifu no himo o nigitte imasu.   *In my household, my*
     wife controls the budget.

---

saisaki 幸先   *future*
   saisaki ga ii 幸先が良い   *to be promising*
   [The future is good.]
   企画の提案で、部長の支持を得たのは幸先がいいです。
     Kikaku no teian de, buchō no shiji o eta no wa saisaki ga ii
     desu.   *It's promising that I got the department chief's support*
     for my proposal for the project.

---

saji 匙   *spoon*
   saji o nageru 匙を投げる   *to give up on something*
   [lit. to throw away a spoon]
   彼にそれをいくら説明しても分からないので、匙を投げま
     した。Kare ni sore o ikura setsumei shitemo wakaranai node,
     saji o nagemashita.   *Since he didn't get it, no matter how*

much I explained it, I gave up.

sajikagen de   匙加減で   *with discretion*
[lit. with the control of a spoonful of medicine]
交渉は、大使の匙加減でうまく行くと思います。Kōshō wa,
taishi no sajikagen de umaku iku to omoimasu.   *I think that
with the ambassador's discretion, the negotiations will turn out
all right.*

---

saki   先   *future; first*
saki ga aru   先がある   *promising*
[lit. There is a future.]
彼女にはハイテクの背景があるので、先があります。
    Kanojo niwa haiteku no haikei ga aru node, saki ga arimasu.
    *Since she has a background in advanced technology, her future
    is promising.*

saki ga mieru   先が見える   *The end is in sight.*
[lit. to be able to see the future]
やっと、この研究も先が見えてきました。Yatto, kono
kenkyū mo saki ga miete kimashita.   *Finally, for this research
the end is in sight.*

saki ni tatsu   先に立つ   *to lead*
[lit. to stand in front of something]
今度の仕事は、私が先に立ってやりました。Kondo no
shigoto wa, watakushi ga saki ni tatte yarimashita.   *I was the
one who led this work.*

saki o kosu   先を越す   *to predict, to anticipate*
[lit. to go beyond the first]
妻の考えの先を越して、二人だけの旅行を提案しました。
    Tsuma no kangae no saki o koshite, futari dake no ryokō o
    teian shimashita.   *Anticipating my wife's wishes, I suggested a
    trip for just two of us.*

sakibō o katsugu   先棒を担ぐ   *to pave the way*
[lit. to carry the front end of a stick]
彼は候補者のために、選挙運動の先棒を担いでいます。

Kare wa kōhosha no tame ni, senkyo undō no sakibō o katsuide imasu. *He is paving the way for the candidate in the election.*

sakibosori   先細り   *decline, failing*
[lit. a skinny end]

彼は新しい事業を始めましたが、期待に反して先細りです。
Kare wa atarashii jigyō o hajimemashita ga, kitai ni hanshite sakibosori desu. *Although he started a new business, despite his hopes, it's failing.*

---

saku   策   *plan*
saku o rōsuru   策を弄する   *to scheme*
[lit. to resort to a plan]

彼女は策を弄して、その地位を得ようとしました。Kanojo wa saku o rōshite, sono chii o eyō to shimashita. *She schemed to gain that position.*

---

sama   様   *appearance*
sama ni narranai   様にならない   *to not have what it takes*
[lit. to be not up to appearance]

彼は先生として、様になりません。Kare wa sensei toshite, sama ni narimasen. *He doesn't have what it takes as a teacher.*

---

saya   鞘   *sheath*
moto no saya ni osamaru   元の鞘に収まる   *to get back together*
[lit. to be put into an original sheath]

彼と彼女は一年の別居の後、元の鞘に収まりました。Kare to kanojo wa ichi nen no bekkyo no ato, moto no saya ni osamarimashita. *After a one-year separation, he and she got back together.*

---

se   背   *back*
se ni hara wa kaerarenu   背に腹は代えられぬ   *to have no choice*

[lit. to be unable to change one's belly for one's back]

急にお金が必要になり、背に腹は代えられないので質屋へ
行きました。Kyū ni okane ga hitsuyō ni nari, se ni hara wa
kaerarenai node shichiya e ikimashita. *Suddenly I needed
money, and because I had no other choice, I went to a
pawnshop.*

se o mukeru　背を向ける　*to turn one's back on
someone or something*

[lit. to direct one's back to someone or something]

彼は、彼女の頼みに背を向けました。Kare wa, kanojo no
tanomi ni se o mukemashita. *He turned his back on her
request.*

sesuji ga samuku naru　背筋が寒くなる　*A chill runs
down one's spine.*

[lit. One's back muscles get cold.]

ひどい交通事故を目撃して、背筋が寒くなりました。Hidoi
kōtsū jiko o mokugeki shite, sesuji ga samuku narimashita.
*Witnessing a terrible traffic accident, a chill ran down my
spine.*

---

sei　精　*spirit*

sei o dasu　精を出す　*to exert oneself to do something, to
work hard*

[lit. to put out one's spirit]

彼女は試験を控えて、勉強に精を出しています。Kanojo wa
shiken o hikaete, benkyō ni sei o dashite imasu. *With the
exam coming up soon, she's exerting herself to study.*

seiippai　精一杯　*all one can do*

[lit. the maximum of one's spirit]

仕事で精一杯で、昼食を食べる時間がありませんでした。
Shigoto de seiippai de, chūshoku o taberu jikan ga arimasen
deshita. *All I could do was work, and I didn't have time to eat
lunch.*

seiippai yaru　精一杯やる　*to do one's best*

[lit. to do something with the maximum of one's spirit]

企画を終わらせようと精一杯やりましたが、締め切りに間に合いませんでした。Kikaku o owaraseyō to seiippai yarimashita ga, shimekiri ni maniaimasen deshita. *I did my best to finish the project, but I couldn't meet the deadline.*

---

seken　世間　*world, public, society*
　seken ga hiroi　世間が広い　*to know many people*
　[lit. One's world is wide.]
　彼女は世間が広いので、選挙に出たら勝つでしょう。
　　Kanojo wa seken ga hiroi node, senkyo ni detara katsu deshō. *Since she knows so many people, she could win an election if she ran.*

　seken ni deru　世間に出る　*to enter the real world*
　[lit. to go out into the world]
　息子は大学を卒業し、仕事を見つけて、世間に出ました。
　　Musuko wa daigaku o sotsugyō shi, shigoto o mitsukete, seken ni demashita. *My son graduated from the university, found a job, and entered the real world.*

　sekenbanashi　世間話　*small talk*
　[lit. a talk about a society]
　彼に仕事の相談に行ったのですが、世間話になってしまいました。Kare ni shigoto no sōdan ni itta no desu ga, sekenbanashi ni natte shimaimashita. *I went to consult with him about my work, but it ended up in small talk.*

　sekenshirazu　世間知らず　*naive*
　[lit. not knowing the world]
　彼女は世間知らずで、誰でもすぐ信用してしまいます。
　　Kanojo wa sekenshirazu de, dare demo sugu shin-yō shite shimaimasu. *Since she's naive, she immediately trusts anyone she meets.*

　sekentei o tsukurou　世間体を繕う　*to keep up appearances*
　[lit. to patch up one's appearances in society]
　彼は世間体を繕うために、娘を私立の学校に行かせています。
　　Kare wa sekentei o tsukurou tame ni, musume o shiritsu no

gakkō ni ikasete imasu.   *He's sending his daughter to a private school to keep up appearances.*

seki   席   *seat*

seki no atatamaru hima mo nai   席の暖まる暇もない
to be very busy

[lit. There is no time for a seat to get warm.]

彼はテレビニュースのレポーターになって以来、席の暖まる暇もありません。Kare wa terebi nyūsu no repōtā ni natte irai, seki no atatamaru hima mo arimasen.   *Since he became a TV news reporter, he has been very busy.*

seki o aratamete   席を改めて   *again on a different occasion*

[lit. by changing a seat]

それについては、席を改めて考えましょう。Sore ni tsuite wa, seki o aratamete kangaemashō.   *Let's consider it again on a different occasion.*

seki o hazusu   席を外す   *to leave a room*

[lit. to get away from one's seat]

数分、席を外してもらえませんか。Sūfun, seki o hazushite moraemasen ka.   *Would you leave the room for a few minutes?*

seki o keru   席を蹴る   *to storm out of the room*

[lit. to kick one's seat]

彼の案が否決されると、彼は席を蹴って会議室を出ていきました。Kare no an ga hiketsu sareru to, kare wa seki o kette kaigishitsu o dete ikimashita.   *When his idea was voted down, he stormed out of the conference room.*

seki o yuzuru   席を譲る   *to give one's position to someone*

[lit. to give one's seat to someone]

彼は、社長の席を娘に譲って引退しました。Kare wa, shachō no seki o musume ni yuzutte intai shimashita.   *He gave his position as president to his daughter and retired.*

---

sekimen   赤面   *red face*
  sekimen no itari   赤面の至り   *to be quite ashamed of
    oneself*
[lit. the height of a red face]
教授を彼女の秘書と間違えて、赤面の至りでした。Kyōju o
kanojo no hisho to machigaete, sekimen no itari deshita.   *I
was quite ashamed of myself at assuming the professor was her
secretary.*

---

sen   線   *line*
  sen ga hosoi   線が細い   *to project insecurity*
[lit. One's line is thin.]
彼には才能があっても線が細いから、この仕事には不向き
です。Kare niwa sainō ga attemo sen ga hosoi kara, kono
shigoto niwa fumuki desu.   *Because he projects insecurity
despite his talent, he's not suitable for this job.*

  sen o hiku   線を引く   *to distinguish*
[lit. to draw a line]
政治家は、公私の別に線を引かねばなりません。Seijika wa,
kōshi no betsu ni sen o hikaneba narimasen.   *Politicians
should distinguish the difference between public and private
affairs.*

  fukusen o haru   伏線を張る   *to forestall*
[to put a line under something]
代替え策を作って、後の反対に伏線を張りました。Daigae
saku o tsukutte, nochi no hantai ni fukusen o harimashita.   *We
forestalled later objections by making an alternate plan.*

  heikōsen o tadoru   平行線をたどる   *to not come to
    agreement*
[lit. to follow parallel lines]
長年の交渉にも関わらず、両者は平行線をたどっています。
Naganen no kōshō nimo kakawarazu, ryōsha wa heikōsen o
tadotte imasu.   *Despite years of negotiations, the two sides
haven't come to agreement.*

  yobōsen o haru   予防線を張る   *to take preventive*

measures

[lit. to outstretch a protective line]

批判される前に言い訳を言って、予防線を張りました。

Hihan sareru mae ni iiwake o itte, yobōsen o harimashita.

I took preventive measures by giving my excuse before being criticized.

---

sente   先手   *first move*

sente o utsu   先手を打つ   *to forestall*

[lit. to take the first move]

競争相手に先手を打って、値引きで契約を申し込みました。

Kyōsō aite ni sente o utte, nebiki de keiyaku o mōshikomimashita.   *By forestalling our competitor, we offered a contract at a cut-rate price.*

---

sentō   先頭   *lead, first*

sentō o kiru   先頭を切る   *to take the lead*

[lit. to venture to be the first]

先頭を切って、週末の仕事を志願しました。Sentō o kitte, shūmatsu no shigoto o shigan shimashita.   *I took the lead and volunteered to work on the weekend.*

---

setsu   節   *principles*

setsu o oru   節を折る   *to yield to someone or something*

[lit. to break one's principles]

子供の願いに節を折って、子猫を飼うことを認めました。

Kodomo no negai ni setsu o otte, koneko o kau koto o mitomemashita.   *Yielding to my children's wishes, I approved of their keeping a kitten.*

---

sewa   世話   *care, trouble, help*

sewa ga nai   世話がない   *astounding*

[lit. There is no care.]

あれほど言ったのにまだ分からないなんて、本当に世話がありません。Are hodo itta noni mada wakaranai nante, hontō

---

ni sewa ga arimasen.   *It's truly astounding that you haven't
gotten it after I've told you so often.*

sewa ga yakeru　世話が焼ける　　*to require care*
[lit. One's help for others burns.]
子供はまだ小さいので、とても世話が焼けます。Kodomo
　wa mada chiisai node, totemo sewa ga yakemasu.   *Since my
　children are still young, they require a lot of care.*

sewa ni naru　世話になる　　*to be under the care of*
　someone
[lit. to get someone's help]
年をとっても、子供の世話になるつもりはありません。
　Toshi o tottemo, kodomo no sewa ni naru tsumori wa arimasen.
　*I have no intention of being under the care of my children, even
　in my old age.*

sewa o yaku　世話を焼く　　*to take care of someone*
[lit. to heat the care of someone]
祖母は、孫の世話を焼くのが好きです。Sobo wa, mago no
　sewa o yaku no ga suki desu.   *My grandmother loves to take
　care of her grandchildren.*

---

shakushi　杓子　*ladle.*
　shakushijōgi　杓子定規　　*to go by the book*
　[lit. a ladle and a ruler]
　彼はいつも杓子定規だから、柔軟性がありません。Kare wa
　　itsumo shakushijōgi dakara, jūnansei ga arimasen.   *Because
　　he always goes by the book, he lacks flexibility.*

---

shi　四　*four*
　shi no go no iu　四の五の言う　　*to find fault*
　[lit. to say four or to say five]
　彼女は何でも四の五の言うので、会議に呼びませんでした。
　　Kanojo wa nandemo shi no go no iu node, kaigi ni yobimasen
　　deshita.   *Since she finds fault with everything, we didn't invite
　　her to the meeting.*

---

shi   死   *death*

shinimizu o toru   死に水を取る   *to be at someone's deathbed*

[lit. to pour water on the mouth of someone who just died]

家族が間に合わず、私が友達の死に水を取りました。
Kazoku ga ma ni awazu, watakushi ga tomodachi no shinimizu o torimashita. *Because my friend's family couldn't make it on time, I was at his deathbed.*

---

shian   思案   *thought*

shian ni amaru   思案に余る   *to be at one's wit's end*

[lit. to exceed one's thought]

彼女と結婚すべきか思案に余って、上司に相談しました。
Kanojo to kekkon subeki ka shian ni amatte, jōshi ni sōdan shimashita. *I conferred with my boss because I was at my wit's end about marrying her or not.*

shian ni kureru   思案に暮れる   *to be preoccupied*

[lit. A day goes by while thinking.]

彼女は離婚した後、どんな仕事を探せばいいのか思案に暮れました。Kanojo wa rikon shita ato, donna shigoto o sagaseba ii no ka shian ni kuremashita. *After the divorce, she was preoccupied with the kind of job she should look for.*

---

shibai   芝居   *drama, theater*

shibai o utsu   芝居を打つ   *to put someone on*

[lit. to run a play]

彼は芝居を打って同情を引いた後で、みんなからお金を借りました。Kare wa shibai o utte dōjō o hiita ato de, minna kara okane o karimashita. *After putting us on to get our sympathy, he borrowed money from everyone.*

shibaigakaru   芝居がかる   *histrionic*

[lit. like a drama]

彼女の芝居がかった話し方が鼻につきます。Kanojo no shibaigakatta hanashikata ga hana ni tsukimasu. *Her histrionic way of talking stinks.*

---

shibire   痺れ   *numbness*
  shibire o kirasu   痺れを切らす   *to get antsy waiting for someone or something*
  [lit. to have pins and needles]
  三十分待っても注文した料理が来ないので、痺れを切らしました。 Sanjuppun mattemo chūmon shita ryōri ga konai node, shibire o kirashimashita.   *We got antsy waiting 30 minutes for the food we ordered.*

---

shifuku   私腹   *one's own belly*
  shifuku o koyasu   私腹を肥やす   *to line one's own pocket*
  [lit. to make one's own belly fat]
  彼が帳簿をごまかして私腹を肥やしていたのを、知りませんでした。 Kare ga chōbo o gomakashite shifuku o koyashite ita no o, shirimasen deshita.   *We didn't know that he was lining his own pocket by cooking the accounts.*

---

shikii   敷居   *threshold (entrance)*
  shikii ga takai   敷居が高い   *to be self-conscious about visiting someone*
  [lit. Someone's threshold is high.]
  彼には借りがあるので、あのうちに行くのは敷居が高いです。 Kare ni wa kari ga aru node, ano uchi ni iku no wa shikii ga takai desu.   *Because I owe him some money, I feel self-conscious about visiting his house.*

---

shimari   締まり   *firmness*
  shimari ga nai   締まりがない   *lax*
  [lit. There is no firmness.]
  今週はボスが出張でいないので、オフィスには締まりがありません。 Konshū wa bosu ga shutchō de inai node, ofisu niwa shimari ga arimasen.   *Because the boss is on a business trip this week, we've been lax in the office.*

---

shimatsu   始末   *management*

shimatsu ni oenai 始末に負えない *unmanageable*
[lit. to be unable to assume management]
昨日友達の子供を預かりましたが、始末に負えませんでした。
Kinō tomodachi no kodomo o azukarimashita ga, shimatsu ni
oemasen deshita. *I took care of my friend's children in my
home yesterday, but they were unmanageable.*

---

shin 真 *reality*
    shin ni semaru 真に迫る *to be true to life*
[lit. to draw near reality]
彼女は真に迫るうそをつきました。Kanojo wa shin ni semaru
uso o tsukimashita. *She told a lie that was true to life.*

---

shinkei 神経 *nerve*
    shinkei ga futoi 神経が太い *to have nerves of steel*
[lit. One's nerves are thick.]
彼は神経が太いから、この仕事には最適です。Kare wa
shikei ga futoi kara, kono shigoto niwa saiteki desu. *Because
he has nerves of steel, he's the best one for this work.*

    shinkei ni sawaru 神経にさわる *to get on one's
nerves*
[lit. to touch one's nerves]
彼の態度は神経にさわります。Kare no taido wa shinkei ni
sawarimasu. *His behavior gets on my nerves.*

    shinkei o suriherasu 神経をすり減らす *to wear
someone down*
[lit. to grind down someone's nerves]
会社の運命を左右する計画をまかされて、神経をすり減ら
しました。 Kaisha no unmei o sayū suru keikaku o
makasarete, shinkei o suriherashimashita. *I was put in charge
of a crucial project for the company, and it wore me down.*

    shinkei o togaraseru 神経をとがらせる *to become
keenly aware of someone or something*
[lit. to sharpen one's nerves]
最近は、未成年の非行に警察が神経をとがらせています。

Saikin wa, miseinen no hikō ni keisatsu ga shinkei o togarasete imasu. *Recently, the police have become keenly aware of juvenile delinquency.*

---

shinmi   親身   *kindness*
  shinmi ni naru   親身になる   *to devote oneself to someone*
[lit. to become kind to someone]
彼女が病気になったので、親身になって世話しました。
Kanojo ga byōki ni natta node, shinmi ni natte sewa shimashita. *Because my girlfriend became ill, I devoted myself to taking care of her.*

---

shinogi   鎬   *the ridges on the sides of a sword blade*
  shinogi o kezuru   鎬を削る   *to compete furiously*
[lit. to scrape the ridges on the sides of a sword blade]
彼らは彼女の注意を引こうと、鎬を削っています。Karera wa kanojo no chūi o hikō to, shinogi o kezutte imasu. *They're competing furiously to get her attention.*

---

shinshō   心証   *impression*
  shinshō o gaisuru   心証を害する   *to make an unfavorable impression*
[lit. to harm one's impression]
仕事の面接で緊張しすぎて、心証を害してしまいました。
Shigoto no mensetsu de kinchō shisugite, shinshō o gaishite shimaimashita. *Because I was too tense at the job interview, I made an unfavorable impression.*

---

shinshoku   寝食   *food and sleep*
  shinshoku o wasurete   寝食を忘れて   *with intense devotion*
[lit. by forgoing food and sleep]
彼女は寝食を忘れて、子供を看病しました。Kanojo wa shinshoku o wasurete, kodomo o kanbyō shimashita. *With intense devotion, she took care of her sick child.*

shintai 進退 *one's course of action*
  shintai kiwamaru 進退窮まる *to be baffled*
  [lit. One's course of action comes to an end.]
  彼は仕事の責任と妻の願いの間で、進退窮まっています。
  Kare wa shigoto no sekinin to tsuma no negai no aida de,
  shintai kiwamatte imasu. *He's baffled at how to reconcile his*
  job responsibilities and his wife's wishes.

shinzō 心臓 *heart*
  shinzō ga tsuyoi 心臓が強い *to have the nerve to do or*
  say something
  [lit. One's heart is strong.]
  彼女は心臓が強くて、言いたいことを誰にでも言います。
  Kanojo wa shizō ga tsuyokute, iitai koto o dare ni demo iimasu.
  She has the nerve to say whatever she wants to say to anyone.

shio 潮 *tide*
  shiodoki o miru 潮時を見る *to wait for a good*
  opportunity
  [lit. to watch for the time of the high or low tide]
  彼は、会社を辞めて自分の事業を始める潮時を見ています。
  Kare wa, kaisha o yamete jibun no jigyō o hajimeru shiodoki o
  mite imasu. *He's waiting for a good opportunity to quit his*
  job and start his own business.

shippo 尻尾 *tail*
  shippo o dasu 尻尾を出す *to reveal the truth*
  [lit. to accidentally reveal one's tail]
  彼は独身の振りをしていましたが、奥さんからの電話で尻
  尾を出してしまいました。Kare wa dokushin no furi o shite
  imashita ga, okusan kara no denwa de shippo o dashite
  shimaimashita. *Although he pretended to be single, the truth*
  was revealed when a phone call came from his wife.

  shippo o furu 尻尾を振る *to ingratiate oneself with*
  someone

[lit. to wag one's tail]

あの俳優は、いつも評論家に尻尾を振っています。Ano haiyū wa, itsumo hyōronka ni shippo o futte imasu. *That actor is always ingratiating himself with critics.*

shippo o maite nigeru   尻尾を巻いて逃げる   *to turn tail*

[lit. to curl one's tail and flee]

彼は仕事が厳しくなると、尻尾を巻いて逃げ出しました。Kare wa shigoto ga kibishiku naru to, shippo o maite nigedashimashita. *When the work got tough, he turned tail.*

shippo o tsukamu   尻尾をつかむ   *to obtain evidence*

[lit. to grasp someone's tail]

その新聞記者は、官僚の汚職の尻尾をつかみました。Sono shinbun kisha wa, kanryō no oshoku no shippo o tsukamimashita. *That newspaper reporter obtained evidence of corruption by the bureaucrats.*

---

shira   白   *white*

shira o kiru   白を切る   *to pretend not to know about something*

[lit. to stick with white]

彼は自分の間違いなのに、白を切っています。Kare wa jibun no machigai nanoni, shira o kitte imasu. *Although he made a mistake, he's pretending not to know about it.*

---

shiri   尻   *buttocks, bottom, hips*

shiri ga karui   尻が軽い   *rash*

[lit. One's buttocks are light.]

彼は尻が軽いたちなので、彼の判断は信用できません。Kare wa shiri ga karui tachi nanode, kare no handan wa shin-yō dekimasen. *He's so rash that you can't trust his judgment.*

shiri ga nagai   尻が長い   *to stay too long*

[lit. One's bottom is stretching.]

彼は尻が長いので、彼が来るといつも食事を出さねばなり

ません。Kare wa shiri ga nagai node, kare ga kuru to itsumo shokuji o dasaneba narimasen. *Because he stays too long, whenever he visits us, we have to serve him a meal.*

shiri ga ochitsukanai   尻が落ち着かない   *to not stay in one place long*

[lit. One's buttocks don't settle down.]

彼女はどんな仕事をしても、尻が落ち着きません。Kanojo wa donna shigoto o shitemo, shiri ga ochitsukimasen. *No matter what kind of job she has, she doesn't stay in one place long.*

shiri ga omoi   尻が重い   *to be slow to act*

[lit. One's buttocks are heavy.]

彼女は尻が重いけれど、一度始めるといい仕事を速くします。Kanojo wa shiri ga omoi keredo, ichido hajimeru to ii shigoto o hayaku shimasu. *She's slow to act, but once she starts, she quickly does a good job.*

shiri ga wareru   尻が割れる   *something bad to be brought to light*

[lit. One's buttocks split.]

彼の社長を失脚させる陰謀は、すぐ尻が割れてしまいました。Kare no shachō o shikkyaku saseru inbō wa, sugu shiri ga warete shimaimashita. *His plot to bring about the president's downfall was instantly brought to light.*

shiri ni hi ga tsuku   尻に火がつく   *Time is fast running out.*

[lit. One's bottom catches fire.]

明日が結婚式ですが、準備のために尻に火がついています。Ashita ga kekkonshiki desu ga, junbi no tame ni shiri ni hi ga tsuite imasu. *My wedding is tomorrow, and the time for preparations is fast running out.*

shiri ni ho o kakeru   尻に帆を掛ける   *to take to one's heels*

[lit. to set a sail to one's bottom]

彼が急に借りの返済を求めたので、尻に帆を掛けて逃げま

した。Kare ga kyū ni kari no hensai o motometa node, shiri ni ho o kakete nigemashita.   *Because he suddenly asked for the repayment of the debt, I took to my heels.*

shiri ni shikareru   尻に敷かれる   *to be under one's wife's thumb*

[lit. A husband is put under a wife's buttocks.]

友達はみんな、私が妻の尻に敷かれていると思っています。 Tomodachi wa minna, watakushi ga tsuma no shiri ni shikarete iru to omotte imasu.   *All my friends think that I'm under my wife's thumb.*

shiri o atatameru   尻を暖める   *to remain at the same place or position*

[lit. to warm one's buttocks]

彼はもう二十年も、助教授として尻を暖めています。Kare wa mō nijū nen mo, jokyōju toshite shiri o atatamete imasu. *He has remained an assistant professor for 20 years already.*

shiri o hashoru   尻をはしよる   *to cut something short*

[lit. to tuck up the bottom of one's kimono]

時間が無くなってきたので、講義の尻をはしょらなければなりませんでした。Jikan ga nakunatte kita node, kōgi no shiri o hashoranakereba narimasen deshita.   *Because time was running out, I had to cut short my lecture.*

shiri o makuru   尻をまくる   *to assume a defiant attitude*

[lit. to pull up the bottom of one's kimono and reveal buttocks]

彼は彼の書いた報告書への批判に、尻をまくりました。 Kare wa kare no kaita hōkokusho e no hihan ni, shiri o makurimashita.   *He assumed a defiant attitude toward criticism of the report he had written.*

shiri o mochikomu   尻を持ち込む   *to complain*

[lit. to bring one's bottom in]

彼女はステーキの品質について、肉屋へ尻を持ち込みました。 Kanojo wa sutēki no hinshitsu ni tsuite, nikuya e shiri o mochikomimashita.   *She complained to the butcher about the quality of the steak.*

shiri o nuguu   尻を拭う   *to clean up someone's mess*
[lit. to wipe someone's bottom]
息子の尻を拭うため、先生に謝りに行きました。 Musuko no
shiri o nuguu tame, sensei ni ayamarini ikimashita. *To clean
up my son's mess, I went to see his teacher to apologize.*

shiri o sueru   尻を据える   *to buckle down*
[lit. to set one's bottom firmly]
来週から、尻を据えてコンピュータの使い方を習います。
Raishū kara, shiri o suete konpyūta no tsukaikata o naraimasu.
*Starting next week, I'll buckle down and learn how to use a
computer.*

shiri o tataku   尻を叩く   *to prod someone to do
something*
[lit. to hit someone's buttocks]
娘の尻を叩いて、ピアノの稽古をさせました。 Musume no
shiri o tataite, piano no keiko o sasemashita. *I prodded my
daughter to practice the piano.*

---

shirōto   素人   *amateur*
shirōtobanare   素人離れ   *to be far from amateurish*
[lit. leaving an amateur behind]
彼女の絵は、素人離れしています。 Kanojo no e wa,
shirōtobanare shite imasu. *Her paintings are far from
amateurish.*

---

shisen   視線   *one's eye*
shisen o abiru   視線を浴びる   *to attract people's
attention*
[lit. to be showered by people's eyes]
彼は会議で独創的な意見を述べて、出席者の視線を浴びま
した。 Kare wa kaigi de dokusōteki na iken o nobete,
shussekisha no shisen o abimashita. *He attracted people's
attention by stating some innovative opinions at the meeting.*

shisshō   失笑   *embarrassing laughter*
  shisshō o kau   失笑を買う   *to cause embarrassed laughter*
  [lit. to buy embarrassing laughter]
  問題を誤解して議論したので、失笑を買ってしまいました。
    Mondai o gokai shite giron shita node, shisshō o katte shimaimashita.   *Because my arguments were based on a misconception, I caused embarrassed laughter.*

---

shita   舌   *tongue*
  shita ga koeru   舌が肥える   *to develop a taste for something*
  [lit. One's tongue gets rich.]
  沢山の美術館へ行って、現代芸術に対する舌が肥えました。
    Takusan no bijutsukan e itte, gendai geijutsu ni taisuru shita ga koemashita.   *After visiting a lot of museums, I have developed a taste for contemporary art.*

  shita ga mawaru   舌が回る   *to be glib*
  [lit. One's tongue spins.]
  彼女は舌がよく回るので、言い訳が上手です。Kanojo wa shita ga yoku mawaru node, iiwake ga jōzu desu.   *Since she's really glib, she's a master at excuses.*

  shita no ne no kawakanu uchi ni   舌の根の乾かぬ内に
  as soon as one says something
  [lit. even before the bottom of one's tongue dries up]
  彼は舌の根の乾かぬ内に、立場を翻しました。Kare wa shita no ne no kawakanu uchi ni, tachiba o hirugaeshimashita.   *As soon as he said it, he flipped his position.*

  shita no saki   舌の先   *only words*
  [lit. the tip of a tongue]
  彼女の約束は、舌の先だけです。Kanojo no yakusoku wa, shita no saki dake desu.   *Her promise is only words.*

  shita o dasu   舌を出す   *to laugh behind someone's back*
  [lit. to stick one's tongue out]
  彼は親の話を聞く振りをしていても、陰では舌を出して

います。Kare wa oya no hanashi o kiku furi o shite itemo, kage dewa shita o dashite imasu.   *He pretends to listen to what his parents say, but he's laughing behind their backs.*

shita o maku   舌を巻く   *to be astounded*
[lit. to curl one's tongue]
彼女の雄弁に舌を巻きました。Kanojo no yūben ni shita o makimashita.   *I was astounded by her eloquent speech.*

shitasaki sanzun   舌先三寸   *glib tongue, sweet talk*
[lit. three inches of a tongue]
彼は説明を求められて、舌先三寸でごまかしました。Kare wa setsumei o motomerarete, shitasaki sanzun de gomakashimashita.   *When he was asked for an explanation, he got through it with his glib tongue.*

shitatarazu   舌足らず   *to not express oneself clearly*
[lit. not enough tongue]
私が舌足らずのため、混乱を引き起こして申し訳ありません。Watakushi ga shitatarazu no tame, konran o hikiokoshite mōshiwake arimasen.   *I'm sorry for causing some confusion because I didn't express myself clearly.*

shitatsuzumi o utsu   舌鼓を打つ   *to eat something with gusto*
[lit. to click one's tongue like a drum]
この前の旅行では、その土地のご馳走に舌鼓を打ちました。Kono mae no ryokō dewa, sono tochi no gochisō ni shitatsuzumi o uchimashita.   *On my last trip, I ate the local delicacies with gusto.*

nekojita   猫舌   *to be sensitive to anything hot (temperature)*
[lit. a cat's tongue]
彼女は猫舌で、熱いお茶は飲めません。Kanojo wa nekojita de, atsui ocha wa nomemasen.   *Since she's sensitive to anything hot, she can't drink hot tea.*

nimaijita o tsukau   二枚舌を使う   *to tell a lie*
[lit. to use two tongues]

彼女は二枚舌を使うので、信用できません。Kanojo wa
nimaijita o tsukau node, shin-yō dekimasen. *Because she tells
lies, you can't trust her.*

shitauchi suru   舌打ちする   *to click one's tongue with
displeasure*

[lit. to make one's tongue hit the palate]

彼は雑用を頼まれて、舌打ちしました。Kare wa zatsuyō o
tanomarete, shitauchi shimashita. *He clicked his tongue with
displeasure when he was asked to do errands.*

---

shita   下   *low, down*

shita nimo okanai motenashi   下にも置かないもてなし
red carpet treatment

[lit. treatment so as not to lay someone down on the ground]

得意先の会社で、下にも置かないもてなしを受けました。
Tokuisaki no kaisha de, shita nimo okanai motenashi o
ukemashita. *We received the red carpet treatment at the
client's company.*

---

shoku   食   *eating*

shoku ga hosoi   食が細い   *small eater*

[lit. One's eating is narrow.]

彼女は食が細いけれど、いつも健康です。Kanojo wa shoku
ga hosoi keredo, itsumo kenkō desu. *She's a small eater, but
she stays healthy.*

shoku ga susumu   食が進む   *to have a big appetite*

[lit. One's eating advances.]

夕べは母の手作りの料理で、食が進みました。Yūbe wa
haha no tezukuri no ryōri de, shoku ga susumimashita. *I had
a big appetite last night since it was my mother's cooking.*

shokushi ga ugoku   食指が動く   *to have an itch for
something*

[lit. An eating (index) finger moves.]

新しい車に、食指が動きます。Atarashii kuruma ni, shokushi
ga ugokimasu. *I have an itch for a new car.*

---

shōmen   正面   *front*
  shōmen kitte   正面切って   *directly*
[lit. by cutting in the front]
正面切って彼を非難することが出来ませんでした。Shōmen
   kitte kare o hinan suru koto ga dekimasen deshita.   *I couldn't
   blame him directly.*

---

shou   背負う   *to carry something on the back*
  shotte tatsu   背負って立つ   *to shoulder the
   responsibility*
[lit. to carry something on the back and stand up]
社長の死後、奥さんが会社を背負って立っています。
   Shachō no shigo, okusan ga kaisha o shotte tatte imasu.   *Since
   the president's death, his wife has been shouldering the
   responsibility for the company.*

---

shu   朱   *vermilion*
  shu o ireru   朱を入れる   *to red-pencil (written material)*
[lit. to insert vermilion]
編集者は、有名な作家の原稿に朱を入れるのをためらいま
   した。Henshūsha wa, yūmei na sakka no genkō ni shu o ireru
   no o tameraimashita.   *The editor hesitated to red-pencil the
   famous writer's manuscript.*

---

shūbi   愁眉   *knitted brows*
  shūbi o hiraku   愁眉を開く   *to breathe freely again*
[lit. to open knotted brows]
子供の高熱が下がって、愁眉を開きました。Kodomo no
   kōnetsu ga sagatte, shūbi o hirakimashita.   *I breathed freely
   again when my child's high fever went down.*

---

shuchū   手中   *inside a palm*
  shuchū ni osameru   手中に収める   *to secure something*
[lit. put something inside one's palm]
彼は首相の座を手中に収めました。Kare wa shushō no za o
   shuchū ni osamemashita.   *He has secured the position of*

prime minister.

---

shukō   趣向   *plan*
  shukō o korasu   趣向を凝らす   *to devise an elaborate plan*
  [lit. to concentrate on a plan]
  彼女は、両親の金婚式のために趣向を凝らしました。
  Kanojo wa, ryōshin no kinkonshiki no tame ni shukō o korashimashita. *She devised an elaborate plan for her parents' golden anniversary.*

---

shūshi   宗旨   *one's religion*
  shūshi o kaeru   宗旨を変える   *to switch one's belief, opinion, job, etc.*
  [lit. to change one's religion]
  彼は最近、革新から保守に政治信念の宗旨を変えました。
  Kare wa saikin, kakushin kara hoshu ni seiji shinnen no shūshi o kaemashita. *He recently switched his political beliefs from liberalism to conservatism.*

---

sode   袖   *sleeve*
  sode ni sugaru   袖にすがる   *to appeal to someone for mercy*
  [lit. to cling to someone's sleeve]
  兄の袖にすがって、宿題を助けてもらいました。Ani no sode ni sugatte, shukudai o tasukete moraimashita. *I appealed to my big brother for mercy and got him to help with my homework.*

  sode ni suru   袖にする   *to rebuff someone*
  [lit. to put hands in sleeves and do nothing]
  彼女は彼を袖にしました。Kanojo wa kare o sode ni shimashita. *She rebuffed him.*

  sode no shita   袖の下   *money under the table, bribe*
  [lit. under the sleeve]
  彼は、袖の下を使って政府の契約をもらったそうです。
  Kare wa, sode no shita o tsukatte seifu no keiyaku o moratta sō

desu.   *He's said to have used money under the table to get the government contract.*

sode o hiku   袖を引く   *to pluck someone's sleeve*
[lit. to pull someone's sleeve]
秘密の話しがあるので、彼女の袖を引きました。Himitsu no hanashi ga aru node, kanojo no sode o hikimashita.   *I plucked her sleeve because I had something secret to tell her.*

sode o nurasu   袖を濡らす   *to weep*
[lit. to wet one's sleeve]
お通夜では、全員が袖を濡らしました。Otsuya dewa, zen-in ga sode o nurashimashita.   *Everyone at the wake wept.*

sode o shiboru   袖を絞る   *to be moved to tears*
[lit. to wring a tear-soaked sleeve]
とても悲しい映画だったので、袖を絞りました。Totemo kanashii eiga datta node, sode o shiborimashita.   *Because it was a very sad movie, I was moved to tears.*

sode o tsuranete   袖を連ねて   *together*
[lit. by lining up sleeves together]
閣僚は、袖を連ねて辞職しました。Kakuryō wa, sode o tsuranete jishoku shimashita.   *The cabinet members resigned together.*

sode o wakatsu   袖を分かつ   *to break off with someone*
[lit. to split a sleeve]
彼と彼女は二年の婚約の後、袖を分かちました。Kare to kanojo wa ni nen no kon-yaku no ato, sode o wakachimashita. *He and she broke off with each other after a two-year engagement.*

---

sojō   俎上   *on the chopping block*
sojō ni noseru   俎上に載せる   *to bring up something for discussion*
[lit. to put something on the chopping block]
政府は、夏休みの延長を俎上に載せています。Seifu wa, natsuyasumi no enchō o sojō ni nosete imasu.   *The*

government has brought up for discussion the subject of longer summer vacations.

sojō no uo　　　祖上の魚　　*to feel quite helpless*
[lit. fish on a chopping block]

病気で明日の試験の準備が出来ず、祖上の魚のような心境です。Byōki de ashita no shiken no junbi ga dekizu, sojō no uo no yō na shinkyō desu.　*I feel quite helpless because I'm sick and can't prepare for tomorrow's exam.*

---

soko　底　*bottom*

soko ga asai　　　底が浅い　　*shallow*
[lit. The bottom is shallow.]

彼女の知識は広いけれど、底が浅いです。Kanojo no chishiki wa hiroi keredo, soko ga asai desu.　*Her knowledge is vast but shallow.*

soko ga wareru　　　底が割れる　　*to fall apart*
[lit. The bottom breaks.]

彼の嘘は、すぐに底が割れてしまいました。Kare no uso wa, sugu ni soko ga warete shimaimashita.　*His lie immediately fell apart.*

soko o tsuku　　　底を突く　　*to run out of something*
[lit. to hit the bottom]

夫が失業し、子供が入院し、貯金が底を突いてしまいました。Otto ga shitsugyō shi, kodomo ga nyūin shi, chokin ga soko o tsuite shimaimashita.　*Because my husband lost his job and our child was hospitalized, our savings ran out.*

soko o watte hanasu　　　底を割って話す　　*to speak one's mind*
[lit. to speak by splitting one's bottom]

夕べは、父と底を割って話す機会がありました。Yūbe wa, chichi to soko o watte hanasu kikai ga arimashita.　*Last night I had an opportunity to speak my mind to my father.*

---

sōkō　相好　*face*

sōkō o kuzusu　　　相好を崩す　　*to be all smiles*

[lit. to soften one's face]

彼女は、娘に子供が生まれて相好を崩しています。Kanojo wa, musume ni kodomo ga umarete sōkō o kuzushite imasu. *She is all smiles because her daughter had a baby.*

---

son   損   *loss*

sontokuzuku de   損得ずくで   *for one's own gain*

[lit. by purely calculating one's gains and losses]

彼は損得ずくで人とつき合います。Kare wa sontokuzuku de hito to tsukiaimasu. *He associates with others for his own gain.*

---

sora   空   *empty, feigned, sham*

soradanomi ni suru   空頼みにする   *to hope in vain*

[lit. to rely on an empty hope]

彼は昇給を受けることを、空頼みにしています。Kare wa shōkyū o ukeru koto o, soradanomi ni shite imasu. *He's hoping in vain to get a raise.*

soraibiki o kaku   空いびきを掻く   *to feign sleep*

[lit. to pretend to be snoring]

父は母の苦情を聞きたくないので、空いびきを掻きました。Chichi wa haha no kujō o kikitakunai node, soraibiki o kakimashita. *My father didn't want to hear my mother's complaints, so he feigned sleep.*

soragoto   空言   *lie*

[lit. empty words]

彼は、言い訳に空言を言いました。Kare wa, iiwake ni soragoto o iimashita. *He told a lie as his excuse.*

soranamida   空涙   *crocodile tears*

[lit. sham tears]

彼は彼女に同情した振りをして、空涙を流しました。Kare wa kanojo ni dōjō shita furi o shite, soranamida o nagashimashita. *He pretended that he sympathized with her and shed crocodile tears.*

sorazorashii   空々しい   *insincere*

[lit. emptiness upon emptiness]

彼女は、上司に空々しいお世辞を言っています。Kanojo wa, jōshi ni sorazorashii oseji o itte imasu.   *She's giving insincere compliments to the boss.*

---

sori   反り   *curve*

sori ga awanai   反りが合わない   *to not see eye to eye*

[lit. Curves don't fit each other.]

彼と私は、反りが合いません。Kare to watakushi wa, sori ga aimasen.   *He and I don't see eye to eye.*

---

soroban   算盤   *abacus*

soroban ga awanai   算盤が合わない   *It doesn't pay.*

[lit. An abacus doesn't fit.]

それをその値段で売っては、算盤が合いません。Sore o sono nedan de uttewa, soroban ga aimasen.   *If you sell it at that price, it doesn't pay.*

soroban o hajiku   算盤をはじく   *to calculate*

[lit. to use an abacus]

彼女は最初に算盤をはじかないと、何にもしません。 Kanojo wa saisho ni soroban o hajikanaito, nannimo shimasen. *She won't do anything unless she calculates beforehand.*

sorobandakai   算盤高い   *to be calculating*

[lit. to be high in calculations]

彼は算盤高くて、得にならないことは決してしません。 Kare wa sorobandakakute, toku ni naranai koto wa kesshite shimasen.   *Being a calculating person, he doesn't do a thing that won't benefit him.*

---

soto   外   *outside*

sotozura ga ii   外面がいい   *to be affable in public*

[lit. An outside face is good.]

彼女は外面はいいけれど、うちではやかまし屋です。 Kanojo wa sotozura wa ii keredo, uchi dewa yakamashiya desu.   *She's affable in public but a nitpicker at home.*

---

suberu   滑る   *to slide, to slip*
  suberikomi de   滑り込みで   *barely*
  [lit. by sliding into something]
  彼は、滑り込みで選挙に当選しました。 Kare wa, suberikomi
  de senkyo ni tōsen shimashita.   *He barely won the election.*

  subettano korondano to iu   滑ったの転んだのと言う
  to complain of one thing or another
  [lit. to say that one slipped or fell down]
  彼女は何をしても、滑ったの転んだのと言います。 Kanojo
  wa nani o shitemo, subettano korondano to iimasu.   *She
  complains of one thing or another no matter what she does.*

---

sui   水   *water*
  suihō ni kisuru   水泡に帰する   *to come to nothing*
  [lit. to return to a water bubble]
  雨で試合が中止になり、厳しい練習が水泡に帰してしまい
  ました。 Ame de shiai ga chūshi ni nari, kibishii renshū ga
  suihō ni kishite shimaimashita.   *Because the game was
  canceled due to rain, our rigorous practice came to nothing.*

  suika mo jisezu   水火も辞せず   *through it all*
  [lit. without rejecting flood or fire]
  彼は水火も辞せず、彼女を助けました。 Kare wa suika mo
  jisezu, kanojo o tasukemashita.   *He helped her through it all.*

---

suji   筋   *line, logic*
  suji ga chigau   筋が違う   *to not stand to reason*
  [lit. Logic is wrong.]
  彼女が私を非難するのは、筋が違います。 Kanojo ga
  watakushi o hinan suru no wa, suji ga chigaimasu.   *It doesn't
  stand to reason that she blamed me.*

  suji ga ii   筋がいい   *to have an aptitude for something*
  [lit. A line is good.]
  息子は、野球の筋が良さそうです。 Musuko wa, yakyū no suji
  ga yosasō desu. *My son seems to have an aptitude for baseball.*

  suji ga tatsu   筋が立つ   *to be logical*

[lit. Logic stands up.]

彼の説明は、筋が立っています。Kare no setsumei wa, suji ga tatte imasu.   *There's logic in his explanation.*

suji o tōsu   筋を通す   *to act according to one's principles*

[lit. to let logic go through something]

協議では、妥協するより筋を通すことを選びました。Kyōgi dewa, dakyō suru yori suji o tōsu koto o erabimashita.   *In the talks, we chose to act according to our principles rather than compromise.*

suji o tōsu   筋を通す   *to go through proper channels*

[lit. to put something through a line]

彼女は筋を通すより、社長に直接昇進を頼みに行きました。 Kanojo wa suji o tōsu yori, shachō ni chokusetsu shōshin o tanomini ikimashita.   *She went directly to the president to request a promotion rather than going through proper channels.*

---

sujigane   筋金   *steel reinforcement*

sujiganeiri no   筋金入りの   *staunch*

[lit. steel-reinforced]

彼は、筋金入りの自由貿易主義者です。Kare wa, sujiganeiri no jiyū bōeki shugisha desu.   *He's a staunch free-trader.*

---

sumi   隅   *corner*

sumi ni okenai   隅に置けない   *There's more to one than meets the eye.*

[lit. to be unable to simply put someone in a corner]

彼女は、週末に小説を書いているそうです。彼女も隅に置けません。Kanojo wa, shūmatsu ni shōsetsu o kaite iru sō desu. Kanojo mo sumi ni okemasen.   *I hear that she has been writing novels on the weekend. There's more to her than meets the eye.*

---

suna   砂   *sand*

suna o kamu yō na   砂を噛むような   *dreary*

319

[lit. like chewing sand]

離婚してからは、砂を嚙むような生活です。Rikon shite kara
wa, suna o kamu yō na seikatsu desu.   *Since my divorce, my
life has been dreary.*

---

sune   すね   *shin*
  sune ni kizu motsu   すねに傷持つ   *to have a shady
    past*
  [lit. to have an old scar on one's shin]

  彼はすねに傷持つ身なので、選挙には出られません。Kare
  wa sune ni kizu motsu mi nanode, senkyo niwa deraremasen.
  Because he has a shady past, he can't run for election.

  sune o kajiru   すねをかじる   *to sponge off one's parent*
  [lit. to gnaw one's parent's shin]

  彼女は、いつまでも親のすねをかじるつもりです。Kanojo
  wa, itsumademo oya no sune o kajiru tsumori desu.   *She.
  intends to sponge off her parent forever.*

---

sushi   鮨   *sushi*
  sushizume   鮨詰め   *to be packed like sardines*
  [lit. to be packed like *sushi*]

  ディスコは、若い人で鮨詰めでした。Disuko wa, wakai hito
  de sushizume deshita.   *In the disco, young people were
  packed like sardines.*

---

suteru   捨てる   *to throw away*
  sutemi de   捨て身で   *in desperation*
  [lit. by throwing one's body away]

  彼は、捨て身でその問題に取り組みました。Kare wa, sutemi
  de sono mondai ni torikumimashita.   *He grappled with his
  problems in desperation.*

  suteta mono dewa nai   捨てた物ではない   *to be not
    altogether worthless*
  [lit. It's not something to throw away.]

  彼女のアイディアも、捨てた物ではありません。Kanojo no
  aidea mo, suteta mono dewa arimasen.

Her idea is not altogether worthless.

suzume 雀 *sparrow*

suzume no namida 雀の涙   *minuscule amount*
[lit. a sparrow's tear]

今度のボーナスは、雀の涙でした。Kondo no bōnasu wa, suzume no namida deshita. *The bonus this time was minuscule.*

kitakiri suzume 着た切り雀   *to wear the same clothes*
[lit. a sparrow with the same clothes]

スーツケースを盗まれて、旅行中は着た切り雀でした。Sūtsukēsu o nusumarete, ryokō chū wa kitakirisuzume deshita. *Because my luggage was stolen, I wore the same clothes throughout the trip.*

T

taga 箍 *hoop*

taga ga yurumu 箍が緩む   *to lose some of one's former vigor*
[lit. A hoop gets loose.]

父も七十を過ぎて、箍が緩んできました。Chichi mo nanajū o sugite, taga ga yurunde kimashita. *My father is now over seventy and has lost some of his former vigor.*

tai 体 *body*

tai o kawasu 体をかわす   *to dodge something*
[lit. to avoid bodily crush]

彼は体をかわして、責任を逃れました。Kare wa tai o kawashite, sekinin o nogaremashita. *He dodged his responsibility.*

tai o nasu 体を成す   *to be organized*
[lit. to achieve a body]

彼女の説明は、あまり体を成していません。

Kanojo no setsumei wa, amari tai o nashite imasen.
Her explanation isn't well organized.

---

taido   態度   *attitude*
　taido ga ōkii   態度が大きい   *to act big*
　[lit. One's attitude is big.]
　彼は新人なのに、態度が大きいです。Kare wa shinjin nanoni,
　taido ga ōkii desu.   *Although he's a new face, he acts big.*

---

taifū   台風   *typhoon*
　taifū no me   台風の目   *a leading figure*
　[lit. the eye of a typhoon]
　学園騒動では、彼らが台風の目になっています。Gakuen
　sōdō dewa, karera ga taifū no me ni natte imasu.   *They're the
　leading figures in the campus revolt.*

---

taigai   大概   *general*
　taigai ni suru   大概にする   *to not carry something too
　far*
　[lit. to remain in a general range]
　人の批判も、大概にするべきです。Hito no hihan mo, taigai
　ni suru beki desu.   *You shouldn't carry your criticism of
　others too far.*

---

taiko   太鼓   *drum*
　taiko o motsu   太鼓を持つ   *to flatter someone*
　[lit. to hold a drum for someone]
　彼女は上司の太鼓を持って、特別待遇を受けています。
　Kanojo wa jōshi no taiko o motte, tokubetsu taigū o ukete
　imasu.   *She's getting special treatment by flattering the boss.*

　taikoban o osu   太鼓判を押す   *to give one's seal of
　approval*
　[lit. to stamp with a large drum-like seal]
　教授は、ピアニストとしての彼女の才能に太鼓判を押しま
　した。Kyōju wa, pianisuto to shite no kanojo no sainō ni
　taikoban o oshimashita.   *The professor gave his seal of*

approval to her talent as a pianist.

---

taisho　大所　*big standpoint*
　taisho kōsho kara　大所高所から　*from a broad perspective*
[lit. from a big and high standpoint]
その問題は、大所高所から接近すべきです。 Sono mondai wa, taisho kōsho kara sekkin subeki desu. *You must approach that issue from a broad perspective.*

---

taisō　大層　*very much*
　taisō mo nai　大層もない　*much too much*
[lit. no less than very much]
その申し出は、私には大層もございません。 Sono mōshide wa, watakushi niwa taisō mo gozaimasen. *Your offer is much too much for me.*

---

taka　高　*amount, high*
　taka ga shireru　高が知れる　*limited*
[lit. The amount is known.]
彼女の知識は、高が知れています。 Kanojo no chishiki wa, taka ga shirete imasu. *Her knowledge is limited.*

　taka o kukuru　高をくくる　*to take something lightly*
[lit. to put the amount together]
易しい試験だと、高をくくっていたのが大きな間違いでした。 Yasashii shiken da to, taka o kukutte ita no ga ōkina machigai deshita. *It was a big mistake for me to take the exam lightly.*

　takabisha ni deru　高飛車に出る　*to act highhanded*
[lit. to advance a rook higher (deeper)]
私が女性のせいか、彼は高飛車に出てきました。 Watakushi ga josei no sei ka, kare wa takabisha ni dete kimashita. *He probably acted highhanded because I was a woman.*

　takami no kenbutsu　高みの見物　*to stand by idly*
[lit. to sightsee from a high point]
彼女は彼らが侮辱し合うのを、高みの見物していました。

Kanojo wa karera ga bujoku shiau no o, takami no kenbutsu shite imashita. *She stood by idly while they were insulting each other.*

otakaku tomaru   お高くとまる   *to be stuck-up*
[lit. to perch high]
彼は有名かも知れないけれど、いつもお高くとまっています。
Kare wa yūmei kamoshirenai keredo, itsumo otakaku tomatte imasu. *He may be famous, but he's always stuck-up.*

---

tama   玉   *jewel*
tama ni kizu   玉に瑕   *a fly in the ointment*
[lit. a scar on a jewel]
素晴らしいバカンスでしたが、一日豪雨が降ったのが玉に
瑕でした。Subarashii bakansu deshita ga, ichi nichi gōu ga futta no ga tama ni kizu deshita. *We had a great vacation; but the fly in the ointment was one day of heavy rain.*

shōchū no tama   掌中の玉   *the apple of one's eye*
[lit. a jewel in one's palm]
あの家族では娘が掌中の玉であることを、みんな知ってい
ます。Ano kazoku dewa musume ga shōchū no tama de aru koto o, minna shitte imasu. *Everybody knows that the daughter is the apple of everyone's eye in that family.*

---

tamoto   袂   *kimono sleeve*
tamoto o tsuranete   袂を連ねて   *acting together*
[lit. by lining up *kimono* sleeves together]
彼らは袂を連ねて、新政党に加わりました。Karera wa tamoto o tsuranete, shin seitō ni kuwawarimashita. *Acting together, they joined a new political party.*

tamoto o wakatsu   袂を分かつ   *to break off with someone*
[lit. to split a *kimono* sleeve]
二人の友達はつまらない議論の後、袂を分かちました。
Futari no tomodachi wa tsumaranai giron no ato, tamoto o wakachimashita. *My two friends broke off with each other*

after an argument over something trivial.

---

tana   棚   *shelf*

   tana ni ageru   棚に上げる   *to ignore something self-indulgently*

[lit. to put something on a shelf]

彼は自分の欠点は棚に上げて、人の批判をします。Kare wa jibun no ketten wa tana ni agete, hito no hihan o shimasu.   *He criticizes other people while self-indulgently ignoring his own shortcomings.*

   tanaage suru   棚上げする   *to shelve*

[lit. to put something on a shelf]

会社は、支店拡張計画を棚上げにしました。Kaisha wa, shiten kakuchō keikaku o tanaage ni shimashita.   *The company shelved the plan for expanding its branches.*

   tanabota   棚ぼた   *windfall*

[lit. a rice dumpling coated with sweet bean paste that fell from a shelf]

円高の棚ぼたで、輸入製品が安くなりました。Endaka no tanabota de, yunyū seihin ga yasuku narimashita.   *Because of the windfall from the yen appreciation, imported goods became cheaper.*

---

tanagokoro   掌   *palm*

   tanagokoro o kaesu yō ni   掌を返すように   *easily*

[lit. like flipping one's palm]

彼女は掌を返すように、質問に答えました。Kanojo wa tanagokoro o kaesu yō ni, shitsumon ni kotaemashita.   *She easily answered the question.*

   tanagokoro o kaesu yō ni   掌を返すように   *suddenly*

[lit. like flipping one's palm]

彼は電話の後、掌を返すように静かになりました。Kare wa denwa no ato, tanagokoro o kaesu yō ni shizuka ni narimashita. *After the telephone call, he suddenly became quiet.*

   tanagokoro o sasu yō ni akiraka   掌を指すように明らか

325

to be as clear as crystal
[lit. to be clear like pointing one's own palm]
彼女が成功することは、掌を指すように明らかでした。
Kanojo ga seikō suru koto wa, tanagokoro o sasu yō ni akiraka
deshita. *It was as clear as crystal that she would be
successful.*

---

tate　盾、楯　*shield*
tate ni toru　盾に取る　*to use something as an excuse*
[lit. to hold something as a shield]
彼は限られた予算を盾にとって、手抜き仕事を正当化しよ
うとしました。Kare wa kagirareta yosan o tate ni totte, te-
nuki shigoto o seitōka shiyō to shimashita. *Using a limited
budget as an excuse, he tried to justify his shoddy work.*

tate no hanmen　盾の半面　*just a part of something*
[lit. one side of a shield]
彼女は盾の半面だけ見て、彼の提案に賛成してしまいました。
Kanojo wa tate no hanmen dake mite, kare no teian ni sansei
shite shimaimashita. *Seeing just a part of it, she agreed with
his suggestion.*

tatetsuku　楯突く　*to rebel against someone*
[lit. to thrust one's shield into the ground]
そのピッチャーは監督に楯突いて、チームを首になりました。
Sono pitchā wa kantoku ni tatetsuite, chīmu o kubi ni
narimashita. *Having rebelled against the manager, the
pitcher was let go from the team.*

---

tazei　多勢　*large number of people*
tazei ni buzei　多勢に無勢　*to be outnumbered*
[lit. a small number of people against a large number of people]
会議では私たちは多勢に無勢で、私たちの提案は否決され
ました。Kaigi dewa watakushitachi wa tazei ni buzei de,
watakushitachi no teian wa hiketsu saremashita. *We were
outnumbered in the meeting, and our proposal was rejected.*

---

tazuna　手綱　*reins*

tazuna o shimeru   手綱を締める   *to rein someone in*
[lit. to tighten the reins]
事業実績を改善するため、社員の手綱を引き締めました。
Jigyō jisseki o kaizen suru tame, shain no tazuna o
hikishimemashita.   *To improve our business performance, I
reined in the employees.*

---

te   手   *hand, palm, arm*
  te ga aku   手が空く   *to have a minute*
  [lit. One's hands get empty.]
  手が空いたら、この仕事をするのを手伝って下さい。Te ga
    aitara, kono shigoto o suru no o tetsudatte kudasai.   *Please
    help me with this job when you have a minute.*

  te ga denai   手が出ない   *to be beyond one's capability*
  [lit. One's hands can't come out and touch something.]
  試験はとても難しくて、手が出ませんでした。Shiken wa
    totemo muzukashikute, te ga demasen deshita.   *The exam was
    so tough that the answers were beyond my capability.*

  te ga fusagaru   手が塞がる   *to have one's hands full*
  [lit. One's hands are occupied.]
  今は手が塞がっているので、また後で来て下さい。Ima wa
    te ga fusagatte iru node, mata ato de kite kudasai.   *Please
    come back later because I have my hands full now.*

  te ga hanareru   手が離れる   *to have some free time*
  [lit. One's hands get off something.]
  子供が保育園に行くので、やっと手が放れます。Kodomo
    ga hoikuen ni iku node, yatto te ga hanaremasu.   *My child will
    start nursery school, so I'll finally have some free time.*

  te ga hayai   手が早い   *to be a womanizer*
  [lit. One's hands are fast.]
  彼は手が早いから、気をつけなさい。Kare wa te ga hayai
    kara, ki o tsukenasai.   *Be careful, since he's a womanizer.*

  te ga kakaru   手が掛かる   *to be a handful*
  [lit. One's hands are needed.]

二人の子供に、手が掛かります。Futari no kodomo ni, te ga
kakarimasu. *My two children are a handful.*

te ga komu   手が込む   *elaborate*
[lit. One's hands are put in.]
それは、非常に手が込んだ策略でした。Sore wa, hijō ni te ga
konda sakuryaku deshita. *It was a very elaborate scheme.*

te ga mawaranai   手が回らない   *no time for something*
[lit. One's hands can't make rounds.]
料理をしていたので、洗濯にまで手が回りませんでした。
Ryōri o shite ita node, sentaku ni made te ga mawarimasen
deshita. *Because I was cooking, there was no time for laundry.*

te ga nai   手がない   *nothing one can do*
[lit. There are no hands.]
交渉では、相手側に譲歩するより手がありませんでした。
Kōshō dewa, aitegawa ni jōho suru yori te ga arimasen deshita.
*There was nothing we could do but make concessions to our
counterpart in the negotiations.*

te ga suku   手がすく   *to have a free moment*
[lit. One's hands get free.]
手がすいたら、休憩してお茶を飲みましょう。Te ga suitara,
kyūkei shite ocha o nomimashō. *When you have a free
moment, let's take a break and have some tea.*

te ga todoku   手が届く   *to be thorough*
[lit. One's hands reach something.]
彼女の家は、庭の手入れまで実に手が届いていました。
Kanojo no ie wa, niwa no teire made jitsu ni te ga todoite
imashita. *At her house, even the gardening was very
thorough.*

te ga tsukerarenai   手が付けられない   *Nothing helps.*
to be out of control
[lit. One can't touch something by hands.]
彼は一度怒り出すと、手が付けられません。Kare wa ichido
okoridasu to, te ga tsukeraremasen. *Once he gets angry,
nothing helps.*

te ga ushiro ni mawaru   手が後ろに回る   *to be arrested*

[lit. One's hands go around one's back.]

彼女は横領の容疑で、手が後ろに回りました。 Kanojo wa ōryō no yōgi de, te ga ushiro ni mawarimashita.   *She was arrested on suspicion of embezzlement.*

te mo ashi mo denai   手も足も出ない   *no match*

[lit. to be unable to put one's hands or legs out]

彼の論理に、手も足もでませんでした。 Kare no ronri ni, te mo ashi mo demasen deshita.   *I was no match for his logic.*

te ni amaru   手に余る   *to be too much for one to handle*

[lit. to be excessive to one's hands]

その仕事は彼の専門外なので、手に余りました。 Sono shigoto wa kare no senmon gai nanode, te ni amarimashita. *Because the work was outside his specialty, it was too much for him to handle.*

te ni noru   手に乗る   *to fall for a scheme*

[lit. to ride in someone's hand]

彼の手に乗って、疑わしい事業に出資してしまいました。 Kare no te ni notte, utagawashii jigyō ni shusshi shite shimaimashita.   *Foolishly, I fell for his scheme to have me invest in his dubious business.*

te ni ochiru   手に落ちる   *to fall into someone else's possession*

[lit. to fall into someone's hands]

ローンが返せずに、担保の土地は銀行の手に落ちてしまいました。 Rōn ga kaesezu ni, tanpo no tochi wa ginkō no te ni ochite shimaimashita.   *When I failed to repay the loan, the land I used as collateral fell into the bank's possession.*

te ni oenai   手に負えない   *to be more than one can handle*

[lit. to be unable to carry someone or something in one's hand]

彼の説明は実に複雑で、私の手には負えませんでした。

329

Kare no setsumei wa jitsu ni fukuzatsu de, watakushi no te niwa oemasen deshita.   *Because his explanation was very complex, it was much more than I could handle.*

te ni suru   手にする   *to have, to gain*
[lit. to put something in one's hand]
彼女は突然大金を手にして、どうしようか迷っています。
Kanojo wa totsuzen taikin o te ni shite, dō shiyō ka mayotte imasu.   *Suddenly having a big sum of money, she doesn't know what to do with it.*

te ni te o totte   手に手を取って   *hand-in-hand*
[lit. to take someone's hand with one's hand]
二社は手に手を取って、新技術の研究・開発を始めました。
Nisha wa te ni te o totte, shin gijutsu no kenkyū・kaihatsu o hajimemashita.   *Hand-in-hand the two companies began research and development on the new technology.*

te ni toru yō ni   手に取るように   *clearly*
[lit. as if picking up something with one's own hand]
彼女は何も言いませんでしたが、気持ちは手に取るように分かりました。Kanojo wa nani mo iimasen deshita ga, kimochi wa te ni toru yō ni wakarimashita.   *Although she said nothing, I understood her feelings clearly.*

te ni tsukanai   手に付かない   *to be unable to bring oneself to do something*
[lit. Something doesn't come in contact with one's hand.]
素晴らしい天気なので、勉強が手に付きません。Subarashii tenki nanode, benkyō ga te ni tsukimasen.   *Because of the beautiful weather, I can't bring myself to study.*

te no uchi o miseru   手の内を見せる   *to show one's hand*
[lit. to reveal what is inside one's hand]
交渉中は、こちら側の手の内をあまり見せないように気をつけました。Kōshō chū wa, kochiragawa no te no uchi o amari misenai yō ni ki o tsukemashita.   *During the negotiations, we were careful not to show our hand too much.*

te no ura o kaesu yō ni　手の裏を返すように　*suddenly*
[lit. just like flipping the back of one's hand]
失業したら、ガールフレンドの態度が手の裏を返すように
冷たくなりました。Shitsugyō shitara, gārufurendo no taido
ga te no ura o kaesu yō ni tsumetaku narimashita.　*Right after
I lost my job, my girlfriend suddenly cooled off toward me.*

te o awaseru　手を合わせる　*to beg someone*
[lit. to put one's open palms against each oher]
姉に手を合わせて、宿題を手伝ってもらいました。Ane ni
te o awasete, shukudai o tetsudatte moraimashita.　*I begged
my big sister to help with my homework.*

te o dasu　手を出す　*to get involved with someone or in
something*
[lit. to thrust one's hand into something]
彼は株に手を出して、大儲けしました。Kare wa kabu ni te o
dashite, ōmōke shimashita.　*By getting involved in the stock
market, he made big bucks.*

te o hiku　手を引く　*to back out of something*
[lit. to draw one's hands away]
彼女は、土地の投機から手を引きました。Kanojo wa, tochi
no tōki kara te o hikimashita.　*She backed out of the land
speculation deal.*

te o hirogeru　手を広げる　*to extend a business*
[lit. to spread one's arms]
彼は短期間に手を広げすぎて、財政難に陥っています。
Kare wa tan kikan ni te o hirogesugite, zaisei nan ni ochiitte
imasu.　*By extending his business too much too soon, he has
fallen into financial difficulties.*

te o ireru　手を入れる　*to go over something*
[lit. to put one's hand in something]
提出する前に、報告書にもう一度手を入れました。
Teishutsu suru mae ni, hōkokusho ni mō ichido te o iremashita.
Before submitting the report, we went over it once more.

te o kae shina o kae　手を替え品を替え　*in many*

different ways
[lit. by changing hands and changing goods]
手を替え品を替え彼女を説得しようとしましたが、無駄で
　　した。Te o kae shina o kae kanojo o settoku shiyō to
　　shimashita ga, muda deshita.　*I tried to persuade her in many
　　different ways, but it didn't work.*

te o kakeru　　手をかける　　*to do something with care and
　　attention*
[lit. to put one's hand on something]
彼は手をかけて、蘭を育てています。Kare wa te o kakete,
　　ran o sodatete imasu.　*He's raising orchids with care and
　　attention.*

te o kariru　　手を借りる　　*to get help*
[lit. to borrow someone's hand]
引っ越ししたとき、友達の手を借りました。Hikkoshi shita
　　toki, tomodachi no te o karimashita.　*I got help from my
　　friends when I moved.*

te o kasu　　手を貸す　　*to help someone*
[lit. to lend one's hands to someone]
父が車を修理するのに手を貸しました。Chichi ga kuruma o
　　shūri suru no ni te o kashimashita.　*I helped my father repair
　　his car.*

te o kiru　　手を切る　　*to sever one's relations with
　　someone*
[lit. to cut one's hand]
彼女は、ボーイフレンドと手を切る決心をしました。
　　Kanojo wa, bōifurendo to te o kiru kesshin o shimashita.　*She
　　decided to sever her relations with her boyfriend.*

te o komaneku　　手をこまねく　　*to look on helplessly*
[lit. to fold one's arms]
火事の現場で、人々は手をこまねくしかありませんでした。
　　Kaji no genba de, hitobito wa te o komaneku shika arimasen
　　deshita.　*At the site of the fire, people could do nothing but
　　look on helplessly.*

te o kudasu　　手を下す　　*to directly involve oneself in something*

[lit. to lower one's hand onto something]

その問題は、社長が手を下して解決しました。Sono mondai wa, shachō ga te o kudashite kaiketsu shimashita. *The president directly involved himself in solving the problem.*

te o kumu　　手を組む　　*to join hand-in-hand*

[lit. to lock each other's arm]

彼らは手を組んで、新しい事業を始めました。Karera wa te o kunde, atarashii jigyō o hajimemashita. *They joined hand-in-hand and started a new business.*

te o kuwaeru　　手を加える　　*to refine something*

[lit. to add one's hand to something]

その企画は、もう一度手を加える必要があります。Sono kikaku wa, mō ichido te o kuwaeru hitsuyō ga arimasu. *You need to refine your planning once more.*

te o mawasu　　手を回す　　*to take measures*

[lit. to go around with one's hand]

状況を改善するために、すでに手を回しておきました。Jōkyō o kaizen suru tame ni, sude ni te o mawashite okimashita. *I've already taken measures to improve the situation.*

te o musubu　　手を結ぶ　　*to cooperate*

[lit. to join hands]

彼女と手を結んで、任務を達成しました。Kanojo to te o musunde, ninmu o tassei shimashita. *I accomplished the task by cooperating with her.*

te o nigiru　　手を握る　　*to come to an agreement*

[lit. to grasp someone's hand]

議論を続けたけれど、最後には手を握りました。Giron o tsuzuketa keredo, saigo niwa te o nigirimashita. *We kept on arguing, but in the end we came to an agreement.*

te o nobasu　　手を伸ばす　　*to expand*

[lit. to stretch one's arms]

最近あの会社は、映画産業にまで手を伸ばしています。
Saikin ano kaisha wa, eiga sagyō ni made te o nobashite imasu.
Recently, that company has even expanded its business to the movie industry.

te o nuku　　手を抜く　　*to cut corners*
[lit. to withdraw one's hand]
地震で、建設会社が工事に手を抜いていたのが分かりました。
Jishin de, kensetsugaisha ga kōji ni te o nuite ita no ga wakarimashita.　*With the earthquake, it appeared that the construction companies had cut corners.*

te o nurasazu　　手を濡らさず　　*without any effort*
[lit. by not wetting one's hands]
彼女は手を濡らさずに、金持ちになりました。Kanojo wa te o nurasazu ni, kanemochi ni narimashita.　*She became rich without any effort.*

te o someru　　手を染める　　*to undertake something*
[lit. to dip one's hand in dye]
彼が趣味として園芸に手を染めてから、十年になります。
Kare ga shumi toshite engei ni te o somete kara, jū nen ni narimasu.　*It's been ten years since he undertook gardening as his hobby.*

te o tsukaneru　　手をつかねる　　*to be at a loss*
[lit. to hold one's arms]
彼女はその問題をどうしたらいいか、手をつかねています。
Kanojo wa sono mondai o dō shitara ii ka, te o tsukanete imasu.　*She's at a loss to know how to deal with the problem.*

te o tsukeru　　手を付ける　　*to take on something*
[lit. to attach one's hand to something]
彼は、新しい研究の分野に手を付けました。Kare wa, atarashii kenkyū no bun-ya ni te o tsukemashita.　*He took on a new field of research.*

te o tsukusu　　手を尽くす　　*to do everything conceivable*
[lit. to exhaust one's hand]
顧客を満足させるために、手を尽くしました。Kokyaku o

manzoku saseru tame ni, te o tsukushimashita. *We did everything conceivable to satisfy our clients.*

te o utsu   手を打つ   *to shake hands on something*
[lit. to clap one's hands]
締め切り日については、今月末で手を打ちました。
Shimekiribi ni tsuite wa, kongetsu matsu de te o uchimashita. *We shook hands on the end of this month as the date of the deadline.*

te o utsu   手を打つ   *to take necessary measures*
[lit. to cast one's hands into something]
どの家庭も、大地震に備えて手を打っておくべきです。
Dono katei mo, ōjishin ni sonaete te o utte oku beki desu. *Every home should take necessary measures for a big earthquake.*

te o wazurawasu   手を煩わす   *to have help*
[lit. to cause someone's hands trouble]
友達の手を煩わせて、丸太小屋を作っています。Tomodachi no te o wazurawasete, marutagoya o tsukutte imasu. *I've been building a log cabin with help from my friends.*

te o yaku   手を焼く   *to have a hard time*
[lit. to burn one's hand]
彼の頑固さに、手を焼いています。Kare no gankosa ni, te o yaite imasu. *We're having a hard time dealing with his stubbornness.*

akago no te o hineru yō   赤子の手を捻るよう   *to be like child's play*
[lit. like twisting a baby's arm]
彼女にとって、テニスで彼を負かすのは赤子の手を捻るようなものでした。Kanojo ni totte, tenisu de kare o makasu nowa akago no te o hineru yō na mono deshita. *It was like child's play for her to beat him at tennis.*

ōde o futte aruku   大手を振って歩く   *to swagger*
[lit. to walk swinging one's extended arms]
彼はテニス大会で優勝してから、クラブの中を大手を振っ

て歩いています。Kare wa tenisu taikai de yūshō shite kara, kurabu no naka o ōde o futte aruite imasu. *Since he won the championship of the tennis tournament, he has been swaggering around the club.*

oku no te　奥の手　*ace in the hole*
[lit. a deep hand]
彼は奥の手を使って、契約を取り付けました。Kare wa oku no te o tsukatte, keiyaku o toritsukemashita. *Using an ace in the hole, he won the contract.*

oteage　お手上げ　*to be unable to do a thing*
[lit. to raise one's hands]
資金不足で、研究はお手上げ状態です。Shikin busoku de, kenkyū wa oteage jōtai desu. *Due to the lack of funds, we can't do a thing in our research.*

otenomono　お手の物　*one's forte*
[lit. something in one's hand]
彼女は、市場分析ならお手の物です。Kanojo wa, shijō bunseki nara otenomono desu. *Market analysis is her forte.*

teashi o nobasu　手足を伸ばす　*to relax*
[lit. to stretch one's arms and legs]
この週末に、やっと手足を伸ばすことが出来ました。Kono shūmatsu ni, yatto teashi o nobasu koto ga dekimashita. *Finally, I was able to relax last weekend.*

teashi to natte　手足となって　*as a devoted helper*
[lit. by becoming someone's hands and legs]
彼は彼女の手足となって、事業の成功のために働きました。Kare wa kanojo no teashi to natte, jigyō no seikō no tame ni hatarakimashita. *He worked as a devoted helper for the success of her business.*

tegusune hiite　手ぐすねひいて　*eagerly*
[by putting wax on an archery string with one's hand]
彼女は彼に仕返しする機会を、手ぐすねひいて待っています。Kanojo wa kare ni shikaeshi suru kikai o, tegusune hiite matte imasu. *She's eagerly waiting for an opportunity to take*

revenge on him.

temawashi   手回し   *arrangement*
[lit. putting one's hands around something]
手回しよく、会議の後で夕食が出ました。 Temawashi yoku,
  kaigi no ato de yūshoku ga demashita.   *With good
  arrangements, they served dinner after the conference.*

teochi   手落ち   *an oversight*
[lit. dropping something from one's hand]
彼の名前をリストに入れなかったのは、私の手落ちです。
  Kare no namae o risuto ni irenakatta nowa, watakushi no teochi
  desu.   *Not including his name on the list was my oversight.*

teshio ni kakeru   手塩にかける   *to raise someone with
    tender care*
[lit. to handle something with salted hands]
彼女は、娘を手塩にかけて育てています。 Kanojo wa,
  musume o teshio ni kakete sodatete imasu.   *She's raising her
  daughter with tender care.*

tetori ashitori   手取り足取り   *with care and tenderness*
[lit. by holding someone's arms and then legs with one's hands]
彼は手取り足取り、彼女にやり方を説明しました。 Kare wa
  tetori ashitori, kanojo ni yarikata o setsumei shimashita.   *With
  care and tenderness, he explained the procedures to her.*

yarite   やり手   *someone capable*
[lit. one with a hand of action]
彼女はやり手だから、その仕事を任せても全く大丈夫です。
  Kanojo wa yarite dakara, sono shigoto o makasetemo mattaku
  daijōbu desu.   *Since she's capable, it's perfectly all right to
  put her in charge of that work.*

---

tedama   手玉   *small ball*
tedama ni toru   手玉に取る   *to lead someone around by
    the nose*
[lit. to handle someone like a small ball]
彼女は、彼を手玉に取っています。 Kanojo wa, kare o tedama

ni totte imasu.   *She's leading him around by the nose.*

---

teko   梃子   *lever*

teko demo ugokanai   梃子でも動かない   *to not budge an inch*
[lit. to not move even if a lever is applied]

彼らは譲歩を強要しましたが、彼は梃子でも動きませんでした。Karera wa jōho o kyōyō shimashita ga, kare wa teko demo ugokimasen deshita.   *They tried to force concessions, but he didn't budge an inch.*

tekoire suru   テコ入れする   *to shore something up*
[lit. to insert a lever]

財界は、政府が銀行部門にテコ入れするのを望んでいます。Zaikai wa, seifu ga ginkō bumon ni tekoire suru no o nozonde imasu.   *Big business wants the government to shore up the banking sector.*

---

tetsu   轍   *track*

tetsu o fumu   轍を踏む   *to fall into the same rut*
[lit. to step on the same track]

私は、サラリーマンとしての父の轍を踏みたくありません。Watakushi wa, sararīman to shite no chichi no tetsu o fumitaku arimasen.   *I don't want to fall into the same rut my father did as an office worker.*

---

tettsui   鉄槌   *an iron hammer*

tettsui o kudasu   鉄槌を下す   *to deal a severe blow*
[lit. to hammer down]

政府は、汚職官僚に鉄槌を下しました。Seifu wa, oshoku kanryō ni tettsui o kudashimashita.   *The government dealt a severe blow to the corrupt bureaucrats.*

---

ten   天   *sky*

ten ni tsuba suru   天に唾する   *to boomerang*
[lit. to spit skyward]

彼を批判したけれど、それは天に唾する結果になりました。

Kare o hihan shita keredo, sore wa ten ni tsuba suru kekka ni narimashita.   *I criticized him, but it boomeranged on me.*

ten o tsuku   天を突く   *very tall*
[lit. hitting the sky]
故郷に帰って、天を突く ビルにびっくりしました。Kokyō ni kaette, ten o tsuku biru ni bikkuri shimashita.   *Returning to my hometown, I was so surprised to see very tall buildings.*

---

tenbin   天秤   *beam*
tenbin ni kakeru   天秤に掛ける   *to weigh the advantages of something*
[lit. to put something on a beam]
どの会社と契約を結ぶか、天秤に掛けました。Dono kaisha to keiyaku o musubu ka, tenbin ni kakemashita.   *We weighed the advantages of concluding a contract with various companies.*

---

tenjō   天井   *ceiling*
tenjōshirazu   天井知らず   *The sky is the limit.*
[lit. to not know the ceiling]
彼女は自尊心にかけては、天井知らずです。Kanojo wa jisonshin ni kakete wa, tenjōshirazu desu.   *Talking about her ego, the sky is the limit.*

---

tenka   天下   *the whole world*
tenka o toru   天下を取る   *to gain absolute control*
[lit. to pick up the whole world]
彼は家電の分野で、天下を取りたいと思っています。Kare wa kaden no bun-ya de, tenka o toritai to omotte imasu.   *He wishes to gain absolute control over the field of home appliances.*

tenkaharete   天下晴れて   *officially*
[lit. with the sky cleared]
彼らは、天下晴れて夫婦になりました。Karera wa, tenkaharete fūfu ni narimashita.   *They officially became husband and wife.*

---

tensū　点数　　*points*
　　tensūkasegi　点数稼ぎ　　*one's personal gain*
　　[lit. to earn points]
　　彼女は点数稼ぎのためなら、何でもします。Kanojo wa
　　　tensūkasegi no tame nara, nandemo shimasu.　*She'll do
　　　anything for her personal gain.*

---

tō　当　　*right*
　　tō o eru　当を得る　　*to be just right*
　　[lit. to gain the right spot]
　　彼の言い分は、当を得ています。Kare no iibun wa, tō o ete
　　　imasu.　*His claim is just right.*

---

todo　とど　　*mullet*
　　todo no tsumari　とどのつまり　　*after all*
　　[lit. the end stage of a mullet's growth]
　　とどのつまり、彼女の意見が正しいことが分かりました。
　　　Todo no tsumari, kanojo no iken ga tadashii koto ga
　　　wakarimashita.　*We learned that her opinion was correct after
　　　all.*

---

todome　止め　　*finishing blow*
　　todome o sasu　止めを刺す　　*to make certain of
　　something*
　　[lit. to stab someone's throat with a finishing blow]
　　息子によく勉強するように、止めを刺しました。Musuko ni
　　　yoku benkyō suru yō ni, todome o sashimashita.　*I made
　　　certain that my son would study hard.*

---

tōge　峠　　*a mountain pass*
　　tōge o kosu　峠を越す　　*to turn the corner*
　　[lit. to go over a mountain pass]
　　日米二国間交渉が、やっと峠を越しました。Nichibei nikoku
　　　kan kōshō ga, yatto tōge o koshimashita.　*The U.S.-Japan
　　　bilateral negotiations finally turned the corner.*

toguro   とぐろ   *coil*
  toguro o maku   とぐろを巻く   *to hang around*
  [lit. to coil oneself]
  彼らは仕事中なのに、いつも喫茶店でとぐろを巻いています。
  Karera wa shigoto chū nanoni, itsumo kissaten de toguro o
  maite imasu.   *Although it's business hours, they hang around*
  the coffee shop all the time.

---

tohō   途方   *direction*
  tohō mo nai   途方もない   *absurd*
  [lit. without a direction]
  彼女は、途方もない夢を追っています。Kanojo wa,
  tohō mo nai yume o otte imasu.   *She's chasing an absurd*
  dream.

  tohō ni kureru   途方に暮れる   *to be at one's wit's end*
  [lit. to spend time trying to find a direction]
  突然首になって、途方に暮れています。Totsuzen kubi ni
  natte, tohō ni kurete imasu.   *I'm at my wit's end at being fired*
  suddenly.

---

tōkaku   頭角   *top of a head*
  tōkaku o arawasu   頭角を現す   *to stand out*
  [lit. to show the top of one's head]
  彼はすでに子供の時に、数学の分野で頭角を現しました。
  Kare wa sude ni kodomo no toki ni, sūgaku no bun-ya de
  tōkaku o arawashimashita.   *Even when he was a child, he*
  stood out in the field of mathematics.

---

toki   時   *time*
  toki o kasegu   時を稼ぐ   *to buy time, to get extra time*
  [lit. to earn time]
  病気を理由に、論文提出の時を稼ぎました。Byōki o riyū ni,
  ronbun teishutsu no toki o kasegimashita.   *With my illness as*
  an excuse, I got extra time for turning in my term paper.

  toki o matsu   時を待つ   *to bide one's time*

[lit. to wait for time]

彼女は声楽とピアノの稽古を受けながら、歌手になる時を
待っています。Kanojo wa seigaku to piano no keiko o
ukenagara, kashu ni naru toki o matte imasu.   *While taking
voice and piano lessons, she's biding her time to become a
singer.*

toki o ushinau   時を失う   *to lose an opportunity*

[lit. to lose time]

不景気になって、転職の時を失ってしまいました。Fukeiki
ni natte, tenshoku no toki o ushinatte shimaimashita.   *With the
downturn of the economy, I lost the opportunity to switch my
job.*

---

tokoro   所   *place*

tokoro o eru   所を得る   *to find one's niche*

[lit. to gain a place]

彼はサラリーマンを辞めて、農業を始めて所を得ました。
Kare wa sararīman o yamete, nōgyō o hajimete tokoro o
emashita.   *He found his niche in farming after quitting office
work.*

tokorokamawazu   所構わず   *no matter where one is*

[lit. to not care about a place]

彼女は、所構わず娘の自慢をします。Kanojo wa,
tokorokamawazu musume no jiman o shimasu.   *She brags
about her daughter no matter where she is.*

---

tora   虎   *tiger*

tora no i o karite   虎の威を借りて   *using someone
else's authority*

[lit. by borrowing a tiger's authority]

彼は社長の虎の威を借りて、社員に超過勤務を強要します。
Kare wa shachō no tora no i o karite, shain ni chōka kinmu o
kyōyō shimasu.   *Using the authority of the president, he
forces the employees to work overtime.*

tora ni naru   虎になる   *to get roaring drunk*

[lit. to become a tiger]

夕べバーを数軒回った後、友達は虎になりました。Yūbe bā o sūken mawatta ato, tomodachi wa tora ni narimashita. *Last night my friend got roaring drunk after visiting several bars.*

tora no ko   虎の子   *one's treasure*

[lit. a tiger cub]

彼は、虎の子の骨董品の壺を割ってしまいました。Kare wa, tora no ko no kottōhin no tsubo o watte shimaimashita. *He broke the antique jar that was his treasure.*

tora no o o fumu omoi de   虎の尾を踏む思いで *gingerly*

[lit. feeling as if one were stepping on the tail of a tiger]

虎の尾を踏む思いで、社長に昇給を頼みました。Tora no o o fumu omoi de, shachō ni shōkyū o tanomimashita. *Gingerly, I asked the president for a raise.*

hariko no tora   張り子の虎   *paper tiger*

[lit. a papier-mache tiger]

彼は張り子の虎だから、恐れる必要はありません。Kare wa hariko no tora dakara, osoreru hitsuyō wa arimasen. *Since he's a paper tiger, you don't need to be afraid of him.*

---

toru   取る   *to take*

toru ni tarinai   取るに足りない   *for the birds*

[lit. not sufficient to take]

彼女の意見は取るに足りません。Kanojo no iken wa toru ni tarimasen. *Her opinions are for the birds.*

torumono mo toriaezu   取る物も取りあえず   *without a moment's delay*

[lit. without taking things one should take]

子供が生まれたという知らせに、取る物も取りあえず病院に向かいました。Kodomo ga umareta to iu shirase ni, torumono mo toriaezu byōin ni mukaimashita. *Hearing that my baby had been born, I headed to the hospital without a moment's delay.*

---

toshi　年　*age*
  toshi ni fusoku wa nai　年に不足はない　*to be old enough*
  [lit. There is no lack in someone's age.]
  彼の年に不足はないけれど、考え方がまだ一面的です。
  Kare no toshi ni fusoku wa nai keredo, kangaekata ga mada ichimenteki desu.　*He's old enough, but his way of thinking is still one-dimensional.*

  ii toshi o shite　いい年をして　*too old to be doing something*
  [lit. with good age]
  彼はいい年をして、いつもお母さんのことを話しています。
  Kare wa ii toshi o shite, itsumo okāsan no koto o hanashite imasu.　*He's too old to be talking about his mother all the time.*

---

tsubu　粒　*grain*
  tsubu ga sorou　粒が揃う　*to be the cream of the crop*
  [lit. The grains are equally excellent.]
  この作業班のメンバーは、粒が揃っています。Kono sagyō han no menbā wa, tsubu ga sorotte imasu.　*The members of this task force are the cream of the crop.*

---

tsubushi　潰し　*making scrap metal*
  tsubushi ga kiku　潰しが利く　*to have a marketable skill*
  [lit. to be able to scrap something]
  彼は色々潰しが利くから、今の仕事を辞めても大丈夫でしょう。Kare wa iroiro tsubushi ga kiku kara, ima no shigoto o yametemo daijōbu deshō.　*Because he has many marketable skills, he'll be all right if he quits his current job.*

---

tsubo　壷　*jar*
  tsubo ni hamatta　壷にはまった　*pertinent*
  [lit. something fitting into a jar]
  彼女は、いつも壷にはまった質問をします。Kanojo wa,

itsumo tsubo ni hamatta shitsumon o shimasu.   *She always asks pertinent questions.*

omou tsubo ni hamaru   思う壺にはまる   *to play into someone's hands*

[lit. to fit into a jar as someone expects]

車を借りに行ったら母の思う壺にはまってしまい、一日中運転させられました。 Kuruma o kari ni ittara haha no omou tsubo ni hamatte shimai, ichinichi jū unten saseraremashita. *Although I had gone to borrow my mother's car, I played into her hands and drove her around all day.*

---

tsue   杖   *cane*

tsue tomo hashira tomo tanomu   杖とも柱とも頼む   *to rely on someone or something a lot*

[lit. to rely on someone or something like a cane or a pillar]

今度の計画では、彼女を杖とも柱とも頼んでいます。 Kondo no kikaku dewa, kanojo o tsue tomo hashira tomo tanonde imasu. *We're relying on her a lot for the new project.*

---

tsuke   付け   *bill*

tsuke ga mawatte kuru   付けが回ってくる   *to come back to haunt one*

[lit. The bill comes to one later.]

この一年間、運動をせずにたくさん食べていた付けが回ってきました。 Kono ichi nen kan, undō o sezu ni takusan tabete ita tsuke ga mawatte kimashita. *My eating a lot without any exercise for the past year has come back to haunt me.*

---

tsuki   月   *moon*

tsuki to suppon   月とすっぽん   *as different as night and day*

[lit. the moon and a terrapin]

彼らは兄弟ですが、性格も趣味も月とすっぽんです。 Karera wa kyōdai desu ga, seikaku mo shumi mo tsuki to suppon desu.   *Although they're brothers, their characters and tastes are as different as night and day.*

---

tsume   爪   *fingernail*

  tsume ni hi o tomosu   爪に灯をともす   *to lead a frugal life*

[lit. to light one's fingernail]

彼女はお金を貯めるため、爪に灯をともして暮らしました。

  Kanojo wa okane o tameru tame, tsume ni hi o tomoshite kurashimashita.   *To save money, she led a frugal life.*

  tsume no aka o senjite nomu   爪の垢を煎じて呑む   *to learn a lesson from someone*

[lit. to brew the dirt from someone's fingernails and drink it]

仕事熱心の彼の爪の垢を煎じて呑みなさい。Shigoto nesshin no kare no tsume no aka o senjite nomimasai.   *You should learn a lesson from him for his devotion to his work.*

  tsume o togu   爪を研ぐ   *to prepare oneself to do something*

[lit. to sharpen one's fingernails]

彼女は離婚以来、前夫に仕返しするために爪を研いでいます。

  Kanojo wa rikon irai, zenpu ni shikaeshi suru tame ni tsume o toide imasu.   *Since the divorce, she's been preparing herself to take revenge against her former husband.*

---

tsumi   罪   *guilt, sin, offense*

  tsumi no nai   罪のない   *innocent*

[lit. no offense intended]

彼は、彼女の罪のない冗談に腹を立てました。Kare wa, kanojo no tsumi no nai jōdan ni hara o tatemashita.   *He got angry at her innocent joke.*

  tsumi o kiseru   罪を着せる   *to pin the blame on someone else*

[lit. to force someone to wear one's guilt]

従業員の不満に、彼女は私に罪を着せようとしました。

  Jūgyōin no fuman ni, kanojo wa watakushi ni tsumi o kiseyō to shimashita.   *To respond to the employees' complaints, she tried to pin the blame on me.*

---

tsumuji   旋毛   *spiral of hair on the crown of the head*

tsumuji o mageru   旋毛を曲げる   *to become nasty*
[lit. to bend the spiral of hair on the crown of one's head]
彼女は彼の言ったことに旋毛を曲げて、仕事を拒否しています。 Kanojo wa kare no itta koto ni tsumuji o magete, shigoto o kyohi shite imasu.   *After what he said, she became nasty and is refusing to work.*

---

tsuna   綱   *rope*

tsunawatari o suru   綱渡りをする   *to take a risk*
[lit. to try to walk across a tightrope]
彼は、先端技術投資で綱渡りしています。 Kare wa, sentan gijutsu tōshi de tsunawatari o shite imasu.   *He's taking a risk by investing in advanced technology.*

tanomi no tsuna   頼みの綱   *one's only hope*
[lit. the rope for one's hope]
この問題を解決するには、彼女が頼みの綱です。 Kono mondai o kaiketsu suru niwa, kanojo ga tanomi no tsuna desu. *She's our only hope to solve this problem.*

---

tsuno   角   *horn*

tsuno o dasu   角を出す   *to get one's back up*
[lit. to reveal one's horns]
妻が角を出さないように、早く帰らなければなりません。 Tsuma ga tsuno o dasanai yō ni, hayaku kaeranakereba narimasen.   *I should go back home early so that my wife won't get her back up.*

tsuno o hayasu   角を生やす   *(for one's wife) to be jealous*
[lit. to grow horns]
妻は理由もなく、秘書と私の関係に角を生やしています。

Tsuma wa riyū mo naku, hisho to watakushi no kankei ni tsuno o hayashite imasu.   *For no reason, my wife is jealous of the relationship between my secretary and me.*

tsuno o oru   角を折る   *to drop one's stubborn attitude*
[lit. to break one's horns]
彼女はやっと角を折って、パーティーに出席することに同意しました。Kanojo wa yatto tsuno o otte, pātī ni shusseki suru koto ni dōi shimashita.   *Dropping her stubborn attitude, she finally agreed to attend the party.*

tsuno o tsukiawaseru   角を突き合わせる   *to be at odds with each other*
[lit. to put horns against each other]
彼らは取るに足りない問題で、角を突き合わせています。Karera wa toru ni tarinai mondai de, tsuno o tsukiawasete imasu.   *They're at odds with each other over minor things.*

---

tsura   面   *face*
tsura no kawa ga atsui   面の皮が厚い   *thick-skinned, insensitive*
[lit. One's facial skin is thick.]
彼は面の皮が厚くて、遠慮を知りません。Kare wa tsura no kawa ga atsukute, enryo o shirimasen.   *Since he's thick-skinned, he doesn't know what modesty is.*

tsurayogoshi   面汚し   *disgrace*
[lit. dirtying someone's face]
彼女は、家族の面汚しです。Kanojo wa, kazoku no tsurayogoshi desu.   *She's a disgrace to the family.*

ii tsura no kawa   いい面の皮   *Serves (someone) right!*
[lit. good for someone's facial skin]
彼は、仕事怠慢で首を切られました。いい面の皮です。Kare wa, shigoto taiman de kubi o kiraremashita. Ii tsura no kawa desu.   *He got fired for his negligence on the job. Serves him right!*

tsuraate ni   面当てに   *out of spite*

[lit. to hit someone's face]

彼は彼女への面当てに、彼女の悪口を言っています。Kare wa kanojo e no tsuraate ni, kanojo no warukuchi o itte imasu. *He's badmouthing her out of spite.*

---

tsuru   鶴   *crane*

tsuru no hitokoe   鶴の一声   *voice of authority*

[lit. a crane's one voice]

父親の鶴の一声で、子供は喧嘩を止めました。Chichioya no tsuru no hitokoe de, kodomo wa kenka o yamemashita. *At the sound of their father's voice, the children stopped fighting.*

U

---

u   鵜   *cormorant*

u no me taka no me de   鵜の目鷹の目で   *with sharp eyes*

[lit. with the eyes of a cormorant or a hawk]

彼女は、鵜の目鷹の目で投資の機会をうかがっています。Kanojo wa, u no me taka no me de tōshi no kikai o ukagatte imasu. *She's waiting with sharp eyes for an investment opportunity.*

unomi ni suru   鵜呑みにする   *to swallow*

[lit. to swallow something as a cormorant does]

人の言うことをすぐ鵜呑みにしないで、最初にそれを確かめなさい。Hito no iu koto o sugu unomi ni shinai de, saisho ni sore o tashikamenasai. *You should examine what others say instead of swallowing it immediately.*

---

udatsu   うだつ   *short pillar supporting a ridgepole*

udatsu ga agaranai   うだつが上がらない   *to be unable to get ahead*

[lit. A short pillar supporting a ridgepole does not go up.]

彼はこの会社で十年になりますが、全然うだつが上がりま
せん。Kare wa kono kaisha de jū nen ni narimasu ga, zenzen
udatsu ga agarimasen. *He's been with this company for ten
years but can't get ahead at all.*

---

ude   腕   *arm*

ude ga agaru   腕が上がる   *One's skill improves.*
[lit. One's arms go up.]
最近、ゴルフの腕が上がりました。Saikin, gorufu no ude ga
agarimashita. *My golf has improved recently.*

ude ga kiku   腕が利く   *to be capable*
[lit. One's arms are effective.]
この仕事には、腕が利く人が必要です。Kono shigoto niwa,
ude ga kiku hito ga hitsuyō desu. *We need someone capable
for this job.*

ude ga naru   腕が鳴る   *to be itching to do something*
[lit. One's arms are ringing.]
明日テニス大会に出るので、腕が鳴っています。Ashita
tenisu taikai ni deru node, ude ga natte imasu. *I'm itching to
play tennis in the competition tomorrow.*

ude ga tatsu   腕が立つ   *skilled*
[lit. One's arms stand out.]
彼女は腕が立つ弁護士です。Kanojo wa ude ga tatsu bengoshi
desu. *She's a skilled lawyer.*

ude ni oboe ga aru   腕に覚えがある   *to be confident of
one's ability*
[lit. to remember something in one's arms]
水泳なら、腕に覚えがあります。Suiei nara, ude ni oboe ga
arimasu. *I'm confident of my ability at swimming.*

ude ni yori o kakeru   腕により をかける   *to outdo
oneself*
[lit. to apply strands to one's arms]
妻は腕によりをかけて、子供の誕生日のためにケーキを焼
きました。Tsuma wa ude ni yori o kakete, kodomo no tanjōbi

no tame ni kēki o yakimashita. *My wife outdid herself baking a cake for our child's birthday.*

ude o furuu   腕を振るう   *to exercise one's skill*
[lit. to arouse one's arms]
夫は週末は、写真に腕を振るっています。Otto wa shūmatsu wa, shashin ni ude o furutte imasu. *My husband is exercising his skill at photography on the weekends.*

ude o kau   腕を買う   *to value someone's skills*
[lit. to buy someone's arms]
会社は彼女の会計の腕を買って、経理部の責任者にしました。Kaisha wa kanojo no kaikei no ude o katte, keiribu no sekininsha ni shimashita. *Valuing her skills, the company put her in charge of the accounting office.*

ude o migaku   腕を磨く   *to polish one's skill*
[lit. to polish one's arms]
彼はイタリア料理の腕を磨くために、ローマへ行きます。Kare wa Itaria ryōri no ude o migaku tame ni, Roma e ikimasu. *He'll go to Rome to polish his skill at Italian cooking.*

udezuku de   腕ずくで   *by force*
[lit. thoroughly by means of one's arms]
彼女は腕ずくで、彼にその計画に同意させました。Kanojo wa udezuku de, kare ni sono keikaku ni dōi sasemashita. *She made him agree to the plan by force.*

---

udo   独活   *udo plant*
udo no taiboku   独活の大木   *big lout*
[lit. an *udo* plant grown to be a tree]
彼は独活の大木で、何の役にも立ちません。Kare wa udo no taiboku de, nan no yaku nimo tachimasen. *He's such a big lout that he isn't good at anything.*

---

ue   上   *top, high*
ue niwa ue ga aru   上には上がある   *to go someone one better*
[lit. There is a top above a top.]

彼女は彼より金持ちだそうです。上には上があるものですね。
Kanojo wa kare yori kanemochi da sō desu. Ue niwa ue ga aru mono desu ne. *I hear that she's richer than he. There's always someone to go you one better.*

ue o shita e no ōsawagi   上を下への大騒ぎ   *chaos*
[lit. confusion in which things that should be kept high are put low and vice versa]
地震でビルの電気が切れ、上を下への大騒ぎになりました。
Jishin de biru no denki ga kire, ue o shita e no ōsawagi ni narimashita. *The loss of electricity in the building during the earthquake caused chaos.*

---

ukime   憂き目   *misfortune*
ukime o miru   憂き目を見る   *to go through hardship*
[lit. to see misfortune]
一年も失業するという憂き目を見ました。Ichi nen mo shitsugyō suru to iu ukime o mimashita. *I went through the hardship of being unemployed for a year.*

---

uma   馬   *horse*
uma ga au   馬が合う   *to get along well with someone*
[lit. A horse is just right.]
彼は、お父さんと馬が合いません。Kare wa, otōsan to uma ga aimasen. *He doesn't get along well with his father.*

shiriuma ni noru   尻馬に乗る   *to follow someone blindly*
[lit. to ride the last horse in a pack]
彼女は人の尻馬に乗ってばかりいて、自分の意見がありません。Kanojo wa hito no shiriuma ni notte bakari ite, jibun no iken ga arimasen. *She always follows other people blindly and doesn't have opinions of her own.*

---

umai   旨い   *delicious*
umai shiru o suu   旨い汁を吸う   *to get all the credit or profit*

[lit. to sip delicious juice]

共同投資なのに、彼は自分だけうまい汁を吸おうとしています。 Kyōdō tōshi nanoni, kare wa jibun dake umai shiru o suō to shite imasu. *Although it's a joint investment, he's attempting to get all the profit for himself.*

---

umi   生み   *giving birth*

umi no kurushimi   生みの苦しみ   *creative anxiety*

[lit. labor pains]

彼女はその本を書くのに、生みの苦しみを味わいました。 Kanojo wa sono hon o kaku noni, umi no kurushimi o ajiwaimashita. *While writing that book, she experienced creative anxiety.*

---

umu   有無   *existence or non-existence*

umu o iwasazu   有無を言わさず   *willy-nilly*

[lit. by not allowing someone to say existence or non-existence]

父は子供たちに有無をいわさず、お使いをさせました。 Chichi wa kodomotachi ni umu o iwasazu, otsukai o sasemashita. *Our father made his children run errands willy-nilly.*

---

un   雲   *cloud*

undei no sa   雲泥の差   *world of difference*

[lit. the difference between clouds and mud]

彼らの背景には、雲泥の差があります。 Karera no haikei niwa, undei no sa ga arimasu. *There's a world of difference in their backgrounds.*

---

unagi   鰻   *eel*

unagi no nedoko   鰻の寝床   *long narrow place*

[lit. an eel's bed]

彼の店は、鰻の寝床のような場所でした。 Kare no mise wa, unagi no nedoko no yō na basho deshita. *His shop was a long narrow place.*

unaginobori ni agaru   鰻登りに上がる   *to skyrocket*

[lit. to go up high as an eel does]

最近の映画の大ヒットで、その俳優の人気は鰻登りに上がりました。Saishin no eiga no dai hitto de, sono haiyū no ninki wa unaginobori ni agarimashita. *With his latest movie a big hit, the actor's popularity has skyrocketed.*

---

ura　裏　*back, reverse side, lining*

ura de ito o hiku　裏で糸を引く　*to maneuver behind the scenes*

[lit. to pull a string from behind]

彼女が交渉を扱っていますが、裏で糸を引いているのは彼です。Kanojo ga kōshō o atsukatte imasu ga, ura de ito o hiite iru nowa kare desu. *She's handling the negotiations, but he's the one who is maneuvering behind the scenes.*

ura no ura o iku　裏の裏を行く　*to outwit someone*

[lit. to go back and behind]

競争相手の裏の裏を行って、契約を取り付けました。Kyōsō aite no ura no ura o itte, keiyaku o toritsukemashita. *We outwitted our competitors and won the contract.*

ura o kaku　裏をかく　*to outsmart someone*

[lit. to scratch someone's back]

彼の裏をかいて、彼女との契約を取り付けました。Kare no ura o kaite, kanojo to no keiyaku o toritsukemashita. *I outsmarted him and got her agreement on a contract.*

ura o toru　裏を取る　*to make certain*

[lit. to check linings]

彼女の言っていることが本当かどうか、裏を取る必要があります。Kanojo no itte iru koto ga hontō ka dō ka, ura o toru hitsuyō ga arimasu. *We need to make certain if what she's saying is true or not.*

urabanashi　裏話　*inside story*

[lit. backtalk]

彼から彼女の過去について、裏話を聞きました。Kare kara kanojo no kako ni tsuite, urabanashi o kikimashita. *I heard the inside story from him about her past.*

urahara   裏腹   *inconsistent*
[lit. a back and a belly]
彼の証言は裏腹です。 Kare no shōgen wa urahara desu.   *His testimony is inconsistent.*

urakata   裏方   *one who remains behind the scenes*
[lit. a stagehand]
彼女は代議士の裏方として、政策を作っています。 Kanojo wa daigishi no urakata to shite, seisaku o tsukutte imasu. *She's formulating policies for the congressman while remaining behind the scenes.*

urame ni deru   裏目に出る   *to backfire*
[lit. to come out inside out]
計画を批判したのが裏目に出て、仕事を任されてしまいました。 Keikaku o hihan shita no ga urame ni dete, shigoto o makasarete shimaimashita.   *My criticism of the plan backfired, and I was put in charge of carrying it out.*

uraomote   裏表   *two-faced*
[lit. back and surface]
彼の態度には裏表があるので、信用できません。 Kare no taido niwa uraomote ga aru node, shin-yō dekimasen.   *We can't trust him because he's two-faced.*

urazuke ga aru   裏付けがある   *to have proof*
[lit. to have a lining]
私の議論には、裏付けがあります。   Watakushi no giron niwa, urazuke ga arimasu. *I have proof for my argument.*

---

urami   恨み   *grudge*
urami o kau   恨みを買う   *to cause someone to hold a grudge*
[lit. to buy someone's grudge]
助言したつもりなのに、彼女の恨みを買ってしまいました。 Jogen shita tsumori nanoni, kanojo no urami o katte shimaimashita.   *I thought I was advising her, but it caused her to hold a grudge against me.*

ushiro 後ろ *back, rear*

ushiro o miseru 後ろを見せる *to reveal a weak point*
[lit. to show one's back]

彼女は彼と議論していて、つい後ろを見せてしまいました。
Kanojo wa kare to giron shite ite, tsui ushiro o misete
shimaimashita. *During the argument with him, she
accidentally revealed her weak point.*

ushirogami o hikareru omoi de 後ろ髪を引かれる思いで
reluctantly
[lit. with feelings as if the hair on the back of one's head is pulled
back]

彼は後ろ髪を引かれる思いで、彼女に別れを告げました。
Kare wa ushirogami o hikareru omoi de, kanojo ni wakare o
tsugemashita. *He said goodby to her reluctantly.*

---

uso 嘘 *lie*

uso de katameru 嘘で固める *to pad one's story with
lies*
[lit. to solidify one's story with lies]

彼女が自分の過去の話しを、嘘で固めていたことが分かり
ました。Kanojo ga jibun no kako no hanashi o, uso de
katamete ita koto ga wakarimashita. *We found out that she
had padded the story about her past with lies.*

uso happyaku 嘘八百 *pack of lies*
[lit. eight hundred lies]

彼の言い訳は、嘘八百でした。Kare no iiwake wa, uso
happyaku deshita. *His excuse was a pack of lies.*

---

usugami 薄紙 *thin paper*

usugami o hagu yō ni 薄紙をはぐように *slowly but
steadily (illness)*
[lit. as if peeling sheets of thin paper]

彼の病気は、薄紙をはぐようによくなっています。Kare no
byōki wa, usugami o hagu yō ni yoku natte imasu. *He's
recovering from his illness slowly but steadily.*

---

utsu 　打つ　　*to hit, to beat*
  uteba hibiku 　打てば響く　　*to be responsive*
  [lit. to make sounds if one hits something]
  彼に用事を頼むと、打てば響くようにしてくれます。Kare
  ni yōji o tanomu to, uteba hibiku yō ni shite kuremasu. *When
  you ask him to do errands, he's very responsive.*

  utte deru 　打って出る　　*to actively enter something*
  [lit. to go out beating a drum]
  彼女は文学賞をもらって、文壇に打って出ました。Kanojo
  wa bungaku shō o moratte, bundan ni utte demashita.
  *Winning a literary award, she actively entered the literary
  world.*

uwa 　上　　*upper, front*
  uwamae o haneru 　上前をはねる　　*to skim a percentage*
  [lit. to flip the front part of a *kimono*]
  彼は、労働者の賃金の上前をはねていました。Kare wa,
  rōdōsha no chingin no uwamae o hanete imashita. *He was
  skimming a percentage of the laborers' wages.*

W

wa 　輪　　*wheel*
  wa o kakeru 　輪をかける　　*to stretch a fact*
  [lit. to put wheels on a talk]
  彼女は、話しに輪をかけました。Kanojo wa, hanashi ni wa o
  kakemashita. *She stretched the facts in her talk.*

  wa o kakete 　輪をかけて　　*more*
  [lit. by carrying someone or something on wheels]
  お母さんは美人ですが、娘はお母さんに輪をかけてきれい
  です。Okāsan wa bijin desu ga, musume wa okāsan ni wa o
  kakete kirei desu. *The mother is beautiful, but her daughter is
  more beautiful.*

waga   我が   *one's own*
  waga i o eru   我が意を得る   *to find something satisfying*
  [lit. to get one's own wishes]
  彼女の意見に我が意を得ました。Kanojo no iken ni waga i o
    emashita.   *I found her opinion satisfying.*

  wagamonogao ni furumau   我が物顔に振る舞う   *to lord it over someone*
  [lit. to act as if something is one's own]
  あの会社では、社長の息子が我が物顔に振る舞っています。
    Ano kaisha dewa, shachō no musuko ga wagamonogao ni
    furumatte imasu.   *In that company, the president's son is
    lording it over the employees.*

---

wakage   若気   *youthful vigor*
  wakage no itari   若気の至り   *youthful folly*
  [lit. the result of youthful vigor]
  彼は若気の至りで上司と口論して、仕事を辞めました。
    Kare wa wakage no itari de jōshi to kōron shite, shigoto o
    yamemashita.   *His youthful folly caused him to have an
    argument with his boss and quit his job.*

---

waki   脇   *side, secondary*
  waki ga amai   脇が甘い   *to take things too lightly*
  [lit. One's side is loose.]
  彼女は何にでも脇が甘いから、すぐにだまされてしまいます。
  Kanojo wa nani ni demo waki ga amai kara, sugu ni damasarete
    shimaimasu.   *She's easily fooled because she takes everything
    too lightly.*

  wakime mo furazu   脇目も振らず   *intently*
  [lit. without casting one's eyes aside]
  彼は、脇目も振らずに仕事しています。Kare wa, wakime mo
    furazu ni shigoto shite imasu.   *He's working intently.*

  wakiyaku ni mawaru   脇役に回る   *to take a backseat*
  [lit. to go around and take a secondary role]
  彼は最近会社の経営を娘に任せて、脇役に回っています。

Kare wa saikin kaisha no keiei o musume ni makasete, wakiyaku ni mawatte imasu.   *Recently, he's been taking a backseat by putting his daughter in charge of managing the company.*

wakiyaku o hatasu   脇役を果たす   *to play second fiddle to someone*

[lit. to fulfill a secondary role]

国際会議では、日本代表の脇役を果たしました。Kokusai kaigi dewa, Nihon daihyō no wakiyaku o hatashimashita.   *I played second fiddle to the chief Japanese delegate at the international conference.*

---

waku   枠   *frame*

waku ni hamaru   枠にはまる   *to be the same old stuff*

[lit. Something fits in a frame.]

彼女の考えは枠にはまっていて、面白くありません。Kanojo no kangae wa waku ni hamatte ite, omoshiroku arimasen.   *Her ideas are the same old stuff and not interesting.*

---

wara   藁   *straw*

wara nimo sugaru   藁にもすがる   *to be desperate (for help)*

[lit. to even cling to a straw]

財布を落として、藁にもすがる思いで道で知らない人にバス代を頼みました。Saifu o otoshite, wara nimo sugaru omoi de michi de shiranai hito ni basudai o tanomimashita. *Because I lost my wallet, I was desperate enough to ask a stranger in the street for bus fare.*

---

warai   笑い   *laugh, smile*

warai ga tomaranai   笑いが止まらない   *to exult*

[lit. One's laugh does not stop.]

彼は買った土地の値段が一年で倍になって、笑いが止まりません。Kare wa katta tochi no nedan ga ichi nen de bai ni natte, warai ga tomarimasen.   *He's exulting because the price of the land doubled within a year after his purchase.*

waraigoto dewa nai   笑い事ではない   *It's no laughing matter.*

[lit. It's not something to laugh about.]

毎晩酔っぱらって帰ってくるなんて、笑い事ではありませんよ。Maiban yopparatte kaette kuru nante, waraigoto dewa arimasen yo. *Every night you come back home drunk. It's no laughing matter.*

waraimono ni naru   笑い物になる   *to make a fool of oneself*

[lit. to become a target of laughter]

会議で全く見当違いの意見を述べて、笑い物になってしまいました。Kaigi de mattaku kentō chigai no iken o nobete, waraimono ni natte shimaimashita. *I made a fool of myself by stating a totally irrelevant view at the meeting.*

---

ware   我   *oneself*

ware ni kaeru   我に返る   *to come to one's senses*

[lit. to return to oneself]

彼女は買い物好きでしたが、去年我に返って投資を始めました。Kanojo wa kaimonozuki deshita ga, kyonen ware ni kaette tōshi o hajimemashita. *She loved shopping, but she came to her senses last year and started investing money.*

ware o wasureru   我を忘れる   *to be absorbed in something*

[lit. to forget oneself]

彼は素晴らしい景色に、全く我を忘れました。Kare wa subarashii keshiki ni, mattaku ware o wasuremashita. *He was totally absorbed in the beautiful scenery.*

waregachi ni   我勝ちに   *everybody for himself or herself*

[lit. by trying to make oneself win]

ビュッフェ式パーティーでは、出席者は我勝ちに鮨を取り始めました。Byuffe shiki pātī dewa, shussekisha wa waregachi ni sushi o torihajimemashita. *It was everybody for himself at the buffet as people started grabbing the sushi.*

warekansezu　我関せず　*indifferent*
[lit. to not get oneself involved in something]
妹がお金に困っているのに、彼は我関せずで助けて上げません。Imōto ga okane ni komatte iru noni, kare wa warekansezu de tasukete agemasen. *His young sister is in a financial mess, but he's indifferent to it and won't help her.*

waremo waremo to　我も我もと　*by competing with one another*
[lit. Me too, me too!]
若者は、我も我もとロックコンサートの券を買おうとしています。Wakamono wa, waremo waremo to rokku konsāto no ken o kaō to shite imasu. *The young people are competing with one another trying to buy rock concert tickets.*

---

wari　割　*rate*

wari ga warui　割が悪い　*low-paying, unfavorable*
[lit. The rate is bad.]
今の仕事は割が悪いので、辞めようと思っています。Ima no shigoto wa wari ga warui node, yameyō to omotte imasu. *Because my current job is low paying, I'm thinking about quitting.*

wari ni awanai　割に合わない　*to be not worth the trouble*
[lit. to not match with a rate]
その申し込みは、問題が多くて割に合いませんでした。Sono mōshikomi wa, mondai ga ōkute wari ni aimasen deshita. *The proposal had so many problems that it wasn't worth the trouble.*

wari o kuu　割を食う　*to be a fall guy*
[lit. to eat an unfavorable rate]
共同作業の失敗で、私だけが割を食わねばなりませんでした。Kyōdō sagyō no shippai de, watakushi dake ga wari o kuwaneba narimasen deshita. *When the joint project failed, I was the only fall guy.*

waru   割る   *to split, to divide*
  warikirenai   割り切れない   *hard to swallow*
  [lit. indivisible]
  彼だけが昇進したのは、割り切れません。Kare dake ga
    shōshin shita nowa, warikiremasen.   *It's hard to swallow the
    fact that only he got a promotion.*

  warikiru   割り切る   *to have a practical attitude*
  [lit. to split something through]
  彼は、会社の人員整理は必要と割り切っています。Kare wa,
    kaisha no jin-in seiri wa hitsuyō to warikitte imasu.   *He has
    the practical attitude that the company's reduction in
    personnel is necessary.*

  wattehairu   割って入る   *to intervene*
  [lit. to split and enter something]
  彼らの口論に、割って入りました。Karera no kōron ni, watte
    hairimashita.   *I intervened in their quarrel.*

---

waru   悪   *bad*
  warufuzake   悪ふざけ   *practical joke*
  [lit. a bad joke]
  彼は、悪ふざけが大好きです。Kare wa, warufuzake ga
    daisuki desu.   *He likes to play practical jokes.*

  warunori suru   悪乗りする   *to get carried away*
  [lit. to take bad rides]
  彼女はパーティーでのお世辞に悪乗りして、そこで直ぐ歌
    を歌い始めました。Kanojo wa pātī de no oseji ni warunori
    shite, soko de sugu uta o utaihajimemashita.   *She got carried
    away with flattery at the party, and started to sing right there.*

---

wata   綿   *cotton*
  wata no yō ni tsukareru   綿のように疲れる   *to be
    dead tired*
  [lit. to get tired like cotton]
  妻は毎日小さい子供の世話で、綿のように疲れています。
    Tsuma wa mainichi chiisai kodomo no sewa de, wata no yō ni

tsukarete imasu.   *Because my wife has to take care of our small children, she's dead tired.*

---

watari   渡り   *ferry*
  watari o tsukeru   渡りを付ける   *to contact someone*
[lit. to make connections at a ferry]
交渉のために、その会社の代表者と渡りを付けました。
Kōshō no tame ni, sono kaisha no daihyōsha to watari o tsukemashita.   *For the negotiations, I contacted the representative of the company.*

Y

---

ya   矢   *arrow*
  ya mo tate mo tamarazu   矢も楯もたまらず   *to have an uncontrollable urge*
[lit. to be unable to hold oneself back despite arrows or shields]
彼は俳優になりたくて、矢も楯もたまらず仕事を辞めました。
Kare wa haiyū ni naritakute, ya mo tate mo tamarazu shigoto o yamemashita.   *He had an uncontrollable urge to become an actor and quit his job.*

  ya no saisoku o suru   矢の催促をする   *to keep pressing someone for something*
[lit. to make an arrow-like demand]
高利貸しは元金と利子を揃えて返すように、矢の催促をしています。Kōrigashi wa gankin to rishi o soroete kaesu yō ni, ya no saisoku o shite imasu.   *The loan shark keeps pressing me for full repayment of the principal with interest.*

  shiraha no ya o tateru   白羽の矢を立てる   *to single out*
[lit. to hit someone with a white-feathered arrow]
政府は諮問委員会の委員長として、彼女に白羽の矢を立てました。Seifu wa shimon iinkai no iinchō toshite, kanojo ni shiraha no ya o tatemashita.   *The government singled her out*

to be the chair of an advisory committee.

yaomote ni tatsu   矢面に立つ   *to bear the thrust of something*

[lit. to stand in front of incoming arrows]

首相は、国民の政府批判の矢面に立っています。Shushō wa, kokumin no seifu hihan no yaomote ni tatte imasu.   *The prime minister is bearing the thrust of the people's criticism of the government.*

---

ya   野   *field*

ya ni kudaru   野に下る   *to leave a government job*

[lit. to go down to the field]

彼は去年野に下って、地方選挙に出馬しました。Kare wa kyonen ya ni kudatte, chihō senkyo ni shutsuba shimashita. *He left his government job last year, and ran for a local election.*

---

yabu   薮   *bush*

yabu kara bō   薮から棒   *out of the blue*

[lit. a stick thrust out of a bush]

薮から棒の結婚の申し込みで、彼女は返事に困りました。Yabu kara bō no kekkon no mōshikomi de, kanojo wa henji ni komarimashita. *Because out of the blue he asked her to marry him, she didn't know what to say.*

yabuhebi ni naru   薮蛇になる   *to backfire*

[lit. to poke at a bush and get a snake]

友達の議論の間に入ったら、薮蛇になって、彼らは私を非難し始めました。Tomodachi no giron no aida ni haittara, yabuhebi ni natte, karera wa watakushi o hinan shihajimemashita. *When I intervened in my friends' argument, it backfired and they started blaming me.*

---

yakebokkui   焼けぼっくい   *charred stick*

yakebokkui ni hi ga tsuku   焼けぼっくいに火がつく

An old flame is rekindled.

[lit. A charred stick caught fire.]

彼らは十年ぶりにあって、焼けぼっくいに火がつきました。
Karera wa jū nen buri ni atte, yakebokkui ni hi ga tsukimashita.
They met for the first time in ten years, and the old flame was rekindled.

---

yaki   焼き   *tempering*

yaki ga mawaru   焼きが回る   *to slow down in one's old age*

[lit. The tempering is complete.]

彼は焼きが回って、物忘れをよくします。Kare wa yaki ga mawatte, monowasure o yoku shimasu. *As he slows down in his old age, he often forgets things.*

yaki o ireru   焼きを入れる   *to teach someone a lesson, to reprimand*

[lit. to temper someone]

彼女は最近遅刻が多いので、焼きを入れました。Kanojo wa saikin chikoku ga ōi node, yaki o iremashita. *Because she was often late to work recently, I taught her a lesson.*

yakimochi o yaku   焼き餅を焼く   *to be jealous*

[lit. to burn grilled rice cakes]

彼は友達が映画女優と結婚したので、焼き餅を焼いています。Kare wa tomodachi ga eiga joyū to kekkon shita node, yakimochi o yaite imasu. *He's jealous because his friend got married to a movie actress.*

---

yakusha   役者   *actor or actress, cast members*

yakusha ga ichimai ue   役者が一枚上   *to be a cut above someone*

[lit. The actor or the actress is one rank above someone.]

説得力にかけては、彼女は彼らより役者が上です。Settokuryoku ni kakete wa, kanojo wa karera yori yakusha ga ichimai ue desu. *In the art of persuasion, she's a cut above them.*

yakusha ga sorou   役者が揃う   *Everyone is present.*

[lit. All the cast members are here.]

役者が揃つたから、会議を始めましょう。Yakusha ga
sorotta kara, kaigi o hajimemashō.   *Since everyone is present,
let's start the meeting.*

yakushazoroi   役者ぞろい   *to have real pros*
[lit. to have many actors and actresses]
あの弁護事務所は、役者ぞろいです。Ano bengo jimusho wa,
yakushazoroi desu.   *They have real pros in their law firm.*

---

yama   山   *mountain*

yama ga ataru   山が当たる   *to guess right*
[lit. The mountain on which one speculated makes a profit.]
試験の問題は山が当たって、満点取りました。Shiken no
mondai wa yama ga atatte, manten torimashita.   *I guessed the
exam questions correctly and got a perfect score.*

yama ga hazureru   山が外れる   *to guess wrong*
[lit. The mountain on which one speculated takes a loss.]
食事が出ると期待していたのに、山が外れてお茶だけでま
した。Shokuji ga deru to kitai shite ita noni, yama ga hazurete
ocha dake demashita.   *Although I expected a meal, I guessed
wrong and they served only tea.*

yama ga mieru   山が見える   *to see the light at the end
of the tunnel*
[lit. to be able to see a mountain]
長年の交渉も、やっと山が見え始めました。Naganen no
kōshō mo, yatto yama ga miehajimemashita.   *After many
years of negotiations, we began to see the light at the end of the
tunnel.*

yama o kakeru   山をかける   *to speculate about
something*
[lit. to bet a mountain on something]
彼は雨が降らないだろうと山をかけて、傘を持たずに出か
けました。Kare wa ame ga furanai darō to yama o kakere,
kasa o motazu ni dekakemashita.   *He speculated that it
wouldn't rain and left home without taking an umbrella.*

yama o kosu　　山を越す　　*to be past the critical point*
[lit. to go over the mountain]
彼らの研究も、やっと山を越したようです。Karera no
　　kenkyū mo, yatto yama o koeta yō desu.　　*It seems that they're
　　finally past the critical point in their research.*

yamaba o mukaeru　　山場を迎える　　*to be at a crucial
　　point*
[lit. to face a crucial moment]
成功するかどうか、彼女の事業は山場を迎えています。
　　Seikō suru ka dō ka, kanojo no jigyō wa yamaba o mukaete
　　imasu.　　*Her business is at a crucial point in terms of whether
　　it's going to succeed or not.*

yamakan　　山勘　　*hunch*
[lit. a calculation on mineral veins in mountains]
おじさんに会いに行ったら、小遣いをくれるという山勘が
　　当たりました。Ojisan ni ai ni ittara, kozukai o kureru to iu
　　yamakan ga atarimashita.　　*My hunch that when I went to see
　　my uncle, he would give me some spending money, turned out
　　to be right.*

---

yamai　　病　　*disease*
yamai kōkō ni iru　　病膏肓に入る　　*Something is
　　incurable.*
[lit. The disease is in a part too innermost to remedy.]
彼の釣りへの没頭ぶりは、今や病膏肓に入っています。
　　Kare no tsuri e no bottōburi wa, imaya yamai kōkō ni itte
　　imasu.　　*His devotion to fishing is incurable by now.*

---

yamu　　止む　　*to stop*
yamu ni yamarenu　　止むに止まれぬ　　*unavoidable*
[lit. to be unable to stop if one tries to stop something]
彼は止むに止まれぬ事情から、学校を辞めなければなりま
　　せんでした。Kare wa yamu ni yamarenu jijō kara, gakkō o
　　yamenakereba narimasen deshita.　　*He had to quit school
　　under unavoidable circumstances.*

---

yari 槍 *spear*

yaridama ni ageru 槍玉にあげる *to blame someone or something*

[lit. to stab someone with a spear]

犯罪の増加原因として、マスコミはテレビの暴力を槍玉に挙げました。 Hanzai no zōka gen-in toshite, masukomi wa terebi no bōryoku o yaridama ni agemashita. *The media blamed the violence on TV for the increase in crime.*

yokoyari o ireru 横槍を入れる *to interfere with something*

[lit. to charge with a spear from the side]

彼女は、私たちの計画に横槍を入れようとしました。 Kanojo wa, watakushitachi no keikaku ni yokoyari o ireyō to shimashita. *She tried to interfere with our plan.*

---

yaseru 痩せる *to become thin*

yasetemo karetemo 痩せても枯れても *as poor as one is*

[lit. no matter how thin or withered one becomes]

痩せても枯れても、汚い仕事には関わりたくありません。 Yasetemo karetemo, kitanai shigoto niwa kakawaritaku arimasen. *As poor as I am, I won't get involved in dirty work.*

yasegaman suru やせ我慢する *to put on a cool act*

[lit. to endure something with a thin disguise]

彼はパーティーに行きたいのに、やせ我慢していきませんでした。 Kare wa pātī ni ikitai noni, yasegaman shite ikimasen deshita. *Although he wanted to go to the party, he put on a cool act and didn't go.*

---

yasui 安い *inexpensive*

yasukarō warukarō 安かろう悪かろう *You get what you pay for.*

[lit. If it's inexpensive, it will not be good.]

安かろう悪かろうと思っていましたが、この間の買い物では、安くていい物をたくさん見つけました。 Yasukarō

warukarō to omotte imashita ga, kono aida no kaimono dewa, yasukute ii mono o takusan mitsukemashita. *Although I believe that you get what you pay for, I found a lot of cheap but good-quality items while shopping the other day.*

---

yo   世   *society, world, era*

yo ga yo nara   世が世なら   *in better times*
[lit. if an era was a good era for someone]
世が世なら、彼女は大政治家になっていたでしょう。Yo ga yo nara, kanojo wa dai seijika ni natte ita deshō. *In better times, she would have become a great politician.*

yo ni deru   世に出る   *to make it*
[lit. to come out in the world]
彼が芸術家として世に出てから、五年になりなす。Kare ga geijutsuka toshite yo ni dete kara, go nen ni narimasu. *It's been five years since he made it as an artist.*

yo no kikoe   世の聞こえ   *reputation*
[lit. hearing in public]
彼女は世の聞こえを気にして、人前ではタバコを吸いません。Kanojo wa yo no kikoe o ki ni shite, hitomae dewa tabako o suimasen. *Because she's concerned about her reputation, she doesn't smoke in public.*

yo o saru   世を去る   *to die*
[lit. to leave the world]
彼は、突然世を去りました。Kare wa, totsuzen yo o sarimashita. *He died suddenly.*

yo o shinobu   世を忍ぶ   *to be in seclusion*
[lit. to hide oneself from society]
彼女は子供の死以来、世を忍んで暮らしています。Kanojo wa kodomo no shi irai, yo o shinonde kurashite imasu. *Since the death of her child, she has been living in seclusion.*

yo o wataru   世を渡る   *to make a living*
[lit. to walk across the world]
彼は小さなレストランのコックとして、世を渡っています。

Kare wa chiisana resutoran no kokku toshite, yo o watatte imasu.   *He makes a living as the chef at a small restaurant.*

yowatari ga umai   世渡りがうまい   *to know how to get ahead*

[lit. to be good at making a living]

彼女は世渡りがうまくて、各界の実力者とつき合っています。 Kanojo wa yowatari ga umakute, kakkai no jitsuryokusha to tsukiatte imasu.   *Because she knows how to get ahead, she's friendly with influential people in many different walks of life.*

---

yo   夜   *night*

yo o hi ni tsuide   夜を日に継いで   *night and day*

[lit. by connecting a night to a day]

鉄道の修復は、夜を日に継いで行われました。 Tetsudō no shūfuku wa, yo o hi ni tsuide okonawaremashita.   *They worked night and day on the repair of the railway.*

yo o tessuru   夜を徹する   *to stay up all night*

[lit. to go through an entire night]

締め切りに間に合わせるために、夜を徹して働きました。 Shimekiri ni maniawaseru tame ni, yoru o tesshite hatarakimashita.   *We stayed up all night and worked to meet the deadline.*

---

yobu   呼ぶ   *to call*

yobigoe ga takai   呼び声が高い   *to be prominently mentioned as something*

[lit. Voices calling for someone are loud.]

彼は、将来首相になるという呼び声が高いです。 Kare wa, shōrai shushō ni naru to iu yobigoe ga takai desu.   *He has been prominently mentioned as a future prime minister.*

yobimizu ni naru   呼び水になる   *to trigger something*

[lit. to become calling (priming) water]

価格競争の呼び水になったのは、安い輸入品の増加でした。 Kakaku kyōsō no yobimizu ni natta no wa, yasui yunyū hin no zōka deshita.   *What triggered the price war was the increase of inexpensive imported goods.*

---

yodare   涎   *saliva*
  yodare o tarasu   涎を垂らす   *to drool with envy*
  [lit. to drip one's saliva]
  彼女は友達の婚約指輪を見て、涎を垂らしました。Kanojo wa tomodachi no kon-yaku yubiwa o mite, yodare o tarashimashita.   *She drooled with envy when she saw her friend's engagement ring.*

---

yoko   横   *side, sideways, lying sideways*
  yoko kara mitemo tate kara mitemo   横から見ても縦から見ても   *every inch*
  [lit. even looking at something sideways or vertically]
  横から見ても縦から見ても、彼は本当の実業家です。Yoko kara mitemo tate kara mitemo, kare wa hontō no jitsugyōka desu.   *He's every inch an industrialist.*

  yoko no mono o tate nimo shinai   横の物を縦にもしない   *won't lift a finger*
  [lit. to not stand up something that is lying on the floor]
  他の人が忙しくても、彼女は横の物を縦にもしません。Hoka no hito ga isogashikutemo, kanojo wa yoko no mono o tate nimo shimasen.   *Even if other people are busy, she won't lift a finger.*

  yoko o muku   横を向く   *to reject something*
  [lit. to look sideways]
  夫は、妻の頼みに横を向きました。Otto wa, tsuma no tanomi ni yoko o mukimashita.   *The husband rejected his wife's request.*

  yokogamiyaburi   横紙破り   *obstinate person*
  [lit. to be difficult to tear Japanese paper sideways]
  彼は横紙破りなので、一緒に仕事は出来ません。Kare wa yokogamiyaburi nanode, issho ni shigoto wa dekimasen.   *Because he's obstinate, we can't work with him.*

yokoguruma o osu　横車を押す　*to force one's will on someone*

[lit. to push a cart sideways]

みんなが彼女の提案に反対したけれど、彼女はそれでも横車を押そうとしました。Minna ga kanojo no teian ni hantai shita keredo, kanojo wa soredemo yokoguruma o osō to shimashita. *Although everyone opposed her proposal, she still tried to force her will on us.*

yokomichi ni soreru　横道にそれる　*to get sidetracked*

[lit. to stray into a side street]

演説が横道にそれて、彼が何をいいたかったのか分かりませんでした。Enzetsu ga yokomichi ni sorete, kare ga nani o iitakatta no ka wakarimasen deshita. *Because he got sidetracked during his speech, we didn't know what he wanted to say.*

---

yoku　欲　*greed, desire*

yoku mo toku mo nai　欲も得もない　*to have no self-interest*

[lit. There is neither greed nor desire for gain.]

彼らの企画に、欲も得もなく助言しました。Karera no kikaku ni, yoku mo toku mo naku jogen shimashita. *With no self-interest I gave my advice on their project.*

yoku o ieba　欲を言えば　*if one could suggest one thing*

[lit. if one can say one's desire]

この計画は素晴らしいですが、欲を言えば統計の裏付けがいります。Kono keikaku wa subarashii desu ga, yoku o ieba tōkei no urazuke ga irimasu. *The plan is wonderful, but if I could suggest one thing, you need statistical backing.*

---

yomi　読み　*reading*

yomi ga fukai　読みが深い　*to be insightful*

[lit. One's reading is deep.]

彼女は景気の読みが深いので、投資の相談には最適です。Kanojo wa keiki no yomi ga fukai node, tōshi no sōdan niwa saiteki desu.   *Because she is insightful about the economic climate, she's a perfect person to consult on investments.*

---

yoru   寄る   *to gather*

yoru to sawaru to   寄ると触ると   *at every opportunity to gather*

[lit. whenever they gather or get in touch with each other]

彼らは、寄ると触ると新しい社長のうわさ話をしています。

Karera wa, yoru to sawaru to atarashii shachō no uwasabanashi o shite imasu.   *At every opportunity to gather, they gossip about the new president.*

yotte takaru   寄ってたかる   *to gang up on someone*

[lit. by gathering and swarming around someone]

外交問題で、野党は寄ってたかって政府を批判しています。

Gaikō mondai de, yatō wa yotte takatte seifu o hihan shite imasu.   *The minority parties are ganging up on the government on diplomatic issues.*

---

yōryō   要領   *point, knack*

yōryō ga ii   要領がいい   *to be shrewd*

[lit. One's knack is good.]

彼女は要領が良くて、自分の得することには協力します。

Kanojo wa yōryō ga yokute, jibun no toku suru koto niwa kyōryoku shimasu.   *Since she's shrewd, she cooperates on things that are advantageous to her.*

yōryō o enai   要領を得ない   *vague*

[lit. to not get someone's point]

彼の説明は、全然要領を得ませんでした。Kare no setsumei wa, zenzen yōryō o emasen deshita.   *His explanation was very vague.*

---

yowai   弱い   *weak*

yowane o haku   弱音を吐く   *to whine*

[lit. to vomit the sound of weakness]

先週は仕事が厳しかったけれど、誰も弱音を吐きませんでした。Senshū wa shigoto ga kibishikatta keredo, daremo

yowane o hakimasen deshita. *Although the work was hard
last week, nobody whined.*

---

yu   湯   *hot water*

yumizu no yō ni tsukau   湯水のように使う   *to throw
money around*

[lit. to spend money like water or hot water]

彼は大きい遺産を相続して以来、金を湯水のように使って
います。Kare wa ōkii isan o sōzoku shite irai, kane o yumizu
no yō ni tsukatte imasu. *Ever since he inherited a large
fortune, he's been throwing money around.*

---

yū   勇   *courage*

yū o kosu   勇を鼓す   *to gather up one's courage*

[lit. to drum up one's courage]

彼女は勇を鼓して、上司に反対意見を述べました。Kanojo
wa yū o koshite, jōshi ni hantai iken o nobemashita.
Gathering up her courage, she gave the opposing view to her boss.

yūmei o haseru   勇名を馳せる   *to win fame for one's
bravery*

[lit. to make one's name run as a brave man]

彼は子供と年寄りを火事から救って、勇名を馳せました。
Kare wa kodomo to toshiyori o kaji kara sukutte, yūmei o
hasemashita. *He won fame for his bravery by rescuing
children and elderly people from a fire.*

---

yubi   指   *finger*

yubi o kuwaeru   指をくわえる   *to look enviously at
something*

[lit. to put a finger in one's mouth]

夫は、隣の家の新車に指をくわえています。Otto wa, tonari
no ie no shinsha ni yubi o kuwaete imasu. *My husband is
looking enviously at our next door neighbor's new car.*

yubi o sasu   指を指す   *to backbite*

[lit. to point one's finger at someone]

彼女に指を指すより、言いたいことがあれば直接言いなさい。

Kanojo ni yubi o sasu yori, iitai koto ga areba chokusetsu
iinasai.   *If you have something to say, you should say it
directly to her instead of backbiting.*

yubi o someru   指を染める   *to take something up*
[lit. to stain one's fingers]

母は五十歳の時に、絵画に指を染めました。Haha wa
gojūssai no toki ni, kaiga ni yubi o somemashita.   *My mother
took up painting when she was fifty.*

yubiori kazoeru   指折り数える   *to look forward to
something*
[lit. to count something on one's fingers]

子供たちは、夏休みが来るのを指折り数えています。
Kodomotachi wa, natsuyasumi ga kuru no o yubiori kazoete
imasu.   *My children are looking forward to summer recess,
counting the days on their fingers.*

yubiori no   指折りの   *prominent*
[lit countable by bending one's fingers]

彼は、指折りの癌の専門家です。Kare wa, yubiori no gan no
senmonka desu.   *He is a prominent cancer researcher.*

ushiroyubi o sasareru   後ろ指を差される   *to be talked
about behind one's back*
[lit. a finger to be pointed at one's back]

後で後ろ指を指されないように、会議では非常に気を付け
て話しました。Ato de ushiroyubi o sasarenai yō ni, kaigi
dewa hijō ni ki o tsukete hanashimashita.   *I spoke extremely
carefully so that I wouldn't be talked about behind my back
later.*

---

yume   夢   *dream*
yume o egaku   夢を描く   *to picture something in one's
mind*
[lit. to draw a dream]

彼女は、いつか医者になる夢を描いています。Kanojo wa,
itsuka isha ni naru yume o egaite imasu.   *She's picturing in
her mind that she'll become a doctor some day.*

yume o idaku　夢を抱く　*to have a dream*
[lit. to embrace a dream]
彼は、来年アメリカの大学に行く夢を抱いています。Kare
　wa, rainen Amerika no daigaku ni iku yume o idaite imasu.
　*He has a dream of going to a university in the United States
　next year.*

yume o miru　夢を見る　*to dream*
[lit. to see a dream]
彼は、いつか金持ちになる夢を見ています。Kare wa, itsuka
　kanemochi ni naru yume o mite imasu.　*He is dreaming of
　becoming rich someday.*

yume o takusu　夢を託す　*to delegate one's hope to
　someone*
[lit. to entrust someone with one's dream]
彼は音楽家になる夢を、息子に託しました。Kare wa
　ongakuka ni naru yume o, musuko ni takushimashita.　*He
　delegated his hope of becoming a musician to his son.*

yumeji o tadoru　夢路をたどる　*to sleep, to fall asleep*
[lit. to follow a dream street]
子供たちは一日泳いでいたので、夕食後直ぐに夢路をたど
　りました。Kodomotachi wa ichinichi oyoide ita node, yūshoku
　go sugu ni yumeji o tadorimashita.　*Because the children were
　swimming all day, they fell asleep right after dinner.*

yumemonogatari　夢物語　*fantasy*
[lit. a dream story]
彼女は、彼の夢物語を信じています。Kanojo wa, kare no
　yumemonogatari o shinjite imasu.　*She believes in his fantasy.*

masayume　正夢　*a dream that comes true*
[lit. a correct dream]
夕べ見た夢が、正夢になりました。Yūbe mita yume ga,
　masayume ni narimashita.　*The dream I had last night came
　true.*

---

yūmei　有名　*famous*

yūmei mujitsu   有名無実   *in name only*
[lit. famous but no content]

あの歌手は有名無実で、歌の才能はありません。 Ano kashu wa yūmei mujitsu de, uta no sainō wa arimasen. *He's a singer in name only; he doesn't have any talent.*

yūmei zei   有名税   *price one has to pay for fame*
[lit. a tax on being famous]

嫌がらせ電話が、彼の有名税の一つです。 Iyagarase denwa ga, kare no yūmei zei no hitotsu desu. *Receiving harassing calls is part of the price he has to pay for fame.*

---

yumi   弓   *bow*

yumi o hiku   弓を引く   *to rebel against someone*
[lit. to pull a bow]

その店員は店主に弓を引いて、競争相手の店で働き始めました。 Sono ten-in wa tenshu ni yumi o hiite, kyōsō aite no mise de hatarakihajimemashita. *The clerk rebelled against the shop owner and started working for a rival shop.*

yumi ore ya tsukiru made   弓折れ矢尽きるまで   *to the end*
[lit. until a bow breaks and arrows are all gone]

一度事業を始めたからには、弓折れ矢尽きるまで頑張るつもりです。 Ichido jigyō o hajimeta kara niwa, yumi ore ya tsukiru made ganbaru tsumori desu. *Now that I've started my own business, I'll hold fast to the end.*

---

yūzū   融通   *adaptability*

yūzū ga kiku   融通が利く   *to be flexible*
[lit. One's adaptability works.]

彼は融通が利くので、彼の意見はとても参考になります。 Kare wa yūzū ga kiku node, kare no iken wa totemo sankō ni narimasu. *Because he's flexible, his comments are quite instructive.*

Z

---

za   座   *seat, occasion*

za ga motenai   座が持てない   *to not be able to carry on something*
[lit. to not be able to sustain an occasion]
彼女に紹介されましたが、その後、座が持てなくて困りました。Kanojo ni shōkai saremashita ga, sono ato, za ga motenakute komarimashita. *I was introduced to her, but I had trouble carrying on a conversation afterward.*

za ga shirakeru   座が白ける   *to spoil an occasion*
[lit. to make an occasion white]
素晴らしいパーティーだったのに、彼が仕事の問題を述べ続けて、座が白けてしまいました。Subarashii pāti datta noni, kare ga shigoto no mondai o nobetsuzukete, za ga shirakete shimaimashita. *Although it was a great party, he spoiled the occasion by carrying on about his problems at work.*

za ni tsuku   座に着く   *to assume a position*
[lit. to arrive at a seat]
会社の再編成の後、私が社長の座に着きました。Kaisha no saihensei no ato, watakushi ga shachō no za ni tsukimashita. *After the reorganization of the company, I assumed the position of president.*

za o hazusu   座をはずす   *to leave a room*
[lit. to get out of a seat]
ちょっと内密の話しがあるので、座をはずしていただけませんか。Chotto naimitsu no hanashi ga aru node, za o hazushite itadakemasen ka. *Since we're having a private talk, would you mind leaving the room?*

za o torimotsu   座を取り持つ   *to act as a mediator*
[lit. to handle an occasion]
彼らの議論が終わりそうもないので、座を取り持つことにしました。Karera no giron ga owarisō mo nai node, za o torimotsu koto ni shimashita. *I decided to act as a mediator*

because otherwise their argument would go on forever.

chūza suru   中座する   *to leave in the middle of something*
[lit. to get out of one's seat in the middle of something]
前からの面会の約束があって、会議の途中で中座しました。
Mae kara no menkai no yakusoku ga atte, kaigi no tochū de chūza shimashita.   *I left in the middle of the meeting because I had a previous engagement.*

---

zehi   是非   *right or wrong*
zehi mo naku   是非もなく   *without question*
[lit. without judging something to be right or wrong]
それは、是非もなくやらせていただきます。Sore wa, zehi mo naku yarasete itadakimasu.   *Without question, I would love to do it.*

---

zen   善   *goodness*
zen wa isoge   善は急げ   *better sooner than later*
[lit. to hurry up with something good]
善は急げで、ダイエットを始めました。Zen wa isoge de, daietto o hajimemashita.   *I've started a diet; better sooner than later.*

---

zengo   前後   *front and rear*
zengo o wakimaezu   前後をわきまえず   *recklessly*
[lit. to not know front or rear]
彼は前後をわきまえず、上司を批判しました。Kare wa zengo o wakimaezu, jōshi o hihan shimashita.   *He criticized his supervisor recklessly.*

zengo o wasureru   前後を忘れる   *to be beside oneself*
[lit. to forget the front from the rear]
彼女は突然の悲しい知らせに、前後を忘れて泣きました。
Kanojo wa totsuzen no kanashii shirase ni, zengo o wasurete nakimashita.   *She was beside herself crying over the sudden sad news.*

zoku 俗 *common, banal*

zoku na 俗な *vulgar*
[lit. too much for common taste]

その雑誌は俗な記事が多いので、取るのを止めました。
Sono zasshi wa zoku na kiji ga ōi node, toru no o yamemashita.
Because there are many vulgar articles in that magazine, I stopped subscribing to it.

zokuaku na 俗悪な *gross*
[lit. worldly bad]

最近は、テレビに俗悪な番組が増えています。Saikin wa, terebi ni zokuaku na bangumi ga fuete imasu. *There are more and more gross programs on TV nowadays.*

zokubutsu 俗物 *a Philistine*
[lit. a banal person]

彼女は政治評論家を装っていますが、実は俗物です。
Kanojo wa seiji hyōronka o yosootte imasu ga, jitsu wa zokubutsu desu. *She pretends to be a commentator on politics, but in reality she's a Philistine.*

---

zu 頭 *head*

zu ga takai 頭が高い *arrogant*
[lit. One's head is high.]

彼は頭が高いので、渉外部には向きません。Kare wa zu ga takai node, shōgai bu niwa mukimasen. *He's so arrogant that he isn't suitable for the public relations department.*

zutsū no tane 頭痛の種 *source of worry*
[lit. the seed of a headache]

あの会社では、労使関係が頭痛の種です。Ano kaisha dewa, rōshi kankei ga zutsū no tane desu. *Labor-management relations are a source of worry in that company.*

---

zu 図 *chart, plan*

zu ni ataru 図に当たる *to be successful*
[lit. to get a plan right]

宣伝活動が図に当たって、我が社の売り上げが急増しました。

Senden katsudō ga zu ni atatte, waga sha no uriage ga kyūzō shimashita.   *Because the advertising campaign was successful, our company's sales jumped up.*

zu ni noru   図に乗る   *to have a swelled head*
[lit. to ride on a plan]
彼女は社長の秘書になって、図に乗っています。Kanojo wa shachō no hisho ni natte, zu ni notte imasu.   *She has had a swelled head since she became the president's secretary.*

zuboshi o sasu   図星をさす   *to hit the nail on the head*
[lit. to point out a star on a chart]
彼は大きい地震を予言しましたが、まさに図星でした。
Kare wa ōkii jishin o yogen shimashita ga, masa ni zuboshi deshita.   *He predicted a big earthquake, and he hit the nail on the head.*

ENGLISH-JAPANESE INDEX

The following is a selective index of useful words from the English translations of Japanese idioms. For example, if you wish to know a Japanese idiom associated with the word "alive," you should go to page 33 and locate "alive," which would be linked with the idiom "chi ga kayotte iru."